THE SHAPING OF EU COMPETITION LAW

Based on a unique and comprehensive database, *The Shaping of EU Competition Law* combines qualitative and quantitative approaches to shed light on the evolution of EU competition law. It brings a new perspective to some of the most topical issues in the field, including due process and the intensity of judicial review. The author's main purpose is to examine how the institutional structure influences the substance of EU competition law provisions. He seeks to identify patterns in the behaviour of the European Commission and the EU courts and how they interact with each other. In particular, his analysis considers how the European Commission reacts to the case law and whether, and in what instances, the EU courts defer to the analysis of the administrative authority. The author's analysis is supported by the database and an unprecedented array of statistics and figures free to view at www.cambridge.org/9781108429429.

PABLO IBÁÑEZ COLOMO is Professor of Law at the London School of Economics and Visiting Professor at the College of Europe (Bruges).

Tables

ACKNOWLEDGEMENTS

This book reflects the evolution of my thinking since I joined the London School of Economics in September 2010. On the substantive side, it is testimony to the effort I have made in order to improve our understanding of the case law and the factors behind its evolution. It also reflects the growing interest in the institutional side of EU competition law, and in particular in the relationship between enforcement and substance. On the methodological side, this monograph shows, more than the rest of my published work, the importance I attach to the comprehensive analysis of data and the careful reading of cases – all cases. The absence of a reliable database of competition law cases, and the resulting frustration, gave the initial impetus to the project.

A successful academic career very much depends on the intellectual environment in which one grows as a scholar. I feel fortunate that my formative years have taken place at three wonderful institutions that I can call home and that have each shaped me in their own way: the College of Europe, the European University Institute and the London School of Economics. Finding inspiring mentors is even more important than the environment. I am immensely grateful to David Kershaw, Heike Schweitzer and Denis Waelbroeck for their time and advice. What I admire in all three, and what they have in common, is that they care deeply – about the law, about Europe, about others. I keep learning from them.

STICERD awarded me the research grant that made it possible to complete the database on which the quantitative part of the monograph is based. I hereby gratefully acknowledge the financial support. Above all, I am grateful that it is through this grant that I met Andriani Kalintiri. I was looking for a research assistant, and was fortunate enough to find a meticulous scholar, a devoted colleague and a good friend. Another recipient of a STICERD grant (and LSE colleague) deserves to be acknowledged: this book, and my thinking, has benefitted immensely from my frequent and lengthy conversations with Eduardo Baistrocchi.

Combining legal discussions and running along the Thames may be unusual, but it has marked much of my time in London.

I am also grateful to Alfonso Lamadrid (friend, co-blogger and someone with whom I spend an inordinate amount of time over the phone). Of his many qualities, I would emphasise his generosity, his common sense and his ability to understand others (and I write all this even though he never managed to read the manuscript before publication!) Last, but certainly not least, this book owes a great deal not only to the rest of my friends and family but to the editorial team at Cambridge University Press for their support and faith in the project.

TABLE OF CASES

1 Decisions of the European Commission

2 Judgments of the General Court of the EU

3 Judgments of the Court of Justice of the EU

PART I

Theory

1

Introduction

1 Institutions and Substance in EU Competition Law

The substantive and institutional aspects of a legal discipline are closely intertwined. One cannot be properly understood without the other. The substantive evolution of a discipline may prompt institutional change. Conversely, the structure through which the law is applied can influence the interpretation of substantive provisions. For instance, a field may evolve differently depending on whether enforcement is entrusted to a generalist court or to a specialist agency instead. The choice of cases – and thus the direction into which the law moves – may vary depending on the model followed. Private parties litigating in court have motivations and incentives that differ from those of an agency acting in the public interest. The approach to the interpretation of the relevant provisions may also be influenced by the institutional structure. Generalist courts may place an emphasis on legal certainty and the administrability of the system. In this sense, they may be inclined to look beyond the outcome of a specific dispute when shaping rules and standards. Expert agencies, on the other hand, may give more weight to the circumstances of each case.[1]

The impact that the institutional structure has had on the evolution of US antitrust is well understood.[2] In this sense, US antitrust provides a prime example of the influence of the enforcement model on the

[1] This is a question that has long attracted the interest of commentators. For some examples specifically related to competition law, see for instance, Joshua D. Wright and Angela M. Diveley, 'Do expert agencies outperform generalist judges? Some preliminary evidence from the Federal Trade Commission' (2013) 1 *Journal of Antitrust Enforcement* 82; Douglas H. Ginsburg and Joshua D. Wright, (2013) 36 *Fordham International Law Journal* 788; and Javier Tapia and Santiago Montt, 'Judicial Scrutiny and Competition Authorities: The Institutional Limits of Antitrust' in Ioannis Lianos and D. Daniel Sokol (eds.), *The Global Limits of Competition Law* (Redwood City: Stanford University Press, 2012).

[2] This issue is covered in Daniel A. Crane, *The Institutional Structure of Antitrust Enforcement* (Oxford: Oxford University Press, 2011).

substantive dimension of a legal discipline. Some of its most salient features are known to be the consequence of the dominance of private enforcement over public enforcement. US antitrust is primarily applied by generalist courts. The constraints faced by such courts inform, and sometimes determine, how substantive analysis is performed. The former are inseparable from the latter. In practice, the question of whether a practice should be declared unlawful – or whether it should be seen as an antitrust matter in the first place – is, at least in part, determined by considerations relating to the ability of generalist courts to impose or supervise the remedy that a finding of infringement would require.[3] More generally, the US antitrust system reflects a concern with the avoidance of enforcement errors by courts – and more precisely the so-called Type I errors, which result from over-enforcing of the law.[4]

This monograph considers how the substantive peculiarities of EU competition law[5] relate to, or have been exacerbated by, the institutional framework in which it operates. The interest of the question lies in the fact that the enforcement model in the EU differs in fundamental respects from the US one. Since its inception, the EU system has revolved, by and large, around expert administrative authorities. As a result, the factors that have marked the evolution of US antitrust are not prominent in the EU. In particular, the concern with Type I errors is far less pressing.[6] The same can be said of the issue of remedies. It is easy to think of cases in which the difficult implementation of a remedy did not deter the European Commission (hereinafter, the 'Commission') from intervening.[7]

[3] On the relationship between remedies and substance, see Phillip Areeda, 'Essential Facilities: An Epithet in Need of Limiting Principles' (1990) 58 *Antitrust Law Journal* 841; and Herbert Hovenkamp, *The Antitrust Enterprise: Principle and Execution* (Cambridge: Harvard University Press, 2005) 50–6. For a concrete practical example in which this factor came into play, see *Verizon Communications v Law Offices of Curtis V Trinko*, LLP, 540 U.S. 398 (2004).

[4] See in this sense Frank H. Easterbrook, 'The Limits of Antitrust' (1984) 63 *Texas Law Review* 1; and Alan Devlin and Michael Jacobs, 'Antitrust Error' (2010) 52 *William & Mary Law Review* 75.

[5] This monograph focuses on Articles 101 and 102 TFEU as well as EU Merger Control. EU State aid law is thus not a central part of the analysis.

[6] See in this sense Giorgio Monti, *EC Competition Law* (Cambridge: Cambridge University Press, 2007) 18.

[7] For instance, the remedies imposed by the Commission in the two *Microsoft* cases included a duty to supply interoperability information and a duty to carry competing applications in the operating system. See in this sense Commission Decision of 24 May 2004 (Case COMP/C-3/37.792 – *Microsoft*) OJ (2007) No. L 32/23 ('*Microsoft I*') and Commission Decision of 16 December 2009 (Case COMP/C-3/39.530 – *Microsoft (tying)*) ('*Microsoft II*').

What is less clear, on the other hand, is whether, and how, the institutional features of the EU system have influenced the evolution of the law.

The institutional structure of EU competition law enforcement has the potential to affect its substantive dimension in various ways. To begin with, it is intuitively appealing to assume that a system revolving around an expert authority is less prone to enforcement errors and inconsistencies. Moreover, unlike generalist courts (which have to rule on the cases that are brought before it), a public agency often has the discretion to devote its efforts to what it deems the most socially important and harmful infringements. On the other hand, the fact that an administrative authority combines the roles of an investigator and a decision-maker may pave the way for opportunistic behaviour. As a result, and somewhat paradoxically, it cannot be excluded that the system eventually becomes less predictable, and also more prone to enforcement errors, than one revolving around generalist courts. Administrative action tainted by opportunism may become less concerned with predictability and consistency and more with advancing the policy objectives of the authority. This attitude may be exacerbated if the review courts show deference to the knowledge of the expert decision-maker.

This question – the link between the substantive and institutional dimensions of the EU competition law system – has not been studied to the same extent as it has in the US. There are many aspects that remain elusive, or that have not been explored in a systematic way in Europe. As a result, some of the most common claims are rarely ever substantiated, if at all. For instance, it is simply accepted as self-evident that the behaviour of, and the interaction between, the Commission and the EU courts has an impact on the evolution of the discipline. In the same vein, greater curial deference to the activity of the authority is generally assumed to lead to the expansion of EU competition law. If the EU courts systematically accept the substantive analysis carried out by the Commission, the intuition suggests, the latter may seek to advance a relatively broad interpretation of the substantive provisions – and thus of the scope of its powers. The fact that the Commission is at the same time investigator and first-instance adjudicator is also seen as problematic insofar as it may be a source of prosecutorial bias.

It is a challenge for commentators to evaluate, beyond received ideas, concerns with the behaviour of the Commission and the EU courts. When raised explicitly, these concerns are generally not supported by theoretical or empirical evidence. As a result, little progress has been made in the understanding of the institutional dimension of EU competition law and its impact on the evolution of the system. Unsubstantiated claims that the EU courts are overly deferential to the Commission, or that the combination of investigation and decision-making powers by the latter is a source of bias, can be – and have been – easily rebutted by commentators.[8] In the absence of an analytical framework against which the accuracy of such views can be assessed, it is indeed difficult to establish whether, and to what extent, the existing institutional structure can explain some of the substantive features of the discipline.

This monograph analyses the patterns underlying the behaviour of the Commission and the EU courts and evaluates the consequences of these patterns for EU competition law provisions. The methodological approach on which the project is based brings together two major strands of the literature. The dominant theme – whether, and how, the enforcement model contributes to shaping the various legal notions – makes it indispensable to do away with the marked tendency of commentators to draw a stark dividing line between substance and procedure and to integrate the two under a common framework. The substantive dimension of the institutional concerns discussed above – the alleged bias of the Commission and the perceived deference of the EU courts – has not been placed at the centre of discussions. Conversely, institutional factors are not systematically considered in the analysis of competition law provisions.

In the current state of the literature, debates about institutional matters often revolve around whether the structure of EU competition law enforcement is compatible with due process principles, in particular as enshrined in Article 6 ECHR. The default approach is to consider the case law of the European Court of Human Rights (hereinafter, the 'ECtHR') and ascertain whether the features of the EU system –the dual role of the Commission as 'prosecutor' and 'judge' and the intensity with which administrative action is reviewed – are in line with the requirements set out in the said provision. Any conclusions about the need to adjust or amend the system are drawn primarily from this exercise. For instance, the need for reform may be inferred from the fact that judicial review is deemed marginal in the EU system. The default approach to the analysis

[8] For an overview of these positions, see Henry Vane, 'The House Always Wins' *Global Competition Review* (London, 29 September 2014) and Wouter Wils, 'The Combination of the Investigative and Prosecutorial Function and the Adjudicative Function in EC Antitrust Enforcement: A Legal and Economic Analysis' (2004) 27 *World Competition* 201.

of these institutional issues is unconvincing – or incomplete – for a number of reasons.

First, this approach presents due process considerations as relating to the institutional set-up of the EU competition law system alone. From this perspective, the only relevant question is whether the current enforcement model should be altered – for instance, by entrusting different bodies with the investigation and the decision-making functions – to make it compatible with fundamental rights principles. As a result, it is an approach that fails to consider the impact of due process (or its absence) on the substantive evolution of the law. This omission seems regrettable if one takes into account that inconsistent and unpredictable enforcement is a likely consequence of biased decision-making that is not subject to appropriate checks. Arguably, due process could be seen as a concern of an essentially substantive, rather than a procedural, nature, at least in the long run. After all, such considerations are closely linked to other fundamental principles, such as legal certainty.

In the same vein, the default approach to the analysis of due process considerations tends to be somewhat formalistic. Typically, it revolves around the compatibility of the system with fundamental rights provisions. This monograph departs from this approach in that it is instead based on the premise that the concerns underpinning the debate on due process are not and cannot be exhausted simply because the EU competition law system is deemed compatible with the ECHR (or any other benchmark). Arguing that the risk of bias disappears simply because the institutional framework is not considered to be in breach of a particular fundamental rights regime is unconvincing. Similarly, prosecutorial bias is unlikely to disappear simply because full review is exercised in the Commission cases that reach the EU courts. What the compatibility of the system with the ECHR (or a comparable regime) suggests, at most, is that the risk of bias and deference in the system is tolerable. Bias and deference – and, more importantly, the concerns underpinning the two phenomena – are independent of, and should not be confused with, the legal status of the institutional structure.

Finally, the default approach does not provide the necessary tools to address or to examine bias and deference concerns and thus to consider the compatibility of the institutional structure with fundamental rights. In this sense, it is not even capable of providing a satisfactory answer to the relatively narrow institutional issues on which it focuses. Under the case law of the ECtHR, the relevant question is whether administrative action is subject to 'full review' by an independent tribunal within the meaning of Article 6 ECHR.[9] This question is not obvious to establish. It cannot be examined in the abstract, or from a purely formal standpoint. For instance, the fact that the review courts declare their commitment to the intense scrutiny of administrative action – or, conversely, that they formally agree to defer to the authority – is insufficient to conclude that decisions are subject to full review – or the opposite. According to the ECtHR, what matters is whether, in practice, full review has actually been exercised. This question is empirical in nature. It requires an analysis of the substance of relevant provisions, which is not undertaken under the default approach.

That the analysis of these institutional questions remains relatively underdeveloped is unsurprising if one considers that the thrust of research efforts in EU competition law is still devoted to the substantive aspects of the discipline. This project is intended to enrich ongoing debates on substance by introducing an institutional dimension, which has so far remained elusive. If at all, institutional considerations have informed the analysis of substantive issues in a fragmentary and anecdotal manner. As a result, there has been no systematic examination of, first, the context in which EU competition law provisions have been shaped and, second, of their evolution over time – including the question of whether the interpretation of a given concept has remained stable or has fluctuated when the Commission and the EU courts have interpreted it.

This monograph provides a comprehensive analysis of the institutional context in which some key substantive concepts in the case law and administrative practice have been defined. The analysis relies on data that sheds light on issues such as the frequency with which a particular substantive concept has been central to the outcome of cases, or the frequency with which it has been litigated before the EU courts. In the same vein, the analysis provides insights about the institutional drivers behind the definition and the shaping of substantive concepts. In some instances, the substantive concept has been framed by the Commission, which has then been followed by the EU courts. In other instances, the EU courts have departed from the substantive approach favoured by the Commission (whether in an administrative decision or in the context of a preliminary reference).

Second, the project develops a set of operational benchmarks that make it possible to evaluate the substantive evolution of EU competition

[9] See in particular *Menarini Diagnostics SRL v Italy* App no 43509/08 (ECtHR 27 September 2011).

law – that is, of the interaction between the Commission and the EU courts over time. The purpose of these benchmarks is to capture the various ways in which the relevant provisions can be construed, and to identify and compare the choices made by the Commission and the EU courts. This is a response to the challenge that scholars face when trying to make sense of administrative action and judicial review, and in particular of the way in which the Commission engages with the case law and, conversely, the way in which the EU courts deal with the decision-making practice of the authority. These questions are not immediately conducive to objective analysis. They are only straightforward when the Commission ostensibly departs from the relevant case law. To take a clear example, the authority never attempted to claim in *Microsoft I* that the firm's refusal to supply its information prevented the emergence of a 'new product', as required in *Magill*.[10] This aspect of the decision was not found to be manifestly incorrect, even though the GC reviewed the legality of the Commission decision against the 'new product' condition.[11] In less obvious cases, however, determining whether the behaviour of the Commission departs from the case law, or is based on a reasonable interpretation of it, may not be easy to establish. For the same reasons, evaluating the behaviour of the EU courts can be equally challenging.

2 Purpose, Scope and Approach

2.1 What This Monograph Is About

This monograph examines, first, how the Commission interprets and enforces EU competition law provisions. It seeks to identify patterns in its approach to the definition of the scope of its powers. The questions considered include, in particular, whether the Commission shapes provisions broadly or narrowly, and how it engages with the case law and with mainstream economic theory. Second, the monograph evaluates the review of administrative action by the EU courts. In this sense, it considers how the EU courts engage with the choices made by the

[10] Compare the conditions set out in Joined Cases C-241/91 P and C-242/91 P, *Radio Telefis Eireann (RTE) and Independent Television Publications Ltd (ITP) v Commission ('Magill')*, EU:C:1995:98 and Case T-201/04, *Microsoft Corp v Commission*, EU:T:2007:289. This is a matter that will be discussed at length in subsequent chapters.

[11] Case T-201/04, *Microsoft I*, para. 665. For an analysis, see also Bo Vesterdorf, 'Article 82 EC: Where do we stand after the Microsoft judgement?' (2008) 1 *Global Antitrust Review* 1.

Commission. More precisely, it seeks to establish whether the EU courts show deference to the interpretations advanced by the authority, and whether there are exogenous factors that influence the intensity with which administrative action is scrutinised. For instance, the EU courts may be reluctant to review a decision in full if they understand that it amounts to questioning the policy choices of the Commission. Conversely, they may be more inclined to do so if administrative action contradicts a long and stable line of case law. The analysis of these questions makes it possible to draw a picture about the evolution of EU competition law over the years. It also provides insights about the consistency and coherence of the system.

As argued by some commentators, an authority that combines the roles of prosecutor and adjudicator may display a bias in favour of establishing an infringement. Prosecutorial bias is a complex phenomenon that is not easy to establish empirically. If it exists, it may be manifested in various ways. Some of the manifestations are intractable, while others are more conducive to analysis. The phenomenon may be reflected, inter alia, in the way facts are established and assessed by the authority, or in the way it applies the law to the facts at hand. The premise of this monograph is that claims of prosecutorial bias are valuable as a proxy. Put differently, they are valuable insofar as they are a powerful reminder that due process has a substantive dimension. Over the long run, due process is important in a legal system not so much for the procedural guarantees it may provide in a specific case, but because administrative action may become arbitrary and unpredictable in the absence of such guarantees. Moreover, establishing bias as such looks like a most daunting challenge. On the other hand, it is possible to assess, as this monograph does, how the Commission crafts EU competition law provisions, and to map how its behaviour has influenced the evolution of the system.

Claims of undue curial deference are equally difficult to establish empirically. Typically, commentators assess deference in light of the rate of annulment of Commission decisions. From this perspective, a judgment upholding a decision would be an indicator of deference, whereas one annulling it would suggest the opposite. The reasons why this approach is unreliable are well known. If a Commission decision is in line with the relevant case law and it is carefully crafted from a factual and a legal standpoint, it is only natural that it is upheld by the EU courts. The reluctance of the EU courts to deviate from a stable line of case law cannot be taken as an indicator of deference. Conversely, the (partial or total) annulment of a Commission decision is compatible with deferential judicial review. As a repeat player, the Commission is not always, or not necessarily, interested in the outcome of an individual case, but in the long-run evolution of the law. It is not difficult to think of 'test cases' where the Commission lost on factual grounds but won on the (substantive) issue of principle. The fundamental flaw of this approach to the analysis of deference claims is that it fails to consider matters of substance, which are indispensable to draw meaningful conclusions about court behaviour. Against this background, the monograph expects to contribute to the understanding of this elusive question by focusing on the reaction of the EU courts to the interpretation of competition law provisions by the Commission, in particular when it deviates from the case law and/or departs from mainstream economic principles.

2.2 *What This Monograph Is Not About*

This work does not seek to dispute some central aspects of the system created by virtue of the TFEU. First, it assumes that EU competition policy is implemented through law. Administrative action is only warranted when it meets the conditions set out in the applicable provisions. Intervention under Article 101 TFEU, for instance, is only possible if it can be shown, inter alia, that the practice involves an agreement that has as its object or effect the restriction of competition. Similarly, Article 102 TFEU does not prohibit dominant positions as such, but only their abuse. Accordingly, administrative action is not justified simply because the authority believes that it would be able to improve the functioning of an industry, or that intervention would be an appropriate response to a perceived market failure (such as a position of dominance). Such claims are in themselves irrelevant if the constitutive elements of an infringement are not met or not established by an authority to the requisite legal standard. In relation to deference and judicial review, this monograph assumes, in line with the letter of the TFEU, that the Commission enjoys no discretion regarding the definition of the substantive scope of EU competition law provisions. As a result, the interpretation of the various provisions by the Commission is subject to full review.

Second, references to the consistency of the EU competition law system are central to the monograph. These references should not be interpreted as a normative claim about the directions in which the field should develop or change. Similarly, they do not intend to suggest that there is such a thing as a doctrine of precedent in EU law, or that administrative authorities cannot, or should not, deviate from the relevant case law. Consistency is mentioned for positive purposes. Thus, conclusions to the effect that like practices are not treated alike, or that a given practice is not treated in the same way across provisions are descriptive in nature. They seek to explain the consequences of enforcement and map the substantive evolution of the field. Above all, the monograph intends to uncover a reality that is not immediately apparent in the absence of systematic analysis.

On the other hand, one should not lose sight of the fact that consistency is an aspiration of EU competition law and the EU law system at large. Consistency seems to be valued as a pre-condition for legal certainty. Pursuant to the TFEU, one of the fundamental tasks of the Court of Justice (hereinafter, the 'Court' or the 'ECJ') is to preserve the 'unity' and 'consistency' of EU law.[12] This aspiration is enshrined in Regulation 1/2003,[13] which provides for several mechanisms to ensure the consistent application of Articles 101 and 102 TFEU across the EU. In particular, it introduces various devices allowing the Commission to monitor the implementation of EU competition law by national courts and authorities and to co-operate and exchange information with them.

Thirdly, the monograph is not concerned with the compatibility of the EU competition law system with Article 6 ECHR and equivalent provisions. Thus, examples that suggest that the Commission tends to depart from the relevant precedents, or that the EU courts may not always have reviewed, in full, the substantive aspects of administrative decisions should not be interpreted as claims that the institutional structure is at odds with fundamental rights and/or that it should be altered. Similarly, the monograph is not concerned with the institutional mechanisms that have been introduced over the years to address concerns with biased decision-making or with their relative effectiveness. Such mechanisms include the possibility for firms to request an oral hearing – chaired by an independent Hearing Officer[14] – and the office of the Chief Competition Economist.[15] In this sense, the monograph aspires to show, at most, that

[12] See in this sense Article 256 TFEU. See also Article 62 and 62b of Protocol (No. 3) on the Statute of the Court of Justice of the European Union.

[13] Council Regulation (EC) No. 1/2003 of 16 December 2002 on the implementation of the rules on competition laid down in Articles 81 and 82 of the Treaty OJ (2003) No. L 1/1.

[14] See in this sense Wouter Wils, 'The Role of the Hearing Officer in Competition Proceedings before the European Commission' (2012) 35 *World Competition* 431.

[15] Lars-Hendrik Röller and Pierre A. Buigues, 'The Office of the Chief Competition Economist at the European Commission' (May 2005) Global Competition Review 122.

debates around bias and deference cannot be confined to the discussion of measures formally addressing these concerns.

Fourthly, the monograph does not take a position on the values and objectives that guide, or that should guide, EU competition law. This question has generated a considerable amount of literature on both sides of the Atlantic, but is not obviously relevant for the positive analysis of the actual behaviour of the Commission and the EU courts. Discussions about the objectives of EU competition law differ from the approach taken in this monograph in at least two important respects. To begin with, they are often normative in nature, in the sense that they are concerned with the way in which the law could be perfected or seek to establish whether individual cases are correctly or incorrectly decided relative to a standard that is deemed appropriate. Second, these discussions are based on a top-down understanding of the discipline, according to which it is possible to assess the EU competition law system against an externally defined benchmark. This monograph follows instead a bottom-up approach, in the sense that it seeks to identify how individual cases are crafted and which factors are considered by the Commission and the EU courts when they assess the lawfulness of a given practice.

In a related vein, the monograph does not seek to dispute the role of economic analysis in EU competition law. Contemporary enforcement cannot be understood without taking into consideration the influence of mainstream economics at several levels. The dimension that has more relevance for this monograph relates to its contribution to the understanding of the nature and likely effects of business practices. By definition, the interpretation of EU competition law provisions involves making assumptions and establishing presumptions about the motivations behind the conduct under examination, and about the instances in which it may prove anti-competitive. Theoretical and empirical evidence contributes to the refinement of these assumptions and presumptions, which are prone to logical fallacies. It is indeed not unusual that formal analysis reveals that practices that look like blatant exclusionary devices are in fact plausibly pro-competitive, in the sense that they have an efficiency justification. Similarly, economic analysis may lead to the conclusion that a practice is only likely to have exclusionary effects in a restrictive set of circumstances. These advances in the economic understanding of business conduct are not called into question.

Finally, the monograph does not seek to establish whether the case law and the administrative practice reflect, or are influenced by, a particular ideology or school of thought. This is a question that has attracted the interest of many commentators in the past decade.[16] It is not considered in the analysis, inter alia, due to the methodological challenges it poses. It looks like an intractable question. It is indeed difficult to claim credibly that a given legal test is the necessary and inevitable consequence of a particular ideology or school of thought. A comprehensive analysis of the case law and administrative practice shows that there is often scope for disagreement about the interpretation of competition law provisions even within a given intellectual climate. Divergences between the Commission and the EU courts have been consistent since the 1960s. Similarly, it is difficult to establish a clear causal link between a particular legal test, on the one hand, and an ideology or school, on the other. This monograph focuses on aspects of the behaviour of the Commission and the EU courts that can be observed and measured. In this sense, it seeks to look at patterns over time.

2.3 Focus

EU competition law has become a vast and complex discipline. Tracing its evolution across the board would require several volumes. The Commission has adopted hundreds of decisions relating to Articles 101 and 102 TFEU,[17] and has decided on the compatibility with the internal market of thousands of mergers since 1990.[18] Against this background, it is indispensable to limit the scope of the inquiry to make the analysis manageable. As already explained, the monograph is exclusively devoted to the substantive evolution of EU competition law provisions. Factual and procedural considerations, which could provide valuable insights, are left outside of its scope. The substantive analysis, in turn, is confined to some of the fundamental conditions for the application of

[16] See for instance Pinar Akman, *The Concept of Abuse in EU Competition Law: Law and Economic Approaches* (Oxford: Hart Publishing, 2012); Liza Lovdahl Gormsen, *A Principled Approach to Abuse of Dominance in European Competition Law* (Cambridge: Cambridge University Press, 2010); and Pierre Larouche and Maarten Pieter Schinkel, 'Continental Drift in the Treatment of Dominant Firms: Article 102 TFEU in Contrast to § 2 Sherman Act' in Roger D. Blair and D. Daniel Sokol (eds.), *The Oxford Handbook of International Antitrust Economics*, 2 vols. (Oxford: Oxford University Press, 2015), vol. 2.

[17] The database on which this study is based shows that the Commission has adopted more than 600 final formal decisions.

[18] The statistics available in September 2017 reveal that more than 6,000 merger cases have been notified to the Commission since 1990.

Articles 101 and 102 TFEU, on the one hand, and the two Merger Regulations, on the other.[19]

More precisely, the monograph explores the interpretation and the substantive evolution of the notion of restriction of competition within the meaning of Article 101(1) TFEU; of the notion of abuse under Article 102 TFEU; and of the substantive criterion against which the legality of mergers has been assessed under the successive Regulations – dominance under Regulation 4064/89[20] and 'significant impediment to effective competition' under Regulation 139/2004.[21] Other key concepts, such as the notion of agreement within the meaning of Article 101(1) TFEU or that of dominance within the meaning of Article 102 TFEU, are left outside the inquiry. As a result, there are entire sub-fields of the discipline, in particular cartels, which are not covered in detail.

Several reasons explain this choice. The abovementioned concepts are understood to be the pivotal ones in each of the provisions, in the sense that it is around them that the line between lawful competition on the merits and prohibited conduct is drawn. Other conditions, namely the notion of agreement within the meaning of Article 101 TFEU, the concept of a dominant position within the meaning of Article 102 TFEU or that of concentration under Regulation 139/2004 define the boundaries of the relevant provisions.[22] The same can be said of the condition requiring that the practice have an effect on trade between Member States, which is common to Articles 101 and 102 TFEU. The question of whether conduct is unlawful, however, is only undertaken, in the strict sense of the expression, once the existence of an agreement or a dominant position has been established and the analysis shifts to the question of whether the practice under consideration has the object or effect of

[19] Council Regulation (EC) No. 139/2004 of 20 January 2004 on the control of concentrations between undertakings OJ (2004) No. L 24/1.

[20] Council Regulation (EEC) No 4064/89 of 21 December 1989 on the control of concentrations between undertakings OJ (1989) No. L 395/1. In accordance with Article 2(3) of the Regulation, '[a] concentration which creates or strengthens a dominant position as a result of which effective competition would be significantly impeded in the common market or in a substantial part of it shall be declared incompatible with the common market'.

[21] In accordance with Article 2(3) of Regulation 139/2004, '[a] concentration which would significantly impede effective competition, in the common market or in a substantial part of it, in particular as a result of the creation or strengthening of a dominant position, shall be declared incompatible with the common market'.

[22] Article 102 TFEU, in addition, requires that the abuse of a dominant position be manifested in the internal market or within a 'substantial part' of it.

restricting competition and/or whether a unilateral practice amounts to an abuse.

One can think of a second reason that pleads in favour of focusing on the abovementioned conditions. Arguably, they are also the most controversial in practice, at least in qualitative terms if not necessarily in quantitative ones. For instance, the circumstances under which an agreement within the meaning of Article 101(1) TFEU is deemed to restrict competition still haunt commentators several decades after the adoption of the EEC Treaty. While there should be little doubt that cartel conduct is restrictive of competition by object, other questions are as topical today as they were 50 years ago.[23] Controversies around the definition of the notion of abuse under Article 102 TFEU, in turn, are probably more recent, but not any less profound. This is at least what the amount of academic commentary on the question published in the course of the past two decades[24] and the initiatives taken by the Commission suggest.[25]

Finally, these three substantive notions lend themselves more easily to systematic analysis than other controversies in EU competition law. The cases where the three notions are relevant are typically 'law-intensive'. 'Law-intensive' disputes revolve around whether the practice under consideration falls within the scope of the prohibition and ultimately on how the latter is defined. In relative terms, the factual aspects of the cases tend to be less contentious (if not undisputed), or easier to establish. For instance, the legal status of most vertical restraints has been

[23] For instance, the boundaries of the notion of restriction of competition by object have attracted the interest of commentators in the past few years. See in this sense Alison Jones, 'Left Behind by Modernisation? Restrictions by Object under Article 101(1)' (2010) 6 *European Competition Journal* 649; David Bailey, 'Restrictions of Competition by Object under Article 101 TFEU' (2012) 49 *Common Market Law Review* 559; and Jean-Philippe Kovar and Robert Kovar, 'L'objet anticoncurrentiel au sens de l'article 101, paragraphe 1, du TFUE: Un objet difficile à identifier' (2016) 1 *Concurrences* 48.

[24] The vast literature cannot be summarised here. For some examples, see Denis Waelbroeck, 'Michelin II: A Per Se Rule Against Rebates by Dominant Companies?' (2005) 1 *Journal of Competition Law & Economics* 149; Renato Nazzini, *The Foundations of European Union Competition Law: The Objective and Principles of Article 102* (Oxford: Oxford University Press, 2011); Lorenzo Federico Pace (ed.), *European Competition Law: The Impact of the Commission's Guidelines on Article 102* (Cheltenham: Edward Elgar, 2011); John Temple Lang, 'How can the problems of exclusionary abuses under Article 102 TFEU be resolved?' (2012) 37 European Law Review 136; and Robert O'Donoghue and Jorge Padilla, *The Law and Economics of Article 102 TFEU*, 2nd edn. (Oxford: Hart Publishing, 2013).

[25] See in this sense Guidance on the Commission's enforcement priorities in applying Article 82 of the EC Treaty to abusive exclusionary conduct by dominant undertakings OJ (2009) No. C 45/7.

established in agreements notified to the Commission, or in preliminary references where the existence of the contract was not challenged as such.[26] Only the compatibility with Article 101 TFEU was contentious. This is in contrast with 'fact-intensive' disputes, in which the legal status of the practice under consideration is generally uncontroversial. The prime example of a 'fact-intensive' case is cartel conduct, which, as already pointed out, is restrictive of competition by object. As a result, controversies in cartel cases relate, first and foremost, to whether the practice has actually taken place (this is the 'fact-intensive' inquiry), and, second, to sanctioning the conduct.

2.4 Approach

2.4.1 The Definition of a Set of Operational Benchmarks

The monograph does not seek to establish bias as such or deference as such. As already explained, these are elusive concepts which escape an easy definition and which can be manifested in ways that are difficult, if not impossible, to evaluate. Instead, it develops a set of operational benchmarks around questions that can be observed and analysed systematically. It is possible to examine in such a way how EU competition law provisions are crafted by the Commission, and how EU courts react to it. The interpretation of EU competition law provisions can be broken down into a number of discrete choices. By the same token, the consistency in the decision-making practice of the Commission and the EU courts can be assessed by reference to whether the choices made in like cases, and over time, are the same. The choices that can be made when construing competition law provisions can be summarised as follows.

To begin with, a court or an authority would need to decide whether the practice under consideration is deemed prima facie prohibited, prima facie lawful or, instead, whether its lawfulness is to be assessed on a case-by-case basis. In order to capture these categories, the monograph distinguishes between rules and standards.[27] Cartels are a textbook example of a practice subject to a prohibition rule and qualitative selective

[26] Some examples include Case 26/76, *Metro SB-Großmärkte GmbH & Co. KG v Commission*, EU:C:1977:167; Case 161/84, *Pronuptia de Paris GmbH v Pronuptia de Paris Irmgard Schillgallis*, EU:C:1986:41; Case C-234/89, *Stergios Delimitis v Henninger Bräu AG*, EU:C:1991:91; or Case C-345/14, *SIA 'Maxima Latvija' v Konkurences padome*, EU:C:2015:784.

[27] The distinction between rules and standards is elaborated in detail in Chapter 2. For an application of the concept in the field of competition law, see Daniel A. Crane, 'Rules Versus Standards in Antitrust Adjudication' (2007) 64 *Washington & Lee Law Review* 49

competition law is vast and diverse, and it would be a challenging task to codify them ex ante, let alone anticipate the emergence of new forms thereof. For instance, the European Commission (hereinafter the 'Commission') has, in the course of the past decade, turned its attention to conduct that had not been examined before and that did not fit neatly into pre-existing categories.[6] Another factor that pleads in favour of the use of flexible provisions has to do with the fact that EU competition law is not intended to be applied in a particular sector, but across the board. Depending on the features of the industry in question and of the relevant market, intervention may take one form or another. Open-textured provisions are also advantageous in that they make it possible to refine intervention in an incremental manner so as to capture theoretical and empirical advances in the field. EU competition policy towards agreements and unilateral practices has undergone major changes in the past twenty years, which have been undertaken without the need to amend the wording of Articles 101 and 102 TFEU.

The use of broad and vague provisions is also a source of challenges, however. This is so, in particular, because the open-textured concepts used in EU competition law only become meaningful when they are fleshed out in concrete factual scenarios. The question of whether, for instance, an agreement restricts competition within the meaning of Article 101(1) TFEU can only be appropriately addressed in the context of a particular case. Competition law is thus a discipline that evolves primarily from the bottom up. As a result, the rationale underpinning the law and the principles guiding intervention are to be inferred from an analysis of the intuitions and assumptions informing – explicitly or implicitly – the outcome of individual cases. Likewise, the extent to which the discipline captures and reflects advances in the field is most reliably assessed by examining specific decisions. Due to the bottom-up nature of competition law, inconsistencies may arise in the interpretation and enforcement of the relevant provisions. Where the law is fleshed out incrementally on a case-by-case basis, there is, indeed, no reason to expect that all individual decisions will be based on similar assumptions or rely on the same premises about, inter alia, the nature, purpose and

[6] It is not difficult to find examples in this regard. New practices include the use of injunctions by holders of standard-essential patents – see in this sense, for instance, Commission Decision of 29 April 2014 (Case AT.39985 – *Motorola – Enforcement of GPRS Standard-Essential Patents*) – or pay-for-delay agreements concluded between patent holders and generic producers in the pharmaceutical sector – see in this sense, for instance, Commission Decision of 19 June 2013 (Case AT.39226 – *Lundbeck*).

impact of business conduct. The concept of *inconsistency* refers hereinafter to instances in which like cases are not decided alike.

1.1 Consistency in the EU Competition Law System

When discussing the issue of consistency in EU competition law, it is useful to distinguish between the static and dynamic dimensions of the concept. *Static inconsistency* is said to exist where, *at a given point in time*, like practices are not treated alike. In such circumstances, it may be difficult to predict the outcome of, inter alia, administrative action. It may also be difficult for firms to be certain that their behaviour will not trigger intervention. When considering the legality of a practice at a given point in time, some cases may suggest a given outcome and others may suggest a conflicting one. The concept of *dynamic inconsistency*, in turn, refers to the treatment of like practices in two separate periods. Thus, dynamic inconsistency arises, for instance, where the treatment of a given practice evolves over time. It may be prohibited in period 1 and authorised in period 2, or vice versa.

1.1.1 The Static Dimension of Consistency

Incoherence is a primary source of static inconsistency. The concept refers to the absence of a uniform approach to the assessment of the lawfulness of practices.[7] If there is incoherence, for instance, the premises underlying, and the approach to, the definition of the notion of 'restriction of competition' may vary from one case to another. In some cases, the notion may be given a relatively broad meaning; in others, a relatively narrow one. Some cases may be grounded on the premise that any agreement restricting the freedom of action of the parties is in breach

[7] The monograph understands the notion of coherence as referring to the overarching rationale (or the absence thereof) within a legal system. It is intended to have the same meaning Ronald Dworkin gave to the notion. See Ronald Dworkin, *Law's Empire* (Cambridge: Harvard University Press, 1986), where the author states that the principles of the system must fit together into a 'single and comprehensive vision of justice'. For an application of this notion in EU competition law (and EU law at large), see Wolf Sauter, *Coherence in EU Competition Law* (Oxford: Oxford University Press, 2016) and Gjermund Mathisen, 'Consistency and Coherence as Conditions for Justification of Member State Measures Restricting Free Movement' (2010) 47 *Common Market Law Review* 1021. Mathisen examines the use of coherence by the Court in free movement case law, and understands it to refer to the question of whether a given measure fits into the system of which it is part. In this sense, it is compatible with the understanding of the notion that forms the basis of this monograph.

balance between rules and standards, as well as about the criteria that should be applied to choose between one and the other in practice. Commentators who favour a relatively expansive interpretation of the role and scope of EU competition law also tend to favour the use of rules over standards.[19] Other commentators emphasise the costs of enforcement errors and favour (structured) standards.[20] For the purposes of this work, the way in which the Commission and EU courts choose between rules and standards, and the criteria they follow to flesh them out in individual cases, is crucial in order to make sense of the sources of static and dynamic inconsistencies.

1.3 Fleshing Out Competition Law Provisions

1.3.1 The Rationale behind Intervention

The question of whether a given practice is anti-competitive comprises several distinct steps. The first step relates to the rationale justifying intervention, which may or may not be made explicit. As depicted in the horizontal axis of Figure 2.1, intervention under EU competition law is a response to a variety of concerns. In some cases, administrative action is a response to a concern with collusion, that is, with coordinated conduct among firms to refrain from competing. One may distinguish between tacit and explicit collusion.[21] In other cases, the concern is with exclusion, in the sense that it relates to the foreclosure of rivals from the relevant market. Rival foreclosure may result from an agreement, a merger or a unilateral practice. Finally, intervention may be driven by a concern with exploitation, that is, with the unilateral exercise of market power to impose unfair terms and conditions on customers or suppliers. The ability to exploit customers and

[19] For an example of an author favouring rules, see Wouter Wils, 'The Judgment of the EU General Court in Intel and the So-Called "More Economic Approach" to Abuse of Dominance' (2014) 37 *World Competition* 405.

[20] See for instance Jorge Padilla and David S. Evans, 'Designing Antitrust Rules for Assessing Unilateral Practices: A Neo-Chicago Approach' (2005) 72 *University of Chicago Law Review* 7.

[21] For an overview of the difference between the two, see Nicolas Petit, 'The Oligopoly problem in EU competition law' in Ioannis Lianos and Damien Geradin (eds.), *Handbook on European Competition Law – Substantive Aspects* (Cheltenham: Edward Elgar, 2013). Tacit collusion is said to exist when competitors in a given market coordinate their conduct without it being necessary for them to engage in an agreement or a concerted practice. Explicit collusion is said to exist when contact between the parties to coordinate their conduct exists.

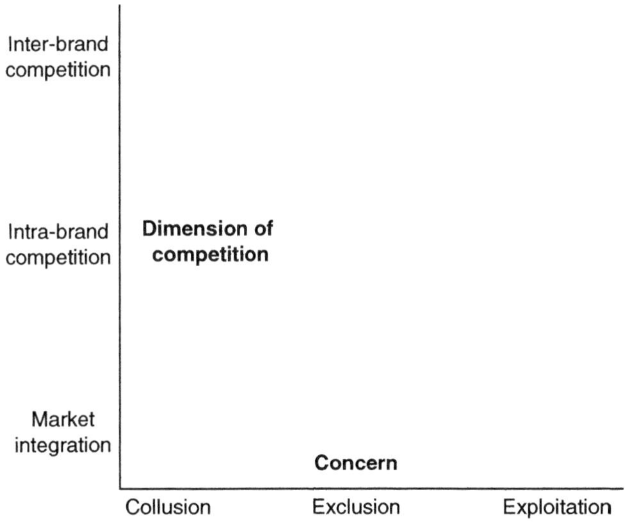

Figure 2.1 The rationale behind intervention

suppliers may result from a dominant position or from a merger – typically a merger between competitors.

The rationale behind intervention also considers, whether explicitly or implicitly, the manifestation of competition that is being protected. This is captured in the vertical axis of Figure 2.1. It is commonplace to distinguish between inter-brand competition (between rival operators at a given level of the value chain) and intra-brand (between distributors of a particular brand). The case law makes it abundantly clear that EU competition law is concerned with both inter-brand and intra-brand competition. However, the single most distinctive feature of the EU competition law system is that it is enforced with the explicit purpose of advancing market integration.[22] In the context of Articles 101 and 102 TFEU, administrative action is justified against practices that would otherwise be pro-competitive (in the sense that they would enhance inter-brand and/or intra-brand rivalry) but that are aimed at partitioning the internal market.[23]

[22] See in this sense Joined Cases C-501/06 P, C-513/06 P, C-515/06 P and C-519/06 P, *GlaxoSmithKline Services Unlimited v Commission*, EU:C:2009:610 (hereinafter '*Glaxo Spain*') and Joined Cases C-468/06 to C-478/06, *Sot. Lélos kai Sia EE and Others v GlaxoSmithKline AEVE Farmakeftikon Proïonton, formerly Glaxowellcome AEVE*, EU: C:2008:504 (hereinafter '*Sot. Lélos*').

[23] The administrative practice of the Commission and the soft law instruments issued in the field suggest that Regulation 139/2004 is not enforced with the explicit purpose of advancing market integration.

1.3.2 The Categorisation of the Practice

The second step relates to the categorisation of the practice. There are recurrent categories of (potentially) anti-competitive conduct. Well-known examples include cartels, rebates and, in EU competition law, agreements giving absolute territorial protection to distributors. It is therefore natural that, when evaluating whether a practice is anti-competitive, competition authorities and courts examine whether it falls within the scope of one of the pre-existing categories or whether it is comparable to them in its nature, purpose and potential effects. For instance, the Court ruled early on that agreements whereby a dominant supplier grants rebates conditional upon exclusivity are prohibited under Article 102 TFEU.[24] In subsequent cases, the Commission considered the lawfulness of practices imposing exclusivity obligations in an indirect way, for instance by making the award of the rebate conditional upon meeting an individualised sales target.[25] If the practice is found to be genuinely new, its lawfulness may have to be established afresh.

It is not difficult to understand, against this background, why this second step is crucial and why inconsistencies may arise when deciding whether a given practice is comparable to pre-existing categories in its nature, scope and potential effects or whether it is genuinely new. If a competition authority (or a claimant) wishes to depart from the legal test that already applies to a given practice, it may seek to argue that the behaviour does not exactly fall within the scope of the pre-existing category. The party wishing to establish an infringement may argue that the factual context is different, or that that there are unique factors that justify a different legal treatment. By giving another label to the practice, the authority or claimant may be able to apply a stricter legal test to the behaviour. This phenomenon may lead to an 'inflation' in the range of practices subject to EU competition law scrutiny and give the impression

[24] Case 85/76, *Hoffmann-La Roche & Co. AG v Commission*, EU:C:1979:36. On the issue of categories in the context of Article 102 TFEU, see Ioannis Lianos, 'Categorical Thinking in Competition Law and the "Effects-Based" Approach in Article 82 EC' in Ariel Ezrachi (ed.), *Article 82 EC: Reflections on Its Recent Evolution* (Oxford: Hart Publishing, 2009). On the issue of categorisation see, more generally, Ioannis Lianos, 'The Principle of Effectiveness, Competition Law Remedies and the Limits of Adjudication' in Philip Lowe and Mel Marquis (eds.), *European Competition Law Annual 2013: Effective and Legitimate Enforcement of Competition Law* (Oxford: Hart Publishing, 2016).

[25] See in particular Case 322/81, *NV Nederlandsche Banden Industrie Michelin v Commission*, EU:C:1983:313 ('*Michelin I*') as well as Case C-95/04 P, *British Airways plc v Commission*, EU:C:2007:166; and Case T-203/01, *Manufacture française des pneumatiques Michelin v Commission*, EU:T:2003:250 ('*Michelin II*').

that every set of factual circumstances is unique and thus fails to provide a reasonable basis to anticipate the outcome of future cases.

1.3.3 The Choice between Rules and Standards

Once the practice has been categorised, it is necessary to decide whether it is subject to a rule or a standard. There are reasons to argue that the divide between rules and standards is hard-wired in the EU competition law system. Article 101(1) TFEU draws a distinction between agreements that restrict competition by object (or 'by their very nature') and by effect, which mirrors the divide between rules and standards. The ECJ has consistently held that these are two alternative conditions.[26] Thus, where an agreement is found to restrict competition by object, it is not necessary to show that it has restrictive effects on competition.[27] Conversely (and as pointed out earlier), some agreements are deemed lawful irrespective of the context of which they are part and of the features of the relevant market. Article 102 TFEU does not formally distinguish between abusive practices by object or effect. However, the divide between rules and standards can be identified in the case law. Some practices are deemed prima facie abusive irrespective of the context in which they are implemented,[28] and some are prima facie lawful.[29] Evidence of an anti-competitive effect is necessary in other cases.[30] Mergers, in turn, are only prohibited if they are shown to be likely to lead to a significant impediment to effective competition, and in this sense they can all be said to be subject to a standard.[31]

[26] Case 56/65, *Société Technique Minière v Maschinenbau Ulm GmbH*, EU:C:1966:38, p. 249; and Case C-8/08, *T-Mobile Netherlands BV, KPN Mobile NV, Orange Nederland NV and Vodafone Libertel NV v Raad van bestuur van de Nederlandse Mededingingsautoriteit*, EU: C:2009:343, para. 28.

[27] Joined Cases 56/64 and 58/64, *Établissements Consten S.à.R.L. and Grundig-Verkaufs-GmbH v Commission*, EU:C:1966:41*('Consten-Grundig')*, p. 342; and Case C-209/07, *Competition Authority v Beef Industry Development Society Ltd and Barry Brothers (Carrigmore) Meats Ltd*, EU:C:2008:643, para. 16.

[28] This category includes exclusive dealing agreements and rebates conditional upon exclusivity. See Case 85/76, *Hoffmann-La Roche*, paras. 89–90.

[29] This category comprises quantity rebates in respect of each individual order. See in this sense Case C-23/14, *Post Danmark II*, para. 28.

[30] This category includes 'margin squeeze' practices, whereby the spread between the wholesale and the retail prices charged by a dominant supplier does not allow its rivals to operate at a profit. See in this sense Case C-52/09, *Konkurrensverket v TeliaSonera Sverige AB*, EU:C:2011:83, paras. 60–77.

[31] As explained above, Article 2 of Regulation 139/2004 provides for a case-by-case assessment of all transactions. The practice of the Commission, as enshrined in its soft law instruments, is consistent with this approach.

This third step is primarily concerned with the criteria that should be followed to establish the divide between rules and standards – that is, the criteria that are followed to make a practice subject to the former or the latter. A rule dispenses from the need to assess the prima facie lawfulness of conduct on a case-by-case basis. By definition, it is based on a *presumption* about the nature of the practice and/or its expected impact on competition. Presumptions in this sense may rely on formal tools (typically, economic analysis) or on intuition and experience alone. The application of a prohibition (or legality) rule may be deemed justified where, for instance, the practice is presumed to be likely (or unlikely) to have negative effects on competition. Alternatively, a rule may be deemed justified for practices that are presumed to serve an anti-competitive (or pro-competitive) purpose. Finally, a presumption may also be based on a combination of these two factors – that is, the nature and likely impact of the practice.

Figure 2.2 seeks to capture the different ways in which the line between rules and standards can be drawn, which depend on the factors that are taken into consideration. As already mentioned, one set of factors – captured in the vertical axis of the figure – relates to the *presumed* impact of the practice on competition (whether it is understood to mean inter-brand competition, intra-brand competition or market integration). The threshold may be set at a higher or a lower level depending on the probability of these effects. It is possible to identify, at the lowest level, a threshold of capability. This term, which is drawn from the case law, is understood to mean that anti-competitive effects are a plausible prospect in light of the nature of the practice and the context of which it is part.[32] For instance, a legality rule could apply to a practice that is not deemed capable of having an impact on the market in which it is implemented. In such a case, it would be safe to presume that the behaviour does not restrict competition that would have existed in its absence. A higher threshold of effects is one of likelihood. The threshold of likelihood would apply where the practice is presumed to be more likely than not

[32] The notion of plausibility is understood to mean that an anti-competitive effect is not against logic and experience. This is the definition of the concept endorsed in Ioannis Lianos, '"Judging" Economists: Economic Expertise in Competition Law Litigation: A European View' in Ioannis Lianos and Ioannis Kokkoris (eds.), *The Reform of EC Competition Law: New Challenges* (Alphen aan den Rijn: Kluwer, 2010). The author cites Oliver Budzinski and Arndt Christiansen, 'Simulating the (Unilateral) Effects of Mergers: Implications of the Oracle/PeopleSoft Case', available at http://ssrn.com/.

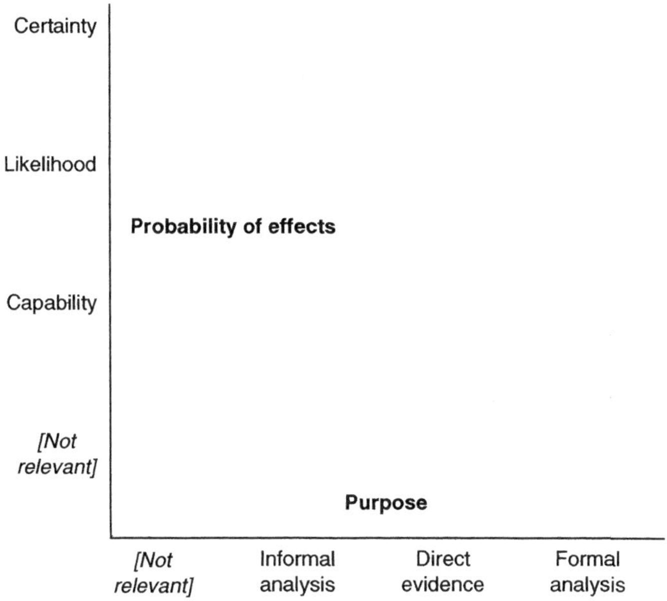

Figure 2.2 The choice between rules and standards

to have a negative impact on competition.[33] Relative to a threshold of plausibility, a threshold of likelihood would require considering alternative scenarios and showing why the scenario leading to anti-competitive effects is more likely than alternative ones.[34] Finally, one can think of a threshold of certainty. In such a case, the practice is presumed to have always, or almost always, a negative impact on competition if implemented.

The horizontal axis seeks to capture the second factor, which revolves around the rationale behind the practice. As observed earlier, presumptions in this sense can be established on the basis of formal or informal tools. At one end of the spectrum, one can think of presumptions based on informal tools, such as experience and/or intuition. At the other end of the spectrum, one can think of formal approaches to the rationale behind the practice. Formal economic tools make it possible to establish presumptions by ascertaining whether the practice under consideration is a plausible source of efficiency gains or whether, instead, it serves no

[33] This understanding is directly drawn from the Opinion of AG Kokott in Case C-23/14, *Post Danmark A/S v Konkurrencerådet*, EU:C:2015:343, para. 82.

[34] See in this sense Case C-12/03 P, *Tetra Laval BV v Commission*, EU:C:2005:87, para. 43.

plausible purpose other than the suppression of competition. Presumptions, whether based on formal or informal tools, can be complemented with direct evidence of a firm's subjective intent in the context of a particular case. An authority or court may dispense of the need to consider the effects of a practice if it is established that the subjective intent of a firm is pro- or anti-competitive.

As shown in the figure, it is also possible to combine the two factors – one based on effects, the other based on the purpose behind the practice – to define the instances in which a rule is justified. For instance, a practice can be made subject to a prohibition rule where it is simultaneously (i) presumed to have an anti-competitive rationale and (ii) deemed capable of having a negative effect on competition. In practice, the two variables can be combined in different ways. An authority or a claimant may be required to establish the two presumptions independently of one another – thereby making it necessary to show that the practice has, first, an anti-competitive purpose and is, second, capable of having (or likely to have, or certain to have) an anti-competitive effect. Alternatively, one of the variables may be inferred from the other. If, for example, an authority or a claimant shows that the practice has an anti-competitive purpose, it can be inferred from that fact that it is also, for instance, capable of having anti-competitive effects.

The approach to the definition of rules and standards can be a major source of inconsistencies in practice. Like cases may not be treated alike if, in some instances, the scope of a rule is defined in accordance with effects-based factors – in the sense that a rule is deemed appropriate when a practice is deemed capable of having, or likely to have, anti-competitive effects – while in other situations purpose-based considerations alone are deemed sufficient to lay down a prohibition rule. Inconsistencies may also arise where there are divergences in the case law and administrative practice about the approach that is followed to establish the rationale behind a practice. Some cases may suggest that a presumption in this sense can be established on the basis of informal factors, while other cases may suggest that formal analysis is required. Indeed, formal and informal approaches to the question are unlikely to lead to the same conclusions in all cases.

1.3.4 Approaches to Standard-Based Analysis

A standard-based approach to the lawfulness of conduct revolves around a case-by-case assessment. The analysis of practices focuses on whether the facts available to the court or authority are consistent with the

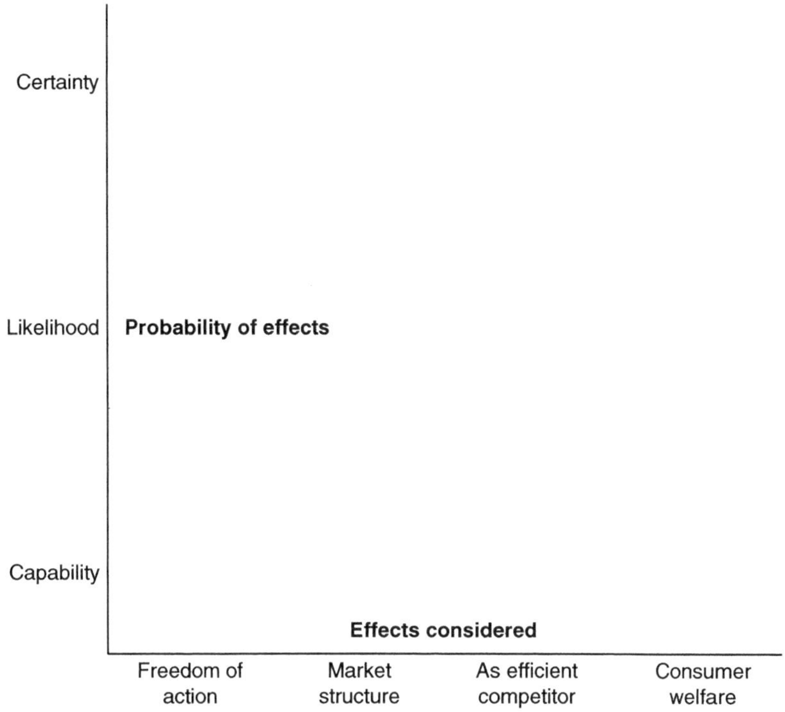

Figure 2.3 Approaches to standard-based analysis

underlying competition concerns. In essence, the application of a standard requires an evaluation of the negative impact of the practice on competition. As shown in Figure 2.3, one dimension of the analysis relates to the probability of anti-competitive effects. It is necessary to determine whether the burden of proving an infringement is discharged by meeting a standard of capability (that is, by showing that the anti-competitive effects are a plausible prospect); one of likelihood (that is, whether the practice is more likely than not to have anti-competitive effects); or one of certainty.

The case-by-case assessment of the compatibility of practices makes it also necessary to give a precise meaning to the notion of effects. This is the second variable captured in the horizontal axis of Figure 2.3. It is necessary, in other words, to decide which phenomenon is equated with an anti-competitive effect. The different meanings that can be attached to the notion can be placed along a continuum. At one end of the spectrum, the notion of effects can be understood to refer to the impact of a practice on firms' freedom of action. At the other end, an anti-competitive effect would be established if there is direct evidence of the impact of a practice on one or more parameters of competition, including prices, output, quality and innovation. For the sake of clarity, this approach to the analysis of effects is referred to as 'consumer welfare'.

It is possible to think of approaches that lie somewhere in between these two extremes, as depicted in the figure. An intermediate approach is one that considers the impact of a practice on the market structure. Under this approach, it would not be sufficient to show that the practice curtails the freedom of action of market players. It would be necessary to show, in addition, that it has negative effects on rivals' ability and incentive to compete. This intermediate approach can be further refined if one takes into account the relative efficiency of market players. If this refinement is introduced, not every effect on the market structure would be unlawful. Intervention would only be justified where the practice has a negative impact on the ability and incentive of equally efficient rivals to compete. The exclusion of rivals that are not able to compete, which would for instance be the case where their products are less attractive in terms of (for instance) price or quality, would not justify intervention. This further refinement would take into account that the departure of such firms is a natural manifestation of the competitive process, and something that can be expected to occur irrespective of the behaviour of other market players.

1.3.5 Objective Justification

It was mentioned in Section 1.2.2 that there is no such thing as unqualified prohibition in EU competition law. Irrespective of the provision, it is possible for firms to advance an objective justification for their practices and, by doing so, to show that they are on the whole pro-competitive or otherwise beneficial. It is clear from the case law that the burden of proving that the practice is objectively justified lies with the firms.[35] An objective justification may be advanced for practices subject to a rule or a standard.[36] The nature of the justification, however, may vary depending on the stage at which it is invoked. If a practice is subject to a rule, an objective justification may be put forward to rebut the presumptions on which the application of the rule is based.

[35] Case C-209/10, *Post Danmark I*, para. 43; and Case C-23/14, *Post Danmark II*, para. 47.

[36] *Post Danmark I* and *Post Danmark II* concerned practices examined in accordance with a standard. An objective justification is open for practices subject to a rule. See in this sense Case T-286/09, *Intel Corp v Commission*, EU:T:2014:547, para. 93. See also C-478/06, *Sot. Lélos*, para. 34.

In particular, it is possible for the firm to show that it does not serve an anti-competitive purpose and that it is, for instance, a source of efficiency gains. If a practice is subject to a standard, the objective justification typically relates to the overall effects on competition. Standard-based analysis focuses on the negative impact of the practice. Once it is found to be prima facie anti-competitive, the objective justification stage allows the firm to establish that the practice has, in addition, pro-competitive effects, and that these effects outweigh the negative effects identified by an authority or claimant.

As is true of the definition of the anti-competitive effects of a practice, it is necessary to define a degree of probability for the pro-competitive effects invoked by firms. If a pro-competitive justification is invoked to rebut a presumption that the practice serves an anti-competitive purpose, for instance, the question is whether it is sufficient that the pro-competitive gains alleged are plausible or whether, instead, it is necessary to show that it is likely or certain that they will be attained. The threshold that is defined for the pro-competitive effects is closely linked to the threshold of anti-competitive effects. If the authority discharges its burden of proof by showing that a given practice is capable of having an anti-competitive effect, the firm would have to show that the pro-competitive effects are more plausible than the negative impact on competition.

1.3.6 The Role of Economic Analysis in the Definition of Rules and Standards

The use of mainstream economic tools has had a major impact on the definition of rules and standards in EU competition law. The progressive incorporation of formal insights in the assessment of practices is arguably the single most important development in the field during the past decades. Economic analysis has influenced the assessment of potentially anti-competitive conduct across all provisions. It has been relied upon both by the Commission and EU courts. The shift in policy undertaken by the authority through the 1990s and early 2000s – which has been labelled the 'more economics-based approach', or 'more economic approach'[37] – has been particularly visible. However, formal economic

37 The idea of the 'more economics-based approach' can be traced back to a speech by Mario Monti, then commissioner for competition. See Mario Monti, 'EU Competition policy after May 2004' (Fordham Annual Conference on International Antitrust Law and Policy, New York, 24 October 2003). See also EAGCP, *An Economic Approach to Article 82* (July 2005), available at http://ec.europa.eu/dgs/competition/economist/eagcp_july_21_05.pdf. The literature on the question is very vast. See, for instance,

Second (and in a related vein), economic analysis imposes discipline in the case-by-case assessment of practices. By rigorously defining the instances in which anti-competitive effects can be expected, it confines the range of scenarios in which intervention would be justified. Take the example of collusive outcomes in oligopolistic markets. From an intuitive perspective, market concentration can be seen with concern insofar as it eases (tacit) collusion between competitors. The consensus among mainstream economists, however, is that an increase in market concentration does not necessarily lead to tacit coordination, and that such an outcome can only be sustained if a relatively narrow set of conditions is met.[46] As a result, credible claims that – for instance – a merger between competitors will lead to tacit collusion would need to show that these circumstances are present. The same can be said of conglomerate mergers. Economic analysis suggests that concerns with the leveraging of a dominant position from one market to a neighbouring one may be intuitively appealing, but are only justified in certain instances.[47]

2 The Institutional Dimension of EU Competition Law

2.1 The Centrality of the Commission in the EU System

The Commission is at the centre of EU competition law and policy-making. This is true not only of EU merger control, where the thrust of enforcement necessarily lies with an administrative authority, but also of Articles 101 and 102 TFEU. Under the system created by the TFEU, it is for the Court of Justice of the European Union ('CJEU') as an institution to state what the law is. In practice, however, the scope of competition law provisions has usually been defined in the cases that the administrative authority has chosen to investigate. Because of the nature and the qualitative significance of these cases, the Commission has often been the one to explore the substantive boundaries of the discipline. It has been the body that gave the initial impetus to some of the defining features of the EU competition law system. While the institutional landscape has changed, and has resulted in a shift in the centre of gravity in law and policy-

[46] For an overview, see Massimo Motta, *Competition Policy: Theory and Practice* (Cambridge: Cambridge University Press, 2004), pp. 142–59.

[47] Simon Bishop, Andrea Lofaro, Francesco Rosati and Juliet Young, *The Efficiency-Enhancing Effects of Non-Horizontal Mergers* (Report prepared by RBB Economics for the Directorate General for Enterprise and Industry, 2005).

making, there are several factors that contribute to the central role of the Commission.

The dominance of public enforcement in Europe is one of these factors. It is conventional wisdom that private disputes shape the legal landscape in the US. Oft-cited studies estimate that there are, or have been, roughly ten private disputes for every case started by a public authority in that country.[48] As a consequence, rules and standards in the US have, to a significant extent, been defined in a decentralised manner without the involvement of administrative authorities. The picture is different in Europe. Historically, private enforcement of the law has, for various reasons, played a relatively minor role in the EU competition law system.[49] The original regime for the enforcement of Article 101 TFEU, which concentrated decision-making powers in relation to agreements with the Commission, contributed to a significant extent to that reality.[50] The absence of a 'competition culture' in post-war Europe is another factor in this sense.[51]

The institutional design of the EU competition law regime is a second factor. It is worth emphasising three key design choices that favour the centrality of the Commission in the system. To begin with, the Commission is an administrative authority that combines the role of investigator and decision-maker. As a consequence, it does not need to rely on a judge to advance its own interpretation of EU competition law provisions. Action leading to the imposition of a fine, blocking a merger or requiring remedies to put an end to an infringement can be adopted by the Commission itself.[52] It is true that these decisions can be

[48] Daniel A. Crane, 'Optimizing Private Antitrust Enforcement' (2010) 63 *Vanderbilt Law Review* 675.

[49] There are at present several attempts by the Commission to encourage the private enforcement of EU competition law. See in particular Directive 2014/104/EU of the European Parliament and of the Council of 26 November 2014 on certain rules governing actions for damages under national law for infringements of the competition law provisions of the Member States and of the European Union OJ (2014) No. L 39/1.

[50] Under the regime established by virtue of Council Regulation 17: First Regulation implementing Articles 85 and 86 of the Treaty, OJ (1962) 13, p. 204/62, the Commission had the competence to examine whether agreements falling under the scope of Article 101(1) TFEU fulfilled the conditions set out in Article 101(3) TFEU.

[51] The Commission has taken the view that part of its remit was the development of such a culture around Europe. See in this sense the White Paper on Modernisation of the Rules Implementing Articles 85 and 86 of the EC Treaty (Brussels, 28 April 1999).

[52] See, in relation to Articles 101 and 102 TFEU, Articles 7, 9 and 23 of Council Regulation (EC) No. 1/2003 of 16 December 2002 on the implementation of the rules on competition laid down in Articles 81 and 82 of the Treaty OJ (2003) No. L 1/1; and, in relation to

subsequently challenged before the EU courts. This said, the Commission remains the first-instance decision-maker, which is of vital importance considering that, as subsequent chapters show, direct actions for annulment are only brought against a fraction of decisions.

Due to the combination of the investigative and adjudicative roles, the interpretation of the relevant provision advanced, or hinted at, in Commission decisions will often become the final word in many proceedings and as such taken as a reliable interpretation of the law. This tendency is reinforced by the incentives of stakeholders, which may not perceive the benefit of challenging a decision before the EU courts. Firms subject to an investigation are not necessarily concerned with the static and dynamic consistency of the system. From their perspective, an outcome that they perceive as efficient and reasonable may be preferred over one that is legally sound. Likewise, the prospect of lengthy proceedings and the possibility of receiving a fine may deter firms from seeking the interpretation of the provisions that they believe is more convincing. This insight is probably more apparent in the context of merger control. Decisions in the field are adopted within a short time frame, as the success of the transaction depends on a quick approval. That a very limited number of merger cases are brought before the EU courts is therefore unsurprising.[53] It is equally unsurprising that firms prefer to propose remedies to obtain clearance.[54]

Regulation 1/2003 provides for several key design choices that favour the central role of the Commission. The authority is entrusted, by virtue of the Regulation, with the task of coordinating and monitoring the implementation of EU competition law by national competition authorities (hereinafter NCAs) and courts. The Regulation introduced mechanisms to ensure the consistent application of Articles 101 and 102 TFEU. These mechanisms allow the Commission to influence the definition of the scope of the two provisions. In accordance with Article 16(1) of Regulation 1/2003, national courts are required to follow any decision either adopted or contemplated by the Commission.[55]

merger control, the Commission Notice on remedies acceptable under the Council Regulation (EC) No. 139/2004 and under Commission Regulation (EC) No. 802/2004 OJ (2008) No. C 267/1.

[53] See Chapter 5.

[54] The number of mergers blocked in over 25 years is also relatively low. The figure stands at 27 at the time of writing.

[55] Article 16(1) of Regulation 1/2003 reads as follows: 'When national courts rule on agreements, decisions or practices under Article 81 or Article 82 of the Treaty which are already the subject of a Commission decision, they cannot take decisions running

The Commission may also become involved in court proceedings at the national level as *amicus curiae*.[56] In turn, the enforcement activity of NCAs is subject to the control of the Commission, which shall be informed of authorities' plans to start an investigation or to adopt a decision.[57] In the same vein, NCAs are relieved of their competence to apply Articles 101 and 102 TFEU when the Commission starts proceedings in a given case.[58]

The Commission has regulatory powers in EU competition law. This is the third factor contributing to its centrality in the system. Individual decisions are a powerful device to advance its interpretation of EU competition law provisions, but it is not the only one. The Commission can adopt block exemption regulations in some areas. These regulations apply to a whole category of agreements within the meaning of Article 101(1) TFEU.[59] Block exemption regulations are typically accompanied by a set of Guidelines that clarify the approach of the Commission and generally expand its scope of application.[60] Comparable pre-commitment devices have also been adopted in the context of Article 102

counter to the decision adopted by the Commission. They must also avoid giving decisions which would conflict with a decision contemplated by the Commission in proceedings it has initiated. To that effect, the national court may assess whether it is necessary to stay its proceedings. This obligation is without prejudice to the rights and obligations under Article 234 of the Treaty'.

[56] See in this sense Article 15(3) of Regulation 1/2003 and Commission Notice on the co-operation between the Commission and the courts of the EU Member States in the application of Articles 81 and 82 EC OJ (2004) No. C 101/54.

[57] See in this sense Article 11 of Regulation 1/2003.

[58] In accordance with Article 11(6) of Regulation 1/2003, '[t]he initiation by the Commission of proceedings for the adoption of a decision under Chapter III shall relieve the competition authorities of the Member States of their competence to apply Articles 81 and 82 of the Treaty. If a competition authority of a Member State is already acting on a case, the Commission shall only initiate proceedings after consulting with that national competition authority'.

[59] In accordance with Article 105(3) TFEU, '[t]he Commission may adopt regulations relating to the categories of agreement in respect of which the Council has adopted a regulation or a directive pursuant to Article 103(2)(b)'. The Block Exemption Regulations adopted by the Commission include Commission Regulation (EU) No. 330/2010 of 20 April 2010 on the application of Article 101(3) of the Treaty on the Functioning of the European Union to categories of vertical agreements and concerted practices OJ (2010) No. L 102/1; and Commission Regulation (EU) No. 316/2014 of 21 March 2014 on the application of Article 101(3) of the Treaty on the Functioning of the European Union to categories of technology transfer agreements (TTBER) OJ (2014) No. L93/17.

[60] See for instance Guidelines on vertical restraints OJ (2010) No. C 130/1 and Guidelines on the application of Article 101 of the Treaty on the Functioning of the European Union to technology transfer agreements OJ (2014) No. C 89/3.

TFEU[61] and merger control.[62] Finally, the reports issued by the Commission in the context of a sector inquiry also provide valuable indications about the practices that might justify intervention.[63]

These instruments allow the Commission to use its resources more efficiently. There is only a limited number of decisions that an administrative authority can adopt at any given point in time. The effectiveness of the system and the deterrence of anti-competitive conduct needs to rely on alternative mechanisms. In this sense, regulations and similar devices of general application allow the Commission to steer firm conduct beyond individual decisions and to focus its enforcement efforts on the most problematic and/or novel infringements. In addition, these instruments can influence the definition of the scope of EU competition law provisions by the Court. It is not difficult to think of Court rulings that reflect a position at which the Commission had already hinted in one of its soft law instruments.[64] Pre-commitment devices can also influence decision-making at the national level.[65]

The potential advantages of centralising the development of competition law and policy within a single administrative authority are obvious. Robert Bork expressed a preference for such a model over the court-based system that prevails in the US.[66] The reasons behind this position are intuitively appealing. Legal fragmentation, and thus legal uncertainty, can be the inevitable outcome of a regime in which enforcement is dispersed across courts and is primarily driven by private disputes.[67]

[61] Guidance on the Commission's enforcement priorities in applying Article 82 of the EC Treaty to abusive exclusionary conduct by dominant undertakings OJ (2009) No. C 45/7.

[62] Guidelines on the assessment of horizontal mergers under the Council Regulation on the control of concentrations between undertakings OJ (2004) No. C 31/5; and Guidelines on the assessment of non-horizontal mergers under the Council Regulation on the control of concentrations between undertakings OJ (2008) No. C 65/6.

[63] In accordance with Article 17 of Regulation 1/2003, the Commission has the power to conduct investigations 'into sectors of the economy and into types of agreements'. Article 17(1) provides specifically that the Commission 'may publish a report on the results of its inquiry into particular sectors'.

[64] This question has been examined systematically in Oana Stefan, *Soft Law in Court: Competition Law, State Aid and the Court of Justice of the European Union* (Alphen aan den Rijn: Kluwer, 2013).

[65] For two examples in which this issue was raised, see Case C-439/09, *Pierre Fabre Dermo-Cosmétique SAS v Président de l'Autorité de la concurrence and Ministre de l'Économie, de l'Industrie et de l'Emploi*, EU:C:2011:649, concerning the Guidelines on vertical restraints; and Case C-23/14, *Post Danmark II*, concerning the Guidance on exclusionary abuses.

[66] See in this sense Bork, *The Antitrust Paradox*, p. 439.

[67] This phenomenon is well identified in the US. For a discussion, see Crane 'Optimizing Private Antitrust Enforcement', at 125–43, who discusses forum shopping; and Douglas

In addition, generalist courts may be unwilling and/or unable to engage with complex legal and economic matters. This question is particularly important in a discipline which, like competition law, is subject to frequent change. Finally, as was explained in Chapter 1, an authority like the Commission can be expected to behave differently to firms in private litigation. The choice of cases, and the arguments, can be expected to be motivated by public-interest considerations, and not by an attempt to obtain a private benefit (such as, for instance, better supply conditions or access to a competitor's facilities).[68] As a consequence, it is reasonable to expect that a system driven by administrative action will cover a broader range of potentially anti-competitive practices. The definition of rules and standards, in turn, can be expected to be closer to the optimal, in the sense that the authority is more likely to pay due regard to the objectives and logic of the competition law system.

2.2 *Due Process Considerations in EU Competition Law*

2.2.1 Claims of Prosecutorial Bias

In spite of the theoretical advantages of a system revolving around an administrative authority, the dual role of the Commission as investigator and adjudicator has become one of the most controversial topics in EU competition law. The potential drawbacks of the model are as apparent as the advantages described earlier. One could argue, to begin with, that allowing an administrative authority to decide on the same cases that it chooses to investigate goes against the basic principle of justice whereby nobody should be a judge in their own cause. Disputes, the argument goes, must be settled by an independent third party. This is probably the single most important factor that makes adverse decisions acceptable for the losing party and, more generally, the fundamental idea underpinning the respect for the legal system.[69] According to this view, the enforcement architecture of EU competition law would be anomalous, even though it is not an unusual setup in the modern administrative state. Expert agencies combining the roles of

H. Ginsburg and Joshua D. Wright, 'Antitrust Courts: Specialists Versus Generalists' (2013) 36 *Fordham International Law Journal* 788.

[68] Wouter Wils, 'The Relationship between Public Antitrust Enforcement and Private Actions for Damages' (2009) 32 *World Competition* 3.

[69] Martin Shapiro, *Courts: A Comparative and Political Analysis* (Chicago: University of Chicago Press, 1986).

investigator and adjudicator have become a common feature of legal systems around the world.[70]

The practical consequences of the combination of roles have been well identified. Where an administrative authority is entrusted with investigative and decision-making powers, a firm may not be subject to what is generally known as a due process of law. The alleged absence of due process may be manifested, first, in the way hearings are conducted, if the firm is not given the chance to advance its position (or does not perceive that its position has been adequately considered by the decision-maker). Even when due process guarantees are formally respected, the combination of roles may be problematic insofar as it may not provide adequate protection against biased decision-making. One could reasonably argue that, where the very authority that has initiated the proceedings is also in charge of adopting a final decision on whether an infringement has taken place, it will be naturally inclined to give more weight to its own views, and particularly so when it has reached the preliminary conclusion that the law has been infringed.

As some practising lawyers have frequently pointed out, where an authority combines the roles of investigator and decision-maker, the outcome of the case may be decided from the early stages of the procedure. As a result, the opposing views advanced by the firms subject to the investigation may have no impact on the predisposition of the officials to establish an infringement or to require remedies.[71] The risk of biased decision-making has been abundantly explored in the literature in recent years, in particular following a seminal contribution by Wouter Wils.[72] Against this background, the fundamental concern with the EU

[70] For an overview of the argument, see Adrian Vermeule, *The Constitution of Risk* (Cambridge: Cambridge University Press, 2014). The author refers to *Withrow v Larkin*, 421 U.S. 35 (1975), where the US Supreme Court rejected the idea that the combination of functions 'necessarily creates an unconstitutional risk of bias in administrative adjudication'. The author also refers to an antitrust case *FTC v Cement Institute et al.*, 333 U.S. 683 (1948).

[71] See in particular Frank Montag, 'The case for a radical reform of the infringement procedure under Regulation 17', (1996) 17 *European Competition Law Review* 428; Donald Slater, Sébastien Thomas and Denis Waelbroeck, 'Competition law proceedings before the European Commission and the right to a fair trial: no need for reform?' (2009) 5 *European Competition Journal* 97; and Ian S. Forrester, 'Due process in EC competition cases: A distinguished institution with flawed procedures' (2009) 34 *European Law Review* 817.

[72] Wouter Wils, 'The Combination of the Investigative and Prosecutorial Function and the Adjudicative Function in EC Antitrust Enforcement: A Legal and Economic Analysis' (2004) 27 *World Competition* 202.

competition law system is that it would not be adequately equipped to correct the prosecutorial bias of the officials in charge of the investigation of an alleged infringement. While the issue of prosecutorial bias has attracted the attention of several commentators, there appears to be an occasional confusion in the literature between the *concept* of bias as such, its *sources* and its *manifestations*.

The concept of prosecutorial bias can be generally defined as a bias in favour of establishing an infringement. Bias may be induced by the policy priorities of the Commission. The enforcement priorities defined by the Directorate General for Competition may influence the analysis of individual cases. There are also broad policy objectives defined at the level of the Commission as a whole. For instance, the Commission has actively supported the liberalisation of the network industries through both legislation and competition law enforcement.[73] Similarly, it has taken several legislative and non-legislative initiatives – including the launch of a Sector Inquiry and the opening of formal competition law proceedings – towards the creation of a Digital Single Market.[74] Where policy objectives and/or enforcement priorities are defined, officials may develop a bias against certain practices that are deemed to be an obstacle to the outcomes that are perceived as desirable. Other sources of bias are cognitive in nature. The latter were explored by Wouter Wils in his seminal piece. In particular, he refers to confirmation bias, which he defined as 'a tendency to search for evidence which confirms rather than challenges one's beliefs, and to accept more readily the conclusion to a syllogism if it corresponds to one's beliefs than if it does not'.[75] He also refers to officials' inclination to show a high level of enforcement.[76]

Prosecutorial bias can lead to erroneous decision-making. A biased authority, in other words, can take action where there are no objective reasons to do so. When thinking about erroneous decision-making, it is useful to refer to the aspects pertaining to the 'external' and the 'internal

[73] Among the most salient examples, see the Commission Directive 88/301/EEC of 16 May 1988 on competition in the markets in telecommunications terminal equipment OJ (1988) No. L 131/73; Commission, 'Towards a new framework for Electronic Communications infrastructure and associated services: The 1999 Communications Review' COM (1999) 539; Commission, 'An Energy Policy for Europe' COM (2007) 1 final.

[74] Commission, 'A Digital Single Market Strategy for Europe' COM (2015) 192 final.

[75] Wils, 'The Combination of the Investigative and Prosecutorial Function and the Adjudicative Function in EC Antitrust Enforcement: A Legal and Economic Analysis', at 215.

[76] Ibid, p. 217.

legality' of administrative acts.[77] Essentially, the former concern the formal and procedural requirements and the latter concern the substantive aspects of the decision. The discussion that follows focuses on the 'internal legality' of administrative acts. One may distinguish, in this regard, between errors of fact and errors of law. Among the former, a biased authority may, for instance, fail to consider all the facts that are relevant for the analysis of a decision. In particular, it may be inclined to disregard, or downplay, evidence that goes against officials' inclination to establish an infringement. A biased authority may also commit errors of law. It may conclude that a given practice is contrary to an EU competition law provision even though the conditions for establishing an infringement are not met in the case. For instance, it may conclude that a practice is prohibited under Article 101(1) TFEU even though it does not qualify as an agreement or it does not have as its object or effect the restriction of competition. An error of law may also result, for instance, from the definition of the wrong legal test. For instance, the Commission may conclude that a practice amounts to an abuse of a dominant position in light of a set of conditions that is not relevant in the context of the case. It may also result from the legal characterisation of facts. Thus, the Commission may rely on the appropriate legal test, but may wrongly apply it to the facts at hand.

The terms of the debate on the lawfulness of the combination of functions within the Commission have generally been defined around the principles set out in the case law of the European Court of Human Rights (hereinafter the 'ECtHR'). This debate has generally been framed as one about compatibility with fundamental rights of the institutional structure of EU competition law enforcement. Because the Commission is a body that adopts decisions in the same cases it investigates, it has often been claimed that the EU system contradicts the principle set out in Article 6(1) ECHR, pursuant to which an individual should be given an impartial hearing before an independent tribunal.[78] For many authors,

[77] This expression is taken from the French tradition of administrative law, which distinguishes between the external legality and the internal legality of administrative acts. The former concerns the procedural aspects of the decision and the latter the substantive ones. For an application of this distinction to actions for annulment in EU law, see Flavien Mariatte and Dominique Ritleng, *Contentieux de l'Union européenne*, 3 vols. (Paris: Lamy, 2011), vol. 1, p. 193.

[78] Article 6(1) ECHR reads as follows: 'In the determination of his civil rights and obligations or of any criminal charge against him, everyone is entitled to a fair and public hearing within a reasonable time by an independent and impartial tribunal established by law. Judgment shall be pronounced publicly but the press and public may be excluded

this question is settled following the ECtHR judgment in *Menarini*.[79] The case concerned the Italian competition law regime. The specific issue raised by the firm in that case related to the scope and intensity of judicial review by administrative courts.

The ECtHR ruled in *Menarini* that fines imposed in competition law proceedings are criminal within the meaning of the Convention.[80] While the imposition of a fine by an administrative authority is not necessarily incompatible with Article 6(1) ECtHR, it is necessary to ensure that all the legal and factual aspects of the decisions adopted by such an authority are reviewed by an independent tribunal with 'full jurisdiction'.[81] From this aspect of the ruling, authors have inferred that the combination of functions by the Commission is not in itself contrary to Article 6(1) ECtHR.[82] The legality of the system would depend on the exercise of 'full jurisdiction' by the EU courts. Immediately following *Menarini*, the EU courts signalled their commitment to the principles outlined in the judgment.[83]

The *Menarini* ruling has not put an end to controversies around due process in the EU competition law system. One of the reasons has to do with the fact that a significant fraction of decisions adopted by the Commission is never challenged before the EU courts. As pointed out earlier, firms do not necessarily have an incentive to engage in lengthy proceedings and may prefer to settle the matter with the authority. In this sense, the use of so-called commitment decisions are a contemporary feature of the framework through which Article 101 and 102 TFEU are enforced. Pursuant to a commitment decision, the Commission decides

from all or part of the trial in the interest of morals, public order or national security in a democratic society, where the interests of juveniles or the protection of the private life of the parties so require, or the extent strictly necessary in the opinion of the court in special circumstances where publicity would prejudice the interests of justice'.

79 *Menarini Diagnostics SRL v Italy* App no 43509/08 (ECtHR 27 September 2011). Contra, see Denis Waelbroeck and Sven Frisch, 'Après l'Arrêt Menarini: l'impact de la Convention européenne de Sauvegarde des Droits de l'Homme et des Libertés fondamentales sur les procédures en droit de la concurrence' in Inge Govaere and Dominik Hanf (eds.), *Scrutinizing Internal and External Dimensions of European Law: Les dimensions internes et externes du droit européen à l'épreuve* (Brussels: PIE Peter Lang, 2013).

80 *Menarini*, para. 42. 81 Ibid, para. 59.

82 See in particular Wouter Wils, 'The Compatibility with Fundamental Rights of the EU Antitrust Enforcement System in Which the European Commission Acts Both as Investigator and as First-Instance Decision Maker' (2014) 37 *World Competition* 5.

83 Case C-386/10 P, *Chalkor AE Epexergasias Metallon v Commission*, EU:C:2011:815; and Case C-389/10 P, *KME Germany AG, KME France SAS and KME Italy SpA v Commission*, EU:C:2011:816.

that there are no longer grounds to continue with an investigation following concessions made by the firms.[84] As a result, errors of law and/or of fact may not be subject to adequate scrutiny. By the same token, the exercise of 'full jurisdiction' by the EU courts may only provide a partial response to due process concerns, in the sense that the prospect of a challenge may not provide an appropriate safeguard. A second reason why controversies have not disappeared relates to the fact that, according to some authors, the EU courts are *unduly* deferential to the Commission and thus fail to comply with the principles set out in *Menarini*. Undue deference, the argument goes, contributes to firms' inclination to reach a negotiated outcome (which reduces the likelihood that enforcement errors will be corrected before the EU courts).[85]

2.2.2 Claims of Curial Deference

The concept of *undue deference* can be defined as a failure to review administrative action in line with the principles set out by the ECtHR in *Menarini*. Crucially, the ECtHR did not approach this question from a formal perspective. Whether courts exercise 'full jurisdiction' over administrative action is to be established on a case-by-case basis. What matters, in other words, is the scope and intensity of the review actually exercised, not the vocabulary used by courts. The Italian administrative courts had declared in the course of the proceedings that the legal characterisation of facts by the competition authority was subject to limited review.[86] The majority did not consider that this fact was sufficient to conclude that 'full jurisdiction' had not been exercised. The concurrent opinion by Judge Sajo emphasised this point. He noted that the scope and intensity of the review de facto exercised by the highest administrative court met the requirements of Article 6 ECHR.[87]

[84] Pursuant to Article 9(1) of Regulation 1/2003: 'Where the Commission intends to adopt a decision requiring that an infringement be brought to an end and the undertakings concerned offer commitments to meet the concerns expressed to them by the Commission in its preliminary assessment, the Commission may by decision make those commitments binding on the undertakings. Such a decision may be adopted for a specified period and shall conclude that there are no longer grounds for action by the Commission'.

[85] For a comprehensive analysis of the interplay of these factors, see Damien Gerard, 'Negotiated remedies in the modernization era: the limits of effectiveness' in Philip Lowe and Mel Marquis (eds.), *European Competition Law Annual 2013: Effective and Legitimate Enforcement of Competition Law* (Oxford: Hart Publishing, 2016).

[86] This is the point emphasised by Judge Pinto de Albuquerque in his dissent in *Menarini*.

[87] Ibid.

The test defined by the ECtHR in *Menarini* is not useful for shedding light on the controversies around the scope and intensity of judicial review in EU competition law. In the EU law system, the task of the EU courts is to state what the law is. The Commission does not enjoy any discretion in this regard. As a result, errors of law and of fact are subject to 'full' or 'comprehensive' review.[88] The Commission may propose a particular interpretation of EU competition law provisions, but the EU courts are not bound by it, even if it is reasonable. The EU courts may very well adopt a different legal test and assess the legality of administrative action against it.[89] This fact suggests that the scope and intensity of review that the EU courts are expected to exercise would meet the standard set by the ECtHR. The review of the Italian courts in *Menarini* was confined to the legality of administrative action, but it was deemed to satisfy the requirements set by Article 6 ECHR.[90]

Controversies around the scope and intensity of judicial review have a formal and a substantive dimension. From a formal perspective, it has been argued that the current system does not meet the conditions set out in *Menarini* insofar as the EU courts have declared that there are exceptions to the principle of full review of the factual and legal aspects of Commission decisions. The EU courts only exercise limited review over the so-called 'complex economic assessments'.[91] In such cases, judicial review is confined to verifying whether 'the evidence relied on is factually accurate, reliable and consistent but also whether that evidence contains all the relevant information which must be taken into account in order to

[88] This principle stems logically from Article 263 TFEU, whereby the CJUE is entrusted with the duty to review the legality of the acts adopted by the EU institutions. For an overview, see Heike Schweitzer, 'Judicial Review in EU Competition Law' in Ioannis Lianos and Damien Geradin (eds.), *Handbook on European Competition Law – Substantive Aspects* (Cheltenham: Edward Elgar, 2013).

[89] See Paul Craig, *EU Administrative Law*, 2nd edn. (Oxford: Oxford University Press, 2012), pp. 405–7. The author refers to this approach as 'substitution of judgment'.

[90] Marco Bronckers and Anne Vallery, 'Business as usual after Menarini?' *MLex* (January-March 2012).

[91] For an overview of this case law and its logic, see Marc Jaeger, 'The Standard of Review in Competition Cases Involving Complex Economic Assessments: Towards the Marginalisation of the Marginal Review?' (2011) 2 *Journal of European Competition Law & Practice* 295; and Renato Nazzini, 'Judicial Review after KME: An Even Stronger Case for the Reform That Will Never Be' (2015) 40 *European Law Review* 490. The principle appears to extend to 'complex technical assessments'. See in this sense Ioannis Lianos and Christos Genakos, 'Econometric evidence in EU competition law: an empirical and theoretical analysis' in Ioannis Lianos and Damien Geradin (eds.), *Handbook on European Competition Law – Enforcement and Procedure* (Cheltenham: Edward Elgar, 2013).

assess a complex situation and whether it is capable of substantiating the conclusions drawn from it'.[92] In light of what was discussed earlier, these formal declarations are not crucial. If the review performed by the EU courts fulfils de facto the *Menarini* conditions, it matters little that they show their willingness to give the Commission a margin of appreciation. In fact, several commentators have identified instances in which the scrutiny of the EU courts was strict and thorough, even though it was formally limited to 'manifest errors'.[93] By the same token, if formal aspects truly determined the scope and intensity of judicial review, the EU courts could effectively address any concerns by simply avoiding any vocabulary suggesting a deferential attitude.[94]

From a substantive standpoint, it has often been argued that, irrespective of what the EU courts formally declare in their judgments, they fail de facto to engage in the full review of administrative action. This is a claim that is very difficult to establish in practice, which is the fundamental reason why it remains controversial and why little progress has been made in establishing (or rejecting) it in a cogent and persuasive way. Many commentators argue that the annulment of a Commission decision is a rare occurrence, and infer from this fact that courts are unduly deferential. For instance, it has often been pointed out that it is very unusual to see a Commission decision quashed in an Article 102 TFEU case.[95] In relation to cartel cases, concerns have also been raised about the intensity with which the EU courts review decisions imposing fines.[96]

[92] Case C-67/13 P, *Groupement des cartes bancaires v Commission*, EU:C:2014:2204, para. 46.

[93] This is a point made by Wils, 'The Compatibility with Fundamental Rights of the EU Antitrust Enforcement System in Which the European Commission Acts Both as Investigator and as First-Instance Decision Maker'. An obvious example in this sense is Case T-5/02, *Tetra Laval BV v Commission*, EU:T:2002:264. The GC, using the vocabulary of limited review and manifest errors of assessment, engaged in a very close scrutiny of the Commission decision.

[94] The avoidance of this vocabulary was suggested, inter alia, in 'Editorial comments, Towards a more judicial approach? EU antitrust fines under the scrutiny of fundamental rights' (2011) 48 *Common Market Law Review* 1405; and Bronckers and Vallery, 'Business as usual after Menarini?'.

[95] This point has been repeatedly made by several authors using different figures. See in particular Christian Ahlborn and David S. Evans, 'The Microsoft Judgment and its Implications for Competition Policy Towards Dominant Firms in Europe' (2009) 75 *Antitrust Law Journal* 887; and Damien Geradin and Nicolas Petit, 'Judicial Review in European Union Competition Law: A Quantitative and Qualitative Assessment' in Massimo Merola and Jacques Derenne (eds.), *The Role of the Court of Justice of the European Union in Competition Law Cases* (Brussels: Bruylant, 2012).

[96] See for instance Luis Ortiz Blanco, Angel Givaja Sanz and Alfonso Lamadrid de Pablo, 'Fine Arts in Brussels: Punishment and Settlement of Cartel cases under EC Competition

The alleged absence of full judicial review in cartel cases would be particularly problematic, according to this view, due to the fact that the fining policy of the Commission is one that has a criminal character within the meaning of the ECtHR case law, and the fact that this is the one area in which EU courts enjoy 'unlimited jurisdiction', by which it is meant that they 'may cancel, reduce or increase the fine or periodic penalty payment imposed'.[97]

The arguments typically raised by commentators in support of their claims are not conclusive. Without a careful analysis of their substantive aspects, the fact that Commission decisions are upheld does not provide unequivocal evidence of undue deference. If a Commission decision follows a well-established line of case law – and it is not difficult to identify clear examples of practices that are always, or almost always, prohibited – it is unsurprising to see it upheld by the EU courts if challenged. For instance, the Courts have consistently held that exclusivity obligations are prima facie prohibited under Article 102 TFEU.[98] As a result, it is uneventful to see the GC dismiss claims that the Commission has erred in law by concluding that the practice is abusive.[99] In the same vein, the absence of annulments is also consistent with judicial activism. If the review of administrative action is consistently intense and thorough, an administrative authority may prefer to adopt a risk-averse strategy and pursue only clear-cut infringements that are certain to be upheld on factual and legal grounds. In reality, it is only possible to draw meaningful conclusions about the deferential nature of judicial review by examining whether the analysis of the Commission conforms to the case law, that is, by considering the link between institutional and substantive matters.

Law' (VIII Conference of the European Lawyers' Union, Treviso, 22–23 May 2008); Ian S. Forrester, 'A Challenge for Europe's Judges: The Review of Fines in Competition Cases' (2011) 36 *European Law Review* 185; and Peter D. Camesasca, Johan Ysewyn, Thomas Weck, and Brian Bowman, 'Cartel Appeals to the Court of Justice: The Song of the Sirens?' (2013) 4 *Journal of European Competition Law & Practice* 215. For some recent concrete examples of how this principle applies in practice, see Eric Barbier de La Serre and Eileen Lagathu, 'The Law on Fines Imposed in EU Competition Proceedings: Fifty Shades of Undertakings' (2015) 6 *Journal of European Competition Law & Practice* 530; and Eric Barbier de La Serre and Eileen Lagathu, 'The Law on Fines Imposed in EU Competition Proceedings: Consolidating the Foundations Before the Tide Goes Out' (2016) 7 *Journal of European Competition Law & Practice* 335.

[97] Article 31 of Regulation 1/2003. [98] Case 85/76, *Hoffmann-La Roche*.

[99] As the GC did in *Intel*. See also Case C-549/10 P, *Tomra Systems ASA and Others v Commission*, EU:C:2012:221.

3 The Interplay between the Institutional and Substantive Dimensions of EU Competition Law

3.1 Bias, Deference and Enforcement Errors

As explained earlier, biased decision-making is generally understood to be problematic insofar as it might lead to enforcement errors.[100] From this perspective, undue deference would be undesirable to the extent that it would fail to fulfil the error-correction role of judicial review.[101] This understanding of bias and deference may fit other legal disciplines well, but is not always a meaningful one in EU competition law. It looks like an appropriate starting point where there is a stable and clearly defined benchmark against which administrative action can be measured. In such circumstances, it may be possible to establish whether a decision is in line with the expected 'but for' outcome and thus whether it is correct. The difficulty with this approach is that it is not always clear what the benchmark is, or should be, in EU competition law. Similarly, this approach assumes that benchmarks are fixed and do not vary over time. A distinct feature of EU competition law is in fact that they fluctuate.

As observed earlier, prosecutorial bias may be manifested, inter alia, in the definition of the legal test by the Commission. If bias exists, the Commission may choose one that makes it relatively easy to establish an infringement. The phenomenon would be manifested at different stages of the definition of the legal test. Bias may come into play, for instance, when the Commission considers whether the practice can be compared in its nature and impact to existing categories. If the available legal tests do not support a finding of infringement, the Commission may depart from them and set a new one. The Commission may take the view that the practice raises novel legal issues that justify defining a new framework. Alternatively, it may decide to refine the existing test, either by incorporating the lessons of experience and economic analysis or by expanding its scope.

The fact that the Commission defines a new legal test, or refines an existing one, does not in itself provide conclusive evidence that the decision is erroneous. The departure from an existing legal test may be

[100] See for instance Wils, 'The Combination of the Investigative and Prosecutorial Function and the Adjudicative Function in EC Antitrust Enforcement: A Legal and Economic Analysis'.

[101] On the error-correction role of judicial review, see Steven Shavell, 'The Appeals Process as a Means of Error Correction' (1995) 24 *Journal of Legal Studies* 379.

plausibly explained on other grounds. It would therefore be misleading to infer from this fact alone that the decision is biased. To complicate matters further, the involvement of the EU courts is not capable of providing conclusive evidence either. The EU courts may uphold the analysis of the Commission and conclude that the authority did not commit an error of law. However, this is not in itself evidence that the decision was correct. As explained earlier, such an outcome is equally consistent with undue deference. Thus, the relative success of the Commission when administrative action is challenged – that is, whether its decisions are annulled or not – does not provide a reliable benchmark either.

An alternative approach is to define a benchmark by reference to a given measure of welfare. Thus, a decision establishing an infringement would be correct if it leads to an improvement in terms of consumer or total welfare and it would be erroneous if it leads to a decrease in this sense. This approach is problematic, first, because it would not be easy to evaluate in practice. The trouble with the precise quantification of the impact of competition law in the economy and in the context of a particular case has been abundantly discussed in the literature.[102] A second reason why this approach would be problematic is that there is no unequivocal indication in the case law suggesting that a particular measure of welfare is the appropriate benchmark to assess administrative action. If anything, the Court has suggested that it is not necessary to establish the precise impact of a practice of consumer welfare in order to establish an infringement.[103] Accordingly, this analysis may well lead to the conclusion that intervention is economically unsound. It would not follow from this conclusion, however, that the Commission had reached an erroneous decision from a legal

[102] On the general impact of competition law on welfare, see Robert W. Crandall and Clifford Winston, 'Does Antitrust Policy Improve Consumer Welfare? Assessing the Evidence' (2003) 17 *Journal of Economic Perspectives* 3; and Gregory J. Werden, 'The Effect of Antitrust Policy on Consumer Welfare: What Crandall and Winston Overlook' (2003) U.S. Department of Justice Antitrust Division Discussion Paper No. EAG 03-2, available at http://ssrn.com. The analysis of the effects of practices ex post does not abound in the literature. See in particular John Kwoka, *Mergers, Merger Control, and Remedies* (Cambridge: MIT Press, 2015); Michael D. Whinston, 'Antitrust Policy toward Horizontal Mergers' in Mark Armstrong and Robert H. Porter (eds.), *Handbook of Industrial Organization*, 3 vols. (Amsterdam: North-Holland, 2007), vol. 3. See also Luca Aguzzoni et al., 'Ex-post analysis of two mobile telecom mergers: T-Mobile/tele.ring in Austria and T-Mobile/Orange in the Netherlands', available at http://ec.europa.eu/competition/publications/reports/kd0215836enn.pdf.

[103] See for instance Joined Cases C-501/06 P, C-513/06 P, C-515/06 P and C-519/06 P, *Glaxo Spain*, para. 63; and Case C-95/04, *British Airways*, para. 106.

standpoint. In this sense, a welfare-based approach is likely to be normative rather than descriptive.

3.2 Bias and Deference as a Substantive Matter

The focus on enforcement errors in the literature is evidence that bias and deference issues tend to be approached from an institutional perspective which, moreover, examines the outcome of intervention by looking at cases in isolation. The fundamental question under this approach is whether, given the institutional structure, the specific case under consideration has been correctly decided. This perspective is said to be institutional in the sense that it is primarily concerned with the structure of enforcement – namely, the combination of roles within the administrative authority and the intensity of judicial review. As a result, other factors that are more relevant for the purposes of EU competition law analysis are not considered. An institutional approach to the two questions fails to capture the substantive dimension of biased decision-making and curial deference. Put differently, it is an approach that does not take into account the dynamic dimension of bias and deference, that is, their impact on the evolution of the discipline as a whole.

Biased decision-making can be manifested in a variety of ways. If manifested at the stage where the legal test is defined, it can become a source of static and dynamic inconsistency. From a static perspective, biased decision-making can become a source of incoherence, if the case law and/or administrative practice lack a single overarching rationale, and inconsistency, if an authority fails to treat like practices alike so as to reach the outcome it prefers. From a dynamic perspective, biased decision-making can lead to the fluctuation of the legal test applied to a given practice. If bias is systematic and is coupled with undue deference, it is likely to have a profound impact on the substantive dimension of the law and its evolution. Seen from a dynamic standpoint, the two phenomena seem problematic not so much because they lead to erroneous outcomes in individual cases, but because they affect the manner in which the boundaries of the discipline are defined and evolve.

If bias and undue deference are pervasive, it may become difficult, if not impossible, to anticipate the outcome of administrative action. In such circumstances, precedents would not provide reliable indications about the likely behaviour of the authority. For instance, the fact that practice A is subject to a standard in period 1 would not exclude, in the presence of biased decision-making, the application of a rule to the same practice in period 2. Similarly, biased decision-making, coupled with undue deference, could lead to the progressive watering-down of a standard or to the unpredictable expansion of the scope of a rule. These phenomena can also be expected to result in uncertainty about the rationale behind intervention. Put differently, it may be difficult to infer from administrative action what the underlying concern is. As already observed, these consequences are a powerful reminder that due process is inextricably linked to values such as legal certainty, consistency and stability and, more generally, a powerful reminder of the close ties between substance and institutions.

3.3 Legal Evolution and the Interactions between the Commission and the EU Courts

Prosecutorial bias and undue deference look like intractable issues. It is difficult to see how direct manifestations of prosecutorial bias (that is, instances of erroneous decision-making in a given case) can be credibly established against a reliable benchmark. The same can be said of instances of undue deference in individual judgments, if one considers that there are typically competing explanations for the behaviour of the EU courts. On the other hand, the debate around these two phenomena points to some fundamental issues that are worth studying in their own right. It has been explained that, in the long run, the consequences of biased decision-making and undue deference are not only procedural but also (and perhaps essentially) substantive in nature. If administrative action is inconsistent, and the review courts are deferential to the authority, it may not be possible to anticipate the outcome of intervention. The analysis that follows focuses on these inconsistencies, which, unlike bias and undue deference, can be the subject of systematic study and yield valuable conclusions about the behaviour of the Commission and the EU courts and thus about the evolution of the system.

The remainder of the monograph traces, first, the choices made by the Commission (i) when it interprets EU competition law provisions and (ii) when it deals with constraints on administrative action. Constraints on administrative action can be endogenous and exogenous in nature. *Endogenous* constraints are those that derive from the EU competition law system itself. These constraints are defined, first and foremost, by the EU courts when they interpret the relevant provisions. The Commission needs to engage with the substantive boundaries of the field if it wishes to depart from them. *Exogenous* constraints on administrative action concern, in particular, those that derive from mainstream economic theory. It has been explained earlier that economic analysis informs the assessment of practices at various stages. The perceived legitimacy of administrative action may suffer if the Commission chooses to ignore these insights or calls them into question.

Considering the peculiarities of EU competition law, judicial deference is defined as the endorsement, by the review courts, of the legal test set by the administrative authority. Approached in this way, judicial deference is not necessarily problematic, in the sense that it may be compatible with the fulfilment by the EU courts of their core tasks. Accepting the legal test chosen by an administrative authority is not necessarily at odds with the thorough scrutiny of the decision. As already pointed out, if the review courts reach the conclusion that the legal test defined by the authority is the *correct* one (and not simply a *reasonable* one), it is natural that they uphold it.[104] At the same time, whether or not courts are deferential to the behaviour of the authority has major consequences for the evolution of the discipline. If there is a systematic tendency to defer to the legal tests defined by the Commission, the latter may be encouraged to define the substantive boundaries of the provisions in a relatively expansive manner.[105] The inconsistencies that result from the relationship between the Commission and the EU courts can be mapped in the literature.

For the purposes of the analysis, it is useful to distinguish between *one-shot* and *repeated* interactions between the Commission and the EU courts.[106] The concept of one-shot interaction refers to an instance in

[104] In line with what has been discussed above, that the full review of Commission decisions implies that the task of the EU courts is to set out the correct legal test, and not simply to review the reasonableness of the test designed by the Commission. See in this sense Craig, *EU Administrative Law*; and Renato Nazzini, 'Administrative Enforcement, Judicial Review and Fundamental Rights in EU Competition Law: A Comparative Contextual-Functionalist Perspective' (2012) 49 *Common Market Law Review* 971. The debate about the choice between correctness and reasonableness is a recurrent theme in Anglo-American legal systems. It became popular in the US following the ruling in *Chevron USA, Inc. v Natural Resources Defense Council, Inc*, 467 U.S. 837 (1984). In that case, the US Supreme Court concluded that, where a statute is 'silent or ambiguous' about a given question, review courts should defer to a reasonable interpretation by an administrative agency. See also, on the same questions, Hanna Wilberg and Mark Elliott (eds.), *The Scope and Intensity of Substantive Review: Traversing Taggart's Rainbow* (Oxford: Hart Publishing, 2015).

[105] Emerson Tiller and Frank B Cross, 'Modelling Agency/Court Interaction' (2007) 121 *Harvard Law Review Forum* 13.

[106] This vocabulary is borrowed from the classic work by Marc Galanter, 'Why the "Haves" Come Out Ahead: Speculations on the Limits of Legal Change' (1974) 9 *Law & Society Review* 95.

which the Commission crafts, for the first time, the legal test that should apply to a given practice. In such cases, the EU courts may be called upon to consider whether the interpretation given by the authority amounts to an error of law. In one-shot interactions, the analysis that follows focuses, first, on whether there are discernible patterns in the behaviour of the Commission when it fleshes out, afresh, the scope of EU competition law provisions. The behaviour of the Commission can be broken down into a number of discrete choices that the authority must make when defining the scope of a provision. These choices are taken as an indirect indicator of whether the Commission acts in a manner that is consistent with the maximisation of the reach of administrative action. Second, it is also necessary to consider, in one-shot interactions, the behaviour of the EU courts – and in particular the factors that might have an impact on their tendency to defer to the legal approach endorsed by the Commission.

The concept of repeated interaction concerns an instance in which the EU courts have already defined the legal test that applies to a given practice. More generally, it is an instance where there may already be a body of case law acting as an endogenous constraint on administrative action. In these circumstances, it is necessary to consider, again, the behaviour of the Commission, and more precisely how it engages with the said constraints. The authority may adopt a conservative approach, and intervene only in cases that fall squarely within the boundaries of the legal test defined by the EU courts. Alternatively, it may adopt a risk-prone attitude. For instance, it may choose to circumvent the legal test, or it may seek to interpret it in an expansive manner. In a repeated interaction, an EU court may decide to remain faithful to the prior line of case law or to validate the analysis of the Commission, even if it gives rise to an inconsistency in the system.

Once the analysis of the behaviour of the Commission and the EU courts is mapped, it is possible to draw a picture about the general features of the EU competition law system and its evolution. In a field that develops incrementally, the emergence of inconsistencies is inevitable. The question is thus not only whether inconsistencies exist and are pervasive, but whether there are factors that contribute to the emergence and the perpetuation of such inconsistencies. These factors are identified as vulnerabilities. Vulnerabilities may arise if a significant fraction of the activity of the Commission is not subject to judicial scrutiny. They may also arise if the persistence of inconsistencies is not acknowledged by the EU courts and specific mechanisms are not devised to prevent the opportunistic behaviour by stakeholders and to ensure that administrative action is predictable.

4 Mapping the Behaviour of the Commission

Due to the open-ended scope of EU competition law provisions, an authority like the Commission is able to take action against a broad range of practices. One can draw a broad distinction between two 'ideal types': 'fact-intensive' and 'law-intensive' cases. Whether a case is predominantly 'fact-intensive' or 'law-intensive' depends on two main variables, which are captured in Figure 2.4. One variable relates to whether the lawfulness of the practice is contentious. This may be the case where the relevant precedents do not unequivocally support the conclusion that the practice under consideration is lawful or unlawful. Uncertainty in this sense may arise where there are doubts about the legal test that applies to a practice – namely, where it is not clear whether the practice in question should be subject to a rule or a standard and/or where the applicable standard is not clear. Uncertainty may also arise where the legal characterisation of facts is contentious, that is, where it is not clear whether the conditions set out in a given standard are fulfilled in the context of the case. The second variable relates to the ease with which the facts underpinning the case can be established.

A 'fact-intensive' case is one that revolves predominantly – if not exclusively – around whether the facts supporting the finding of infringement have been established to the requisite legal standard. It is typically clear beyond doubt, in cases falling under this category, that the practice under consideration is unlawful. As shown in Figure 2.4, an 'ideal type' of a 'fact-intensive' case is a cartel. It has always been clear that cartel-type agreements are prohibited under Article 101(1) TFEU and very unlikely to fulfil the conditions set out in Article 101(3) TFEU. More often than not, firms involved in the practice attempt to conceal it as a result. The Commission policy in relation to 'fact-intensive' cases focuses on the detection and sanctioning of the practices, as well as on deterrence. The soft law instruments issued by the authority reflect this focus well. In essence, the purpose of the Guidelines on leniency is to facilitate the detection of prohibited conduct.[107] The Guidelines on fines, in turn, are conceived to ensure deterrence.[108] In the same vein, the Notice on settlements provides for

[107] Commission Notice on immunity from fines and reduction of fines in cartel cases OJ (2006) No. C 298/17, as amended.

[108] Guidelines on the method of setting fines imposed pursuant to Article 23(2)(a) of Regulation No. 1/2003 OJ (2006) No. C 210/2.

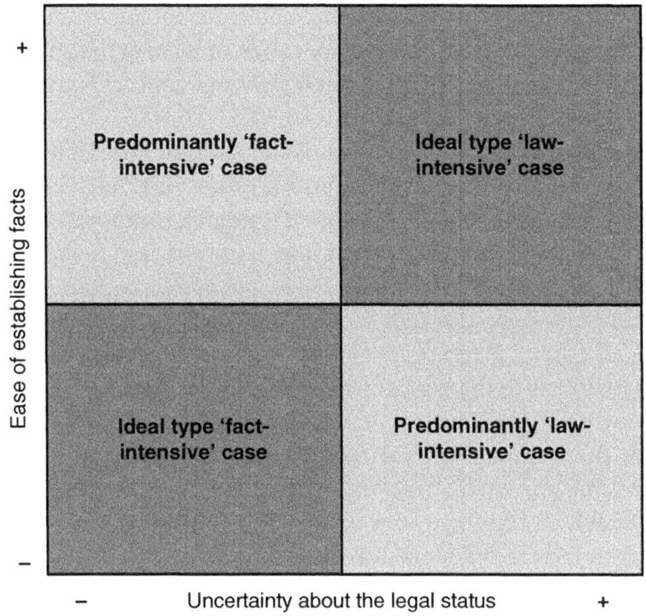

Figure 2.4 'Law-intensive' and 'fact-intensive' cases

a mechanism to reduce the procedural burden and ease the finding of infringement.[109]

A 'law-intensive' case, in turn, is one in which the controversy relates, first and foremost, to whether a given set of facts – around which there is often little or no controversy – is prohibited under EU competition law. 'Ideal types' of a 'law-intensive' case include practices enshrined in contracts, such as a distribution agreement providing for one or several vertical restraints and, in the same vein, a software licence given by a developer to a computer manufacturer. Notified mergers, by definition, fall within this category. 'Law-intensive' practices are not presumed to be unlawful and thus are, more often than not, subject to a standard. Where the legal status of a practice depends on a 'case-by-case' assessment, enforcement focuses on ensuring that the practice in question conforms to the principles laid down in the case law and/or to the outcomes that the Commission seeks to favour from a policy-making standpoint. This focus is reflected in the various soft law instruments issued by the authority,

[109] Commission Notice on the conduct of settlement procedures in view of the adoption of Decisions pursuant to Article 7 and Article 23 of Council Regulation (EC) No. 1/2003 in cartel cases OJ (2008) No. C 167/1.

such as the Guidelines on vertical restraints and on technology transfer agreements.[110] These instruments define the range of factors that firms should consider when assessing whether their conduct conforms to EU competition law.

The monograph concerns the behaviour of the Commission and the EU courts when defining the scope of substantive provisions. As a result, it focuses virtually exclusively on 'law-intensive' cases. A comprehensive analysis of the administrative practice of the Commission makes it possible to identify patterns in its behaviour. The behaviour is examined in light of the different steps through which the Commission must go when examining whether a given practice is unlawful. These steps range from the legal instrument to the way in which it engages with exogenous constraints on administrative action. Every step can be presented as a distinct choice that, among several options, the Commission must make. The options at one end of the spectrum allow the Commission to maximise the reach of administrative action. The options at the other end of the spectrum reduce the scope for intervention.

4.1 The Definition of the Scope of Legal Provisions

4.1.1 The Rationale behind Intervention

It would be natural for a competition authority to spell out the rationale behind intervention. Clarity about this point allows firms to understand why administrative action takes place and what the overarching concerns are. In this sense, it can be seen as one of the fundamental aspects in the motivation of a decision. At the same time, one can think of the reasons why an authority may be reluctant to be explicit – or overly explicit – about the rationale underlying administrative action. By setting out the concerns and the reasons why it believes action is justified, the authority may expose the weaknesses of – and inconsistencies in – its reasoning. For instance, firms may challenge the decision if there is a mismatch between the declared rationale and the substantive analysis. Such a mismatch can be expected to exist, for instance, when intervention is influenced by policy considerations that are in principle alien to EU competition law analysis.

An authority can minimise risks in this sense in two main ways. It may remain elusive about the rationale behind intervention or may rely upon

110 See in this sense the Guidelines on vertical restraints and Guidelines on technology transfer agreements.

generalities and/or open-ended concepts. If an authority follows this approach, it may be able to shift the focus to the factual aspects of the decision. Thus, instead of spelling out a cogent theory behind intervention, the authority may more modestly claim that action is justified in the specific factual circumstances of the case, which allegedly support a finding of infringement. Alternatively, the authority may invoke several concerns, or claim that it is simultaneously protecting different manifestations of competition. For instance, the authority may argue that it is concerned with exclusion and with exploitation, and that it seeks to protect simultaneously inter-brand competition and market integration. On the one hand, such an approach may create confusion about the actual factors driving administrative action. On the other, it might increase the chances that the decision will be upheld if challenged.

4.1.2 The Choice between Rules and Standards

The choice between a prohibition rule and a standard has a significant impact on the ease with which an infringement can be established. If a practice is subject to a prohibition rule, the authority would just have to show, to the requisite legal standard, that it has been implemented. Evidence in this sense would suffice to reverse the burden of proof and require the firm to advance an objective justification if it wishes to avoid intervention. Where a practice is subject to a standard, it is necessary to show, in addition, that it has restrictive effects on competition (however these are defined). The question of whether an administrative agency is inclined to favour rules over standards provides insights about its behaviour. Other things being equal, a competition authority like the Commission will face lower hurdles to advance its policy objectives if a practice is subject to a rule. The evolution of the law may be very different if the former are systematically favoured over the latter, or vice versa.

4.1.3 The Fleshing Out of Rules and Standards

There is not a unique way in which rules and standards, as defined in the present work, can be approached. Differences may exist, first, with regard to the categorisation of practices. The scope of a prima facie rule – the 'trigger', if one uses Schlag's expression[111] – may be defined in a 'hard' or a 'soft' way. In other words, the behaviour that is subject to the rule may be defined in accordance with a set of operational criteria –

[111] Schlag, 'Rules and Standards'.

a 'hard' trigger – or in relatively vague terms that can change from one case to another – a 'soft' trigger. Other things being equal, a 'soft' trigger gives more leeway to the authority, in the sense that it is amenable to ex post and ad hoc interpretation. The nebulous boundaries of the rule would make it easier for the authority to expand its scope at a subsequent stage. An authority faces a similar choice when fleshing out standards. As pointed out earlier, standards may be structured or unstructured. The behaviour of an authority can be expected to be less constrained in one-shot and repeated interactions where it opts for an unstructured approach to establishing the anti-competitive effects of a practice. This is so because such a standard leaves more aspects to the case-by-case assessment and the specific circumstances of each case, and thus, again, greater leeway to the authority.

Differences may also exist with regard to the way rules and standards are fleshed out. The relevant variables have already been identified earlier. The probability of effects is one of them, and is common to rules and standards. An authority must determine whether evidence of anti-competitive effects is necessary to intervene and, if so, the requisite threshold of effects – that is, whether the threshold is set at the level of capability, likelihood or certainty. Other things being equal, intervention is easier where the probability of effects is not a relevant factor, or, alternatively, where capability is deemed sufficient. As far as the fleshing out of rules is concerned, the behaviour of an authority is less constrained ex ante where the presumed rationale behind a practice is established on the basis of experience and/or intuition alone, as opposed to formal analysis. As already explained, it is not unusual that formal analysis leads to the conclusion that findings based on intuition and/or experience alone lack nuance, if they are not plain incorrect. As far as the fleshing out of standards is concerned, intervention by an authority is easier where the effects are equated with the freedom of action of market players or with the impact of the practice on the market structure – as opposed to consumer welfare, which would typically require a deeper enquiry.

4.2 Enforcement Instruments

An authority can choose between different legal instruments when dealing with 'law-intensive' cases. Figure 2.5 seeks to capture the different options available to the Commission when applying Articles 101 and 102

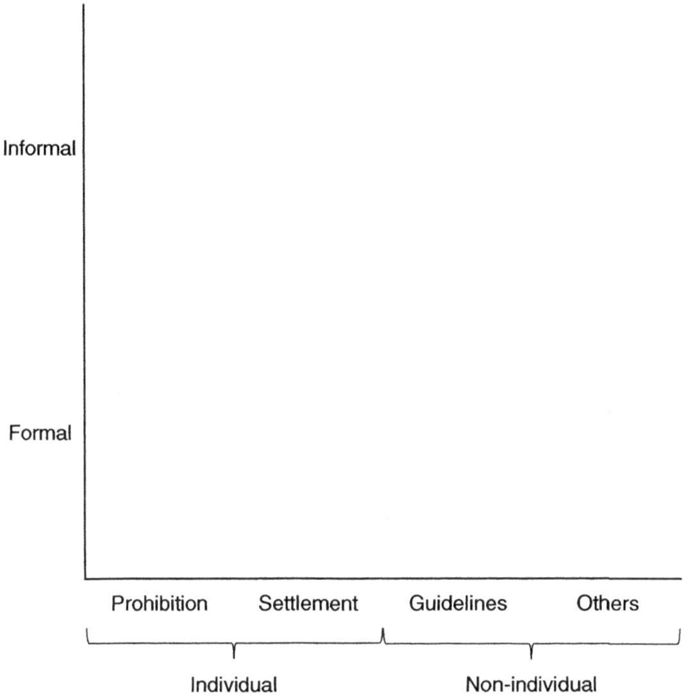

Figure 2.5 Enforcement instruments

TFEU.[112] The concerns raised by 'law-intensive' cases can be addressed in a formal or an informal manner. Firms can in fact seek informal guidance from the Commission.[113] This is so because these cases typically revolve around the instances in which a practice is a source of concerns and around how firms should adapt their conduct to conform to the outcome for which the Commission might have a preference. Similarly, it is not unusual that, as soon as an investigation is opened, a firm reacts by changing its commercial practices to address the concerns raised in the investigation. If that is the case, it may not be in the interest of the

[112] Merger control cases are always dealt with in a formal manner. The Commission has introduced a simplified procedure for transactions below a certain turnover or unlikely to give rise to competition concerns. See the Commission Notice on a simplified procedure for treatment of certain concentrations under Council Regulation (EC) No. 139/2004 OJ (2013) No. C 366/5.

[113] Commission Notice on informal guidance relating to novel questions concerning Articles 81 and 82 of the EC Treaty that arise in individual cases (guidance letters) OJ (2004) No. C 101/78.

authority to proceed to the formal stage. It has in fact been reported that a substantial fraction of the cases examined by the Commission are closed informally.[114]

The horizontal axis of Figure 2.5 shows that the Commission can adopt individual and non-individual instruments. The different instruments can be placed along a continuum. Non-individual instruments give the Commission greater flexibility, in the sense that they do not place significant procedural constraints on the authority and allow it to advance its own interpretation of EU competition law provisions. At the other end of the spectrum there are instruments that provide for extensive procedural guarantees but are more effective insofar as they allow the Commission to deter conduct through fines and to make some obligations binding on specific firms. The importance of soft law instruments in contemporary EU competition law has already been outlined. These instruments can be used by the Commission to steer firm behaviour towards the outcomes it prefers and to spell out its policy priorities. For instance, the Guidelines on horizontal co-operation agreements set out in detail the principles that standard-setting organisations must follow to bring their behaviour in line with Article 101(1) TFEU.[115] Similarly, the reports issued in the context of a sector inquiry allow it to give indications about the practices that are deemed prima facie problematic and about the ways in which the concerns raised by the Commission can be addressed.[116]

If the Commission issues an individual decision in Article 101 and 102 TFEU cases, it has the choice between a negotiated outcome and the adoption of a decision formally establishing an infringement, providing for (positive or negative) obligations and perhaps imposing a fine (that is, a 'prohibition decision').[117] Negotiated outcomes can be achieved by means of a commitment decision.[118] As already explained, these instruments do not formally establish that the behaviour under examination amounts to an infringement of EU competition law. They simply provide that, following the concessions offered by the parties, there

[114] For a quantitative overview, see Pablo Ibáñez Colomo, 'Three Shifts in EU Competition Policy: Towards Standards, Decentralisation, Settlement' (2013) 20 *Maastricht Journal of European and Comparative Law* 363.

[115] Guidelines on the applicability of Article 101 of the Treaty on the Functioning of the European Union to horizontal co-operation agreements OJ (2011) No. C 11/1, paras. 257–307.

[116] For a clear example, see Commission, 'Inquiry pursuant to Article 17 of Regulation (EC) No. 1/2003 into the European gas and electricity sectors (Final Report)' COM(2006) 851 final.

[117] Article 7 of Regulation 1/2003.

[118] Article 9 of Regulation 1/2003.

are no longer grounds for it to intervene. As a result, the Commission can afford to be less specific, and more speculative, about the legal test and about whether it is consistent with the case law and its past practice.[119] Because the decision would be the result of a negotiated outcome, moreover, the likelihood that the commitment decision will be challenged before the EU courts is significantly reduced.[120]

Against this background, assessing whether there is a systematic tendency on the part of the Commission to choose between negotiated outcomes over prohibition decisions provides valuable insights about its behaviour in 'law-intensive' cases. This is so, in particular, because the Commission enjoys discretion, by virtue of Regulation 1/2003, to accept the commitments proposed by the parties and make them binding on them or to adopt a formal decision establishing an infringement. In *Alrosa*, the Court confirmed that the choice of the enforcement instrument is a matter that is subject to limited review by the EU courts.[121] This judgment appears to be in line with prior case law, according to which the Commission has discretion to define its enforcement priorities and manage its limited resources.[122]

4.3 Constraints on Administrative Action

4.3.1 Repeated Interactions and Endogenous Constraints on Administrative Action

Endogenous constraints set the substantive boundaries of the EU competition law system. They are primarily defined by the EU courts when they interpret the Treaty and secondary legislation. For instance, the EU courts may lay down the conditions under which a concentration gives rise to the creation of a collective dominant position within the meaning of the applicable Merger Regulation.[123] Similarly, the EU courts may identify the instances in which a refusal to license an intellectual property right amounts to an abuse of dominance within the meaning of Article

[119] This issue was identified early on. See in this sense Heike Schweitzer, 'Commitment Decisions under Art. 9 of Regulation 1/2003: The Developing EC Practice and Case Law' in Claus-Dieter Ehlermann, Mel Marquis (eds.), *European Competition Law Annual 2008 – Antitrust Settlements under EC Competition Law* (Oxford: Hart Publishing, 2010).

[120] For an analysis of the relevant data in this regard, see Chapter 6.

[121] Case C-441/07 P, *Commission v Alrosa Company Ltd*, EU:C:2010:377.

[122] On this question, see Wouter Wils, 'Discretion and Prioritisation in Public Antitrust Enforcement, in Particular EU Antitrust Enforcement' (2011) 34 *World Competition* 353.

[123] Case T-342/99, *Airtours plc v Commission*, EU:T:2002:146.

102 TFEU.[124] The Commission may also choose to constrain its own behaviour by means of a pre-commitment device. If the administrative authority promises to follow a particular course of conduct in a soft law instrument, firms may develop an expectation that it will be subsequently followed in individual cases. Endogenous constraints can intervene at various instances of the definition of a legal test by the EU courts. They may come into play when defining the criteria to draw the line between rules and standards, or when clarifying the effects that should be considered when evaluating the unlawfulness of a given practice.

The reaction of the Commission to endogenous constraints on administrative action has important consequences for the static and dynamic consistency of the system. Importantly for the purposes of the present monograph, it is also a behaviour that can be mapped in light of the analytical framework sketched earlier. In presence of a constraint on administrative action, the Commission can follow two strategies. Once the boundaries to intervention have been defined by the EU courts, the authority can adopt a *risk-averse* strategy and take action only in those cases that meet the conditions set out in the case law. A *risk-prone* strategy is one that seeks to stretch the outer boundaries of the legal test. For instance, the Commission may, at the stage of the categorisation of the practice, conclude that it is different in its nature and/or impact and that a different legal test is justified as a result. Alternatively, it may redefine or adopt an expansive interpretation of the conditions set out by the EU courts.

4.3.2 Economic Analysis as an Exogenous Constraint on Administrative Action

Economic analysis can expose the weaknesses of the premises underpinning administrative action. It has already been explained that the definition of a legal test is necessarily based on a set of assumptions and presumptions about the nature of a practice and its effects. Formal tools may reveal that the said assumptions and/or presumptions are misguided. If administrative action is at odds with mainstream economic analysis, the likelihood of a successful challenge before the EU courts is higher. As already pointed out, such a behaviour may also cast doubts on the legitimacy of intervention. It may not be easy for the Commission to justify why it chooses to ignore the findings of an expert body of knowledge developed incrementally over the years. This is so, in particular, if

[124] As explained above, this question was addressed in Case C-418/01, *IMS Health*.

the Commission is not able to advance a compelling theory justifying such departure.

Economic analysis may come into play in one-shot and repeated interactions. Where the Commission examines the legal status of a practice for the first time, formal tools may be relied upon to inform or challenge its approach. As with endogenous constraints on administrative action, the Commission may choose to ignore the lessons of economic analysis or to minimise their relevance. It is not a secret that economic theory may not lead to univocal conclusions.[125] Thus, the Commission may expose the ambiguities that are inherent in economic research to favour the outcome it prefers from a policy-making standpoint. In repeated interactions, the reasoning of the Commission may be questioned in light of economic analysis. For instance, formal tools may suggest that it is incorrect to make a practice subject to a rule insofar as the presumptions about the purpose behind the practice and/or its impact on competition do not withstand rigorous scrutiny. In such instances, the Commission may argue that claims about the pro-competitive gains of the practice under consideration, insofar as they can be advanced as an objective justification, need not lead to a change in the legal test.

5 Mapping the Behaviour of the EU Courts

A distinct feature of the EU competition law system is that the Commission enjoys no discretion to define the legal test that applies to potentially anti-competitive conduct. It is for the EU courts to spell out the rationale behind intervention, and to lay down the conditions under which a given practice is deemed unlawful and the instances in which it can be objectively justified. At the same time, there may be factors influencing the courts' willingness to engage in the full review of administrative action. Some of these factors may make the EU courts more inclined to scrutinise the analysis of the Commission, and other factors

125 On this question, see, in general, Lianos, '"Judging" Economists: Economic Expertise in Competition Law Litigation: A European View'; and Sibony, *Le juge et le raisonnement économique en droit de la concurrence*. See also Giorgio Monti, *EC Competition Law* (Cambridge: Cambridge University Press 2007), who goes as far as to claim that 'bar some shared ground, there is no such thing as mainstream economics'. For a criticism of mainstream thinking and a discussion of its flaws, see Wils 'The Judgment of the EU General Court in Intel and the So-Called "More Economic Approach" to Abuse of Dominance'.

may have the opposite effect. Among the former, one can think of constraints that are exogenous to the EU competition law system, and in particular economic analysis and the case law of the ECtHR. Among the latter, the perception that judicial review could interfere with the policy choices of the Commission might make the EU courts reluctant to scrutinise administrative action beyond a standard of reasonableness. These factors are examined in turn hereinafter.

5.1 *Judicial Review between Law and Policy-Making*

It has already been pointed out that the Commission has discretion to define its enforcement priorities and set out the objectives it seeks to achieve. For instance, it may decide to focus its efforts on what it perceives to be the most problematic infringements (for instance, cartel conduct and practices aimed at restricting parallel trade) and/or on the sectors that it considers to be decisive for economic growth and the well-being of European citizens (for instance, network and innovation-driven industries). The fundamental consequence of the discretion enjoyed by the Commission in this regard is that the policy choices it makes are subject, if at all, to limited review. A decision to reject a complaint, for instance, will only be annulled if the Commission makes a manifest error of assessment.[126]

The discretion enjoyed by the Commission in policy-related matters coexists with the lack of discretion in relation to issues of law, over which the EU courts exercise full review. This gives rise to a duality of standards of review in practice. Such a duality can be problematic because law and policy-making are mutually intertwined. In EU competition law, policy is often formulated through the choice of individual cases, and thus by establishing that a given line of conduct is in breach of a legal provision. As a result, a successful challenge of the legal aspects of a decision has an indirect impact on policy considerations. Questioning the law, in other words, may be tantamount to questioning the underlying strategy of the authority. Following a successful challenge of a decision, the Commission may not be able to pursue as many cases as it would have desired from a strict policy-making standpoint, or may not be able to take action against a given line of conduct at all. The likely impact of a judgment

[126] Case T-427/08, *Confédération européenne des associations d'horlogers-réparateurs v Commission*, EU:T:2010:517, para. 65 (see also Case T-712/14, *Confédération européenne des associations d'horlogers-réparateurs v Commission*, pending).

on competition policy may make the EU courts reluctant to question the substantive aspects of a decision unless they find them to be unreasonable.[127] If this reluctance becomes systematic, it may influence the evolution of the law insofar as it can lead to inconsistencies in the long-run.

5.2 *Judicial Review in One-Shot and Repeated Interactions*

5.2.1 The Procedural Context

The case law may develop very differently depending on the procedural context in which the legal tests are defined and refined. EU competition law provisions are interpreted primarily in the context of annulment proceedings brought against Commission decisions and in the context of preliminary references submitted by national courts in accordance with Article 267 TFEU.[128] It is possible to think of various reasons why the behaviour of the EU courts may vary significantly depending on the procedural context in which they are called upon to interpret competition law provisions. These reasons relate to the nature of, respectively, annulment and preliminary reference proceedings, of the role that the EU courts are expected to play in each of them as well as the relative influence of policy considerations.

The very purpose of the preliminary reference procedure is to provide an interpretation of an EU law provision. As a result, the Court[129] is expected to be explicit about the conditions against which the lawfulness of a practice must be assessed, and to provide insights about the rationale behind intervention. The references submitted by national courts, moreover, may pay more attention to the administrability of the legal test, which may in turn influence the approach of the Court to the question. Finally, policy considerations may, other things being equal, weigh less than in the context of annulment proceedings. Because the reference relates to a dispute at the national level, it does not necessarily relate to

[127] Some judges and référendaires have expressed an opinion that is consistent with this view. See in particular Hubert Legal, 'Le contentieux communautaire de la concurrence entre contrôle restreint et pleine juridiction' (2005) 2 *Concurrences* 1; and Pascal Gilliaux, 'L'intensité du contrôle de la légalité par les juridictions communautaires' (2009) 17 *Journal de droit européen* 37.

[128] Pursuant to Article 267 TFEU, the CJUE as an institution has jurisdiction to give preliminary rulings on the interpretation of the Treaties.

[129] In accordance with Article 256(3) TFEU, the GC can be given jurisdiction to give preliminary rulings 'in specific areas laid down by the Statute'. At the time of writing, however, the CJUE has not relied upon this possibility.

the cases that the Commission perceives to be an enforcement priority, or the issues with which it has dealt in the past, either in individual decisions or in its soft law instruments. The role of the Commission is also different. Even though it may submit its observations to the Court, its choices and preferences are not necessarily the main drivers of the dispute.[130]

The opposite is true in direct actions brought in accordance with Article 263 TFEU. In line with what has been suggested earlier, this is the procedural instance in which the EU courts are more likely to prove deferential to the substantive choices made by the administrative authority. In the context of direct action, the task of the EU courts is to control the legality of a decision. Inevitably, the analysis of the Commission – including its policy choices – is at the centre of the case brought before the EU courts. In particular, the legal test set out in the decision is the default starting point of the scrutiny. As already explained, this reality may influence the analysis of the EU courts at various levels. Moreover, some of the considerations that are relevant in the context of a preliminary reference, such as the administrability of the legal test, are less prominent in the context of a procedure that is intended to ascertain whether the legal test set out by the Commission is correct.

5.2.2 A Dynamic Perspective on the Evolution of the Case Law

The fundamental conclusion that follows from the above is that the approach of the EU courts to the definition of the legal test may be influenced by the underlying procedural context. A dynamic dimension on the question shows, in addition, that the case law may evolve differently depending on whether the scope of a provision is primarily defined in the context of preliminary references or annulment proceedings instead. The attitude of the EU courts in each of the proceedings, which is discernible in one-shot interactions, can potentially be exacerbated if one procedure clearly dominates over the other. It has been suggested earlier that, in the context of a preliminary reference, the Court may be more likely to be explicit about the legal test and the underpinning rationale, as well as more likely to take administrability into consideration. In the long run, these features may have an impact on the stability of the case law (and thus on its consistency). It has also been

130 See in this sense Article 23 of Protocol (no. 3) on the Statute of the Court of Justice of the European Union.

suggested that, in the context of annulment proceedings, the EU courts may be more likely to defer to the analysis of the Commission and less likely to be concerned with administrability. As pointed out earlier, the relatively deferential attitude may encourage the administrative authority to adopt a risk-prone strategy, and thus to depart from existing tests or to interpret them in an expansive manner. If so, the case law could become less stable and thus less consistent.

As can be seen, the likelihood that any given Commission decision will be annulled may depend on the procedural context in which the case law has evolved. Where preliminary references dominate over annulment actions, the case law may become not only more stable, but also more *resilient*. As a consequence, the EU courts may more readily react against attempts by the Commission to depart from the existing test and/or its underlying rationale. Conversely, the case law may be less stable, and thus less resilient, where annulment actions dominate. If the legal test defined by the EU courts has not been subsequently confirmed in a number of judgments, it may be progressively modified by the Commission through its administrative practice. The likelihood that any given decision will be annulled would also be lower (and might decrease with any given decision).

5.3 *Exogenous Constraints and Judicial Review*

5.3.1 Economic Analysis as an Exogenous Constraint

Economic analysis may influence the likelihood of deference to the analysis of the Commission. As already explained, it may be difficult for an administrative authority to justify ignoring, or departing from, consensus positions among economists. From the perspective of a review court, mainstream economics provides a reliable benchmark against which various stages of the reasoning of the Commission can be assessed. If the approach advocated by the Commission appears to be less plausible, or is deemed to be less persuasive, the EU courts may be more inclined to annul the decision. Similarly, a choice to ignore or to downplay a body of knowledge around which there is a consensus may be perceived as arbitrary or unreasonable by the judges reviewing the decision. By the same token, the position of the applicant will typically look stronger if it is supported by robust economic research.

The likelihood that economic insights will be incorporated in the analysis may depend on whether it is introduced when the legal test is defined for the first time, or at a later stage, where there is already a body of case law defining the status of the practice under consideration. In the first scenario, which corresponds to a one-shot interaction, the review court would not be required to depart from prior positions and thus to introduce an element of dynamic inconsistency. As a result, it may be more likely that it will engage with economic analysis. The opposite is true where the EU courts have already validated a decision that is found to be at odds with consensus positions. In such a case, economic arguments would not simply relate to the control of administrative action, but to the very status of the case law. As a result, concerns with the stability and predictability of the system might be taken into consideration.

5.3.2 The Case Law of the ECtHR

Menarini has emerged as an exogenous benchmark against which the scope and intensity of judicial review by the EU courts can be assessed. Even though the *Menarini* case concerned the compatibility of the Italian system with Article 6 ECHR, commentators immediately assumed that the ruling would have significant implications for EU competition law. The expectation was that the EU courts would bring their behaviour in line with the principles set out in *Menarini*. Even if, at the time of writing, the EU is not a member to the Convention,[131] the EU law system is expected to provide a level of protection that is at least equivalent to that provided under the ECHR. More generally, the credibility of the EU courts may suffer if there is a perception that they do not fulfil their core tasks, or if the ECtHR holds administrative action to a stricter standard.

The statements found in *KME* and *Chalkor* (issued immediately after the ECtHR judgment in *Menarini*) provide a valuable example of the way in which exogenous factors of a legal nature may influence the behaviour of the EU courts. These two rulings have been interpreted as the expression of a commitment to full judicial review by the EU courts and, if not the abandonment, the confinement of the doctrine whereby 'complex economic assessments' are controlled for 'manifest errors' alone to relatively exceptional circumstances.[132] Some commentators have noted that

[131] See in this sense Article 6(2) TFEU; Protocol (No 8) relating to article 6(2) of the Treaty on European Union on the accession of the Union to the European Convention on the Protection of Human Rights and Fundamental Freedoms; and Opinion 2/13 of the Court, EU:C:2014:2454.

[132] Carol Harlow and Richard Rawlings, *Process and Procedure in EU Administration* (Oxford: Hart Publishing, 2014), p. 219.

the vocabulary of 'manifest error' has even disappeared from subsequent rulings, thereby suggesting a more thorough review of administrative action.[133] In the same vein, there are examples, post-*Menarini*, where the Court has set aside a ruling of the GC due to the fact that the judicial review of administrative action was not deemed thorough enough.[134]

6 Methodology

6.1 Scope of the Analysis

Part II examines the case law and the administrative practice relating to the interpretation of three key notions of EU competition law. As already explained in Chapter 1, these are: the notion of restriction of competition within the meaning of Article 101(1) TFEU; the notion of abuse within the meaning of Article 102 TFEU; and the substantive criterion for the assessment of mergers with a Union dimension. The categorisation of the practice, the definition of the legal test or the analysis of whether it is objectively justified are all undertaken under these conditions. The monograph considers only issues of law, which relate directly to the emergence of substantive inconsistencies and can be reliably measured and examined in light of the analytical framework described earlier. Thus, issues of fact, as well as the legal characterisation of facts, are left out of the analysis. The two issues may provide valuable insights, but are not easily measured.

6.2 Research Questions

Part II seeks to identify, first, the institutional context in which the abovementioned conditions have been fleshed out. The institutional context considers both the procedural framework in which the EU courts engaged with the definition of the condition and the institution (the Commission or the EU courts) that took the lead in this regard. Second, Part II examines the evolution in the interpretation of the provision in light of the behaviour of the Commission and the EU courts. This analysis includes one-shot and repeated interactions. In one-shot interactions, the questions examined include the role of exogenous

133 See for instance Wils, 'The Compatibility with Fundamental Rights of the EU Antitrust Enforcement System in Which the European Commission Acts Both as Investigator and as First-Instance Decision Maker'.

134 See in particular Case C-67/13 P, *Cartes Bancaires*, paras. 89–92.

constraints on the behaviour of the Commission and issues of static consistency. In repeated interactions, the analysis considers whether the Commission has adopted a risk-prone or a risk-averse strategy once the EU courts have intervened to define the boundaries of the prohibition as well as the reaction of the latter.

6.3 *Structure*

All three chapters in Part II follow the same structure. The first section of each chapter – *substantive context* – provides an overview of the relevant condition, and outlines the way in which it can be crafted. In particular, it shows how the line between rules and standards can be drawn, the sort of practices to which the provision may apply and the nature of the controversies. The second section provides the *institutional context* in which the scope of the condition has been defined. This is achieved with the aid of descriptive statistics. As already explained, the EU courts engage with EU competition law provisions in two main ways: through preliminary reference procedures and in the context of annulment actions. This section thus outlines whether the former weighs more than the latter in the definition of the concept, or vice versa. A second question relates to the relative importance of the condition in the case law and the administrative practice, that is, the number of cases in which the definition of the scope of the condition was a central aspect. The descriptive statistics rely upon a comprehensive database that was last updated on 15 September 2017.[135]

Against the background of the statistical analysis, the third section – a dynamic analysis of the notion – considers the behaviour of the Commission and the EU courts. It is possible to identify, for each of the conditions, some broad trends in the case law that give an accurate picture of the factors influencing the emergence of inconsistencies in the system. In the context of Article 101(1) TFEU, the notion of restriction of competition has been contentious in three broad areas: (i) distribution agreements and vertical restraints; (ii) licensing of intellectual property; and (iii) horizontal co-operation agreements. In the context of Article 102 TFEU, the behaviour of the Commission becomes apparent when examining the application of the provision to (i) predatory pricing and

[135] The database, which classifies the relevant case law and administrative practice on the basis of a number of variables, is available on the Cambridge University Press website under Resources at www.cambridge.org/9781108429429. It is accessible in Microsoft Access format.

related practices; (ii) exclusive dealing and rebates; and (iii) leveraging strategies. Finally, Chapter 5 is based on the usual dividing line between (i) horizontal (including transactions giving rise to both coordinated and non-coordinated effects) and (ii) non-horizontal mergers (vertical and conglomerate transactions).

3

Restrictions of Competition under Article 101(1) TFEU

1 Substantive Context

1.1 Substantive Choices

Two of the most salient features of Article 101 TFEU are relevant for the purposes of this study. First, Article 101(1) TFEU distinguishes between agreements that restrict competition by object and by effect. It is apparent from the Treaty that these are alternative conditions. The Court has consistently confirmed this point.[1] As explained earlier in Chapter 2, the divide between 'by object' and 'by effect' restrictions mirrors the divide between rules and standards, which can be said to be built into the provision. Some agreements, like cartels, are prohibited irrespective of their impact on competition, whereas others are only subject to the prohibition insofar as they have restrictive effects. Second, Article 101 TFEU has a bifurcated structure. The prohibition laid down in the first paragraph of the provision may be declared inapplicable to agreements that fulfil the conditions set out in its third paragraph. In other words, Article 101(3) TFEU provides for an explicit mechanism to justify conduct that is subject to the prima facie prohibition but that is on the whole pro-competitive.

These two features are at the heart of the substantive choices that the Commission must make when fleshing out the scope of Article 101(1) TFEU. In line with the framework set out in Chapter 2, the first choice relates to the criteria to establish the divide between rules and standards.

[1] The principle was introduced in Joined Cases 56 and 58/64, *Établissements Consten S.à.R. L. and Grundig-Verkaufs-GmbH v Commission*, EU:C:1966:41 ('*Consten-Grundig*') ('for the purpose of applying Article [101(1)], there is no need to take account of the concrete effects of an agreement once it appears that it has as its object the prevention, restriction or distortion of competition'). Some judgments that have reiterated this principle include Case C-209/07, *Competition Authority v Beef Industry Development Society Ltd and Barry Brothers (Carrigmore) Meats Ltd*, EU:C:2008:643 ('*BIDS*'), para. 16; and Case C-8/08, *T-Mobile Netherlands BV, KPN Mobile NV, Orange Nederland NV and Vodafone Libertel NV v Raad van bestuur van de Nederlandse Mededingingsautoriteit*, EU:C:2009:343, para. 29.

The second relates to the criteria for the assessment of restrictive effects. These two choices, combined, determine whether, and to what extent, the divide between rules and standards has meaningful consequences in practice. If the restrictive effects of potentially anti-competitive conduct can be established as easily as its restrictive object, the difference between object and effect may not be a particularly relevant one. In that case, choosing one route or the other would not have significant implications for the authority or the claimant. The way in which object and effect are defined also has consequences for the relative scope of, respectively, Articles 101(1) and 101(3) TFEU. Where the threshold to establish a prima facie restriction under Article 101(1) TFEU is low, the thrust of the analysis takes place under the third paragraph. The opposite is true where the analysis of the restrictive object and/or effects of a practice under Article 101(1) TFEU is thorough.

At one extreme, one can think of a substantive choice in which the scope of Article 101(1) TFEU is broad and in which the thrust of the analysis is conducted under Article 101(3) TFEU as a result. Under this approach, the vast majority of agreements would be restrictive of competition, whether by object or effect. Such would be the case where the notion of restriction of competition is built around informal presumptions about the purpose behind the practice, or where a breach can be established simply by showing that the agreement is capable of having anti-competitive effects. The scope of Article 101(1) TFEU would also be relatively broad where a restriction on the freedom of action of the parties is equated with a restriction of competition. By definition, co-operation between firms curtails firms' freedom of action in one way or another.[2] Where the threshold to establish a restriction is set at such a level, an authority or a court can confidently conclude, in virtually every case, that the agreement under consideration amounts to a prima facie infringement of Article 101(1) TFEU. In such circumstances, the analysis would revolve almost exclusively around whether the agreement fulfils the conditions set out in Article 101(3) TFEU.

It is also possible to think of alternative approaches in which the thrust of the analysis takes place under Article 101(1) TFEU. This would be the case, for instance, where the application of a rule is confined to instances

[2] See in this sense Valentine Korah, 'EEC Competition Policy – Legal Form or Economic Efficiency' (1986) 39 *Current Legal Problems* 85. For a different perspective on the question, see Giuliano Marenco, 'La notion de restriction de concurrence dans le cadre de l'interdiction des ententes' in Marianne Dony and Aline De Walsche (eds.), *Mélanges en hommage à Michel Waelbroeck* (Brussels: Bruylant 1999).

in which a practice is deemed likely (or certain) to have a negative impact on competition, or to instances in which formal analysis suggests that it is safe to presume that the agreement can only be plausibly explained as an attempt to restrict competition. Similarly, the range of measures caught by Article 101(1) TFEU would be reduced where a restriction on the freedom of action is deemed insufficient to establish the anti-competitive effects of an agreement – and evidence of likely to harm consumer welfare and/or to the exclusion of equally efficient competitors is required instead. If any of these approaches were followed, Article 101 (3) TFEU would only come into play to address the lawfulness of a smaller subset of agreements.

1.2 *Principles of the Case Law*

1.2.1 Scope of Article 101 TFEU

According to the consensus among economists that has informed enforcement in the past decades, competition law analysis should focus on inter-brand rivalry.[3] In this sense, mainstream economics suggests that restrictions of intra-brand competition – including restrictions to cross-border trade – can (should) be tolerated by courts and authorities insofar as they may lead to more vigorous rivalry among producers. Accordingly, vertical restraints, as opposed to collusive arrangements among rivals, would typically be unproblematic. Distribution agreements and similar practices would only be a source of concerns if it can be established, case-by-case, that they lead to collusion or exclusion at one or several levels of the value chain. This consensus is reflected in the current Commission policy, according to which vertical restraints are only considered to be problematic where there is insufficient inter-brand competition.[4]

[3] For a review of the relevant literature, see Vincent Verouden, 'Vertical Agreements: Motivation and Impact' (2008) 3 *Issues in Competition Law and Policy* 1813, who observes that 'when there is sufficient interbrand competition consumers are likely to benefit from the agreement in question as competition will force sellers to pass possible efficiency gains on. As a bottom line, it is highly improbable that consumers will suffer in this case, since there are plenty of alternatives available. Second, the analysis also shows that the strategic effects, e.g., the use of vertical agreements to soften competition, are less strong when competition in the product market is fiercer'.

[4] Guidelines on vertical restraints OJ (2010) No. C 130/1, para. 6: 'For most vertical restraints, competition concerns can only arise if there is insufficient competition at one or more levels of trade, that is, if there is some degree of market power at the level of the supplier or the buyer or at both levels. Vertical restraints are generally less harmful than horizontal restraints and may provide substantial scope for efficiencies'.

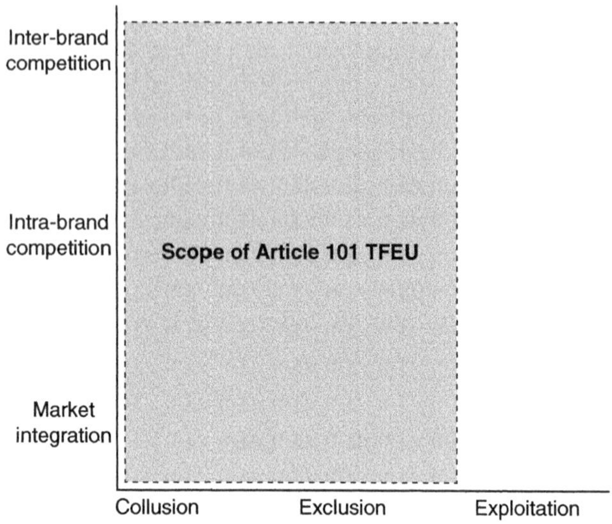

Figure 3.1 Scope of Article 101 TFEU

This position, however, does not reflect the state of Article 101 TFEU. It is clear from the case law that the provision is not only concerned with inter-brand competition; it comprises all dimensions of competition, as depicted in Figure 3.1. From the very early years, the Court emphasised that market integration is an autonomous objective of EU competition law. Thus, an agreement aimed at partitioning the internal market is in principle contrary to Article 101 TFEU.[5] More importantly, the Court has ruled that this conclusion holds true irrespective of whether the agreement in question would increase inter-brand rivalry,[6] and irrespective of whether consumers would be made better off.[7] It is also clear from the case law that intra-brand competition is worthy of protection in and of itself. For instance, a selective distribution

[5] See in particular Joined Cases 56 and 58/64, *Consten-Grundig*, and also Joined Cases C-403/08 and C-429/08, *Football Association Premier League Ltd and Others v QC Leisure and others and Karen Murphy v Media Protection Services Ltd*, EU:C:2011:631, para. 139.

[6] This point was made explicit in Joined Cases 56 and 58/64, *Consten-Grundig*, where (regarding intra-brand rivalry) the Court observed that ('Although competition between producers is generally more noticeable than that between distributors of products of the same make, it does not thereby follow that an agreement tending to restrict the latter kind of competition should escape the prohibition of Article [101] (1) merely because it might increase the former').

[7] Joined Cases C-501/06 P, C-513/06 P, C-515/06 P and C-519/06 P, *GlaxoSmithKline Services Unlimited v Commission*, EU:C:2009:610 ('*Glaxo Spain*'), para. 63.

agreement may be caught by Article 101(1) TFEU where it unduly restricts rivalry among distributors, irrespective of the intensity of inter-brand competition faced by the supplier. Accordingly, members of a selective distribution system should, for instance, be able to sell their products via the Internet.[8]

Similarly, there is little doubt that Article 101 TFEU is concerned with both collusive and exclusionary behaviour. Collusive behaviour may involve firms at the same or different levels of the value chain. Thus, the notion comprises both an agreement between rivals to refrain from competing[9] (such as a cartel) and also an agreement between, for instance, a supplier and a distributor to limit (intra-brand) competition at one level of the value chain.[10] A vertical agreement aimed at prohibiting active and passive sales by distributors is an example of collusive behaviour in the latter sense. Agreements may also have an exclusionary object or effect. For instance, a group of firms may implement a collective boycott against a rival.[11] A vertical agreement providing for an exclusive dealing obligation, in turn, may lead to the foreclosure of competing suppliers.[12] The unilateral exercise of market power, on the other hand, falls outside the scope of Article 101 TFEU.

1.2.2 Practices That Are Deemed Restrictive of Competition by Object

Over the years, the Court has laid down a set of principles about the notion of restriction of competition. There are some practices which, according to the case law, are clearly prima facie prohibited by object (or 'by their very nature'). At the same time, there is some uncertainty

[8] Case C-439/09, *Pierre Fabre Dermo-Cosmétique SAS v Président de l'Autorité de la concurrence and Ministre de l'Économie, de l'Industrie et de l'Emploi*, EU:C:2011:649.

[9] See for instance Case C-209/07, *BIDS*, which concerned an arrangement to encourage certain producers to leave the market.

[10] An example in this sense is that of an agreement giving absolute territorial protection to a distributor, examined in Joined Cases 56 and 58/64, *Consten-Grundig*, and an agreement requiring a distributor not to sell competing products, which the Court examined in Case C-234/89, *Stergios Delimitis v Henninger Bräu AG*, EU:C:1991:91.

[11] This was the issue at stake in Case C-68/12, *Protimonopolný úrad Slovenskej republiky v Slovenská sporiteľňa a.s.*, EU:C:2013:71.

[12] See in this sense Case C-234/89, *Delimitis*, para. 15 ('it is necessary to analyse the effects of a beer supply agreement, taken together with other contracts of the same type, on the opportunities of national competitors or those from other Member States, to gain access to the market for beer consumption or to increase their market share and, accordingly, the effects on the range of products offered to consumers').

around the outer boundaries of the category.[13] 'By object' infringements include cartels, which can take various forms depending on the nature of the industry and the conditions of competition prevailing therein. The letter of Article 101(1) TFEU refers to some of the most common manifestations of cartel conduct, including price-fixing, market-sharing and the restriction of output.[14] In any event, the case law and administrative practice show that cartel-like arrangements are sometimes concealed as pro-competitive or innocuous ventures.[15] In other cases, they may take an elaborate form that does not fall neatly within existing categories.[16] According to the Court, the relevant question is whether rivals knowingly substitute 'practical cooperation between them' for 'the risks of competition'.[17] A feature that is common to all cartels is the absence of a credible pro-competitive motivation. They can only be plausibly explained as a means to restrict competition and extract rents from suppliers or customers.[18]

The setting of fixed or minimum prices by a supplier is also restrictive of competition by object under Article 101(1) TFEU.[19] This is so in spite of the explicit recognition by the Court that, unlike cartels, this practice may have ambivalent effects on competition. Finally, and as already pointed out, agreements aimed at partitioning the internal market, and in particular those providing for absolute territorial protection,[20] are in

[13] 'By object' and 'by their very nature' are used hereinafter as synonymous, which is the way in which they appear to be used in the case law.

[14] Article 101(1) TFEU refers to agreements that '(a) directly or indirectly fix purchase or selling prices or any other trading conditions; (b) limit or control production, markets, technical development, or investment; (c) share markets or sources of supply; (d) apply dissimilar conditions to equivalent transactions with other trading parties, thereby placing them at a competitive disadvantage; (e) make the conclusion of contracts subject to acceptance by the other parties of supplementary obligations which, by their nature or according to commercial usage, have no connection with the subject of such contracts'.

[15] Joined Cases 96–102, 104, 105, 108 and 110/82, *NV IAZ International Belgium and others v Commission*, EU:C:1983:310.

[16] See for instance Case T-5/00, *Nederlandse Federatieve Vereniging voor de Groothandel op Elektrotechnisch Gebied and Technische Unie BV v Commission*, EU:T:2003:342, in which collusion took the form of a 'collective exclusive dealing' arrangement that precluded firms based in other Member States from entering the Dutch market.

[17] This expression has been frequently used in the case law. See for instance Case C-8/08, *T-Mobile*, para. 61; and Case T-588/08, *Dole Food Company, Inc. and Dole Germany OHG v Commission*, EU:T:2013:130, para. 369.

[18] See OECD, 'Competition Policy and Efficiency Claims in Horizontal Agreements' OCDE/GD(96)65.

[19] Case 243/83, *SA Binon & Cie v SA Agence et messageries de la presse*, EU:C:1985:284.

[20] Joined Cases 56 and 58/64, *Consten-Grundig*.

principle restrictive of competition by object. For instance, it seems clear beyond doubt that a distribution agreement that provides for an export prohibition or allows the buyer to control parallel trade is prohibited by its very nature if it concerns tangible property (such as a book, a record or a television set).[21] Practices having an equivalent object and effect are treated in the same way. For instance, the Court held in *Glaxo Spain* that an agreement that applies a dual price depending on whether a tangible good is intended for export or for domestic consumption is restrictive of competition by its very nature.[22] Practices that limit the ability of distributors to sell goods via the Internet are seen in the same light.[23]

1.2.3 The Analysis of the Restrictive Nature of an Agreement

The case law defines a fundamental set of principles to establish whether a practice is restrictive of competition within the meaning of Article 101 (1) TFEU. In *Société Technique Minière*, the Court explained that the question of whether an agreement is caught by that provision, whether by object or effect, requires an assessment of its nature, the content of its provisions and the economic and legal context of which it is part.[24] This framework makes it necessary to evaluate the conditions of competition that would exist with the agreement and in its absence. An agreement falls outside the scope of Article 101(1) TFEU if the analysis of the counterfactual reveals that it is not capable of restricting competition that would have existed in its absence. This may be the case, for instance, where the practice is objectively necessary for a supplier to enter a given geographic market.[25] Similarly, the counterfactual analysis may reveal that a firm would not have engaged in a practice in the absence of some core clauses protecting, for instance, its brand image, know-how or

[21] See in this sense Case 19/77, *Miller International Schallplaten v Commission*, EU:C:1978:19.

[22] Joined Cases C-501/06 P, C-513/06 P, C-515/06 P and C-519/06 P, *Glaxo Spain*.

[23] Case C-439/09, *Pierre Fabre*; and Guidelines on vertical restraints, paras. 52–4.

[24] Case 56/65, *Société Technique Minière v Maschinenbau Ulm GmbH*, EU:C:1966:38 ('The fact that these are not cumulative but alternative requirements, indicated by the conjunction "or", leads first to the need to consider the precise purpose of the agreement, in the economic context in which it is to be applied. This interference with competition referred to in Article [101] (1) must result from all or some of the clauses of the agreement itself'). See also, inter alia, Joined Cases C-501/06 P, C-513/06 P, C-515/06 P and C-519/06 P, *Glaxo Spain*, para 58; and Case C-439/09, *Pierre Fabre*, para. 35.

[25] Ibid. ('it may be doubted whether there is an interference with competition if the said agreement seems really necessary for the penetration of a new area by an undertaking').

have been able to achieve, alone, the aims of the agreement), it is not prohibited under Article 101(1) TFEU. That a restriction in the freedom of action is insufficient to show that an agreement has restrictive effects of competition is a point that the Court would implicitly and explicitly confirm in subsequent years.[35] The implications of the early case law are captured in Figure 3.3. The seminal rulings revealed that, at the very least, it is necessary to consider the impact of a practice on the market structure in order to establish a restriction of competition.

2 Institutional Context

2.1 Annulment Proceedings

2.1.1 Prohibition Decisions

Charts 3.1 and 3.2 reveal much about the nature of litigation in the context of Article 101 TFEU. The former shows that only around half of prohibition decisions adopted since the 1960s have been challenged. Of these, as seen in Chart 3.2 (and Table 3.1 in the Appendix), only 12% related to the notion of restriction of competition. This finding is not surprising. On the one hand, the Commission has devoted its limited resources to what it considers to be the most serious infringements. More and more of its efforts focus on cartel cases. If one considers the annulment proceedings started in the past decade, it appears that the overwhelming majority of prohibition decisions challenged before the GC relate, indeed, to cartel-like arrangements.[36] In the past, a substantial proportion of the resources of the authority was devoted to distribution agreements aimed at restricting trade between Member States, which are also clear 'by object' violations of Article 101(1) TFEU.[37] As a result of

[35] The point would be made explicit in Case C-309/99, *JCJ Wouters, JW Savelbergh and Price Waterhouse Belastingadviseurs BV v Algemene Raad van de Nederlandse Orde van Advocaten*, EU:C:2002:98, para. 97 ('not every agreement between undertakings or every decision of an association of undertakings which restricts the freedom of action of the parties or of one of them necessarily falls within the prohibition laid down in Article [101(1)] of the Treaty').

[36] Of a total of over 40 prohibitions decisions adopted (and challenged before the GC) since January 2007, only six of them concerned non-cartel matters. This feature is examined at greater length below.

[37] For some examples, see Case 19/77, *Miller International*; Case 277/87, *Sandoz prodotti farmaceutici SpA v Commission*, EU:C:1989:363; Case 279/87, *Tipp-Ex GmbH & Co. KG v Commission*, EU:C:1989:230; Case T-49/95, *Van Megen Sports Group BV v Commission*, EU:T:1996:186; and Case T-13/03, *Nintendo Co., Ltd, established in Kyoto (Japan) and Nintendo of Europe GmbH*, EU:T:2009:131.

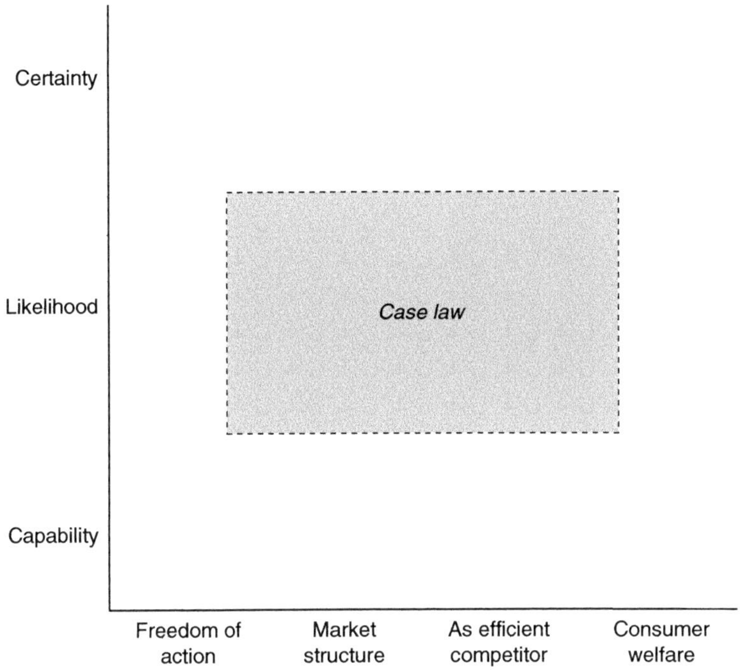

Figure 3.3 Approach to the analysis of effects in the case law

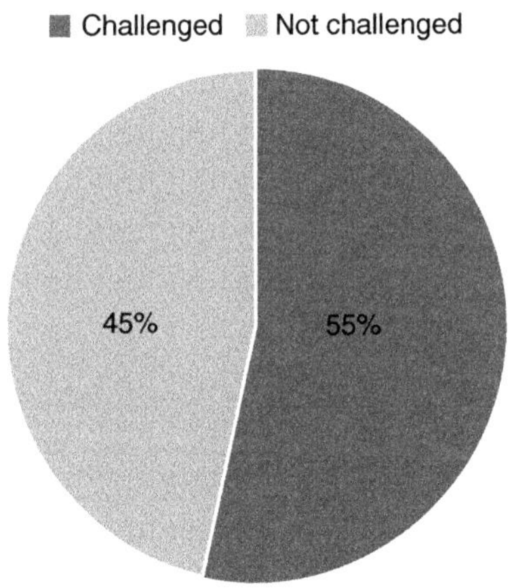

Chart 3.1 Proportion of prohibition decisions challenged before the EU courts

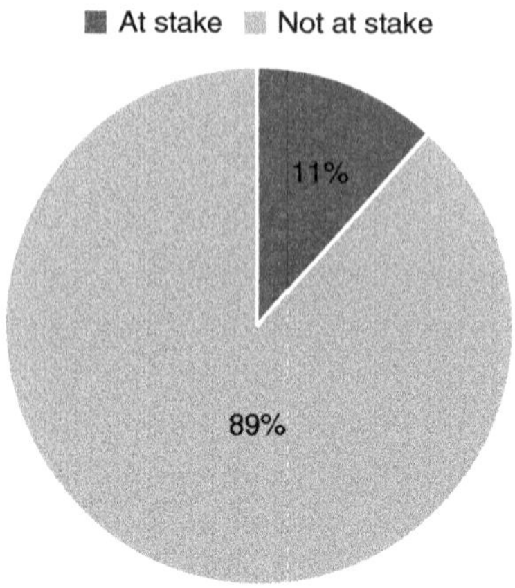

Chart 3.2 Relevance of the notion of restriction of competition in challenged prohibition decisions

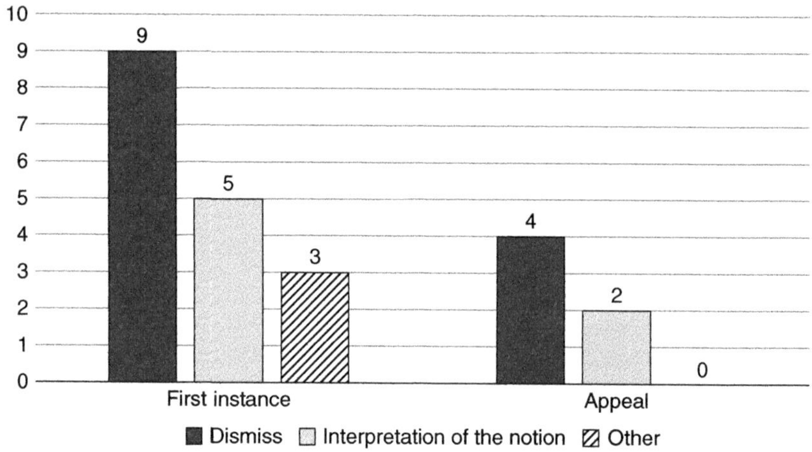

Chart 3.3 Outcome of cases engaging with the notion of restriction

these enforcement priorities, a relatively small percentage of prohibition decisions challenged before the EU courts can be qualified as 'law-intensive'. The pool of prohibition decisions that has contributed to the definition of the scope of restriction of competition is thus limited.

The outcome of litigation in 'law-intensive' cases engaging with the notion of restriction of competition is depicted in Chart 3.3. As can be seen, the rate of annulment of decisions in this limited pool of cases is relatively high. More importantly, the majority of annulments relate

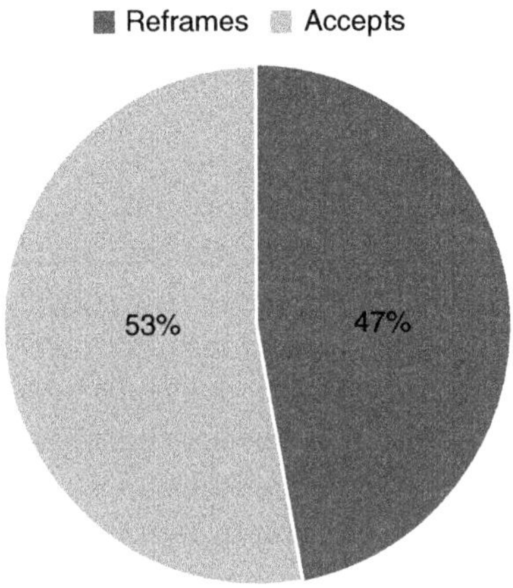

Chart 3.4 Approach to the notion of restriction (exemption decisions), percentages

directly to the interpretation of the notion of restriction of competition by the Commission, or to the legal characterisation of the facts in the context of the case. This finding is a first indicator that the narrative of undue deference does not appear to fit the reality of litigation – or at least not in this context. The impression that the EU courts engage meaningfully with the notion of restriction of competition is confirmed when one considers other factors, and in particular appeals as well as those cases in which the EU courts, without annulling the decision, reframed the analysis undertaken by the Commission. Chart 3.4 seeks to capture these other factors.

An analysis of the substance of appeals is suggestive of a vigorous exchange of views – and occasional disagreement – about the boundaries of Article 101(1) TFEU between the Commission and the EU courts, and between the GC and the Court. Emblematic examples in this regard include *Glaxo Spain*,[38] where the GC took the view that the economic and legal context justified a finding that the agreement in the case was not restrictive of competition by object (and this in spite of the fact that the contentious clauses were an ostensible attempt to limit trade between Member States), while the Court disagreed. Another example is *Cartes Bancaires*,[39] which will be examined in detail below,

[38] Case T-168/01, *GlaxoSmithKline Services Unlimited v Commission*, EU:T:2006:265. Compare with Joined Cases C-501/06 P, C-513/06 P, C-515/06 P and C-519/06 P, *Glaxo Spain*.

[39] Case T-491/07, *Groupement des cartes bancaires v Commission*, EU:T:2012:633. Compare with Case C-67/13 P, *Cartes Bancaires*.

and which revealed a difference of views about the relevance of the economic and legal context for the finding that the agreement was not a 'by object' infringement.

Even more revealing is, arguably, the question of whether the EU courts reframe the legal interpretation of Article 101(1) TFEU found in the decision or whether they defer to the choices made by the authority instead. It appears that the EU courts have often rectified the framework crafted by the authority in its decisions, even in cases in which the conclusions were ultimately upheld. Suffice it to mention some examples in this regard. The idea that a restriction in the freedom of action is insufficient to establish a restriction of competition was confirmed in a series of challenges against prohibition decisions taking the opposite view, including *Nungesser*[40] and *BAT*[41] (in relation to the exploitation of intellectual property rights), and *Langnese-Iglo*[42] and *Schöller*[43] (concerning distribution agreements). The latter three judgments are particularly notable in that the actions for annulment were dismissed. In spite of this fact, the GC departed from the legal framework defined by the Commission in its decision and restated the principles defined by the Court in the seminal case law.

2.1.2 Exemption, Negative Clearance and Commitment Decisions

Exemption and negative clearance decisions played a prominent role under the system created in 1962 by virtue of Regulation 17.[44] From the perspective of the Commission, they were particularly useful instruments to spell out its policy with regard to 'law-intensive' cases, which were typically notified by firms to obtain certainty about the legality of their conduct. The Commission would declare the compatibility of the practice with Article 101 TFEU, sometimes after modifications introduced by the parties. Often, the exemption would come with conditions and/or obligations. Against this background, it is not surprising that the proportion of exemption and negative clearance decisions that were challenged before the Court

40 Case 258/78, *L.C. Nungesser KG and Kurt Eisele v Commission*, EU:C:1982:211.

41 Case 35/83, *BAT Cigaretten-Fabriken GmbH v Commission*, EU:C:1985:32.

42 Case T-7/93, *Langnese Iglo GmbH v Commission*, EU:T:1995:98; and Case C-279/95 P, *Langnese-Iglo GmbH v Commission*, EU:C:1998:447.

43 Case T-9/93, *Schöller Lebensmittel GmbH & Co. KG v Commission*, EU:T:1995:99.

44 Regulation No. 17: First Regulation implementing Articles 85 and 86 of the Treaty OJ (1962) No. 13/204. References are confined to Regulation 17 to streamline the argument.

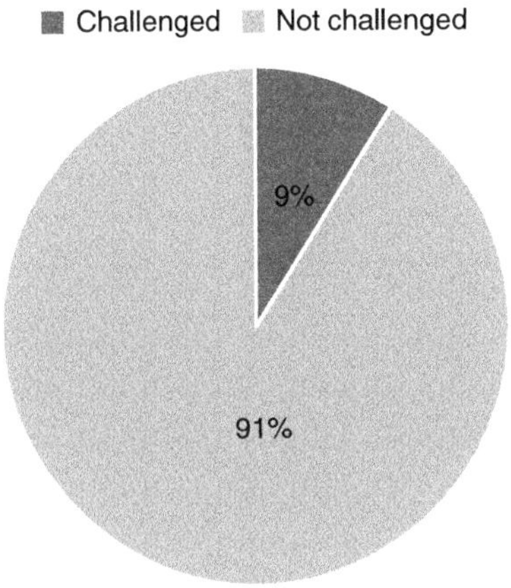

Chart 3.5 Proportion of exemption and negative clearance decisions challenged before the EU courts

was relatively low. Typically, addressees would be satisfied with the outcome of a negotiated solution with the authority. As shown in Chart 3.5, the legality of contested decisions was challenged only in under 10 per cent of cases. The incentive for third parties to bring a direct action against an exemption decision was also low. The EU courts held, early on, that the Commission enjoyed a margin of discretion when applying Article 101(3) TFEU.

While the proportion of challenged decisions is relatively low, Chart 3.6 shows that the notion of restriction of competition is significantly more relevant in this context than in one in which the dispute revolves around a prohibition decision. Details of these decisions can be found in Table 3.2 in the appendix. Again, there is nothing surprising about this finding. Insofar as exemption and negative clearance decisions are generally 'ideal type' 'law-intensive' cases, it is only natural that disputes tend to focus on the boundaries of Article 101(1) TFEU. In several cases, the firms having received an exemption subsequently challenged the finding that the practice amounted to a restriction of competition in the first place. This is the issue at stake, for instance, in landmark rulings like *O2*,[45] *Métropole Télévision*[46] and *European Night Services*,[47] which clarified some central

[45] Case T-328/03, *O2 (Germany) GmbH & Co. OHG v Commission*, EU:T:2006:116.
[46] Case T-112/99, *Métropole télévision (M6), Suez-Lyonnaise des eaux, France Télécom and Télévision française 1 SA (TF1) v Commission*, EU:T:2001:215.
[47] Joined Cases, T-374/94, T-375/94, T-384/94 and T-388/94, *European Night Services Ltd and others v Commission*, EU:T:1998:198.

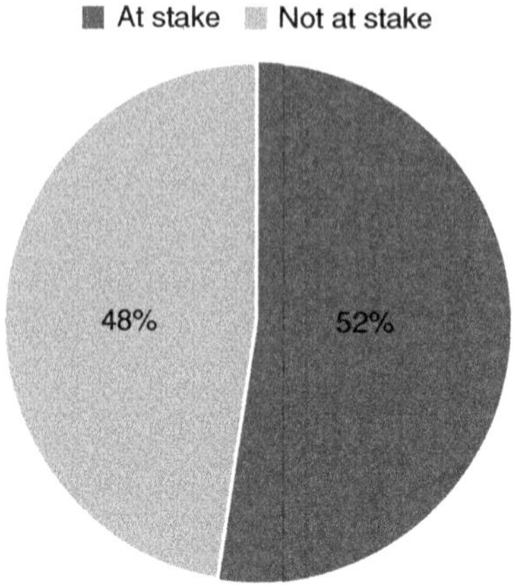

Chart 3.6 Relevance of the notion of restriction of competition in challenged exemption and negative clearance decisions

aspects about the approach to establish a restriction and about the relationship between Articles 101(1) TFEU and 101(3) TFEU. In other cases, including the *Metro* saga and *Givenchy*, actions were brought by third parties, which often challenged the analysis under Article 101(3) TFEU.

The outcome of litigation in cases addressed by means of exemption and negative clearance decisions is captured in Charts 3.7 and 3.8. It confirms the impression given by the analysis of prohibition decisions. When the two charts are considered together, there is nothing that suggests that the EU courts have been generally deferential to the analysis of the Commission. Chart 3.7 shows that, more often than not, the EU courts annulled a Commission decision for reasons relating to the interpretation of the notion of restriction of competition. More importantly (and this is something that Chart 3.8 captures only imperfectly), the annulment of these decisions was typically the result of a disagreement about the applicable legal framework. In *European Night Services* and *O2*, both mentioned above, the annulment was the consequence of the failure of the Commission to consider the conditions of competition that would have existed in the absence of the practice. The EU courts engaged with the interpretation of Article 101(1) TFEU advanced by the authority even in cases in which the action was dismissed. *Metro I*, in which the ECJ defined the boundaries of the legality rule applying to selective distribution agreements, is a good example in this regard.

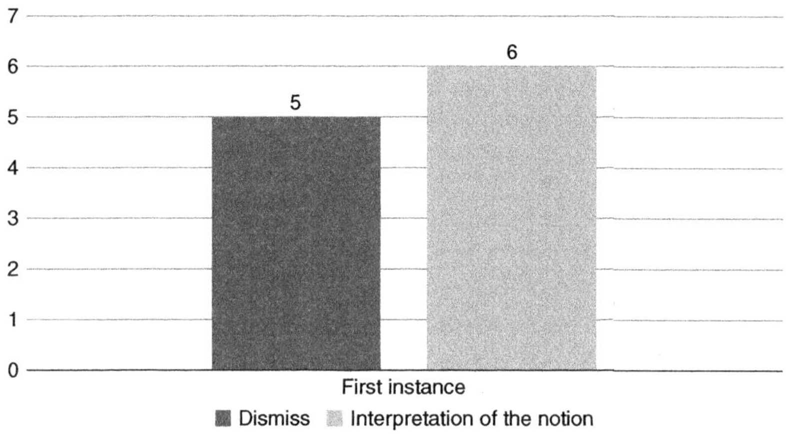

Chart 3.7 Outcome of cases engaging with the notion of restriction

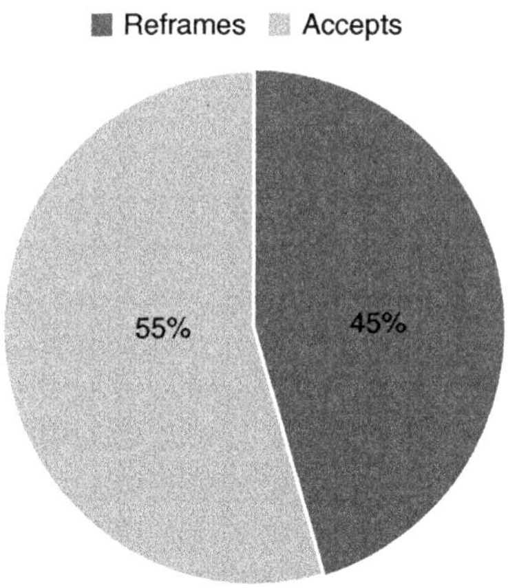

Chart 3.8 Approach to the notion of restriction, percentages

Following the adoption of Regulation 1/2003, the Commission no longer has the monopoly to apply Article 101(3) TFEU, and neither does it have the obligation to rule on whether the conditions of the provision are fulfilled in the context of a given case. Regulation 1/2003 introduced two instruments that could replace, in theory, exemption and negative clearance decisions. One of them is the finding of inapplicability, pursuant to which the Commission is entitled to declare, by means of a formal decision, that a practice falls outside the scope of Article 101(1) TFEU or fulfils the conditions set out in Article 101(3)

TFEU. Article 10 of Regulation 1/2003[48] gives the Commission discretion to adopt a decision of this kind where it believes that doing so is in the public interest. At the time of writing, the authority has not adopted a single finding of inapplicability. As a result, the gap left by exemption and negative clearance decisions has been filled in practice by commitment decisions, which is another instrument introduced by Regulation 1/2003. The nature and operation of commitment decisions has already been described in Chapter 2. Considering that this instrument does not establish whether EU competition law has been infringed, the parties to an agreement do not have a clear incentive to bring a direct action before the GC following a negotiated outcome with the Commission. The observable behaviour of stakeholders over the past decade suggests that this intuition is correct. Out of 19 decisions concerning a potential infringement of Article 101 TFEU, only two have been challenged before the EU courts.[49]

2.2 *Preliminary References*

Preliminary references have played a vital role in the definition of the scope of Article 101(1) TFEU. It is in this procedural context that the legal status of a wealth of practices, including (among many others) exclusive distribution,[50] exclusive dealing[51] or franchising,[52] has been clarified. This is so for quantitative and qualitative reasons. From a quantitative perspective, a significant number of references concerning the interpretation of the notion of restriction of competition has reached the Court since the 1960s. Overall, the analysis of the case law shows that the absolute number of preliminary references that engage meaningfully with the notion is higher than the absolute number of cases having reached the EU courts through direct actions. When one considers specific practices, it appears

[48] Pursuant to Article 10 of Regulation 1/2003: 'Where the Community public interest relating to the application of Articles [101] and [102] of the Treaty so requires, the Commission, acting on its own initiative, may by decision find that Article [101] of the Treaty is not applicable to an agreement, a decision by an association of undertakings or a concerted practice, either because the conditions of Article [101(1)] of the Treaty are not fulfilled, or because the conditions of Article [101(3)] of the Treaty are satisfied'.

[49] Case T-274/06, *Estaser El Mareny, SL v Commission*, EU:T:2007:323; and Case T-873/16, *Groupe Canal+ v Commission*, pending.

[50] Case 56/65, *Société Technique Minière*; and Case 22/71, *Béguelin Import Co. v S.A.G.L. Import Export*, EU:C:1971:113.

[51] Case C-234/89, *Delimitis*. [52] Case 161/84, *Pronuptia*.

that for every judgment addressing the question in the context of a direct action, there are typically two or more preliminary rulings. Inevitably, the latter make a more important contribution to the definition of the legal status of the practice. From a qualitative perspective, a substantial number of the references submitted by national courts raise fundamental issues about the boundaries of the notion of restriction of competition.

Chart 3.9 provides a quantitative perspective on the question. As can be seen, 24 per cent of the preliminary references have been found to engage with the notion of restriction. Details of the rulings can be found in Table 3.3 in the appendix. Chart 3.10, in turn, seeks to identify the topics raised in the references. As can be seen, it is possible to identify three broad categories in this sense: horizontal agreements, vertical agreements and issues relating to the exploitation of intellectual property rights. Each of the categories have been subdivided. As far as horizontal agreements are concerned, for instance, it makes sense to single out cases addressing the status of exchanges of information (which range from the prima facie lawful[53] to the prima facie unlawful)[54] and those that deal with what can be labelled quasi-legislation, and which include, in particular, the activities of professional associations.[55] Other practices range from cartel-like conduct[56] to pro-competitive co-operation arrangements, such as joint purchasing co-operatives.[57]

Concerning, second, vertical restraints, Chart 3.10 shows that some categories – exclusive distribution, exclusive dealing and selective distribution – feature prominently in the case law. Predictably, the questions regarding these practices have gained in sophistication over time. They range from the question of whether the practice should be considered restrictive by object or effect[58] to the methodology that should be

[53] Case C-238/05 *Asnef-Equifax, Servicios de Información sobre Solvencia y Crédito, SL v Asociación de Usuarios de Servicios Bancarios*, EU:C:2006:734.

[54] Case C-8/08, *T-Mobile*.

[55] See in particular Case C-309/99, *Wouters*. See also Case C-136/12, *Consiglio nazionale dei geologi v Autorità garante della concorrenza e del mercato*, EU:C:2013:489; and Case C-1/12, *Ordem dos Técnicos Oficiais de Contas v Autoridade da Concorrência*, EU:C:2013:127.

[56] See for instance Joined Cases C-295/04 to C-298/04, *Vincenzo Manfredi v Lloyd Adriatico Assicurazioni SpA, Antonio Cannito v Fondiaria Sai SpA and Nicolò Tricarico and Pasqualina Murgolo v Assitalia SpA*, EU:C:2006:461; and Case 319/82, *Société de Vente de Ciments et Bétons de l'Est SA v Kerpen & Kerpen GmbH und Co. KG*, EU:C:1983:374.

[57] Case C-399/93, *H.G. Oude Luttikhuis and others v Verenigde Coöperatieve Melkindustrie Coberco BA*, EU:C:1995:434; and Case C-250/92, *Gøttrup-Klim e.a. Grovvareforeninger v Dansk Landbrugs Grovvareselskab AmbA*, EU:C:1994:413.

[58] See for instance Case C-234/89, *Delimitis*, paras. 11–3.

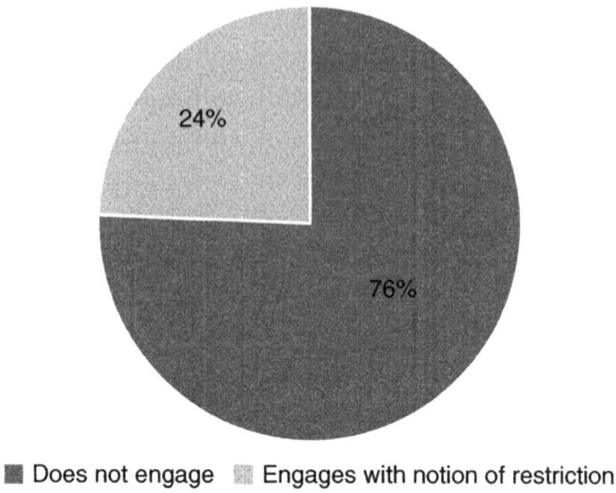

Chart 3.9 Preliminary references dealing with Article 101 TFEU

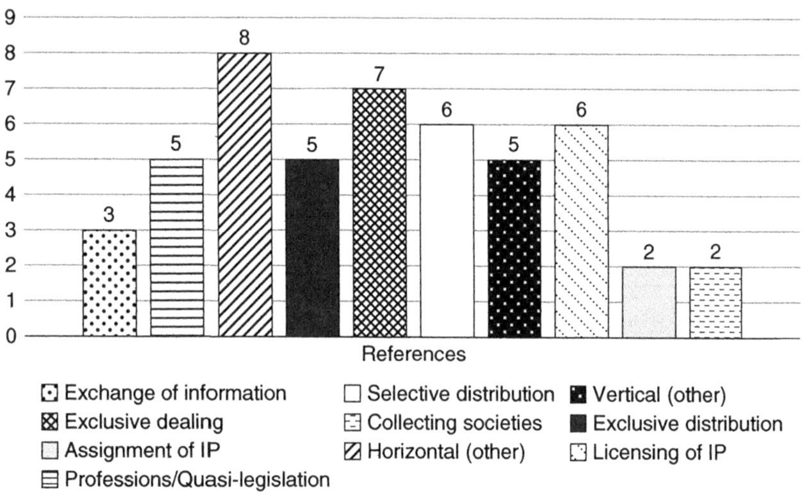

Chart 3.10 Preliminary references engaging with the notion of restriction

followed to establish its restrictive impact on competition;[59] or to whether a de facto ban on online sales is compatible with Article 101(1) TFEU.[60] Often, the questions are very fact-specific.[61] References

[59] Case C-384/13, *Estación de Servicio Pozuelo 4, SL v GALP Energía España SAU*, EU:C:2014:2425.

[60] Case C-439/09, *Pierre Fabre.*

[61] See for instance the questions raised in Case C-32/11, *Allianz Hungária Biztosító Zrt. and Others v Gazdasági Versenyhivatal*, EU:C:2013:160; Case C-70/93, *Bayerische*

concerning other vertical restraints are no less important. For instance, the legal status of vertical price-fixing has been clarified in a series of preliminary rulings, in particular *Binon*.[62] The same can be said of franchising, the status of which the Court considered in *Pronuptia*.[63]

Finally, the interface between competition law and intellectual property features prominently in the case law – this is true across both Articles 101 and 102 TFEU, as shown in Chapter 4. A question that reached the Court early on related to the status of agreements providing for the assignment of intellectual property rights, which, as the ECJ itself and the Commission would quickly realise, can be an effective device to partition the internal market.[64] As shown in the chart, moreover, a sizeable stream of references concerns the status of some clauses included in licensing agreements. The questions raised range from the lawfulness of exclusive territorial licensing[65] to whether no-challenge clauses amount to a restriction of competition.[66] Finally, the licensing activities of collecting societies – to which Article 101(1) TFEU applies insofar as right holders co-operate to license their works jointly – were raised in *Tournier*[67] and *Lucazeau*.[68]

2.3 *Joint Analysis*

The first conclusion that follows from the above is that, as far as the interpretation of the notion of restriction of competition is concerned, the tone has been set, by and large, in preliminary references. The principles of the applicable case law, described in Section 1, were introduced in the context of a dialogue between the ECJ and national courts. As already pointed out, the observed pre-eminence of preliminary rulings can in part be attributed to the higher number of references

Motorenwerke AG v ALD Auto-Leasing D GmbH, EU:C:1995:344; and Case 23/67, *SA Brasserie de Haecht*.

[62] Case 243/83, *Binon*. [63] Case 161/84, *Pronuptia*.

[64] See Case C-9/93, *IHT Internationale Heiztechnik GmbH and Uwe Danzinger v Ideal-Standard GmbH and Wabco Standard GmbH*, EU:C:1994:261; and Case 40/70, *Sirena S.r.l. v Eda S.r.l. and others*, EU:C:1971:18. A trade mark assignment was in fact the device used by the supplier in Joined Cases 56 and 58/64, *Consten-Grundig*.

[65] Case 262/81, *Coditel SA, Compagnie générale pour la diffusion de la télévision, and others v Ciné-Vog Films SA and others*, EU:C:1982:334.

[66] Case 65/86, *Bayer AG and Maschinenfabrik Hennecke GmbH v Heinz Süllhöfer*, EU:C:1988:448.

[67] Case 395/87, *Ministère public v Jean-Louis Tournier*, EU:C:1989:319.

[68] Joined Cases 110/88, 241/88 and 242/88, *François Lucazeau and others v Société des Auteurs, Compositeurs et Editeurs de Musique (SACEM) and others*, EU:C:1989:326.

efforts on agreements directly aimed at restricting parallel trade (and in particular those providing for absolute territorial protection and export prohibitions). During the 1970s and 1980s, these agreements amounted to a significant fraction of the enforcement activity of the Commission, as they were perceived to be particularly deleterious for the integration of Member States' economies. There were, however, some cases in which the Commission examined agreements that did not seek to restrict parallel trade. In these cases, the analysis of Article 101(1) TFEU did not consider the factors set out in *Société Technique Minière*.

The *Omega* case, for instance, concerned the two levels of a distribution system. The wholesale level gave (non-absolute) territorial protection to the distributors. The Commission concluded, in that regard, that the agreements amounted to a restriction of competition for the same reasons that it advanced in its 1965 decisions. Thus, the mere fact that the agreement gave a single firm the right to obtain supplies from a given territory was deemed sufficient to trigger Article 101(1) TFEU.[80] A similar restriction was found in *Junghans*, decided in 1977.[81] In addition, the set of agreements considered in that decision contained an obligation on some distributors not to engage in active selling in other Member States. The Commission argued that this clause 'substantially restricted' the competition opportunities of these distributors in other Member States. When reaching this conclusion, however, the authority did not evaluate, as *Société Technique Minière* would require, whether distributors in other Member States would have accepted the restraints in the absence of protection from active sales from other distributors.

3.2.2 Exclusive Dealing

Under the traditional approach favoured by the Commission, an exclusive dealing agreement is necessarily restrictive of competition. By definition, single branding requirements curtail the freedom of action of the distributor, which is precluded by virtue of the agreement from selling products competing with those of the supplier. The Court's approach to these agreements is markedly different from that of the Commission. It was laid down early on, in *Brasserie de Haecht*. As pointed out above, this is precisely one of the rulings in which the Court emphasised the need to consider the restrictive nature of the agreement in the economic and legal

[80] Commission Decision 70/488/EEC of 28 October 1970 (Case IV/10.498, 11.546, 12.992, 17.394, 17.395, 17.971, 18.772, 18.888 and ex 3.213 – *Omega*) OJ (1970) No. L 242/22.

[81] Commission Decision 77/100/EEC of 21 December 1976 (Case IV/5715 – *Junghans*) OJ (1972) No. L 30/10.

context of which it is part. *Brasserie de Haecht* suggested that an exclusive dealing agreement does not in itself restrict competition, even if it precludes the distributor from selling products from rival manufacturers.

The early administrative practice of the Commission shows that the authority interpreted *Brasserie de Haecht* in a narrow manner. According to this view, beer supply agreements tend to fall outside the scope of Article 101(1) TFEU, but not because they fail to restrict competition. The reason, instead, is that they are generally not capable, in and of themselves, of affecting trade between Member States. Accordingly, an agreement requiring a single retailer not to sell competing brands can only be expected to have a cross-border effect when combined with other similar agreements. This is in fact the position the Commission took in the Preamble to Regulation 1984/83.[82] Under this interpretation of Article 101(1) TFEU, an exclusive dealing agreement has as its object or effect the restriction of competition unless it is de minimis.

The decision in *Goodyear Italiana* captures the early approach of the Commission well.[83] This case concerned an agreement that combined exclusive distribution – covering the whole of the territory of a Member State – and exclusive dealing – the exclusive distributor agreed not to sell brands competing with those of the supplier. As the agreement covered cross-border activities (it included prohibitions relating to sales outside the allocated territory) it was clear that it was at least capable of affecting trade between Member States. In such circumstances, the Commission concluded that the exclusive dealing aspect of the agreement amounted to a restriction of competition – the distributor's freedom to sell competing products was curtailed and rivals' access to the market was limited. Insofar as the distributor was an important player, the restriction was of an appreciable nature.[84] The *Spices* case, whereby a supplier required

[82] See the Commission Regulation (EEC) No. 1984/83 of 22 June 1983 on the application of Article 85(3) of the Treaty to categories of exclusive purchasing agreements OJ (1983) No. L 173/5, Recital 3: 'Whereas exclusive purchasing agreements of the categories defined in this Regulation may fall within the prohibition contained in Article [101(1)] of the Treaty; whereas this will often be the case with agreements concluded between undertakings from different Member States; whereas an exclusive purchasing agreement to which undertakings from only one Member State are party and which concerns the resale of goods within that Member State may also be caught by the prohibition; whereas this is in particular the case where it is one of a number of similar agreements which together may affect trade between Member States'.

[83] Commission Decision 75/94/EEC of 19 December 1974 (Case IV/23.013 – *Goodyear Italiana-Euram*) OJ (1975) No. L 38/10.

[84] Ibid., para. 6: 'Euram, by virtue of the exclusive dealing agreement is prevented from selling any product which could compete with those to which the agreement relates; this has the effect not only of restricting the freedom of Euram to do business but also affects

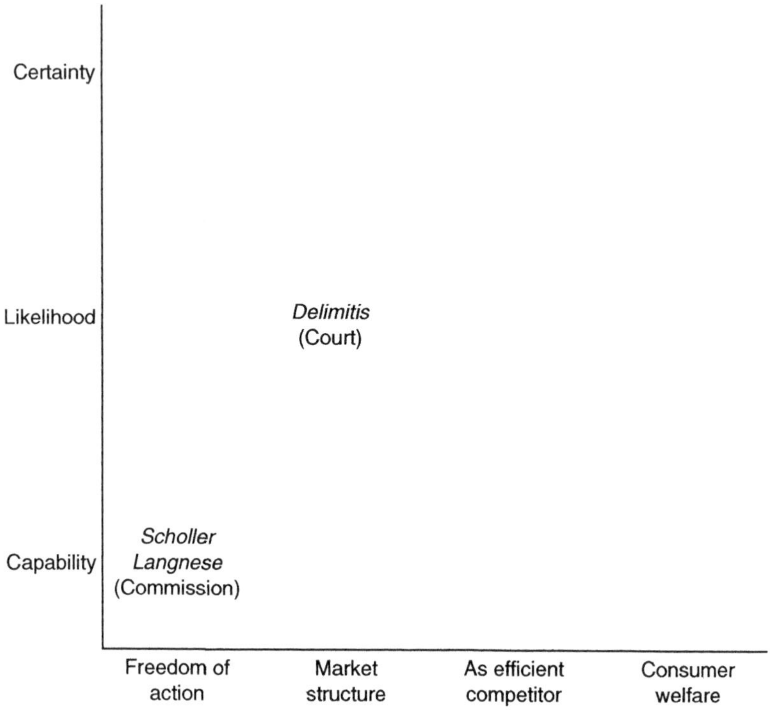

Figure 3.6 The effects of exclusive dealing agreements

Langnese-Iglo.[90] In contrast with the Court ruling, these two decisions equate competition with firms' freedom of action. According to the Commission's understanding of *Delimitis*, an exclusive dealing agreement has restrictive effects on competition if it is not de minimis within the meaning of *Völk*. Thus, any agreement that is above the thresholds defined by the Commission in its Notice would be presumptively prohibited if it is capable of affecting trade between Member States. The central question in *Delimitis*, namely whether the agreement, alone or in combination with others, would result in market foreclosure, is irrelevant under the approach endorsed in *Schöller* and *Langnese-Iglo*. According to the Commission, the test devised by the Court – that is, the analysis of the cumulative effect of parallel networks of agreements – would only be of

[90] Commission Decision 93/406/EEC of 23 December 1992 (Case IV/34.072 – *Langnese-Iglo GmbH*) OJ (1993) No. L 183/19.

relevance where the agreements concluded by individual suppliers fall below the de minimis threshold.

When adopted, *Schöller* and *Langnese-Iglo* were criticised by commentators for contradicting a literal reading of *Delimitis.*[91] In fact, nowhere in the latter ruling did the Court hold or suggest that the legal test was confined to agreements of minor importance. In addition, it made clear, as already pointed out, that restrictive effects had to be assessed by reference to the impact of the agreement(s) on market access, not by reference to the freedom of action of the distributor or competing suppliers. *Schöller* and *Langnese-Iglo* were not annulled on substantive grounds when challenged before the EU courts.[92] However, the Commission's narrow and controversial reading of *Delimitis* was not upheld. According to the GC, the fact that an agreement exceeds the de minimis thresholds set by the Commission in its soft law instrument is not in itself sufficient to establish a restriction of competition.[93] In addition, the GC examined the legality of the Commission decision in light of the criteria defined by the Court in *Delimitis*.

3.2.3 Ancillary Restraints

The ancillary restraints doctrine can be seen as a variation on the evaluation of the counterfactual. It is therefore an area in which the divergent approaches of the Commission and the Court become apparent. According to the doctrine, the clauses that are objectively

91 See in this sense Valentine Korah, 'Exclusive purchasing obligations: *Mars v Langnese* and *Scholler*' (1994) 15 *European Competition Law Review* 171, who claimed that '[t]he published decisions of the Commission [...] show no signs that the early part of the judgment in *Delimitis* has been read'; and James Veltrop, 'Tying and Exclusive Purchasing Agreements under EC Competition Law' (1994) 31 *Common Market Law Review* 549, who noted that the interpretation of the Commission in *Schöller* and *Langnese-Iglo* 'is contradicted by the express language of *Delimitis*'s two-part test'.

92 Case T-7/93, *Langnese-Iglo* and Case T-9/93, *Schöller.* The two decisions were partially annulled for reasons relating to the remedy, the application of which is in turn related (at least in part) to the interpretation of Article 101(1) TFEU advanced by the Commission. See in this sense *Langnese-Iglo*, paras. 205–11; and *Schöller*, paras. 158–65.

93 Case T-9/93, *Schöller*, para. 75, where the GC pointed out that 'it cannot be inferred from [the De Minimis Notice] with any certainty that a network of exclusive purchasing agreements is automatically liable to prevent, restrict or distort competition appreciably merely because the ceilings laid down in it are exceeded. Moreover, it is apparent from the actual wording of paragraph 3 of that notice that it is entirely possible, in the present case, that agreements concluded between undertakings which exceed the ceilings indicated affect trade between Member States or competition only to an insignificant extent and consequently are not caught by Article [101(1)] of the Treaty'.

necessary to achieve the pro-competitive aim sought by the agreement are not capable of restricting competition within the meaning of Article 101(1) TFEU. As a result, they are prima facie lawful. The underlying rationale is that, absent these clauses, the main transaction would not have taken place. The doctrine is potentially applicable in a variety of scenarios.[94] In the context of a merger, for instance, a buyer may not be willing to acquire a business if it does not have assurances that it will be able to capture the goodwill that is associated with the assets transferred. This is an idea that the Commission accepted early on in its administrative practice, prior to the formal implementation of a merger control regime.[95]

The goodwill associated with a business is typically protected by means of a non-compete obligation. In the context of a distribution agreement, for instance, a supplier is likely to rule out selling through independent distributors if doing so risks undermining its brand image. Similarly, distributors may be reluctant to undertake the necessary investments for the sale of a product absent guarantees that other distributors would not take a free ride on these investments. Selective distribution systems are effective devices to preserve the brand image of the manufacturer and the investments of resellers, and as such ideal candidates for the application of the ancillary restraints doctrine. What is peculiar about selective distribution is that the supplier chooses its resellers on the basis of qualitative conditions pertaining, inter alia, to the training of the employees, the service provided in the store and/or to the presentation of the products. The corollary to these restraints is a prohibition on the distributors to sell the products in question to operators that are not members of the system. Such a prohibition seems objectively necessary to ensure the appropriate functioning of the network. Accordingly, it would not be caught by Article 101(1) TFEU.

In several decisions adopted during the 1970s, including *Omega* and *Junghans*, mentioned above, the Commission considered the compatibility of selective distribution with Article 101 TFEU. In its decision in

[94] For an application of the concept to these agreements, see F. Enrique González Díaz, 'The Notion of Ancillary Restraints Under EC Competition Law' (1995) 19 *Fordham International Law Journal* 951.

[95] Commission Decision 83/670/EEC of 12 December 1983 (Case IV/30.389 – *Nutricia/de Rooij* and IV/30.408 – *Nutricia/Zuid-Hollandse Conservenfabriek*) OJ (1983) No. L 376/22.

SABA,[96] which would give rise to the *Metro I* judgment,[97] the Commission did not endorse the ancillary restraints doctrine. It accepted the principle whereby a supplier is entitled to appoint its distributors on the basis of conditions relating, in particular, to the qualifications of the latter (and their employees), the suitability of the trading premises or the provision of guarantees and after-sales services. Such conditions were found to fall outside the scope of Article 101(1) TFEU insofar as they were deemed objective and were imposed without discrimination to all dealers. On the other hand, any restraints requiring distributors to keep a certain range of products from the supplier, to meet some supply targets or to achieve a minimum turnover were deemed to fall within the scope of Article 101(1) TFEU. Clauses prohibiting distributors from selling to non-members of the network were also deemed restrictive of competition and this insofar as they constrained their commercial freedom.[98]

The Court upheld the analysis of the Commission when challenged by Metro, a third party. The ruling is notable in that it departs in some respects from the principles of the case law as defined in *Société Technique Minière* and *Brasserie de Haecht*. Several passages of the ruling suggest that a restriction in the freedom of action is sufficient to make a clause fall within the scope of Article 101(1) TFEU. For instance, the Court argued that an obligation on the part of the wholesalers to participate in the creation of a distribution network is restrictive of competition insofar as it binds such distributors to a particular manufacturer. According to the judgment, 'the function of a wholesaler is not to promote the products of a particular manufacturer but rather to provide for the retail trade supplies obtained on the basis of competition between manufacturers'.[99] It is not obvious to see how this position can be reconciled with other rulings in which the Court accepted that exclusivity obligations – and in particular exclusive dealing – are not necessarily restrictive of competition, and that an analysis of the economic and legal context is necessary in any circumstance. In particular, the Court

[96] Commission Decision 76/159/EEC of 15 December 1975 (Case IV/847 – *SABA*) OJ (1976) No. L 28/19.

[97] Case 26/76, *Metro SB-Großmärkte GmbH & Co. KG v Commission*, EU:C:1977:167 ('*Metro I*').

[98] *SABA* Decision, para. 26: '[t]hese obligations restrict the commercial freedom of SABA and its dealers. They have as the object and effect the restriction of competition within the common market to a perceptible degree'.

[99] Case 26/76, *Metro I*, para. 40.

did not consider whether a supplier would have relied upon independent wholesalers absent a certain degree of commitment on their part. The same can be said of some conditions requiring the retailers to achieve a particular turnover, which were also deemed to fall within the scope of Article 101(1) TFEU.[100] In this regard, the risk of free-riding, which had been identified in *Société Technique Minière*, is not considered.[101]

There is some tension between the analysis in *Metro I* and that found in *Pronuptia*,[102] a preliminary reference concerning the lawfulness of franchising agreements under Article 101(1) TFEU. This tension is captured in Figure 3.7. *Pronuptia* laid down a legality rule for clauses in a franchising agreement that are aimed at protecting the know-how of the franchisor and the reputation and uniformity of the distribution system. First, the Court held, on the basis of formal analysis, that franchising agreements are plausibly pro-competitive. In this sense, it identified, as in *Delimitis*, the benefits for both parties to the agreement.[103] Second, the Court concluded, in light of the counterfactual, that the abovementioned clauses were not capable of restricting competition, and as such fell prima facie outside the scope of Article 101(1) TFEU. A supplier may not be willing to rely upon independent retailers, the ECJ explained, if it fears that its know-how might benefit competitors, whether directly or indirectly. Thus, it may be justified to impose a non-compete obligation on distributors. Similarly, a supplier may not be willing to allow third parties to use its name if it perceives that doing so might undermine its brand image. Thus, it may be entitled to require distributors to use its business methods and know-how, or to provide for obligations relating to the location of the stores, or the quality of the goods and services supplied.[104]

100 Ibid., para. 37.

101 Valentine Korah and Denis O'Sullivan, *Distribution Agreements Under the EC Competition Rules* (Oxford: Hart Publishing, 2002).

102 Case 161/84, *Pronuptia*.

103 Ibid., para. 15. The Court pointed out that franchising 'is a way for an undertaking to derive financial benefit from its expertise without investing its own capital'. In addition, it 'gives traders who do not have the necessary experience access to methods which they could not have learned without considerable effort and allows them to benefit from the reputation of the franchisor's business name'. Accordingly, it concluded that this arrangement, 'which allows the franchisor to profit from his success, does not in itself interfere with competition'.

104 The idea that vertical restraints may fall outside the scope of Article 101(1) TFEU when they seek to preserve the brand image of a manufacturer was not explicitly accepted in *Metro I*, but would be endorsed by the Commission in subsequent cases. See in this sense Commission Decision 92/428/EEC of 24 July 1992 (Case No IV/33.542 – *Parfums Givenchy system of selective distribution*) OJ (1992) No. L 236/11. See also Guidelines

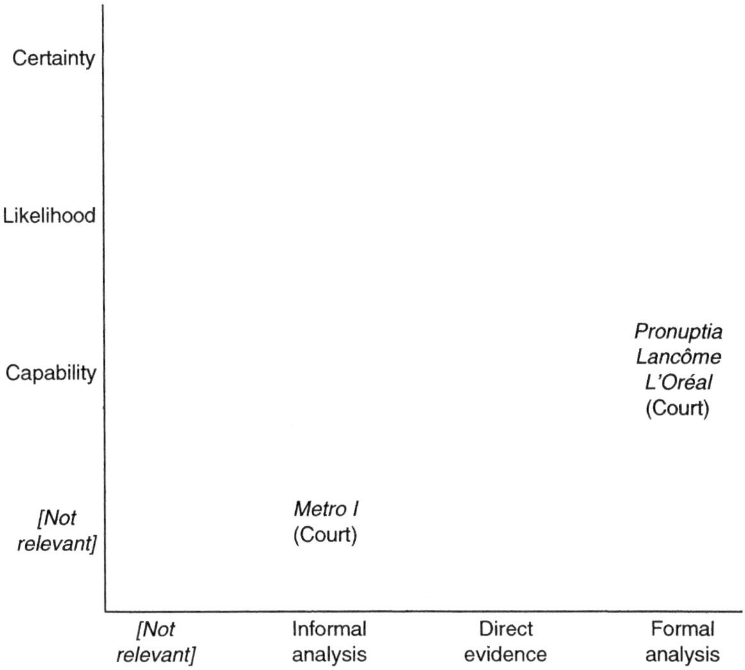

Figure 3.7 Ancillary restraints

The tension between *Metro I* and *Pronuptia* is not present in subsequent preliminary references dealing with the lawfulness of selective distribution systems. In these subsequent cases, the Court held that restraining the retailers' freedom of action does not necessarily amount to a restriction of competition. Thus, the restrictive nature of a selective distribution system could not simply be inferred from the fact that the conditions laid down in *Metro I* are not fulfilled. In three judgments delivered in 1980 and 1981 – *Lancôme*,[105] *L'Oréal*[106] and

on vertical restraints, para. 107: 'A vertical restraint may help to create a brand image by imposing a certain measure of uniformity and quality standardisation on the distributors, thereby increasing the attractiveness of the product to the final consumer and increasing its sales. This can for instance be found in selective distribution and franchising'.

105 Case 99/79, *SA Lancôme and Cosparfrance Nederland BV v Etos BV and Albert Heyn Supermart BV*, EU:C:1980:193.

106 Case 31/80, *NV L'Oréal and SA L'Oréal v PVBA 'De Nieuwe AMCK'*, EU:C:1980:289.

Salonia[107] – the Court emphasised that, even when the requirements imposed on distributors go beyond what was considered to be objectively necessary in the seminal ruling, it would still be necessary to evaluate the counterfactual, as well as the features of the relevant market and the position of the parties therein.[108]

3.3 *Licensing Agreements*

3.3.1 Overview

Agreements providing for the licensing of intellectual property put the traditional approach of the Commission to test. This is so because, in some instances, licensing agreements do not appear to restrict competition that would have existed in their absence. There are, to begin with, instances where a licence does not go beyond the substantive scope of the intellectual property right. When a licensee is allowed to authorise or prohibit the same range of acts that the licensor would have been able to authorise or prohibit, one could argue that any resulting restriction is not attributable to the agreement, but to the intellectual property right. Second, one should consider that intellectual property is a public good,[109] and as such inherently fragile. As a result, a right holder may not be willing to license its intellectual property if doing so would undermine the value of the technology in question. Similarly, the licensee may not be willing to undertake the investments necessary for the exploitation of a technology if it is unable to capture its value. These factors plead in favour of a systematic assessment of the counterfactual to evaluate whether the licensing agreement would have been concluded in the absence of some restraints.

Against this background, it would be insufficient to show that the agreement restricts the freedom of action of one or more of the parties to the agreement. It would be irrelevant, for instance, that an exclusive territorial licence precludes the licensor from exploiting the technology itself in a given territory and the licensee from exploiting the technology in territories other than the one covered by the licence. Insofar as it is objectively necessary for the transaction to take place and/or not capable of restricting competition that would have existed in its absence, it would

[107] Case 126/80, *Maria Salonia v Giorgio Poidomani and Franca Baglieri, née Giglio*, EU:C:1981:136.

[108] See in this sense Case 31/80, *L'Oréal*, para. 19; and Case 99/79, *Lancôme*, para. 24.

[109] See for instance Richard Posner, 'Intellectual Property: The Law and Economics Approach' (2005) 19 *Journal of Economic Perspectives* 57.

not restrict competition. This is the position at which the Commission originally hinted in its 1962 Notice on patent licensing agreements (hereinafter, the '1962 Notice').[110] In this document, the Commission expressed the view that some of the clauses included in such agreements are not caught by Article 101(1) TFEU.

The 1962 Notice is based on the idea that the clauses that remain within the substantive scope of the patent are not restrictive of competition. Such clauses, in other words, do not go beyond the range of acts that the patentee would be in a position to control by virtue of its exclusive right.[111] Thus, contractual provisions that, inter alia, limit the scope of the licence to certain uses (the so-called 'field of use' restrictions), the amount to be produced in accordance with the licence and – more importantly – the territory from which the product is to be exploited were all deemed to fall outside the scope of Article 101(1) TFEU.[112] The 1962 Notice also took the view that clauses whereby the licensor commits not to licensing its technology to third parties or not to exploiting it itself are not caught by the prohibition, due to the fact that they were not deemed to affect trade between Member States at the time.[113]

In the years that followed the adoption of the Notice, the Commission progressively moved away from the principles underpinning it and endorsed its traditional understanding of the notion of restriction of competition. The principles of the case law, however, proved resilient. The Court acknowledged that the ideas sketched in *Société Technique Minière* are relevant in the context of the exploitation of intellectual property rights – and this on account of the investments required for the development of new technologies. The case law also displays an understanding of the nature of intangible property. Thus, there are several cases that suggest that, where the agreement remains within the substantive scope of the exclusive right, it is not restrictive of competition (at least not by object).

[110] Notice on patent licensing agreements OJ (1962) 2922.

[111] Ibid., at p. 2923: '*Les engagements énumérés au point I/A ne sont pas visés par l'interdiction édictée par l'article [101], paragraphe 1, parce qu'ils sont couverts par le brevet. Ils impliquent uniquement le maintien partiel du droit d'interdiction que comporte le droit exclusif du breveté vis-à-vis du licencié par ailleurs autorisé à exploiter l'invention. L'énumération du point I/A ne constitue pas une délimitation exhaustive des droits conférés par le brevet*'.

[112] Ibid., at p. 2922. [113] Ibid., at p. 2923.

3.3.2 Territorial Licensing

The move away from the principles set out in its 1962 Notice became apparent a decade later when the Commission adopted its first formal decisions concerning agreements providing for the licensing of intellectual property.[114] This shift is perhaps best explained by reference to *Davidson Rubber*.[115] In that case, the Commission concluded that an exclusive territorial licensing agreement was caught by Article 101(1) TFEU insofar as it restricted the licensor's freedom of action to grant the licence to third parties or to exploit the technology itself in the relevant territory.[116] The restriction at stake in the case was deemed appreciable due to the importance of the technology.[117] Interestingly, the Commission considered that the clauses included in the agreement were objectively necessary for the launch of the product. In this regard, it accepted that the licensees would not have accepted the agreements in the absence of some degree of territorial protection. However, such considerations were only deemed relevant for the assessment in the context of Article 101(3) TFEU.[118]

It was necessary to wait until the eighth decision adopted by the Commission to see a challenge before the Court. In *Nungesser*,[119] the authority declared a licensing agreement to be caught by Article 101(1) TFEU. In addition, it refused to grant an exemption in accordance with the third paragraph of the provision. The main difference between *Davidson Rubber* and *Nungesser* is that, in the latter, the licensor sought to protect the licensee against sales by third parties, thereby conferring absolute territorial protection upon it. The analysis in *Nungesser* reflected, again, the traditional approach of the Commission. Thus, the authority concluded in its decision that the clauses in the agreement whereby the licensor refused to grant a licence to third parties and to exploit the product itself were restrictive of competition. Moreover, it held that the clauses aimed at preventing third parties from importing the contractual products were caught by Article 101(1) TFEU.

[114] The shift in the position of the Commission is explained in Valentine Korah, *Intellectual Property Rights and the EC Competition Rules* (Oxford: Hart Publishing, 2006), p. 30; and Inge Govaere, *The Use and Abuse of Intellectual Property Rights in EC Law* (London: Sweet & Maxwell, 1996), pp. 115–6.

[115] Commission Decision 72/237/CEE of 9 June 1972 (Case IV/17.545, 6.964, 26.858, 26.890, 18.673, 17.448 – *Davidson Rubber Co.*) OJ (1972) No. L 143/31.

[116] Ibid., para 7. [117] Ibid., para. 8. [118] Ibid., paras. 11–5.

[119] Commission Decision 78/823/EEC of 21 September 1978 (Case IV/28.824 – *Breeders' rights – maize seed*) OJ (1978) No. L 286/23.

The judgment of the Court in *Nungesser* is a landmark in EU competition law.[120] It is notable in that the analysis departed substantially from that of the Commission. As in the cases relating to distribution agreements, the Court refused to equate a restriction in the freedom of action of the parties with a restriction of competition. The Court considered that an agreement that gives a licensee the exclusive right to use a technology in a given territory is not necessarily caught by Article 101(1) TFEU. In this regard, it drew a distinction between the so-called open exclusive licences, which are not necessarily restrictive, and closed licences, which are in principle caught by the prohibition.[121] The difference between the two depends on whether the licence limits the ability of third parties to sell the product into the territory covered by the agreement.[122]

The divide between open and closed licences echoes the position of the German Government, which, in its submission, claimed that agreements that remain within the substantive scope of the intellectual property right are not in themselves contrary to Article 101(1) TFEU. An open exclusive licence which does not affect the position of third parties does not grant to the licensee more rights than those granted to the holder of the intellectual property by virtue of the relevant legislation. Considering that the purpose of intellectual property is to reward the investments made in the development of new technologies, an approach that would consider every exclusive territorial licence as contrary to Article 101(1) TFEU would have a negative impact on firms' incentives to grant new licences. As a result, small players that lack the ability to invest in the development of their own facilities would be penalised and, by the same token, larger groups favoured.

The Court noted, in the same vein, that the development of the product had been the result of 'research and experimentation' and that it led to a variety that was unknown in the Member State covered by the licence. In this sense, the concerns raised by Germany were deemed justified.[123] In addition, it took into account the fact that the licensee may not have been willing to invest in the cultivation and sale of the product. In such circumstances, an open exclusive licence was deemed to fall outside the scope of Article 101(1) TFEU.[124] As can be

[120] Case 258/78, *Nungesser*. [121] Ibid., para. 53.
[122] Ibid.: 'the second case [a closed exclusive licence] involves an exclusive licence or assignment with absolute territorial protection, under which the parties to the contract propose, as regards the products and the territory in question, to eliminate all competition from third parties, such as parallel importers or licensees for other territories'.
[123] Ibid., para. 55. [124] Ibid., para. 58.

seen, the judgment was a reminder that the question of whether an agreement is restrictive of competition needs to consider the counterfactual. As Korah has consistently noted, a restriction cannot be merely assessed from an ex post perspective, that is, without taking into consideration the ex ante incentives to invest and innovate.[125]

The *Nungesser* case can be interpreted in two main ways. The arguments that the Court advanced to leave open licences outside the scope of Article 101(1) TFEU are, at least in principle, common to all intellectual property rights. Patents and related rights (such as plant variety rights, at stake in *Nungesser*) are only granted to reward investments in technologies that fulfil certain conditions, including novelty.[126] Therefore, the factors identified by the Court in the case could be easily transposed to any other instance in which valid patents and plant varieties – and, by extension, any other intellectual property right – are at stake. This was the position taken by the German Government, for which intellectual property protection was in itself an indication that the licence was not restrictive of competition.[127] Under this approach, open exclusive licences would be presumptively compatible with Article 101(1) TFEU. In other words, one could infer from *Nungesser* a (qualified) legality rule for agreements that remain within the substantive scope of the intellectual property right. In this case, and coming back to the vocabulary used in Chapter 2, the rule would have a 'hard' trigger. The applicability of the rule would depend on the validity of the intellectual property right.

An alternative interpretation of the judgment is to confine its meaning to the narrow circumstances of *Nungesser*. From this perspective, a licensing agreement would only escape the prima facie prohibition if it can be shown, in the specific circumstances of the case, that the technology is new and that substantial investments have been devoted to its development. This approach makes it necessary to test the counterfactual on a case-by-case basis. Thus, EU competition law would not defer to the logic of intellectual property rights. The question of whether the level of investment and the novelty of the product are important enough to leave the agreement outside the scope of

[125] See for instance Valentine Korah, 'Draft block exemption for technology transfer' (2004) 25 *European Competition Law Review* 247.

[126] See in this sense Article 52 of the European Patent Convention and Article 6 of Council Regulation (EC) No. 2100/94 of 27 July 1994 on Community plant variety rights OJ (1994) No. L 227/1.

[127] See in this sense the arguments of the German Government found in ECR [1982] 2044.

Article 101(1) TFEU would have to be examined by a court or a competition authority. In this sense, EU competition law would determine the appropriate level of protection for the technology or creation. Under this approach, the rule laid down in *Nungesser* would have a 'soft' trigger.

Consistent with the behaviour observed in other areas, the Commission chose a 'soft' trigger after *Nungesser*. By not deferring to the logic and operation of intellectual property systems, it was able to define the scope of the ruling on a case-by-case basis. In the practice that followed *Nungesser*, the Commission took the view that the judgment was confined to the specific circumstances of the case, and thus could only apply to instances where the parties can show in concreto, to the requisite standard, that substantial investments have been undertaken. Commentators noted that in all subsequent decisions the authority concluded that the technology was not new and thus that the agreement was caught by Article 101(1) TFEU.[128] By favouring this approach (and thus shifting the burden of proof to the companies), the Commission was able to define the instances in which technology licensing is in line with Article 101 TFEU. Shortly after *Nungesser*, moreover, it adopted a Block Exemption Regulation covering technology licensing agreements.[129] The Regulation diluted the difference between the agreements that are not restrictive of competition – even under a narrow reading of *Nungesser* – and those that require an exemption under Article 101(3) TFEU.[130] In practice, stakeholders would inevitably follow the principles set out on the Regulation. The approach of the Commission to technology licensing, and in particular to territorial restraints limiting the ability of licensees to sell in other territories, was developed in the

[128] See in this sense Valentine Korah, 'EEC Licensing of Intellectual Property' (1993) 4 *Fordham Intellectual Property, Media and Entertainment Law Journal* 55, at 74–5.

[129] Commission Regulation (EEC) No. 2349/84 of 23 July 1984 on the application of Article 85(3) of the Treaty to certain categories of patent licensing agreements OJ (1984) No. L 219/15.

[130] Mario Siragusa, 'The Millenium Approaches: Rethinking Article 85 and the Problems and Challenges in the Design and Enforcement of the EC Competition Rules' (1997) 21 *Fordham International Law Journal* 650, at 654 ('Two years after *Nungesser*, the Commission adopted the Patent Licence Regulation. 4 Article 1 of the Regulation provides that all open exclusive licensing agreements are exempted. This has blurred the distinction between open exclusive licenses related to the introduction and protection of a new technology, that were deemed to fall outside the scope of Article [101(1)], and other open exclusive licenses which were not').

successive versions of the block exemption.[131] In 2004, it adopted a set of Guidelines,[132] which were reviewed in 2014.[133]

3.3.3 No-Challenge Clauses

A licensor may wish to provide for a clause pursuant to which the licensee agrees not to challenge the validity of the intellectual property right. A plausible rationale for such a clause is the preservation of the value of intangible property. By definition, no-challenge clauses limit the freedom of action of the licensee, which may suffer a competitive disadvantage as a result. There should be little doubt that, under the traditional approach of the Commission, these clauses are caught by Article 101(1) TFEU. This was in fact the conclusion reached by the authority in *Vaessen/Moris*.[134] It is equally unsurprising that no-challenge clauses were excluded from the benefit of the exemption in the first version of the Block Exemption Regulation.[135] The question would eventually reach the Court in *Windsurfing*,[136] in which it validated the analysis of the Commission. However, the rationale for the 'by object' prohibition of no-challenge clauses appeared to be that such clauses fall outside the scope of the intellectual property right.[137] In this regard, *Windsurfing* is not necessarily incompatible with *Nungesser*.

Windsurfing contrasts with *Bayer v Süllhöfer*,[138] a preliminary ruling delivered two years later, in 1988. The case concerned a no-challenge

[131] See for instance Commission Regulation (EC) No. 240/96 of 31 January 1996 on the application of Article 85(3) of the Treaty to certain categories of technology transfer agreements OJ (1996) No. L 31/2; Commission Regulation (EC) No. 772/2004 of 27 April 2004 on the application of Article 81(3) of the Treaty to categories of technology transfer agreements OJ (2004) No. L 123/11; and Commission Regulation (EU) No. 316/2014 of 21 March 2014 on the application of Article 101(3) of the Treaty on the Functioning of the European Union to categories of technology transfer agreements OJ (2014) No. L 93/17. Regulation 240/96 defined 'passive competition' in Recital 11 of the Preamble as the 'prohibition on the licensee from selling the licensed product in territories granted to other licensees'.

[132] Guidelines on the application of Article 81 of the EC Treaty to technology transfer agreements OJ (2004) No. C 101/2.

[133] Guidelines on the application of Article 101 of the Treaty on the Functioning of the European Union to technology transfer agreements OJ (2014) No. C 89/3.

[134] Commission Decision 79/86/EEC of 10 January 1979 (Case IV/C-29.290 – *Vaessen/Moris*) OJ (1979) No. L 19/32.

[135] Article 3 of Regulation 2349/84.

[136] Case 193/83, *Windsurfing International Inc. v Commission*, EU:C:1986:75; and Commission Decision 83/400/EEC of 11 July 1983 (Case IV/29.395 – *Windsurfing International*) OJ (1983) No. L 229/1.

[137] Case 193/83, *Windsurfing*, para. 92.

[138] Case 65/86, *Bayer v Süllhöfer*.

clause introduced in the context of a settlement agreement. In line with its position in *Windsurfing*, the Commission argued in its submission that no-challenge clauses are in principle restrictive of competition, but that they could be compatible with Article 101(1) TFEU in the context of a settlement agreement where certain conditions are fulfilled.[139] The analysis of the Advocate General and the Court did not follow this approach. On the one hand, Advocate General Darmon emphasised the need to consider the counterfactual. According to the view expressed in his opinion, it cannot be concluded that a given clause violates Article 101 (1) TFEU without considering, in addition, whether the licensor would have been willing to license its technology in its absence.[140] By reference to the Opinion of the Advocate General in *Société Technique Minière*, he expressly disagreed with the submission of the Commission, which he claimed was overly formalistic.[141]

The Court, in the same vein, took the view that the analysis of this question must consider the relevant economic and legal context. It held that a no-challenge clause is not restrictive of competition by its very nature, and that it can fall outside the scope of Article 101(1) TFEU in certain circumstances. In addition, it reiterated its long-held view whereby limiting the freedom of action of the licensee would not be sufficient to establish a breach of Article 101(1) TFEU. Accordingly, it would be necessary to assess whether the clause in question has an appreciable effect on competition in light of the position of the parties on the relevant market.[142] This position is in contrast with its judgment in *Windsurfing*, where some of the passages – including the one concerning the lawfulness of no-challenge clauses – appeared to equate a

[139] Ibid., para. 14.

[140] Opinion of AG Darmon in Case 65/86, *Bayer AG and Maschinenfabrik Hennecke GmbH v Heinz Süllhöfer*, EU:C:1987:336.

[141] Ibid., para. 17: 'It would thus be unjustifiable to prohibit a no-challenge clause which is essential to the equilibrium of an agreement the effects of which proved in reality not to restrict, and even to encourage, competition. So, on the assumption that, since no royalties were charged for the licence, the licensees were placed in a situation similar to that in which they would have been if there had been no patent, it is difficult to see how competition might be affected'.

[142] Case 65/86, *Bayer v Süllhöfer*, para. 19: 'It should, however, be pointed out that, if the national court were to consider that the no-challenge clause contained in the licence granted subject to payment of royalties does involve a limitation of the licensee's freedom of action, it would still have to verify whether, given the positions held by the undertakings concerned on the market for the products in question, the clause is of such a nature as to restrict competition to an appreciable extent'.

restriction of competition with a restriction in the freedom of action of the parties.[143]

3.3.4 *Erauw-Jacquery* and Export Prohibitions

The approach sketched in *Nungesser* was developed in *Erauw-Jacquery*, a preliminary ruling.[144] The case concerned the compatibility with Article 101(1) TFEU of, inter alia, an agreement banning the export of basic seed protected by plant variety rights. Even though an export prohibition is in principle restrictive by object as inimical to market integration, the Court held that in circumstances comparable to those at stake in *Nungesser* (that is, where investments have been undertaken in the development of new seeds and there is intellectual property protection) such a restraint is not caught by Article 101(1) TFEU.[145] Part of the interest of *Erauw-Jacquery* relates to the position taken by the Commission in its submission. As noted by the Court, the Commission argued that an export prohibition in the circumstances of the case is not restrictive of competition insofar as it remains within the substantive scope of plant variety rights.[146] This position is in line with a broad understanding of *Nungesser*.

3.3.5 *Coditel II* and Absolute Territorial Protection

A few months after *Nungesser*, the Court delivered a preliminary ruling in *Coditel II*.[147] The two cases are similar insofar as they both concerned the territorial licensing of intellectual property rights. The similarity also relates to the practical outcome that the parties achieved by virtue of the agreement. As in *Nungesser*, the agreement in *Coditel II* gave absolute territorial protection to the licensee and, in this sense, looked, on its face, like a clear 'by object' infringement. The legal outcome, however, was different. The Court held in *Coditel II* that the agreement in question was not in itself contrary to Article 101(1) TFEU (that is, not restrictive by

143 The factors identified by the Court in *Bayer v Süllhöfer* were not given any relevance in the analysis in *Windsurfing*. Korah has suggested that the tension between the two rulings is to be solved in favour of the former insofar as it was delivered by a larger chamber. See Valentine Korah, *Intellectual Property Rights and the EC Competition Rules* (Oxford: Hart Publishing, 2006), p. 39.

144 Case 27/87, *SPRL Louis Erauw-Jacquery v La Hesbignonne SC*, EU:C:1988:183.

145 Ibid., para. 10.

146 Ibid., para. 9. The Commission argued that the clause in question 'falls within the ambit of the plant breeder's rights'.

147 Case 262/81 *Coditel SA, Compagnie générale pour la diffusion de la télévision, and others v Ciné-Vog Films SA and others*, EU:C:1982:334 ('*Coditel II*').

object).[148] In this sense, this case provides a prime example of the importance given to the economic and legal context of a practice in the case law. The difference in outcome between *Nungesser* and *Coditel II* can be explained by the different nature of the intellectual property right at stake in the latter.

Coditel II concerned the legality with Article 101 TFEU of an exclusive territorial licensing agreement concluded between a film producer and a film distributor. By virtue of the agreement, the licensee was given the right to authorise or prohibit all communications to the public taking place within the territory covered by the licence. In particular, the agreement allowed the licensee to prohibit the retransmissions of broadcasts originating in other Member States. In its submission to the Court, the Commission argued that the agreement had as its object the restriction of competition. More precisely, the Commission claimed that such an exclusive territorial licence provided for 'typical restrictions on freedom of economic action which generally fall within the scope of Article [101 (1)] of the Treaty'.[149] As in *Nungesser*, it argued that any considerations relating to the specific features of the cinematographic industry would only be relevant under Article 101(3) TFEU.[150]

As in *Bayer v Süllhöfer*, the Court did not follow the Commission, and refused to equate a restriction in the freedom of action with a restriction of competition. In line with the Advocate General,[151] it ruled that, even though the agreement gave absolute territorial protection to the licensee, it was not contrary to Article 101(1) TFEU by its very nature. In this regard, *Coditel II* went further than *Nungesser*, which was delivered shortly before it. The reason why the Court accepted an outcome resulting in absolute territorial protection can be explained by the fact that the right of communication to the public, at stake in the case, is not subject to exhaustion. The substantive scope of the right indeed comprises every single communication to the public. Thus, an exclusive territorial licence that allows the licensee to prohibit broadcasts originating in other Member States does nothing more than replicate the operation of the intellectual property right. In other words, it remains within its substantive scope.[152]

[148] Ibid., para. 16. [149] [1982] ECR I-3389. [150] Ibid., at p. 3390.

[151] Opinion of AG Reischl in Case 262/81 *Coditel SA, Compagnie générale pour la diffusion de la télévision, and others v Ciné-Vog Films SA and others*, EU:C:1982:290.

[152] Case 262/81 *Coditel II*, para. 12. The Court points out that the right to authorise or prohibit any communication to the public 'is part of the essential function of copyright'. This point was also raised by the Advocate General, for whom 'the right to require fees

3.4 *Horizontal Agreements*

3.4.1 Overview

As a rule, horizontal agreements are deemed more problematic from a competition law standpoint than distribution and licensing agreements. This fact does not mean, however, that they are necessarily prohibited under Article 101 TFEU. The Commission acknowledged early on in its practice that some horizontal agreements are potentially pro-competitive, in the sense that they may allow the parties to achieve efficiency gains and/or to compete more effectively on the relevant market. A series of decisions issued in the late 1960s and early 1970s clarified that agreements between competitors with modest market shares – involving, for instance, joint selling – fall outside the scope of Article 101(1) TFEU where they are unlikely to have appreciable restrictive effects on competition. This was the stance of the Commission in, for instance, its 1971 decision in *SAFCO*.[153] The agreement brought together a group of small French vegetable producers that intended, inter alia, to promote the export of their products and to buy inputs jointly. Even though it required the parties not to take part in competing organisations, the horizontal arrangement was left outside the scope of Article 101(1) TFEU altogether.

The Commission also granted exemptions in relation to agreements with appreciable restrictive effects insofar as these were deemed to lead to efficiency gains within the meaning of Article 101(3) TFEU. In particular, the early practice of the authority sought to make it explicit that research and development, as well as specialisation agreements, were seen favourably by the authority. Consider, for instance, an agreement between Clima Chappée and Buderus, exempted in 1969, whereby the parties reciprocally agreed to focus on the production of certain goods and to distribute each other's products.[154] In 1971, it cleared an agreement setting up a research and development joint venture between Henkel and Colgate-Palmolive.[155] The positive stance in relation to these

for any showing of a film is part of the essential function of copyright in this type of literary and artistic work, and therefore the rules of the Treaty cannot in principle constitute an obstacle to the geographical limits which the parties to contract of assignment have agreed upon in order to protect the author and his assigns in this regard'.

[153] Commission Decision 72/23/EEC of 16 December 1971 (Case IV/23 514 – *SAFCO*) OJ (1972) No. L 13/44.

[154] Commission Decision 69/241/EEC of 22 July 1969 (Case IV/26.625 – *Clima Chappée-Buderus*) OJ (1969) No. L 195/1.

[155] Commission Decision 72/41/CEE of 23 December 1971 (Case IV/26917 – *Henkel/Colgate*) OJ (1972) No. L 14/14.

agreements would crystallise in the adoption of two block exemption regulations concerning these two categories.[156]

The favourable policy stance vis-à-vis horizontal co-operation did not have an impact on the legal analysis of the Commission, which generally followed its traditional approach throughout the 1970s, 1980s and 1990s. The agreement between Clima Chappée and Buderus, for instance, was deemed restrictive of competition insofar as it limited the freedom of action of two undertakings that could have undertaken these activities on a stand-alone basis.[157] The features of the relevant market and the position of rivals were not considered in the analysis. The creation of the joint venture between Henkel and Colgate-Palmolive was found to be caught by Article 101(1) TFEU insofar as it eliminated in practice the possibility for the parties to engage in research and development activities and that research and development was an important parameter of competition in the industry.[158] The fact that the parties faced competition from two larger rivals – and that the agreement could thus promote, rather than restrict, competition–, was not deemed relevant in this regard.

At the same time, perhaps more than in other areas – and somewhat paradoxically – the Commission occasionally showed some flexibility and thus some willingness to take the counterfactual into consideration in the analysis. It adopted several negative clearance decisions finding that the agreement did not restrict competition that would have existed in its absence. The Commission came to the conclusion that the parties, alone, would not have been in a position to achieve the objectives of the agreement. This outcome was reached, for instance, in *Elopak/Metal Box – Odin*,[159] decided in 1990. In *Konsortium ECR 900*, concerning the creation of a joint venture for the development of the GSM system,[160] the Commission concluded, in the same vein, that the scale of the

[156] The Commission had been empowered to adopt block exemption regulations in these two areas by virtue of Regulation (EEC) No 2821/71 of the Council of 20 December 1971 on application of Article 85(3) of the Treaty to categories of agreements, decisions and concerted practices OJ (1971) No. L 285/46. For an overview of the early steps taken by the Commission in this area, see Joanna Goyder and Albertina Albors-Llorens, *Goyder's EC Competition Law*, 5th edn. (Oxford: Oxford University Press), pp. 484–97.

[157] Commission Decision of 22 July 1969, *Clima Chappée-Buderus*, at p. 3.

[158] Commission Decision of 23 December 1971, *Henkel/Colgate*, at p. 16.

[159] Commission Decision 90/410/EEC of 13 July 1990 (Case IV/32.009 – *Elopak/Metal Box – Odin*) OJ (1990) No. L 209/15.

[160] Commission Decision 90/446/EEC of 27 July 1990 (Case IV/32.688 – *Konsortium ECR 900*) OJ (1990) No. L 228/31.

investments required would not have allowed a single operator to undertake the project individually.

Another notable aspect of this area of practice is the relative paucity with which Commission decisions were challenged. While decisions in cases relating to horizontal agreements having as their object the restriction of competition – and in particular cartels – were challenged before the Court with some regularity,[161] there are limited examples of direct actions brought against decisions concerning efficiency-enhancing agreements between competitors. In any event, these limited examples confirmed the general principles on which the case law is based. In particular, the Court emphasised the need to consider the conditions of competition that would have existed in the absence of the contested restraints as well as the fact that a restriction in the firms' freedom of action does not necessarily amount to a restriction of competition. These principles were also reiterated in the context of references for a preliminary ruling.

In *Remia*, the Court followed the Commission in holding that a non-compete obligation that is objectively necessary for the sale of a business falls outside the scope of Article 101(1) TFEU.[162] This idea is even more apparent in the context of agreements relating to the exercise of intellectual property rights. In *BAT*,[163] the Court held that a trade mark delimitation agreement between competing firms is not as such restrictive of competition, whether by object or effect. It would only be caught by the prima facie prohibition where its objective purpose is not only to delineate the respective areas in which the operators are able to use their trade marks but also to share markets.[164] In line with the submission of the

[161] To mention some examples from the formative years, see Case T-6/89, *Enichem Anic SpA v Commission*, EU:T:1991:74; Joined cases C-89/85, C-104/85, C-114/85, C-116/85, C-117/85 and C-125/85 to C-129/85, *A. Ahlström Osakeyhtiö and others v Commission*, EU:C:1993:120; Case 240/82, *Stichting Sigarettenindustrie and others v Commission*, EU:C:1985:488; Case 73/74, *Groupement des fabricants de papiers peints de Belgique and others v Commission*, EU:C:1975:160; Joined Cases 40 to 48, 50, 54 to 56, 111, 113 and 114/73, *Coöperatieve Vereniging 'Suiker Unie' UA and others v Commission*, EU:C:1975:174; Case 8/72, *Vereeniging van Cementhandelaren v Commission*, EU:C:1972:84; and Case 48/69, *Imperial Chemical Industries Ltd. v Commission*, EU:C:1972:70.

[162] Case 42/84, *Remia BV and others v Commission*, EU:C:1985:327.

[163] Case 35/83, *BAT*.

[164] Ibid., para. 33: 'The Court acknowledges that, as the applicant and the Government of the Federal Republic of Germany submit and the Commission also concedes, agreements known as "delimitation agreements" are lawful and useful if they serve to delimit, in the mutual interest of the parties, the spheres within which their respective trade marks may be used, and are intended to avoid confusion or conflict between them. That is not to say,

German government, the Court appeared to suggest that an agreement that remains within the substantive scope of the intellectual property right is as such not capable of having restrictive effects on competition. The analysis of the Court departed from that of the Commission, in the sense that the latter did not appear to give any deference to the operation of intellectual property systems.[165]

Agreements relating to the exploitation of intellectual property rights also featured in references for a preliminary ruling. In *Ideal Standard*, the Court held that an agreement providing for the assignment of a trade mark is not always restrictive of competition, even though it leads, by definition, to the partitioning of the internal market.[166] According to the ruling, the object of such an assignment is not necessarily anti-competitive. It may be part of an efficiency-enhancing transaction – and in particular the sale of a business. In *Tournier*, the Court held that agreements relating to the activities of copyright collecting societies may fall outside the scope of Article 101(1) TFEU altogether insofar as they are necessary to allow the said societies to perform their function.[167] This is so in spite of the fact that the licensing of the catalogue of a collective society necessarily amounts to price-fixing by the participating members.[168]

It is also in the context of preliminary references that the Court emphasised that a restriction in the freedom of action of competing firms does not necessarily amount, in and of itself, to a restriction of competition. In *Gottrup-Klim*[169] and *Oude Luttikhuis*,[170] the Court suggested that the compatibility of a joint purchasing agreement with Article 101(1) TFEU depends on an analysis of the features of the market, including the nature of the product and the position of suppliers and

however, that such agreements are excluded from the application of Article [101] of the Treaty if they also have the aim of dividing up the market or restricting competition in other ways'.

165 Commission Decision 82/897/EEC of 15 December 1982 (Case IV/C-30.128 – *Toltecs-Dorcet*) OJ (1982) No. L 379/19. An analysis of the Commission decision in the case in fact suggests that it examined the likelihood of confusion between the two trade marks – an issue that typically falls within the realm of national intellectual property systems. See in this sense p. 25 of the Decision ('the Commission cannot find any serious risk of confusion between the word mark Dorcet and the word/device mark Toltecs. There is still no serious risk of visual or phonetic confusion if the pictorial component registered and used by Mr Segers [. . .] is disregarded').

166 Case C-9/93, *Ideal Standard*.

167 Case 395/87, *Tournier*.

168 See in this sense *Broadcast Music Inc. v Columbia Broadcasting System Inc.*, 441 U.S. 1 (1979), in which this question is explicitly acknowledged.

169 Case C-250/92 *Gøttrup-Klim*.

170 Case C-399/93, *Oude Luttikhuis*.

competitors. These factors, and not the freedom of action of the parties, were deemed the relevant criteria to establish a breach of Article 101(1) TFEU. Thus, a joint purchasing agreement would not have restrictive effects if the parties are relatively small, they face large suppliers and the price paid for the inputs depends on the volume of the orders.[171] The principle underlying this line of case law was made even more explicit in *Wouters*, which concerned a decision restricting the ability of the members of the Dutch Bar Association to form partnerships with accountants.[172]

In any event, the evaluation of the counterfactual by the Commission was far from coherent, let alone systematic, in its practice. It is therefore unsurprising that, from the limited pool of decisions challenged before the EU courts, several of them were, as mentioned earlier, annulled due to the failure of the authority to consider the conditions of competition that would have prevailed in the absence of the practice. It is equally unsurprising to note the tendency of the Commission to equate a restriction of competition with a restriction in firms' freedom of action. It is remarkable in this regard that it took some time for the shift in policy proclaimed in the 1990s to become visible in all individual decisions. Interestingly, as the divide between restrictions of competition by object and by effect became starker, the Commission displayed a tendency to construe horizontal agreements as 'by object' infringements. This tendency has led to some frictions in proceedings before the EU courts.

3.4.2 Pre-Modernisation Practice

In the pre-modernisation era, the evaluation of the counterfactual by the Commission was not systematic. This aspect of the administrative practice is exemplified by *European Night Services*[173] and *Eurovision I*.[174] In the first of these decisions, the Commission considered the compatibility with Article 101(1) TFEU of a joint venture involving the incumbent railway operators in several Member States. It argued that the agreement in question had as its object and effect the restriction of competition. The Commission drew this conclusion from the fact that the relevant regulatory framework allowed the parties to compete with each other for the provision of the services covered by the

[171] Case C-250/92 *Gøttrup-Klim*, paras. 32–3. [172] Case C-309/99, *Wouters*, para. 97.
[173] Commission Decision 94/663/EC of 21 September 1994 (Case IV/34.600 – *Night Services*) OJ (1994) No. L 259/20.
[174] Commission Decision 93/403/EEC of 11 June 1993 (Case IV/32.150 – *EBU/Eurovision System*), OJ (1993) No. L 179/23.

agreement.[175] According to the decision, the creation of the joint venture – alone and together with other overlapping ventures - inevitably has the effect of eliminating competition between the incumbent operators, which continued to hold a dominant position in their domestic markets (in particular in relation to the activities covered by the agreement) and of preventing market entry by third parties.[176]

When challenged, the analysis of the Commission was found to be vitiated by an error of assessment.[177] In line with *Société Technique Minière*, the GC held that the conditions of competition prevailing in a particular market cannot be considered in the abstract.[178] Thus, a restriction cannot simply be established by holding that the regulatory framework allows, in theory, for market entry. As shown in Figure 3.8, this approach does not make it possible to establish whether an agreement is capable of having restrictive effects. It is necessary to consider, in addition, whether the economic conditions prevailing on the relevant market give real, concrete possibilities for the parties to enter the relevant market and thus to be deemed potential competitors.[179] In the specific circumstances of the case, the Commission had failed to provide any evidence in support of its theory.

Eurovision I is based on a similar approach. This case concerned the joint acquisition of the television rights to sports events of pan-European interest (such as the Olympics, the World Cup or the World Athletics Championships) by the members of the European Broadcasting Union (or EBU), most of which are public service broadcasters. The Commission concluded that the Eurovision system had as its object and effect the restriction of competition.[180] According to the decision, it precluded competition between the broadcasters. In this sense, the Commission

[175] Commission Decision of 21 September 1994, *Night Services*, para. 39: 'Under Article 10 of Directive 91/440/EEC international groupings of railway undertakings providing passenger transport have a right of access to the railway infrastructures of the Member States of establishment of their constituent railways and transit rights on the infrastructures of other Member States in order to enable them to provide international services'.

[176] Ibid., para. 45.

[177] Joined Cases, T-374/94, T-375/94, T-384/94 and T-388/94, *European Night Services*.

[178] Ibid., para. 136: 'Before any examination of the parties' arguments as to whether the Commission's analysis as regards restrictions of competition was correct, it must be borne in mind that in assessing an agreement under Article [101(1)] of the Treaty, account should be taken of the actual conditions in which it functions, in particular the economic context in which the undertakings operate, the products or services covered by the agreement and the actual structure of the market concerned'.

[179] Ibid., para. 142. [180] Commission Decision of 11 June 1993, *Eurovision I*, para. 47.

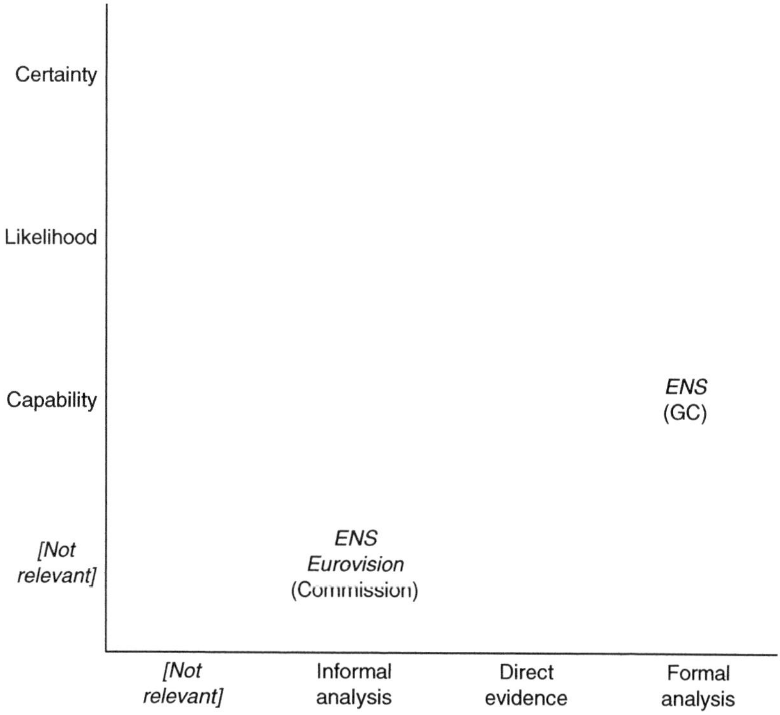

Figure 3.8 Horizontal co-operation agreements

failed to consider two important factors that were relevant in *European Night Services*. First, markets for broadcastings services were (and still are) national in scope.[181] As a result, the majority of members of the EBU were not competitors for the acquisition of the television rights. Second, the Commission did not consider whether there would have been 'real, concrete possibilities' for the individual members – or at least for some of them – to acquire the rights in other territories in the absence of a joint purchasing arrangement. In any event, the arrangement was found to fulfil the conditions of Article 101(3) TFEU. The GC annulled the decision for reasons unrelated to the Commission assessment under Article 101(1) TFEU.[182]

[181] This point has been accepted by the Commission in its later practice. See Commission Decision of 11 September 2014 (Case COMP/M.7332 – *BSkyB/Sky Deutschland/Sky Italia*).

[182] Joined Cases T-528/93, T-542/93, T-543/93 and T-546/93, *Metropole télévision SA and Reti Televisive Italiane SpA and Gestevisión Telecinco SA and Antena 3 de Televisión v Commission*, EU:T:1996:99.

3.4.3 Transition Period

The adoption of a set of Guidelines, together with the adoption of a new version of the Block Exemption Regulations applying to specialisation and research and development agreements, heralded the shift to a new approach to the assessment of horizontal co-operation agreements. As already pointed out, these instruments are best understood as a pre-commitment device to carefully assess the object and effect of agreements in the economic and legal context of which they were part. The shift involves, in particular, a careful assessment of the counterfactual and of the impact of the agreement on the dynamics of the relevant market. The adoption of this approach by the Commission was incremental. In the early 2000s, some decisions were still based on the traditional interpretation of Article 101(1) TFEU that the GC censored in *European Night Services*. A clear example in this sense is *Eurovision II*,[183] adopted shortly before the publication of the Guidelines on horizontal co-operation agreements, and which did not depart in approach from *Eurovision I*.[184]

Another example is *UEFA Champions League*, decided in 2003.[185] The case concerned the compatibility with Article 101(1) TFEU of a joint licensing arrangement of the rights to a football championship. The interest of the case lies in the fact that the teams taking part in the competition were not rivals in the strict sense of the word. Insofar as the relevant market considered by the Commission in its decision was the championship as a whole (as opposed to the individual matches), they were, more than rivals, members of a joint venture contributing an input to allow for the creation of a complex product. From this perspective, the arrangement was more similar to the licensing activities of copyright collecting societies or of patent pools. By the same token, it did not appear to be obvious whether the joint licensing of the rights restricted competition that would otherwise have existed. Alone, the individual teams would not have been in a position to license the rights

[183] Commission Decision 2000/400/EC of 10 May 2000 (Case IV/32.150 – *Eurovision*) OJ (2000) No. L 15/18.

[184] *Eurovision II* would also be annulled, again, for reasons relating to the interpretation and application of Article 101(3) TFEU. See Joined Cases T-185/00, T-216/00, T-299/00 and T-300/00, *Métropole Télévision SA (M6), Antena 3 de Televisión, SA, Gestevisión Telecinco, SA and SIC – Sociedade Independente de Comunicação, SA v Commission*, EU:T:2002:242.

[185] Commission Decision 2003/778/EC of 23 July 2003 (Case COMP/C.2–37.398 – *Joint selling of the commercial rights of the UEFA Champions League*) OJ (2003) No. L 291/25.

to the event in question, but only to a portion thereof.[186] These are factors that the Commission did not consider in its analysis. It concluded in the decision that the practice restricted the ability of individual teams to license their rights and amounted to the joint fixing of prices and other trading conditions.[187]

The Commission displayed a similar approach in *O2*,[188] which concerned a network sharing agreement involving two mobile telephone operators in Germany. The Commission had found in its decision that an aspect of the co-operation agreement, while not restrictive of competition by object, was caught by Article 101(1) TFEU.[189] This aspect concerned co-operation between the parties in relation to roaming.[190] According to the Commission, reliance on the network of a competitor necessarily restricts competition in relation to certain parameters of competition insofar as the parties would not be in a position to differentiate their offer in relation to the coverage, quality and transmission rates.[191] In this regard, the Commission appeared to assume that, in the absence of the agreement, the parties would have rolled out competing networks, at least in densely populated areas. However, it did not provide any evidence in support of this conclusion. This is the reason why the GC annulled the Commission decision. More precisely, the GC noted that the Commission did not envisage the hypothesis that O2 would have been absent from the relevant market.[192] In addition, it pointed out that the findings in relation to roaming services were not in any way specific to the position in which the parties found themselves and thus could have been argued in relation to any agreement.

3.4.4 The Rebalancing of Issues Post-Modernisation

The enforcement practice of the Commission following the application of Regulation 1/2003 is suggestive of a different approach to horizontal

186 This is something that the Commission acknowledged in its decision. See ibid., paras. 139–42.

187 Ibid., paras. 113–6.

188 Commission Decision 2004/207/EC of 16 July 2003 (Case COMP/38.369 – *T-Mobile Deutschland/O2 Germany: Network Sharing Rahmenvertrag*) OJ (2004) No. L 75/32.

189 Ibid., paras. 91–3. 190 Ibid., paras. 107–12.

191 See for instance para. 109: ‘Given the resulting constraints on the ability of O2 Germany and T-Mobile to compete on coverage, on quality, on transmission rates, and on wholesale prices, 3G national roaming between O2 Germany and T-Mobile has an impact on competition in all 3G network markets in Germany including the market for wholesale national roaming access for 3G communications services and the market for wholesale airtime access to 3G services’.

192 Case T-328/03, *O2*.

agreements. Under the traditional approach, the divide between restrictions by object and effect was blurred and made irrelevant in practice. This is not the case, however, in the post-modernisation era. If, as advocated in the different soft law instruments issued by the Commission, the effects of the agreement are to be established by reference to the market power enjoyed by the parties, the difference between object and effect is real and has concrete practical consequences. Under the new approach, the hurdles faced by the authority when establishing a breach of Article 101(1) TFEU are significantly higher where it chooses the 'by effect' route. Against this background, it is not surprising to note that 'by effect' cases have become a rarity following the adoption of Regulation 1/2003. Two techniques, one substantive and one procedural, explain the phenomenon.

A look at the practice since 2004 shows that the Commission has a marked preference for crafting cases as 'by object' infringements. The technique, in other words, consists of favouring rules over standards. An authority may choose to favour the 'by object' route even when a 'case-by-case' analysis would have been justified. An analysis of its enforcement practice since 2004 suggests, first, that the Commission has prioritised 'fact-intensive' cases, for which the 'by object' label is uncontroversial. As shown in Chart 3.11, 85 per cent of the decisions adopted during the said period is classified as cartel conduct by the authority itself. If one examines the remaining 15 per cent it appears that the overwhelming majority of infringement decisions adopted by the Commission concern non-cartel practices qualified as restrictive of competition by object. This phenomenon was identified and documented by Gerard in 2012.[193] Of the 14 non-cartel prohibition decisions adopted since 2004, which include several horizontal agreements,[194] only in two

[193] Damien Gerard, 'The Effects-Based Approach under Article 101 TFEU and Its Paradoxes: Modernisation at War with Itself?' in Jacques Bourgeois and Denis Waelbroeck (eds.), *Ten years of effects-based approach in EU competition law – State of play and perspectives* (Brussels: Bruylant, 2012).

[194] Commission Decision of 9 July 2014 (Case AT.39612 – *Perindopril-Servier*); Commission Decision of 10 December 2013 (Case AT.39685 – *Fentanyl*); Commission Decision of 19 June 2013 (Case AT.39226 – *Lundbeck*); Commission Decision of 23 January 2013 (Case AT.39839 – *Telefónica/Portugal Telecom*); Commission Decision of 8 December 2010 (Case AT.39510 – *ONP*); Commission Decision of 8 July 2009 (Case COMP/39.401 – *E.ON/GDF*); Commission Decision of 16 July 2007 (Case COMP/C2/38.698 – *CISAC*); Commission Decision of 19 December 2007 (Case COMP/34.579 – *Mastercard*; COMP/36.518 – *EuroCommerce*; and COMP/38.580 – *Commercial Cards*); Commission Decision of 17 October 2007 (Case COMP/D1/38.606 – *Groupement des Cartes Bancaires 'CB'*); Commission Decision of 3 October 2007 (Case COMP/D1/

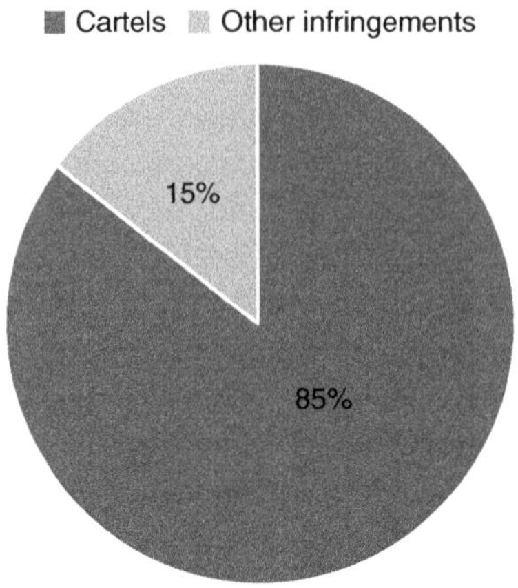

Chart 3.11 Article 101 TFEU prohibition decisions post-Regulation 1/2003, by type

of them did the Commission choose the 'by effect' route.[195] This breakdown of cases is captured in Chart 3.12.

An analysis of the individual infringement decisions suggests that some of the non-cartel prohibition decisions relate to clear-cut infringements.[196] In other cases, however, the 'by object' label was controversial. Inevitably, the observed preference for rules over standards has given rise to frictions, which have been addressed by the EU courts. *Cartes Bancaires*, which the ECJ examined on appeal, has emerged as an emblematic example in this regard. The case concerned a series of measures adopted in the context of a co-operative joint venture among French banks. The Commission argued in the case that the said measures had as their object and effect the restriction of competition coming from new participants in the joint venture. More precisely, the alleged purpose of the contentious measures was to raise the costs of the issuing of cards for these new entrants, thereby inflicting a competitive disadvantage upon them and favouring established players. The Commission likened these measures to a collective boycott.[197]

37.860 – *Morgan Stanley/Visa International and Visa Europe*); Commission Decision of 26 October 2004 (Case COMP/38.662 – *GDF/ENEL*); and Commission Decision of 24 June 2004 (Case COMP/38.549 – *Belgian architects' fee system*).

[195] Commission Decision of 19 December 2007, *MasterCard* and Commission Decision of 3 October 2007, *Morgan Stanley/Visa*.

[196] For a clear example, see Commission Decision of 7 December 2005 (Cases COMP/E2/36.623, 36.820, 37275 – *SEP and others/Automobiles Peugeot SA*), which concerned a distribution agreement aimed at restricting trade between Member States.

[197] Commission Decision of 17 October 2007 (Case COMP/D1/38.606 – *Groupement des Cartes Bancaires 'CB'*), in particular para. 251.

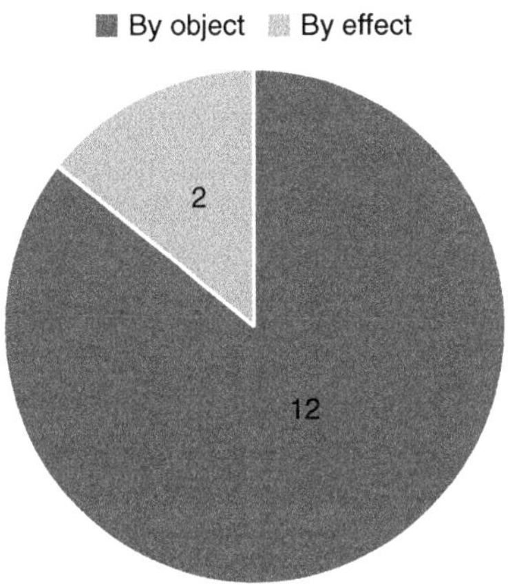

Chart 3.12 Article 101 TFEU non-cartel prohibition decisions post-Regulation 1/2003

On appeal, the ECJ found that the decision in *Cartes Bancaires* was vitiated by an error of law.[198] The crux of the disagreement related to the analysis of the objective purpose of the practice. The Court concluded that the Commission and the GC had failed to acknowledge the implications of some of the features of the relevant market, and in particular its two-sided nature.[199] Insofar as the contentious measures related to a legitimate objective – that is, the need to address free-riding concerns – it could not be claimed, according to the Court, that it was restrictive of competition by object.[200] In this sense, it provides a valuable example of the commitment to formal analysis in the case law. It also confirms the impression that agreements that are a plausible source of efficiency gains are not caught by Article 101(1) TFEU by their very nature.[201]

A second phenomenon is the frequent recourse to commitment decisions, in which horizontal agreements feature prominently.[202] Cartel

[198] Case C-67/13 P, *Cartes Bancaires.*

[199] Ibid., para. 73. The Court noted that, due to the two-sided nature of the market, the two economic activities at stake in the case were interdependent and thus indispensable for the operation of the system.

[200] Ibid., para. 74.

[201] See in this sense Opinion of AG Wahl in Case C-67/13 P, *Groupement des cartes bancaires v Commission*, EU:C:2014:1958, para. 56: 'Only conduct whose harmful nature is proven and easily identifiable, in the light of experience and economics, should therefore be regarded as a restriction of competition by object, and not agreements which, having regard to their context, have ambivalent effects on the market or which produce ancillary restrictive effects necessary for the pursuit of a main objective which does not restrict competition'.

[202] For a detailed analysis, see Chapter 6.

cases aside, the Commission has adopted more commitment than prohibition decisions in the context of Article 101 TFEU since the adoption of Regulation 1/2003. This outcome is not surprising if one considers the analytical framework crafted in Chapter 2. One would expect an authority like the Commission to prefer informal and/or negotiated solutions over formal ones in 'law-intensive' cases, which are typically those addressed by means of a commitment decision. It is reasonable, for instance, that the cases building on *UEFA Champions League* were closed following commitments offered by the parties.[203] Similarly, it is only natural that the issues raised by the so-called alliances between airlines are addressed in a negotiated manner – such alliances are known to be a source of efficiency gains, and require remedies that are similar in nature to those found in merger decisions.[204]

[203] Commission Decision of 22 March 2006 (Case COMP/C-2/38.173 – *Joint selling of the media rights to the FA Premier League*); and Commission Decision of 19 January 2005 (Case COMP/C-2/37.214 – *Joint selling of the media rights to the German Bundesliga*).

[204] Commission Decision of 12 May 2015 (Case AT.39964 – *Air France/KLM/Alitalia/Delta*); Commission Decision of 23 May 2013 (Case COMP/AT.39595 – *Continental/United/Lufthansa/Air Canada*); and Commission Decision of 14 July 2010 (Case COMP/39.596 – *BA/AA/IB*).

APPENDIX TO CHAPTER 3

Table 3.1 *Challenged prohibition decisions engaging with the notion of restriction of competition*

Decision	First instance	Outcome	Reframes?	Appeal	Outcome	Reframes?
Servier	T-691/14 (and others)	Pending	–	–	–	–
Lundbeck	T-472/13 (and others)	Dismiss	No	C-591/16 P	Pending	–
Telefónica/Portugal Telecom	T-216/13 and T-208/13	Dismiss (substance), Annul (fine)	No	–	–	–
E.ON/GDF	T-360/09 and 370/09	**Annul (law)**	**Yes**	–	–	–
MasterCard	T-111/08	Dismiss	No	C-382/12 P	Dismiss	No
Groupement des cartes bancaires	T-491/07	Dismiss	No	C-67/13 P	**Set aside**	**Yes**
Morgan Stanley/Visa (and other)	T-461/07	Dismiss	No	–	–	–
Glaxo Wellcome (and others)	T-168/01 (and others)	**Annul (law)**	**Yes**	C-501/06 (e.a.)	**Set aside**	No
Van den Bergh Foods Limited	T-65/98	Dismiss	No	C-552/03 P	Dismiss	No
Schöller Lebensmittel GmbH&Co KG	T-9/93	**Annul (other)**	**Yes**	–	–	–
Langnese-Iglo GmbH	T-7/93	**Annul (other)**	**Yes**	C-279/95 P	Dismiss	No
UK Tractor	T-34/92 and 35/92	Dismiss	No	C-7/95 P and C-8/95 P	Dismiss	No

Table 3.1 (*cont.*)

Decision	First instance	Outcome	Reframes?	Appeal	Outcome	Reframes?
Nutricia/de Rooij (and other)	42/84	Dismiss	No	–	–	–
Windsurfing International	193/83	**Annuls (legal characterisation)**	No	–	–	–
Toltecs/Dorcet	35/83	Dismiss	**Yes**	–	–	–
Breeders' Rights – Maize Seeds	258/78	**Annul (law)**	**Yes**	–	–	–
Kali und Salz/Kali Chemie	19/74 and 20/74	**Annul (other)**	No	–	–	–
Grundig-Consten	56/54 and 58/64	**Annul (law)**	**Yes**	–	–	–

Table 3.2 *Challenged exemption and negative clearance decisions engaging with the notion of restriction of competition*

Decision	First instance	Outcome	Reframes?	Appeal	Outcome	Reframes?
ARA	T-419/03	Dismiss	No	–	–	–
T-Mobile Deutschland/ O2 Germany	T-328/03 (and others)	**Annul (law)**	**Yes**	–	–	–
EPI code of conduct	T-144/99	**Annul (legal characterisation)**	No	–	–	–
TPS	T-112/99	Dismiss	No	–	–	No
Eurotunnel	T-79/95 and T-80/95	**Annul (facts)**	No	–	–	**Yes**
European Night Services	T-374/94 (and others)	**Annul (law)**	**Yes**	–	–	–
Ford/Volkswagen	T-17/93	Dismiss	No	–	–	
Parfums Givenchy	T-87/92 and T-88/92	**Annul (law)**	**Yes**	–	–	–
Yves Saint-Laurent	T-19/92	**Annul (law)**	**Yes**	–	–	No
SABA	75/84	Dismiss	No	–	–	No
SABA	26/76	Dismiss	**Yes**	–	–	No

Table 3.3 *Preliminary rulings engaging with the notion of restriction of competition*

Case number	Parties	Issue
C-567/14	*Genentech Inc. v Hoechst GmbH and Sanofi-Aventis Deutschland GmbH*	Licensing of IP
C-345/14	*SIA 'Maxima Latvija' v Konkurences padome*	Exclusive dealing
C-172/14	*ING Pensii, Societate de Administrare a unui Fond de Pensii Administrat Privat SA v Consiliul Concurenţei*	Horizontal (other)
C-384/13*	*Estación de Servicio Pozuelo 4 SL v Galp Energía España SAU*	Exclusive dealing
C-136/12	*Consiglio nazionale dei geologi v Autorità garante della concorrenza e del mercato*	Professions/quasi-legislation
C-68/12	*Protimonopolný úrad Slovenskej republiky v Slovenská sporiteľňa a.s.*	Horizontal (other)
C-1/12	*Ordem dos Técnicos Oficiais de Contas v Autoridade da Concorrência*	Professions/quasi-legislation
C-32/11	*Allianz Hungária Biztosító Zrt. and Others v Gazdasági Versenyhivatal*	Vertical (other)
C-439/09	*Pierre Fabre Dermo-Cosmétique SAS v Président de l'Autorité de la concurrence and Ministre de l'Économie, de l'Industrie et de l'Emploi*	Selective distribution
C-403/08 and C-429/08	*Football Association Premier League Ltd and Others v QC Leisure and others* and *Karen Murphy v Media Protection Services Ltd*	Licensing of IP
C-8/08	*T-Mobile Netherlands BV, KPN Mobile NV, Orange Nederland NV and Vodafone Libertel NV v Raad van bestuur van de Nederlandse Mededingingsautoriteit*	Exchange of information
C-506/07*	*Lubricantes y Carburantes Galaicos SL v GALP Energía España SAU*	Exclusive dealing
C-209/07	*Competition Authority v Beef Industry Development Society Ltd and Barry Brothers (Carrigmore) Meats Ltd*	Horizontal (other)

Table 3.3 (*cont.*)

Case number	Parties	Issue
C-238/05	*Asnef-Equifax, Servicios de Información sobre Solvencia y Crédito, SL v Asociación de Usuarios de Servicios Bancarios*	Exchange of information
C-295/04 (and others)	*Vincenzo Manfredi v Lloyd Adriatico Assicurazioni SpA, Antonio Cannito v Fondiaria Sai SpA* and *Nicolò Tricarico and Pasqualina Murgolo v Assitalia SpA*	Exchange of information
C-309/99	*J. C. J. Wouters, J. W. Savelbergh and Price Waterhouse Belastingadviseurs BV v Algemene Raad van de Nederlandse Orde van Advocaten*	Professions/quasi-legislation
C-214/99	*Neste Markkinointi Oy v Yötuuli Ky and Others*	Exclusive dealing
C-306/96	*Javico International and Javico AG v Yves Saint Laurent Parfums SA*	Selective distribution
C-230/96	*Cabour SA and Nord Distribution Automobile SA v Arnor 'SOCO' SARL*	Exclusive distribution
C-215/96 and C-216/96	*Carlo Bagnasco and Others v Banca Popolare di Novara soc. coop. arl. and Cassa di Risparmio di Genova e Imperia SpA*	Horizontal (other)
C-399/93	*H. G. Oude Luttikhuis and others v Verenigde Coöperatieve Melkindustrie Coberco BA*	Horizontal (other)
C-70/93	*Bayerische Motorenwerke AG v ALD Auto-Leasing D GmbH*	Vertical (other)
C-9/93	*IHT Internationale Heiztechnik GmbH and Uwe Danzinger v Ideal-Standard GmbH and Wabco Standard GmbH*	Assignment of IP
C-393/92	*Municipality of Almelo and others v NV Energiebedrijf Ijsselmij*	Exclusive dealing
C-376/92	*Metro SB-Großmärkte GmbH & Co. KG v Cartier SA*	Selective distribution
C-250/92	*Gøttrup-Klim e.a. Grovvareforeninger v Dansk Landbrugs Grovvareselskab AmbA*	Horizontal (other)

Table 3.3 (*cont.*)

Case number	Parties	Issue
C-234/89	*Stergios Delimitis v Henninger Bräu AG*	Exclusive dealing
110/88 and others	*François Lucazeau and others v Société des Auteurs, Compositeurs et Editeurs de Musique (SACEM) and others*	Collecting societies
395/87	*Ministère public v Jean-Louis Tournier*	Collecting societies
320/87	*Kai Ottung v Klee & Weilbach A/S and Thomas Schmidt A/S*	Licensing of IP
27/87	*SPRL Louis Erauw-Jacquery v La Hesbignonne SC*	Licensing of IP
136/86	*Bureau national interprofessionnel du cognac v Yves Aubert*	Professions/quasi-legislation
66/86	*Ahmed Saeed Flugreisen and Silver Line Reisebüro GmbH v Zentrale zur Bekämpfung unlauteren Wettbewerbs e.V.*	Horizontal (other)
65/86	*Bayer AG and Maschinenfabrik Hennecke GmbH v Heinz Süllhöfer*	Licensing of IP
31/85	*ETA Fabriques d'Ébauches v SA DK Investment and others*	Exclusive distribution
161/84	*Pronuptia de Paris GmbH v Pronuptia de Paris Irmgard Schillgallis*	Vertical (other)
243/83	*SA Binon & Cie v SA Agence et messageries de la presse*	Vertical (other)
319/82	*Société de Vente de Ciments et Bétons de l'Est SA v Kerpen & Kerpen GmbH und Co. KG*	Horizontal (other)
262/81	*Coditel SA, Compagnie générale pour la diffusion de la télévision, and others v Ciné-Vog Films SA and others*	Licensing of IP
126/80	*Maria Salonia v Giorgio Poidomani and Franca Baglieri, née Giglio*	Selective distribution
31/80	*NV L'Oréal and SA L'Oréal v PVBA 'De Nieuwe AMCK'*	Selective distribution
99/79	*SA Lancôme and Cosparfrance Nederland BV v Etos BV and Albert Heyn Supermart BV*	Selective distribution

Table 3.3 (*cont.*)

Case number	Parties	Issue
90/76	*S.r.l. Ufficio Henry van Ameyde v S.r.l. Ufficio centrale italiano di assistenza assicurativa automobilisti in circolazione internazionale*	Horizontal (other)
22/71	*Béguelin Import Co. v S.A.G.L. Import Export*	Exclusive distribution
1/71	*Société anonyme Cadillon v Firma Höss, Maschinenbau KG*	Exclusive distribution
40/70	*Sirena S.r.l. v Eda S.r.l. and others*	Assignment of IP
23/67	*SA Brasserie de Haecht v Consorts Wilkin-Janssen*	Exclusive dealing
56/65	*Société Technique Minière v Maschinenbau Ulm GmbH*	Exclusive distribution

* Order

4

The Notion of Abuse within the Meaning of Article 102 TFEU

1 Substantive Context

1.1 Scope of Article 102 TFEU

It is unequivocal from the letter of Article 102 TFEU that it is concerned with the exercise of market power vis-à-vis customers or suppliers. It was argued early on by commentators that the non-exhaustive list of practices mentioned in the provision only refers to exploitative conduct, including practices such as unfair pricing and discrimination.[1] The case law clarified that action against the exploitation of market power may address all the manifestations of competition described in Chapter 2. Thus, Article 102 TFEU may apply where an airport discriminates between competing airlines, thereby harming inter-brand rivalry.[2] It may also apply to an instance in which a dominant supplier discriminates between its customers, thus distorting intra-brand competition.[3] Finally, the abusive exploitation of a dominant position may be perceived to be problematic not only because it inflicts a competitive disadvantage on a firm or group thereof but also because it affects the integration of Member States' economies.[4]

In *Continental Can*, the Court confirmed that Article 102 TFEU applies to exclusionary conduct.[5] Typically, when administrative action

1 René Joliet, *Monopolization and Abuse of Dominant Position: A Comparative Study of the American and European Approaches to the Control of Economic Power* (The Hague: Martinus Nijhoff, 1970).

2 See for instance Case C-163/99, *Portugal v Commission*, EU:C:2001:189.

3 This is an issue present in rebate cases. See for instance Case C-322/81, *NV Nederlandsche Banden Industrie Michelin v Commission*, EU:C:1983:313 ('*Michelin I*'); and Case T-203/01 *Manufacture française des pneumatiques Michelin v Commission*, EU:T:2003:250 ('*Michelin II*').

4 See for instance Joined Cases C-468/06 to C-478/06, *Sot. Lélos kai Sia EE and Others v GlaxoSmithKline AEVE Farmakeftikon Proïonton, formerly Glaxowellcome AEVE*, EU:C:2008:504.

5 Case 6/72, *Europemballage Corporation and Continental Can Company Inc. v Commission*, EU:C:1973:22.

is driven by a concern with rival foreclosure, it is intended to preserve inter-brand competition. This is the case, for instance, where a dominant firm engages in a below-cost price campaign against a rival,[6] or when it decides to stop supplying an input to a downstream customer with which it is in competition.[7] However, intervention may also be driven by market integration considerations. Such considerations may be relevant, for instance, where a below-cost price campaign is intended to prevent, or has the effect of preventing, the entry of a rival based in a neighbouring Member State,[8] or where a vertically integrated operator discriminates against producers based in other Member States.[9] An abuse may also exist where the incumbent postal operator delays or refuses to deliver international mail originating from a centralised mail distribution centre.[10]

1.2 Substantive Choices

Article 102 TFEU applies to firms that are in a dominant position. This factor necessarily influences the interpretation of the notion of abuse. The controversies surrounding the latter notion cannot be understood without addressing the scope and meaning of dominance. According to the case law, a firm in a dominant position is able to 'prevent effective competition being maintained on the relevant market' and to 'behave to an appreciable extent independently of its competitors, customers and ultimately of its consumers'.[11] In other words, Article 102 TFEU applies to instances in which the conditions of competition are substantially weakened, that is, in instances in which a firm enjoys a position of substantial market power.[12] As a result, some practices that would

[6] See for instance Case C-62/86, *AKZO Chemie BV v Commission*, EU:C:1991:286.

[7] See for instance Joined Cases 6 and 7/73, *Istituto Chemioterapico Italiano S.p.A. and Commercial Solvents Corporation v Commission*, EU:C:1974:18.

[8] Case T-228/97, *Irish Sugar plc v Commission*, EU:T:1999:246.

[9] Commission Decision of 26 November 2008 (Cases COMP/39.388 – *German Electricity Wholesale Market* and COMP/39.389 – *German Electricity Balancing Market*) OJ 2009 No. C 36/8.

[10] Commission Decision 2001/892/EC of 25 July 2001 (Case COMP/C-1/36.915 – *Deutsche Post AG – Interception of cross-border mail*) OJ (2001) No. L 331/40.

[11] Case 85/76, *Hoffmann-La Roche & Co. AG v Commission*, EU:C:1979:36, para. 38. This is the classic definition of the concept of single dominant position. For a definition of the concept of collective dominance, see Case T-342/99, *Airtours plc v Commission*, EU:T:2002:146, paras. 61–2.

[12] For a definition of substantial market power, which appears to capture the essence of the notion of dominance, see ICN Unilateral Conduct Working Group, Dominance/

otherwise be unproblematic may be prohibited as prima facie abusive. This idea is encapsulated in the case law. The Court has consistently held that dominant firms have a 'special responsibility' not to impair 'genuine undistorted competition'.[13]

1.2.1 Substantive Choices and Exclusionary Conduct

Against this background, a strict stance vis-à-vis potentially abusive conduct seems defensible. Because dominance is defined as the power to exclude, it would only be natural, as some commentators argue, to outlaw any behaviour that is known to be a potential source of exclusionary effects, irrespective of the (objective or subjective) purpose of the dominant firm and irrespective of its actual or likely impact in the specific context in which it is implemented. Under this approach, the most common categories of practices routinely scrutinised by competition authorities would be prima facie prohibited under Article 102 TFEU. The prohibition rule would apply, inter alia, to tying, exclusive dealing or loyalty rebates, all of which are known to be capable of having exclusionary effects. These practices would only escape the prohibition if the dominant firm is in a position to put forward an objective justification.

However, a rule-based approach applying to the most common categories of potentially exclusionary behaviour – while reasonable – is not uncontroversial. To begin with, rule-based approaches typically fail to acknowledge that the majority of practices scrutinised under Article 102 TFEU are capable of having pro-competitive effects. As a result, they seem to provide no basis to presume that conduct has an anti-competitive rationale. In addition, the fact that a practice is capable of being exclusionary does not mean that anti-competitive effects would necessarily result from its implementation in concrete scenarios. In fact, it would seem that such effects can only be expected to arise when some, more or less restrictive, conditions are met. This is so even when the firm enjoys a dominant position. These views reflect consensus positions among economists, and are typically relied upon to argue that the scope of the prohibition should be narrower or, alternatively, that potentially abusive practices should at least be subject to a standard requiring a case-by-case assessment.[14]

Substantial Market Power Analysis Pursuant to Unilateral Conduct Laws, available at www.internationalcompetitionnetwork.org/uploads/library/doc317.pdf.

[13] Case 322/81, *Michelin I.*

[14] For an expression of this consensus, see EAGCP, *An economic approach to Article 82* (July 2005), available at http://ec.europa.eu/dgs/competition/economist/eagcp_july_21_05.pdf

As an alternative to an approach that would ban prima facie all potentially exclusionary conduct, some tests narrowing the scope of the prohibition have been proposed. These approaches include the 'no economic sense' test and the 'equally efficient competitor' test.[15] Under the first, the prima facie rule would only apply to conduct that makes no economic sense other than the exclusion of competition. The scope of the prohibition would be confined to practices that are presumed to serve an anti-competitive purpose. The purpose would be typically established by means of formal analysis. The Areeda-Turner rule is a prime example of the 'no economic sense' test.[16] The basic insight underlying this framework is that it is in principle irrational for firms to charge prices below average variable costs. As a result, an instance in which a dominant firm prices below that level can be safely presumed to be an attempt to drive rivals out of the market.

The 'as efficient competitor' test, on the other hand, would involve the application of a standard to all potentially exclusionary strategies. Under this approach, conduct would be lawful or unlawful depending on its impact on the ability and incentive to compete of equally efficient rivals. This test can be modulated depending on the requisite probability. As explained in Chapter 2, there is a difference between requiring that the behaviour be capable of having exclusionary effects and requiring the certainty of such effects. Alternatively, it is possible to craft a standard that is based on the impact of the practice on consumers. Under this approach, the prohibition would only be established following a balancing of the pro- and anti-competitive effects of the practice.[17] This is the

and US Department of Justice, *Competition and Monopoly: Single-Firm Conduct Under Section 2 of the Sherman Act* (2008), available at www.justice.gov/atr/competition-and-monopoly-single-firm-conduct-under-section-2-sherman-act.

15 For an analysis of these tests see, in general, Renato Nazzini, *The Foundations of European Union Competition Law: The Objective and Principles of Article 102* (Oxford: Oxford University Press, 2011).

16 For the first version of the test, see Phillip Areeda and Donald F. Turner, 'Predatory Pricing and Related Practices under Section 2 of the Sherman Act' (1975) 88 *Harvard Law Review* 697. As explained by the authors (p. 698, 'predatory pricing would make little economic sense to a potential predator unless he had (1) greater financial staying power than his rivals, and (2) a very substantial prospect that the losses he incurs in the predatory campaign will be exceeded by the profits to be earned after his rivals have been destroyed'). For an overview of the test, see Herbert Hovenkamp, 'The Areeda-Turner Test for Exclusionary Pricing: A Critical Journal' (2015) 46 *Review of Industrial Organization* 209.

17 For a test that considers the need to balance the pro- and anti-competitive effects of a practice, see David Spector, 'From Harm to Competitors to Harm to Competition: One More Effort, Please!' (2006) 2 *European Competition Journal* 145.

approach that comes naturally to economists, even though the difficulties relating to its implementation have been widely acknowledged – including by economists themselves.[18]

1.2.2 Substantive Choices and Exploitative Conduct

The substantive choices relating to some categories of exploitative conduct are not fundamentally different from those that apply to exclusionary practices. This is true, in particular, of discriminatory behaviour. The application of dissimilar conditions to equivalent transactions can be deemed prima facie abusive in and of itself, or may only be prohibited insofar as it has an anti-competitive effect on the relevant market in which the customers (or suppliers) of the dominant firm operate. In the latter case, it would be necessary to decide, when crafting the legal test, whether the prima facie prohibition applies where the anti-competitive effects are merely plausible or, instead, virtually certain to arise. Similarly, it would be necessary to determine whether discrimination is problematic merely when it inflicts a competitive disadvantage on some customers (or suppliers) or, instead, where the market structure and/or one or more parameters of competition can be expected to be affected by the behaviour.

The definition of substantive choices is more complex in relation to other exploitative behaviour, such as the setting of excessive prices and other unfair practices. Because a dominant firm is able to 'behave to an appreciable extent independently of its competitors, customers and ultimately of its consumers', it is also in a position to charge supra-competitive prices for its products. It is, in other words, in a position to demand prices that are above the level that would prevail in a competitive market. As a result, one could argue that all prices charged by a dominant firm are by definition excessive and that action is thus justified always and everywhere.[19] Alternatively, it would be possible to define a benchmark against which the abusive nature of the price can be established.[20] Finally, one

[18] For an analysis of the difficulties of full-scale balancing, see Robert O'Donoghue and Jorge Padilla, *The Law and Economics of Article 102 TFEU*, 2nd edn. (Oxford: Hart Publishing, 2013), p. 237.

[19] Ibid., pp. 732–41.

[20] For an overview of the different approaches, see Richard Whish and David Bailey, *Competition Law*, 8th edn. (Oxford: Oxford University Press, 2015), pp. 763–4. See also Opinion of AG Wahl in Case C-177/16, *Biedrība 'Autortiesību un komunicēšanās konsultāciju aģentūra – Latvijas Autoru apvienība' v Konkurences padome*, EU: C:2017:286.

could confine intervention to a narrow set of exceptional circumstances, which are then to be identified on a case-by-case basis.[21]

1.3 Principles of the Case Law

1.3.1 Horizontal Issues

In *Continental Can*, the Court held that a practice may fall within the scope of Article 102 TFEU even when there is no causal link between the dominant position and the alleged abuse. In other words, it is possible to take action even when the contentious practice is not a manifestation of the ability of the firm to 'prevent effective competition' or to 'behave independently' of suppliers and customers. This early substantive choice had important consequences for Article 102 TFEU. It allowed for a significant expansion of the scope of the prohibition. For instance, the acquisition of a competing undertaking may amount to an abuse of a dominant position.[22] Article 102 TFEU may also come into play where a dominant firm provides misleading information to an office in charge of the award of intellectual property rights.[23] By the same token, the prohibition may come into play when a firm implements a practice on a market other than the one in which it enjoys a dominant position.[24] Thus, the award of cross-subsidies to finance activities on non-dominated markets could, for instance, fall within the scope of Article 102 TFEU.[25]

On the other hand, the case law suggests that the Court requires a causal link between the practice and the anti-competitive effects that are alleged. Thus, if the – observed, assumed or presumed – effects on the relevant market are not, or would not, be attributable to the behaviour of the dominant firm, Article 102 TFEU is not applicable.[26] One can think

[21] This is an approach advocated in Massimo Motta and Alexandre de Streel, 'Excessive Pricing in Competition Law: Never say Never?', *The Pros and Cons of High Prices* (Stockholm: Konkurrensverket, 2007).

[22] This was the issue at stake in Case 6/72, *Continental Can* and in Case T-51/89, *Tetra Pak Rausing SA v Commission*, EU:T:1990:41.

[23] Case T-321/05, *AstraZeneca AB and AstraZeneca plc v Commission*, EU:T:2010:266 and Case C-457/10 P, *AstraZeneca AB and AstraZeneca plc v Commission*, EU:C:2012:770.

[24] Case C-333/94 P, *Tetra Pak International SA v Commission*, EU:C:1996:436 ('*Tetra Pak II*'); and Case T-83/91, *Tetra Pak International SA v Commission*, EU:T:1994:246 ('*Tetra Pak II*').

[25] On this question, see the classic work by Leigh Hancher and José Luis Buendía Sierra, 'Cross-Subsidization and EC Law' (1998) 35 *Common Market Law Review* 901.

[26] Case C-23/14, *Post Danmark A/S v Konkurrencerådet*, EU:C:2015:651 ('*Post Danmark II*'), para. 47, where the Court holds that intervention requires evidence that the effects be 'attributable' to the dominant undertaking.

of many instances in which there is no link between a practice and its presumed or expected impact on competition. For instance, the exclusion of a rival from the relevant market may be the result of the operation of the regulatory framework, not of an allegedly abusive strategy.[27] It may also be the case that rivals are unable to meet consumer demand in terms of price, quality and innovation, and leave the market as a result of this inability.[28] The latter example is not fundamentally different from the 'failing firm' defence that has long been recognised in merger control.[29]

Contrary to what is true in the context of Article 101 TFEU, the Court has consistently held that it is not necessary to show that the exclusionary effect of a practice is 'appreciable' for Article 102 TFEU to apply.[30] Thus, there is no threshold below which a practice can be deemed to have a de minimis impact on competition. According to the Court, the fact that the conditions of competition are already weakened as a result of the presence of the dominant firm means that any further weakening of the market structure may amount to an abuse of a dominant position.[31] In such circumstances, any practice implemented by a dominant firm may have restrictive effects on competition, or may even lead to the exclusion of rivals.[32]

1.3.2 Practices Subject to a Rule

The letter of Article 102 TFEU does not distinguish between abuses by object and by effect. However, there are some categories of practices that are subject to a qualified prohibition rule. At the time of writing, cases involving these practices are thus fact-intensive, in the sense that intervention does not require evidence of their impact on competition. To begin with, it is prima facie prohibited for a dominant company to impose an obligation of exclusivity and quasi-exclusivity on its

[27] This question was discussed in Case C-280/08 P, *Deutsche Telekom AG v Commission*, EU:C:2010:603.

[28] Case C-209/10, *Post Danmark A/S v Konkurrencerådet*, EU:C:2012:172 ('*Post Danmark I*'), para. 22.

[29] See in particular Joined Cases C-68/94 and C-30/95 *France and Société commerciale des potasses et de l'azote and Entreprise minière et chimique v Commission*, EU:C:1998:148 ('*Kali & Salz*') and Guidelines on the assessment of horizontal mergers under the Council Regulation on the control of concentrations between undertakings OJ (2004) No. C 31/5 ('Horizontal Merger Guidelines'), paras. 12–3.

[30] Case C-23/14, *Post Danmark II*, para. 73.

[31] Ibid., para. 72.

[32] Ibid., para. 73. According to the Court, an anti-competitive practice implemented by the dominant firm is, 'by its very nature, liable to give rise to not insignificant restrictions of competition, or even of eliminating competition on the market on which the undertaking concerned operates'.

customers.[33] It is also prima facie prohibited to award rebates conditional upon its customers obtaining all or most of their requirements from the dominant supplier.[34] The subsequent case law shows that the rule applies not only to schemes that are formally conditional upon exclusivity or quasi-exclusivity, but also to rebates having an equivalent object and effect. For instance, a system of rebates that is conditional upon the customer meeting an individualised target that corresponds to all or most of its requirements would also be prima facie prohibited as abusive.[35]

The second category of practices subject to a qualified prohibition rule is predatory pricing. Thus, it is prima facie prohibited for a dominant firm to price below average variable cost.[36] The Court clarified in subsequent cases that this rule does not require evidence of the ability of the dominant firm to recoup the losses incurred during the predatory pricing campaign.[37] In other words, the prima facie prohibition does not depend on the (presumed or expected) anti-competitive effects of the practice, but on the fact that it is deemed to serve an anti-competitive purpose.[38] It is also prima facie abusive for a dominant firm to price below average total costs but above average variable costs where the competition authority or the claimant can show that the below-cost pricing campaign is the expression of a plan to eliminate a competitor.[39] Finally, tying practices are also deemed abusive without it being necessary to show that they have a negative impact on competition.[40]

The case law suggests that at least two practices are subject to a qualified legality rule. Rebates that are based on volume are prima facie lawful under Article 102 TFEU. While this rule was laid down in *Hoffmann-La Roche*, it is only in *Post Danmark II* that its scope was defined with precision. Only rebates that (i) depend on the quantity supplied and (ii) are granted in respect of individual orders are deemed compatible with Article 102 TFEU.[41] Accordingly, rebate schemes that

33 Case 85/76, *Hoffmann-La Roche*, paras. 89–90. 34 Ibid.

35 Case 322/81, *Michelin I*, para. 73. 36 Case C-62/86, AKZO, para. 71.

37 Case C-202/07, *France Télécom SA v Commission*, EU:C:2009:214 ('*Wanadoo*'), paras. 103–14.

38 This is an idea that is made explicit in Case C-62/86, *AKZO*, para. 71 ('[a] dominant undertaking has no interest in applying such prices except that of eliminating competitors so as to enable it subsequently to raise its prices by taking advantage of its monopolistic position'). This point was reiterated in case C-202/07, *Wanadoo*, para. 109.

39 Case C-62/86, *AKZO*, para. 72.

40 Case T-30/89 *Hilti AG v Commission*, EU:T:1991:70 and Case T-83/91 *Tetra Pak II*.

41 Case C-23/14, *Post Danmark II*, paras. 27–8.

are retroactive in nature – and thus applied to all units acquired from the dominant firm – fall outside the scope of the legality rule. Following the ruling in *Post Danmark I*, it would seem that an aggressive pricing campaign – which may include the application of selective price cuts to the customers of a rival – does not amount to an exclusionary abuse if the dominant firm does not sell below cost.[42]

1.3.3 Practices Subject to a Standard

Other common categories of potentially abusive conduct are subject to a standard. First, it is only in 'exceptional circumstances' that a dominant firm may be required to deal with a rival. As a result, an abuse may only be established where a set of restrictive conditions is met. Thus, it is necessary to show, at the very least, that dealing with the dominant firm is 'indispensable' to compete on a neighbouring market and that the refusal would lead to the elimination of 'all competition' therein.[43] In relation to intellectual property rights, the Court has expressly held that it is necessary to show that the refusal would prevent the emergence of a new product for which there is potential consumer demand.[44] Second, a 'margin squeeze', whereby the wholesale prices charged by a vertically integrated firm prevent downstream rivals from competing, is not abusive in itself. It is necessary to show that the practice has an exclusionary effect.[45] In the same vein, pricing below average total costs but above average variable costs is not prohibited absent evidence of anti-competitive intent. It is only caught by Article 102 TFEU where it can be shown to have a negative impact on competition.[46] It would seem that the same can be said of standardised rebate schemes that are not subject to the prima facie legality rule set out in *Hoffmann-La Roche* and are thus

[42] Case C-209/10, *Post Danmark I*, paras. 22 and 30.

[43] See in particular Case C-7/97, *Oscar Bronner GmbH & Co. KG v Mediaprint Zeitungs- und Zeitschriftenverlag GmbH & Co. KG, Mediaprint Zeitungsvertriebsgesellschaft mbH & Co. KG and Mediaprint Anzeigengesellschaft mbH & Co. KG*, EU:C:1998:569; and Case C-418/01, *IMS Health GmbH & Co. OHG v NDC Health GmbH & Co. KG*, EU:C:2004:257. As will be explained in greater detail below, this condition was reinterpreted in Case T-201/04, *Microsoft Corporation v Commission*, EU:T:2007:289 ('*Microsoft I*').

[44] This principle was introduced in Joined Cases C-241/91 P and C-242/91 P, *Radio Telefis Eireann (RTE) and Independent Television Publications Ltd (ITP) v Commission*, EU:C:1995:98 ('*Magill*'), para. 54. The reception of this test by the Commission and the GC is examined below.

[45] Case C-280/08, *Deutsche Telekom*, paras. 250–1.

[46] This principle can be inferred from Case C-209/10, *Post Danmark I*, paras. 38–40.

halfway between those presumptively allowed and those presumptively prohibited.[47]

2 Institutional Context

2.1 Annulment Proceedings

Two issues become immediately apparent when reviewing the enforcement practice of the Commission in the context of Article 102 TFEU. The first is that administrative action took off relatively late. It was necessary to wait until 1971 – that is, nine years after the adoption of Regulation 17 – to see the first decisions concerning dominant firms. In general, the volume of Article 102 TFEU cases is lower than that of merger and Article 101 TFEU cases. This is not necessarily a consequence of the fact that Article 102 TFEU was 'neglected' by the Commission, as some commentators have argued.[48] The paucity of abuse cases is probably something inevitable if one considers that dominant positions can be expected to be relatively rare in a market economy, whereas agreements (and mergers) are pervasive. One must consider, in addition, that many industries in which dominant positions tend to emerge were organised around legal monopolies during the 1970s.

The second aspect that is immediately noticeable is that decisions in Article 102 TFEU cases are more contentious than Article 101 TFEU and merger decisions. As will be explained in greater detail below, the percentage of formal prohibition decisions that is challenged before the EU courts is significantly higher than in the other two areas. Several factors may explain this difference. First, it is not easy to think of an obvious cartel-like, 'fact-intensive' practice in the context of Article 102 TFEU – by which it is meant that the most common categories of potentially abusive conduct are a plausible source of efficiency gains. Another factor is institutional in nature. Until the adoption of Regulation 1/2003 (and given the available instruments), the Commission faced, at least formally speaking, a binary choice between prohibiting a practice and closing the file.[49] The category of

[47] Case C-23/14, *Post Danmark II*, paras. 28–46.

[48] This expression is taken from John Temple Lang, 'How can the problems of exclusionary abuses under Article 102 TFEU be resolved?' (2012) 37 *European Law Review* 136, at 145.

[49] In practice, to be sure, the Commission had recourse to negotiated procedures, which could be closed formally (with a finding that there were no grounds for action) or informally. For two examples in this sense, see: Commission Decision 84/233/EEC of 18 April 1984 (Case IV/30.849 – *IBM personal computer*) OJ (1984) No. L 118/24 and

decisions, whereby the authority concludes that a practice is acceptable subject to conditions, did not exist under that regime. Inevitably, the proportion of contentious *formal* decisions was higher as a result.

2.1.1 Prohibition Decisions

Turning more specifically to prohibition decisions, Chart 4.1 depicts the proportion of these decisions that have been challenged before the EU courts. As can be seen, direct actions have been brought against a relatively high number of Commission decisions. The proportion is significantly higher than that found in Chapters 3 and 5. Chart 4.2 (as well as Table 4.2 in the Appendix) is even more telling about the peculiarities of litigation in the context of Article 102 TFEU. As can be seen, the notion of abuse is at stake in about 90 per cent of the challenges brought against prohibition decisions, which suggests that it is central in the vast majority of disputes. This figure stands in stark contrast with that observed in the context of Article 101 TFEU, where, as explained in Chapter 3, most direct actions concern disputes in which the notion of restriction of competition is not at stake. Put differently, Article 102 TFEU cases tend to be 'law-intensive' in nature.

Chart 4.3 focuses on the outcomes of these actions in first instance. It suggests that, on the whole, the annulment of decisions by the EU courts has not been infrequent. This finding goes against the popular narrative of undue deference.[50] Chart 4.4 helps understand why this discourse has emerged as a popular one. As can be seen, the thrust of the annulment of Commission decisions can be traced back to the very early years of enforcement. The Chart shows that seeing a Commission decision quashed became a relative rarity during the 1990s, and that the trend has continued to this day. It would seem that, at most, decisions are partially annulled for errors of fact (as was the case in *AstraZeneca*)[51] or for reasons other than the interpretation of Article 102 TFEU (as in *Microsoft I*).[52] In the same vein, Chart 4.5 shows that

Commission, 'The European Commission accepts an undertaking from Digital concerning its supply and pricing practices in the field of computer maintenance services' (IP/97/868, 10 October 1997).

50 For an example of these views, see Christian Ahlborn and David S. Evans, 'The Microsoft Judgment and its Implications for Competition Policy towards Dominant Firms in Europe' (2009) 75 *Antitrust Law Journal* 887.

51 As in Case T-321/05, *AstraZeneca*.

52 See for instance Case T-201/04, *Microsoft I*.

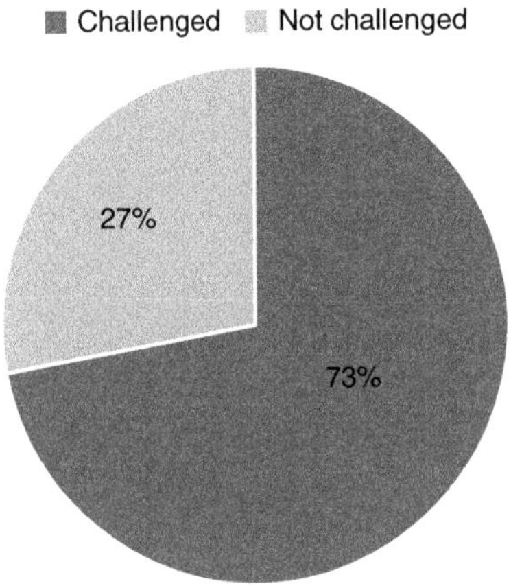

Chart 4.1 Proportion of prohibition decisions challenged before the EU courts

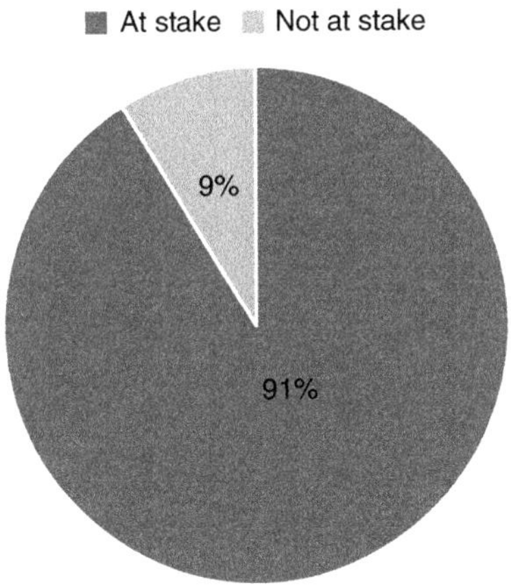

Chart 4.2 Relevance of the notion of abuse in challenged prohibition decisions

appeals on points of law before the Court have proved unsuccessful in virtually every case.

These figures can be interpreted in more than one way. The idea that the EU courts changed their behaviour and became more deferential during the 1990s is only one possible explanation of the trend, and perhaps not the most persuasive one. The observed pattern – frequent annulments in the first years, followed by a period in which most actions are dismissed – is also compatible with a risk-averse attitude of an

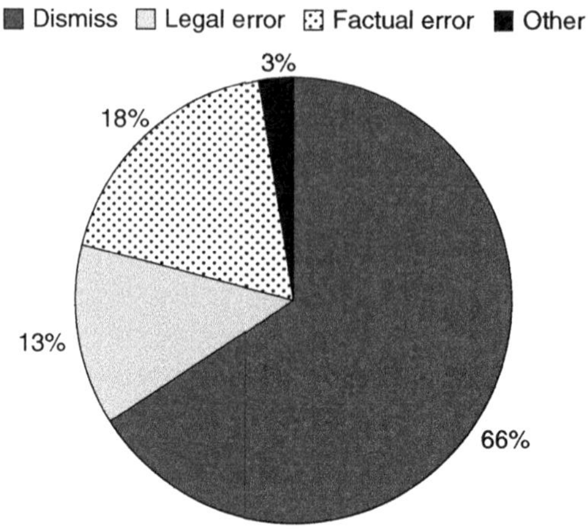

Chart 4.3 Prohibition decisions engaging with the notion of abuse: outcome in first instance

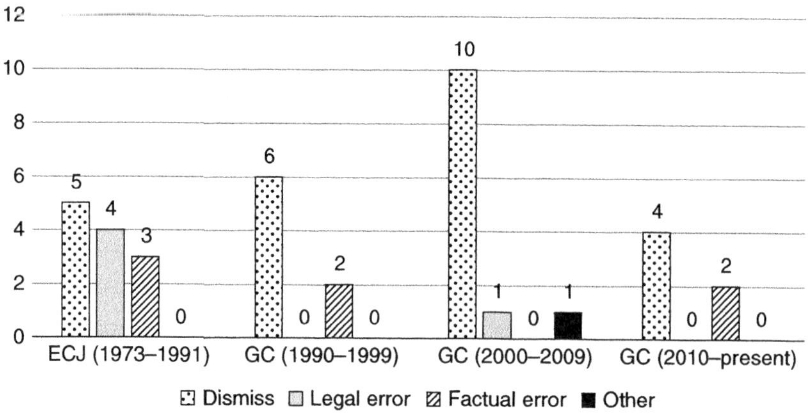

Chart 4.4 Prohibition decisions engaging with the notion of abuse: outcome by year and court

authority that, once the boundaries of the prohibition are defined with clarity, chooses to pursue clear-cut infringements. The trend is also compatible with the behaviour of a relatively risk-prone competition authority that carefully construes, in law and in fact, its decisions and thus justifies the expansion of the boundaries of the provision. Thus, it is only possible to come to conclusions by examining, as is done in Section 3, the substantive choices made by the Commission, and how

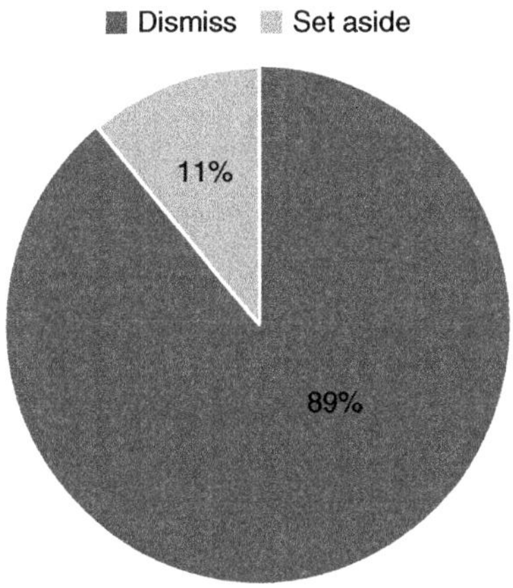

Chart 4.5 Outcome (substance) of appeals against rulings engaging with the notion of abuse

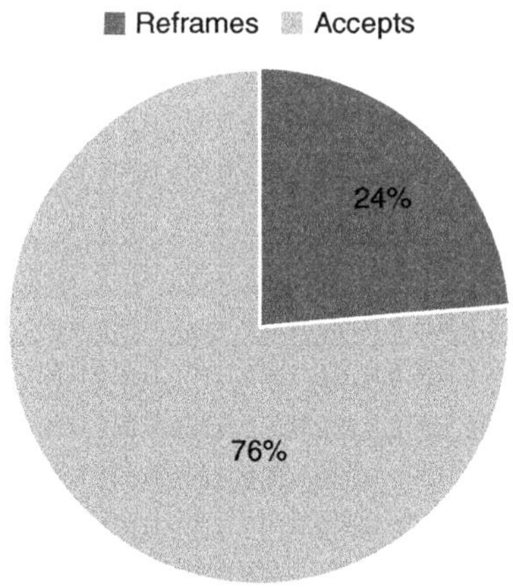

Chart 4.6 Approach to the notion of abuse, percentages

these choices compare against the relevant precedents. Chart 4.6 helps shed some light on this question. It considers the instances in which the EU courts have not deferred to the interpretation of the notion of abuse advanced by the Commission, but have redefined it – even when the

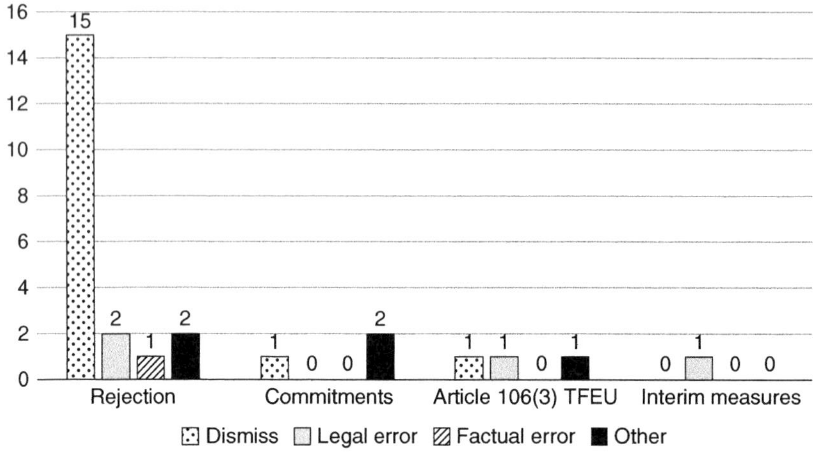

Chart 4.7 Article 102 TFEU decisions: outcomes in first instance, by type (other decisions)

Commission decision would eventually be upheld on substantive grounds. It shows that such instances are not infrequent.

2.1.2 Other Decisions

Chart 4.7 seeks to capture the outcomes in first instance of actions brought in cases other than those concerning prohibition decisions. Some of the findings seem unsurprising. One would expect, for instance, the rate of annulment in cases brought against rejection decisions to be lower. Applicants in such cases have to overcome a well-established principle according to which the Commission has the discretion to define its enforcement priorities, and thus to reject decisions if there are insufficient grounds for pursuing the case.[53] Thus, decisions in such cases are subject to marginal review when challenged.[54] Even though the figures are less reliable – rejection decisions are not systematically published by the Commission – it is also apparent (and equally unsurprising) from the available data that an action for annulment is brought in a relatively small proportion of cases. This fact has not prevented the EU courts from

[53] See in this sense Article 7 of Commission Regulation (EC) No. 773/2004 of 7 April 2004 relating to the conduct of proceedings by the Commission pursuant to Articles 81 and 82 of the EC Treaty OJ (2004) No. L 123/18.

[54] Case T-24/90, *Automec Srl v Commission*, EU:T:1992:97. For an analysis, see Luis Ortiz Blanco, *EU Competition Procedure*, 3rd edn. (Oxford: Oxford University Press, 2013), at 12.19.

introducing some valuable legal principles in challenges against rejection decisions. In *Micro Leader*,[55] for instance, the GC clarified some points relating to the interface between competition law and intellectual property, and about the status of exploitative abuses. In *Meca Medina*,[56] the EU courts dealt with the status of sporting rules and in *Laurent Piau*[57] with the concept of collective dominance. It is equally unsurprising to note that the proportion of actions brought against commitment decisions is low – probably even lower. This said, it is worth noting that *Alrosa*, where the Court ruled on the standard of review to which such decisions are subject, concerned the status of a practice under Article 102 TFEU.[58]

The outcome of challenges brought against other decisions comes across as less intuitive. The Commission has only adopted a limited number of decisions in accordance with Article 106(3) TFEU.[59] Of the 15 decisions that have been adopted for a breach of Articles 106(1) and 102 TFEU, only three were challenged before the EU courts. Of these, two decisions were annulled in first instance, one for a breach of procedural requirements[60] and the second one for a legal error.[61] The latter judgment, which was then set aside on appeal by the Court, is an important landmark in the case law addressing the joint application of Articles 106 and 102 TFEU. Interim measures feature equally marginally in quantitative terms. In qualitative terms, however, it is worth noting that the interim measures in *IMS Health*[62] contributed decisively to the clarification of the scope of the notion of abuse.

[55] Case T-198/98, *Micro Leader Business v Commission*, EU:T:1999:341.

[56] Case T-313/02, *David Meca-Medina and Igor Majcen v Commission*, EU:T:2004:282; and Case C-519/04 P, *David Meca-Medina and Igor Majcen v Commission*, EU:C:2006:492.

[57] Case T-193/02, *Laurent Piau v Commission*, EU:T:2005:22; and Case C-171/05 P, *Laurent Piau v Commission*, EU:C:2006:149.

[58] Case T-170/06, *Alrosa Company Ltd v Commission*, EU:T:2007:220; and Case C-441/07 P, *Commission v Alrosa Company Ltd*, EU:C:2010:377.

[59] A complete list of decisions can be found at http://ec.europa.eu/competition/general/liberalisation_en.html.

[60] Joined Cases C-48/90 and C-66/90, *Koninklijke PTT Nederland NV and PTT Post BV v Commission*, EU:C:1992:63.

[61] See in this sense Case T-169/08, *Dimosia Epicheirisi Ilektrismou AE v Commission*, EU:T:2012:448; and Case C-553/12 P, *Commission v Dimosia Epicheirisi Ilektrismou AE*, EU:C:2014:2083.

[62] Case T-184/01 R, *IMS Health Inc. v Commission*, EU:T:2001:259.

2.2 Preliminary References

A steady stream of references has reached the Court since the 1970, even before the Commission adopted its first decision enforcing the provision. However (and contrary to what is true in the context of Article 101 TFEU), the resulting rulings have done little to clarify the scope of the notion of abuse. As shown in Chart 4.8 (and Table 4.3 in the Appendix), only around a third of the references engage meaningfully with the notion. In many cases, Article 102 TFEU was of peripheral relevance for the outcome of the dispute. This is true, in particular, of preliminary references that concern primarily the compatibility of national legislation with EU law – and only as a secondary, if not marginal, matter whether the behaviour of the firm amounts to an abuse. There are two main categories of cases in this regard. Some relate to legislation that restricts competition in some way (in particular by fixing prices) and that is challenged under Article 4(3) TEU jointly with other Treaty provisions.[63] Other cases concern the application of Article 106(1) TFEU together with Article 102 TFEU, and often fail to clarify any aspect concerning the notion of abuse. *Corbeau*, in which the Court appeared to assume that the behaviour necessarily amounted to a breach of Article 102 TFEU, is an emblematic example in this regard.[64]

The preliminary references in which the interpretation of the notion of abuse was relevant for the outcome of the case are peculiar insofar as the vast majority of them raise a relatively narrow set of recurring issues. It is possible to identify four main categories of references, which are identified and summarised in Chart 4.9. A first category concerns the exploitation of intellectual property rights by a single right holder. The questions raised in these cases relate not only to the allegedly excessive nature of the prices charged by the right holder,[65] but also to whether a refusal to license an intellectual property right,[66] or to bring an injunction before a

[63] Examples of these decisions include Case C-412/93, *Société d'Importation Edouard Leclerc-Siplec v TF1 Publicité SA and M6 Publicité SA*, EU:C:1995:26; Joined Cases C-140/94, C-141/94 and C-142/94, *DIP SpA v Comune di Bassano del Grappa, LIDL Italia Srl v Comune di Chioggia and Lingral Srl v Comune di Chiogga*, EU:C:1995:330; and Case C-38/97, *Autotrasporti Librandi Snc di Librandi F. & C. v Cuttica spedizioni e servizi internationali Srl*, EU:C:1998:454.

[64] Case C-320/91, *Criminal proceedings against Paul Corbeau*, EU:C:1993:198.

[65] Disputes about this question are found in the earliest references. See for instance Case 78/70, *Deutsche Grammophon Gesellschaft mbH v Metro-SB-Großmärkte GmbH & Co. KG*, EU:C:1971:59.

[66] See for instance Case 238/87, *AB Volvo v Erik Veng (UK) Ltd*, EU:C:1988:477; and Case C-418/01, *IMS Health*.

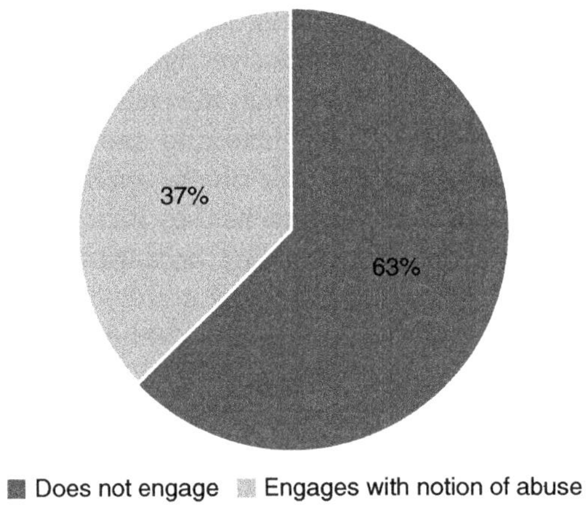

Chart 4.8 Preliminary references dealing with Article 102 TFEU

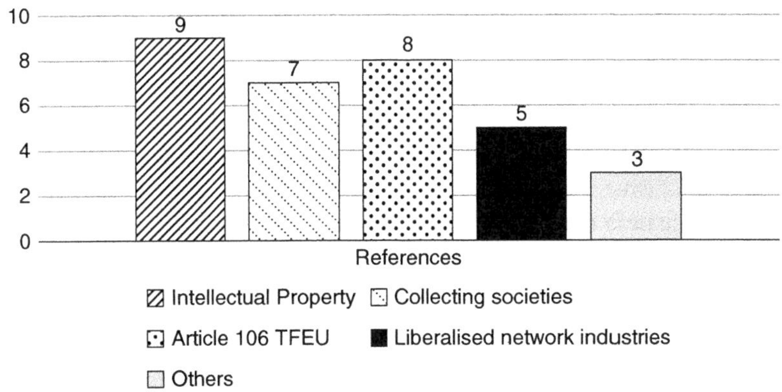

Chart 4.9 Preliminary references engaging with the notion of abuse

court,[67] amount to an abuse. A second category revolves around the collective exploitation of these rights. The activities of collecting societies, and in particular the abusive and/or discriminatory nature of their tariffs,[68] are often contentious at the national level, and have a

[67] Case C-170/13, *Huawei Technologies Co. Ltd v ZTE Corp. and ZTE Deutschland GmbH*, EU:C:2015:477.

[68] See for instance Case 395/87, *Ministère public v Jean-Louis Tournier*, EU:C:1989:319; Joined Cases 110/88, 241/88 and 242/88, *François Lucazeau and others v Société des Auteurs, Compositeurs et Editeurs de Musique (SACEM) and others*, EU:C:1989:326; Case 402/85, *G. Basset v Société des auteurs, compositeurs et éditeurs de musique*, EU:

by-case basis. In other words, the authority expressed, early on, a preference for 'soft' triggers. Typically, it was by taking several criteria together – which may or may not amount to an individual breach of Article 102 TFEU – that the Commission concluded to the existence of an abuse. As a result of this tendency, the administrative practice suggested that the outcome in each case was explained by the peculiar factual circumstances surrounding it. The factors that proved decisive in a particular context were not necessarily important in another one. For instance, the fact that costs-based considerations are relevant in a particular case on predatory pricing does not mean, according to this approach, that such considerations are relevant across the board.

In the same vein, the Commission displayed an inclination to make potentially abusive practices subject to rules rather than standards. Article 102 TFEU cases were traditionally built as fact-intensive ones. The legal analysis, on the other hand, is relatively thin in these cases. The Commission traditionally favoured an understanding of the provision according to which a finding of abuse follows logically from the specific set of facts at hand. Predatory pricing, exclusive dealing and 'margin squeeze' abuses have all been examined in this way. Due to the preference for a rule-based approach to enforcement, the assessment of the anticompetitive effects of the practice on competition is typically absent from the analysis. At most, the capability of the practice having such effects is an implicit aspect of the assessment, not one that needs to be shown in order to establish an abuse.

A third feature is the tendency to conflate exclusionary and exploitative considerations. Several of the practices that are examined below were deemed problematic not only because of their potential to drive rivals out of the market but because they amounted to unfair pricing and/or exploitative discrimination. It would seem that in many instances the concern was essentially exclusionary, but exploitative considerations were included to make the analysis more robust. This is, in particular, a key feature of the Commission practice in relation to rebates until the mid-2000s. The conflation of the two concerns makes it more difficult to anticipate the exact boundaries of the prohibition. This is so, in particular, because the Commission has never provided any clear guidance in relation to exploitative conduct.[88]

[88] Notably, exploitative abuses were left outside the modernisation efforts undertaken by the Commission during the 2000s. In particular, such abuses were not included in the Guidance Paper issued in 2009.

As shown above, it is not immediately obvious to argue that the EU courts have been systematically deferential to the interpretation advanced by the Commission when observed from a static perspective. The substantive analysis that follows this introduction reveals that, in one-shot interactions, the Court and the GC have departed in some cases from the approach favoured by the Commission. The examples of predatory pricing and refusal to deal are eloquent in this regard. In the two cases, the EU courts crafted a structured legal test that was at odds with the holistic, 'soft trigger' approach adopted by the administrative authority. The court's structured approach, moreover, reflected consensus positions about the appropriate way to tackle the practices in question and incorporated the insights from economic analysis. The recalibration of the legal test by the EU courts, however, has not always resulted in the annulment of the relevant Commission decision on substantive grounds.

From a dynamic perspective, the behaviour of the Commission is also consistent with the idea that it tends to adopt an expansive interpretation of the scope of its powers. It has often, and across the board, chosen a risk-prone approach to enforcement. This approach has been manifested in two main ways. First, the tendency of the authority – in relation to several abusive practices – has been to depart from the legal tests devised in the case law, or to alter them so as to broaden the reach of intervention. This inclination can be observed in relation to predatory pricing and refusals to deal. Second, the administrative practice of the Commission has resulted in the progressive broadening of the scope of prohibitions. This pattern is particularly apparent in relation to rebates and similar conduct. The qualified rule that initially applied to exclusivity agreements and loyalty rebates was progressively expanded to cover schemes based on quantity.

In repeated interactions, the EU courts have been less inclined to correct the (risk-prone) legal interpretation advanced by the Commission. The case law, in other words, has not proved to be resilient. In relation to predatory pricing, the Court dismissed challenges against decisions that deviated from the principles it had itself laid down in *AKZO*.[89] In relation to refusals to deal, the GC concluded[90] that the Commission decision in *Microsoft I*[91] met the conditions laid down by the Court in *Magill*, even though the analysis of the authority deviated

[89] Case C-62/86, *AKZO*. [90] Case T-201/04, *Microsoft I*.

[91] Commission Decision of 24 May 2004 (Case COMP/C-3/37.792 – *Microsoft*) OJ (2007) No. L 32/23 ('*Microsoft I*').

ostensibly from some of them. The fluctuations in the case law fuelled the widespread perception that the notion of abuse lacks clear boundaries and that there are no overarching principles capable of providing legal certainty.

Remarkably, the first reaction against the perceived legal uncertainty created by the case law came from the Commission itself. The authority developed a pre-commitment device to constrain its discretion and to anticipate the instances in which it is likely to take action. In 2005, it issued a Discussion Paper,[92] in which it outlined a new approach to the enforcement of Article 102 TFEU. The analytical framework devised in the document sought to bring administrative action in line with mainstream economic principles.[93] This shift entails a move away from rules towards standards at the prioritisation stage. The move was justified by the fact that the most common categories of conduct are capable of having both pro- and anti-competitive effects. In addition, it involves a systematic analysis of the likely impact of the practice on equally efficient rivals and/or on consumers.[94] Eventually, the Commission would adopt a Guidance Paper, which is narrower in scope but has the same objective.[95]

The reaction by the EU courts has been more cautious and incremental. The case law has not been overhauled in the way the enforcement priorities of the Commission were. In the years that have followed the adoption of the Guidance Paper, the Court has been confronted with some of the inconsistencies that emerged in the case law, including in relation to predatory pricing (and comparable behaviour) and rebate schemes. Judgments like *Post Danmark I, Post Danmark II* and *Intel* reflect the ambition to apply uniform principles across the board. In the aftermath of these rulings, it appears safe to claim that Article 102 TFEU is concerned, at least in principle, with rivals that are as efficient as the dominant firm. In addition, these judgments seek to minimise inconsistencies by bringing the case law closer to mainstream positions.

[92] DG Competition Discussion Paper on the application of Article 82 of the Treaty to exclusionary abuses (December 2005).

[93] The Discussion Paper builds on the advice given by a group of mainstream economists. See EAGCP, *An economic approach to Article 82.*

[94] See Discussion Paper, paras. 54–60, and in particular para. 56 ('[t]he central concern of Article 82 with regard to exclusionary abuses is thus foreclosure that hinders competition and thereby harms consumers').

[95] Guidance on the Commission's enforcement priorities in applying Article 82 of the EC Treaty to abusive exclusionary conduct by dominant undertakings OJ (2009) No. C 45/7.

3.1.2 Case Selection

The dynamic analysis that follows below focuses on three broad families of exclusionary practices: aggressive pricing (namely predatory pricing and related behaviour); exclusive dealing and rebates; and leveraging conduct (in particular outright and constructive refusals to deal). Exploitative practices are left outside the scope of the analysis. A systematic review of the administrative practice reveals that they have never been a priority for the Commission. Decisions dealing with excessive pricing and exploitative discrimination have been adopted by the authority, in particular in the early years. Similarly, the Court has routinely ruled on preliminary references addressing these questions. However, these practices have not been consistently enforced at the EU level and thus reveal little about the behaviour of the Commission.

The three categories of practices selected, on the other hand, are representative in quantitative and in qualitative terms. From a quantitative perspective alone, the decisions listed in Table 4.1 make up, overall, over half of the prohibition decisions challenged before the EU courts and represent the clear majority of decisions adopted since the 1990s. This is not surprising, considering that they constitute some of the most common categories of potentially abusive conduct. The Guidance Paper issued by the Commission focuses on the abovementioned categories (including other forms of leveraging, such as tying and mixed bundling). The preliminary references that have reached the Court in the 2000s suggest that these practices are also quantitatively

Table 4.1 *Case selection*

	Period 1	Period 2	Period 3
Pricing	*AKZO*	*Irish Sugar, CMB*	*Wanadoo*
Exclusivity and rebates	*Suiker Unie Hoffmann-La Roche Michelin I*	*Solvay* (saga), *BPB, British Airways, Michelin II, Van den Bergh Foods*	*Tomra, Intel*
Vertical leveraging	*Commercial Solvents, Magill*	*Microsoft, Clearstream, Deutsche Telekom*	*Telefónica, Telekomunikacja Polska, Google*

important at the national level, and that they represent a significant fraction of the activity of NCAs.

From a qualitative perspective, the focus on these practices allows for an appropriate dynamic analysis. As shown in Table 4.1, it is possible to distinguish, in each of them, three broad generations of cases, something that is not possible in the case of other practices. In Period 1, the legal status of the practice is addressed for the first time in one or several decisions. For instance, the conditions under which a policy of aggressive pricing by a dominant firm amounts to an abuse was systematically addressed for the first time, by the Commission and the Court, in *AKZO*. In period 2, the Commission explores the boundaries of the applicable case law. It is, in other words, the context in which the lack of resilience of the case law becomes apparent. Finally, the influence of exogenous constraints on administrative action becomes clear in Period 3 cases, which often reflect an attempt by the Commission to roll back the reach of the scope of Article 102 TFEU and to provide a structured approach to the assessment of some practices.

3.2 *Predatory Pricing and Related Practices*

3.2.1 The Rule in *AKZO*

AKZO[96] defined the standards applicable to predatory pricing by dominant companies in EU competition law. The divergence between the legal tests defined by the Commission and the Court is a noticeable aspect of the case. The framework crafted by the authority set a markedly lower thershold than that eventually defined by the ECJ. As shown in Figure 4.1, the Commission defined a legal test that did not focus on the anti-competitive potential of the predatory pricing campaign but on its presumed or established rationale. The anti-competitive object, in turn, was to be established, according to this test, on the basis of direct evidence and informal analysis. The substantive threshold defined by the Court, on the other hand, did not ignore the anti-competitive effects of the practice. Thus, it held that predatory pricing is only caught by Article 102 TFEU when it is at least capable of driving equally efficient rivals out of the relevant market. In addition, for a predatory pricing claim to be successful, it would be necessary to show, on the basis of formal analysis or of direct evidence, that the aggressive pricing campaign is the expression of a plan to exclude a rival from the relevant market.

96 Case C-62/86, *AKZO*.

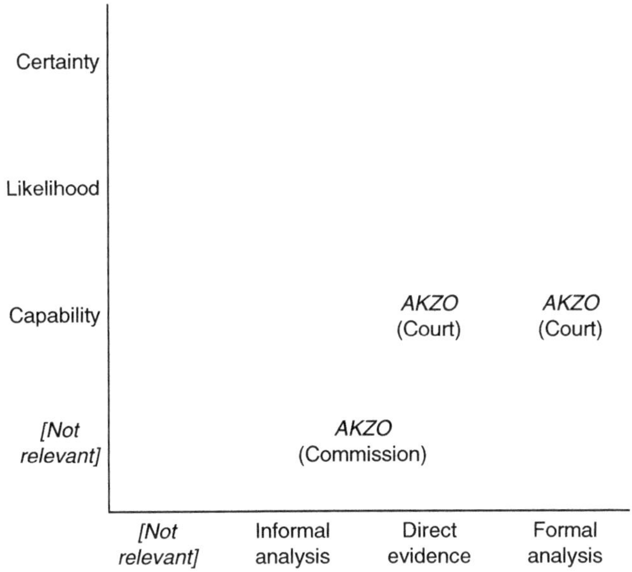

Figure 4.1 *AKZO*

In the proceedings before the Commission, AKZO argued that a campaign of aggressive pricing by a dominant firm could only be considered abusive if prices were to fall below an appropriate cost measure. In this regard, the firm relied upon the Areeda-Turner test, which consists of examining whether the prices charged by the dominant firm fall below average variable costs.[97] As pointed out above, this test is based on the premise that it is in principle irrational for a firm to price at such a level. In such circumstances, the pricing strategy can be safely presumed to have no economic sense other than the exclusion of competition. In addition, the firm considered that the prima facie prohibition of an above-cost pricing campaign would be problematic insofar as it would lead, through the protection of less efficient rivals, to allocative inefficiency.[98]

[97] Commission Decision of 14 December 1985, *AKZO*, para. 75: 'AKZO however argues that the only criterion for assessing the legality or otherwise of its conduct is whether the prices it charged were above its average variable costs (used as a proxy for marginal costs)'.

[98] Ibid.: 'The rationale for this argument is said to be that only less efficient firms will be harmed by pricing above average variable cost. A higher level than average variable cost will, according to AKZO, mean first that less efficient competitors will remain in business

The Commission argued in its decision that a legal test based on cost alone would be unduly narrow and would, as such, be at odds with the system of undistorted competition that the Treaty of Rome sought to establish.[99] According to the decision, any 'unfair' practice implemented by a dominant firm would be prima facie prohibited as abusive irrespective of the form that it may take in practice. In the Commission's view, even though aggressive pricing was the primary means through which AKZO sought to exclude rivals, it was not the only one. As it would do in other cases, the Commission took the view that the various practices implemented by the dominant firm could not be examined in isolation. Instead, they have to be examined together as the expression of a plan to exclude a rival.

The Commission, in other words, set out an unstructured test, based on a 'checklist' approach that resulted in a 'soft' trigger. Rather than providing a set of conditions against which the lawfulness of a practice could be examined, it identified a series of factors which, in the specific circumstances of the *AKZO* case, supported the conclusion that the behaviour amounted to an abuse of a dominant position. This approach does not make it possible to dissociate the predatory pricing campaign from other strategies. Instead, it requires considering them holistically. For instance, the Commission claimed that AKZO had cut its prices selectively to the customers of its main rival while maintaining substantially higher prices for its own customers. This behaviour was taken as an indication of the abusive nature of the strategy, insofar as it would amount to unlawful price discrimination within the meaning of Article 102(c) TFEU.[100] More generally, the Commission argued that it was an expression of an overall plan to drive AKZO's main rival out of the market, which included direct threats against it.[101]

and secondly that the higher prices will lead to lower output and a misallocation of resources'.

99 In para. 73, ibid., the Commission argued that '[a]ny behaviour by a dominant undertaking which undermines the purpose of Article 3 (f) and endangers the structure of competition might therefore constitute an abuse of a dominant position under Article [102]'; in para. 74, it concluded that '[a]ny unfair commercial practices on the part of a dominant undertaking intended to eliminate, discipline or deter smaller competitors would thus fall within the scope of the prohibition of Article 86 if the other conditions for its application were fulfilled' and claimed, by the same token, that 'Article [102] does not prescribe any cost-based legal rule to define the precise stage at which price-cutting by a dominant firm may become abusive'.

100 Commission Decision of 14 December 1985, *AKZO*, para. 82.

101 Ibid.

The Commission decision was only partially annulled by the ECJ on factual grounds. The Court found that some of the discrimination claims were not appropriately substantiated, as the two groups of customers were not found to be in a comparable position.[102] The substantive analysis, however, differs significantly from the 'checklist' approach defended by the Commission. According to the Court, a predatory pricing campaign would only be abusive in two instances: where the prices charged by the dominant firm would fall below average variable costs[103] and where they fall below average total costs but it can be established that they are the expression of a plan to eliminate a competitor.[104] Compared with the holistic approach favoured by the Commission, the substantive standard defined by the Court stands out as introducing a 'hard' trigger that can be defined in advance and that is grounded on formal analysis. Because there was clear evidence that AKZO had articulated a plan to drive its main rival out of the market,[105] and that the dominant firm had engaged in below-cost pricing, most of the claims made by the Commission were upheld. On the other hand, the legal test defined by the Court constrained significantly the scope for intervention in predatory pricing cases in the sense that it allowed the authority to intervene in a narrower set of circumstances. In particular, the logical consequence of the *AKZO* test is that aggressive pricing is deemed presumptively lawful so long as it remains above cost.

3.2.2 The Move Away from *AKZO*

The first expansion of the logic of *AKZO* took place in *Tetra Pak II*.[106] The Commission argued in this case that a strategy of predatory pricing can fall within the scope of Article 102 TFEU even when implemented on a market other than the one in which a firm holds a dominant position. In a sense, the expansion is uneventful as it was clear since *Continental Can* that there need not be a causal link between the dominant position and the abuse for Article 102 TFEU to come into play. However, the Court felt the need to qualify its position. In its appeal judgment, it held that a finding of infringement 'presupposes a link between the dominant position and the alleged abusive conduct'.[107] At the same time, the Court held that the departure from this principle could be justified in 'special circumstances'.[108] These circumstances were deemed to be present in

[102] Case C-62/86, *AKZO*, paras. 118–20. [103] Ibid., para. 71. [104] Ibid., para. 72.
[105] Ibid., paras. 76–82. [106] Case C-333/94, *Tetra Pak II*. [107] Ibid., para. 27.
[108] Ibid.

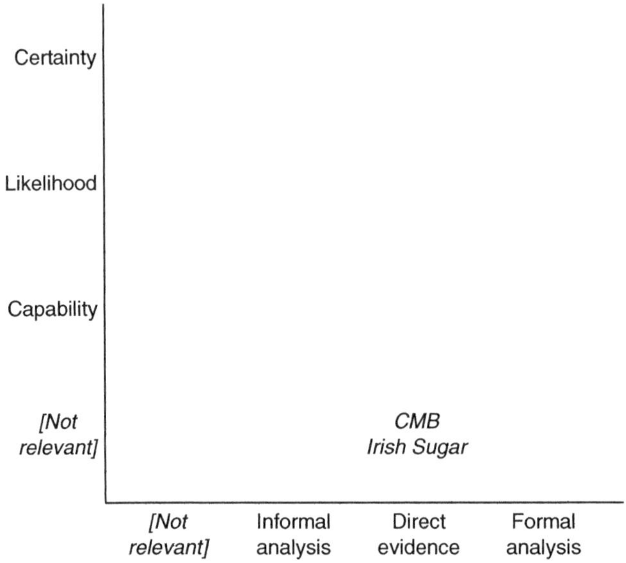

Figure 4.2 *CMB* and *Irish Sugar*

the case. The Court took the view that, even though it was not dominant, Tetra Pak held a leading position. In addition, there were close links between the two markets.[109]

In subsequent cases, the Commission resorted to the approach it originally advanced in its *AKZO* decision. Thus, the authority argued that a strategy of aggressive pricing can amount to an abuse even when there is no evidence of below-cost pricing. The decision that would lead to the *Compagnie Maritime Belge* judgment is the first example in this regard.[110] The case concerned, inter alia, the practices of a shipping conference (Cewal) that operated a route between Europe and West and Central Africa. The Commission raised concerns about a strategy of 'fighting ships', whereby Cewal set lower prices for ships when the dates of sailing were closest to the dates of sailing of a rival's (G&C) ships. The strategy of 'fighting ships' would be problematic, according to the Commission, due to the fact that the prices would be set with a view to matching or lowering the rates charged by G&C.[111] In addition, the

[109] Ibid., para. 28.
[110] Commission Decision 93/82/EEC of 23 December 1992 relating to a proceeding pursuant to Articles 85 (Case IV/32.448 and IV/32.450 – *Cewal, Cowac and Ukwal*) OJ (1993) No. L 34/20.
[111] Ibid., para. 81.

Commission put an emphasis on the fact that the strategy of 'fighting ships' was known in the industry and that sectoral regulation asked shipping conferences to refrain from engaging in it.[112]

According to the Commission, the above factors led to the conclusion that the behaviour was part of a plan to drive a rival out of the market. On the other hand, the Commission never attempted to show that the strategy of 'fighting ships' amounted to below-cost pricing, as *AKZO* would require. In the circumstances of the case, the Commission did not consider this factor to be relevant. It argued that the price cuts in response to entry by G&C would be problematic insofar as they would amount to cross-subsidisation (from this perspective, the profits obtained with the regular tariffs would subsidise the aggressive pricing campaigns).[113] In addition, the Commission claimed that the strategy of 'fighting ships' could lead to the exclusion of an equally efficient rival, irrespective of whether it amounts to below-cost pricing.[114] As in rebate cases, the decision conflated exclusionary and exploitative concerns. Even though the case was ostensibly driven by exclusionary considerations, the Commission argued, in addition, that the aggressive pricing strategy also amounted to exploitative discrimination within the meaning of Article 102(c) TFEU.[115]

The finding of abuse was validated by the EU courts.[116] One of the most notable aspects of the first instance ruling is the absence of references to *AKZO*. In addition, the GC failed to define a legal test against which the legality of the behaviour was to be assessed. In spite of this fact, the analysis of the first instance judgment appears to suggest that direct evidence of anti-competitive intent – which was found to have been established in the case – can lead, alone, to a finding that a dominant firm has abused its dominant position.[117] In this sense, the behaviour was deemed to go beyond competition on the merits, and beyond what was

[112] Ibid., paras. 74–6. [113] Ibid., para. 82.

[114] Ibid.: 'subsidization of the cost of fighting rates by the conference's normal rates charged on its other sailings is in itself in the case at issue abusive, anti-competitive conduct which might have the effect of eliminating from the market an undertaking which is perhaps as efficient as the dominant conference but which, because of its lesser financial capacity, is unable to resist the competition practised in a concerted and abusive manner'.

[115] Ibid., para. 83.

[116] Joined Cases T-24/93, T-25/93, T-26/93 and T-28/93, *Compagnie maritime belge transports SA and Compagnie maritime belge SA, Dafra-Lines A/S, Deutsche Afrika-Linien GmbH & Co. and Nedlloyd Lijnen BV v Commission*, EU:T:1996:139.

[117] Ibid., para. 147.

necessary for the shipping conference to protect its commercial interests.[118] The appeal judgment engaged with the apparent contradiction between *AKZO* and the analysis of the Commission in its decision. In that respect, however, the Court was far less explicit than AG Fennelly. The advocate general suggested that, as a matter of principle, above-cost pricing cannot be considered to be in breach of Article 102 TFEU.[119] On the other hand, he argued that a finding of abuse in the context of the case could be rationalised due to the fact that the practice involved a position of super-dominance that was, in addition, collectively enjoyed by the members of the conference.[120] These are the factors at which the Court hinted in its succinct assessment. In a single paragraph, the Court holds that, given that the conference enjoyed a market share above 90 per cent and that the purpose of the strategy was to eliminate its only rival from the market, a finding of abuse was appropriate.[121] As in *Tetra Pak II*, a departure from *AKZO* was deemed justified in light of the specific (or 'special') circumstances of the case.

Irish Sugar concerned several practices implemented by a firm approaching a position of monopoly on the relevant market. One of the practices, which the Commission labelled 'selective rebates', consisted in the application of different prices to customers based in the border area with Northern Ireland. According to the decision, the purpose of this practice was to reduce imports from the UK. As 'fighting ships', the strategy was implemented whenever there was a risk that the price differential would increase cross-border trade.[122] Accordingly, the policy was not deemed justified by any objective cost differences relating to the supply of customers along the border with Northern Ireland, or by the

[118] Ibid., para. 148: 'Since the purpose of the practice was to remove their only competitor, the Court considers that the applicants cannot effectively argue that they merely reacted to an infringement by G & C of the monopoly legally granted to Cewal, compensated for discrimination which they suffered at the hands of Ogefrem, entered into a price war started by the competitor or even responded to expectations of their customers'.

[119] Opinion of AG Fennelly in Joined Cases C-395/96 P and C-396/96 P, *Compagnie Maritime Belge NV and Dafra-Lines v Commission*, EU:C:1998:518.

[120] Ibid., para. 132, where AG Fennelly states that departing from *AKZO* could be justified 'where an undertaking which enjoys a position of dominance approaching a monopoly, particularly on a market where price cuts can be implemented with relative autonomy from costs, implements a policy of selective price cutting with the demonstrable aim of eliminating all competition'.

[121] Joined Cases C-395/96 P and C-396/96 P, *Compagnie Maritime Belge Transports SA, Compagnie Maritime Belge SA and Dafra-Lines A/S v Commission*, EU:C:2000:132.

[122] Commission Decision 97/624/EC of 14 May 1997 (Case IV/34.621, 35.059/F-3 – *Irish Sugar plc*) OJ (1997) No. L 258/1, para. 128.

fact that these customers ordered larger volumes of sugar.[123] Instead, it was considered to be part of a 'systematic' policy aimed at deterring imports into the relevant market.[124] Crucially, the Commission referred to *AKZO* in support of the proposition that a policy of selective price cuts by a dominant firm is abusive irrespective of whether it leads to below-cost pricing.[125] As in *Compagnie Maritime Belge*, moreover, it suggested that a policy of selective price cuts amounts to the application of dissimilar conditions to equivalent transactions and is thus in breach of Article 102(c) TFEU as a form of exploitative discrimination.[126]

The GC ruled that the Commission had not erred in law by holding that the selective rebates amounted to an abuse of a dominant position. In its analysis, the GC noted that the thrust of the disagreement concerned the question of whether such rebates can be abusive even when they do not amount to below-cost pricing.[127] The reasoning is notable for two main reasons. First, there are no references to the issue of costs, which was central in *AKZO*, and no attempt to reconcile the ruling with prior case law, even though it is cited. Second, the GC introduced market integration considerations, which did not feature in the Commission decision.[128] In addition, the judgment suggested that a finding of exploitation could in itself suffice to establish an abuse of a dominant position.[129] Even though an appeal was lodged against the first instance ruling, this point of law was not considered by the Court.[130]

3.2.3 The Recalibration of Principles in *Post Danmark I*

Following *Compagnie Maritime Belge* and *Irish Sugar*, the standards that applied to aggressive pricing campaigns were unclear. If *AKZO* suggested that only below-cost pricing could amount to a breach of Article 102 TFEU, *Compagnie Maritime Belge* and *Irish Sugar* suggested that, at least

[123] Ibid., para. 129. [124] Ibid, para. 133.
[125] Ibid., para. 134: 'In the Commission's final decision in *ECS/AKZO* it was held to be abusive for a company with a 50% or more market share to offer selectively low prices to customers of a small competitor while maintaining substantially higher prices for its existing customers. This principle was upheld by the Court'.
[126] Ibid., para. 129, which refers to a practice of 'selective and discriminatory pricing'.
[127] Case T-228/97, *Irish Sugar*, para. 182: 'Whilst there is no dispute between the parties that an undertaking holding a dominant position has a particular responsibility with regard to competition on its market [. . .], they differ as to whether or not special rebates to customers facing competition constitute a reaction that is compatible with that responsibility, in so far as the prices in question are not predatory within the meaning of the case-law'.
[128] Ibid., para. 185. [129] Ibid., para. 183.
[130] Case C-497/99 P, *Irish Sugar plc v Commission*, EU:C:2001:393.

in certain circumstances, above-cost prices can be abusive. Commentators rationalised the latter by pointing to the unusually high market shares of the firms, and to the fact that the aggressive pricing campaign was part of a wider pattern of anti-competitive conduct. Moreover, the anti-competitive purpose and/or the anti-competitive nature of the practice had not been called into question. In *Irish Sugar*, for instance, the GC placed an emphasis on the fact that the dominant firm suspected that its behaviour infringed Article 102 TFEU.[131] In *Compagnie Maritime Belge*, the Court noted that the anti-competitive purpose behind the 'fighting ships' strategy had been acknowledged in the course of the proceedings.[132]

After *Compagnie Maritime Belge* and *Irish Sugar*, it was no longer possible to argue that costs are, always and everywhere, a decisive factor in the assessment of the abusive nature of an aggressive pricing campaign. In this sense, the original position of the Commission in *AKZO* appeared to have been eventually validated. It is against this background that AG Mengozzi had to examine the lawfulness of the selective pricing campaign at stake in *Post Danmark I*.[133] This is the first preliminary reference in which the practice played a prominent role. The case is interesting for several reasons. First, the position of Post Danmark at the time of the facts was in some respects comparable to that of Irish Sugar and Cewal. As an incumbent in a market recently open to competition, it enjoyed a privileged position, which was strengthened by structural advantages.[134] Second, there was no evidence that the selective price cuts were part of a plan by the dominant firm to exclude its rival from the relevant market. In this sense, the case addressed a 'blind spot' in the case law. Finally, there was evidence suggesting that, at least with respect to one of the clients, the prices were below average total costs.

AG Mengozzi's Opinion discusses the interpretation suggested by the Commission in the proceedings. The Commission's submission did not depart fundamentally from the stance it took in *Irish Sugar*.[135] It argued,

[131] Ibid., para. 183.

[132] Joined Cases C-395/96 P and C-396/96 P, *Compagnie Maritime Belge*, para. 119.

[133] Opinion of AG Mengozzi in Case C-209/10, *Post Danmark A/S v Konkurrencerådet*, EU:C:2011:342 ('*Post Danmark I*').

[134] Ibid., para. 19.

[135] Ibid., para. 52: 'FK, the Danish and Italian Governments, the EFTA Surveillance Authority and, to a certain extent, the Commission, take the opposite view [. . .]. In broad outline, those interested parties submit that, irrespective of costs, selective pricing by a dominant undertaking in relation to customers of its only genuine competitor leads, or may very likely lead, to the exclusion of the latter if such pricing is not justified on

as it did in that case, that a policy of selective price cuts implemented by an incumbent in a recently liberalised industry could be deemed prima facie abusive. This is so because a policy of selective price cuts such as the one considered in *Post Danmark I* was not justified by any cost savings. Selective price cuts were merely driven by an attempt to attract the customers away from its competitor. The fact that the Commission did not rely on any cost considerations is particularly remarkable given that, at the time when the preliminary reference reached the Court, it had already issued its Guidance Paper, which suggested that the lawfulness of practices such as the one at stake in *Post Danmark I* would be assessed by reference to a variation of the Areeda-Turner test.[136]

AG Mengozzi directly addressed the contradiction between *AKZO*, on the one hand, and *Compagnie Maritime Belge* and *Irish Sugar*, on the other. He took the view that the latter two cases could be explained by the unusual circumstances surrounding the practice and that, as a matter of principle, selective price cuts are only abusive if they lead to predatory pricing within the meaning of *AKZO*. If, as in *Post Danmark I*, prices are above average variable costs[137] and there is no evidence of a plan to exclude a competitor, the practice should fall outside the scope of Article 102 TFEU. The Court followed the advocate general on this point. Crucially, it laid down two general principles that plead against the idea that above-cost pricing can – at least as a matter of principle – amount to an abuse of a dominant position.

First, the Court held that the exclusion of less efficient competitors is beyond reproach, as it is a natural manifestation of the process of rivalry between firms and the expected consequence of competition on the merits.[138] Second, it held that the application of selective price cuts is not, as such, evidence of an exclusionary abuse.[139] Thus, the fact that the lower prices are not justified by cost differences cannot justify, in and of itself, a finding of a breach of Article 102 TFEU. Crucially, the Court did

economic grounds, particularly economies of scale. That is said to be the situation in the main proceedings'.

[136] Guidance Paper, paras. 63–74. These paragraphs describe a cost-test framework that requires, in addition, evidence of anti-competitive foreclosure. The Commission suggests in para. 72 that the selective nature of the price cuts may make it easier for the dominant firm to foreclose competition.

[137] Or an equivalent cost measure. In Case C-209/10, *Post Danmark I*, the predatory nature of the prices was not established in light of average variable costs, but in light of average incremental costs, which appear to be suited for a network industry. See in this sense, para. 31 of the judgment and para. 26 of the Guidance Paper.

[138] Case C-209/10, *Post Danmark I*, para. 22. [139] Ibid., para. 30.

not follow the Commission on this point. In the circumstances of the case (no pricing below average variable costs, no plan to exclude competition), the selective price cuts at stake in the case would only be caught by the prohibition, the Court explained, if there is evidence of them having an anti-competitive effect. The Court pointed out that an equally efficient competitor is 'as a general rule' able to match prices that are below average total costs but above average incremental costs.[140] If the Court suggested in *AKZO* that such prices are capable of driving equally efficient competitors out of the relevant market, it added that exclusionary effects are unlikely to occur.

The preliminary reference asked whether the practice implemented by Post Danmark amounted to an exclusionary abuse. As a result, some aspects of the case law were not explicitly addressed by the Court. Even though *Compagnie Maritime Belge* and *Irish Sugar* were primarily driven by exclusionary concerns, exploitative considerations were introduced by the Commission to support the finding of abuse. It is not clear from the case law whether exploitative discrimination would have sufficed, in and of itself, to establish a breach of Article 102 TFEU. Another question left open by the preceding case law is whether market integration considerations alter the analysis of the abusive nature of the practice, as suggested by the GC in *Irish Sugar*. If they do, the substantive test laid down in *Post Danmark I* could be easily circumvented by arguing that the practice prevents cross-border trade – or, as in *Post Danmark I*, that it prevents operators based in other Member States from entering a recently liberalised market.

3.3 *Exclusive Dealing and Related Practices*

3.3.1 The Principles of *Hoffmann-La Roche*

The legal principles applying to exclusive dealing and similar practices under Article 102 TFEU were sketched by the Court in *Suiker Unie*.[141] However, *Hoffmann-La Roche* remains the reference and starting point.[142]

[140] Ibid., para. 38. The Court went on to suggest, in para. 39, that the practice had not had any exclusionary effects ('it is worth noting that it appears from the documents before the Court that Forbruger-Kontakt managed to maintain its distribution network despite losing the volume of mail related to the three customers involved and managed, in 2007, to win back the Coop group's custom and, since then, that of the Spar group').

[141] Joined cases 40 to 48, 50, 54 to 56, 111, 113 and 114–73, *Coöperatieve Vereniging 'Suiker Unie' UA and others v Commission*, EU:C:1975:174, para. 505.

[142] Case 85/76, *Hoffmann-La Roche*.

This is so because the Court explained at relative length the rationale behind the application of a prohibition rule to exclusive dealing and loyalty rebates, and contrasted them with quantity rebates, which it deemed prima facie lawful. There was a difference in approach between the Commission and the Court in *Hoffmann-La Roche*. In its prohibition decision, the Commission placed an emphasis on the restrictive potential of exclusive dealing, loyalty rebates and other practices having the same object.[143] On the one hand, the authority equated competition with freedom of action.[144] From the perspective of the authority, any practice that prevents customers from obtaining supplies from other producers is restrictive of competition by its very nature and thus prima facie prohibited. On the other, the Commission noted that the rebates were offered across the board, and therefore increased customers' incentives to acquire their products exclusively from the dominant firm.[145] As in predatory pricing cases, the Commission also argued that, in addition to them being capable of having exclusionary effects, exclusive dealing and loyalty rebates are discriminatory within the meaning of Article 102(c) TFEU.[146]

The Court confirmed that exclusivity and quasi-exclusivity obligations, as well as rebates conditional on the customer obtaining all or most of its supplies from the dominant firm, are prima facie abusive within the meaning of Article 102 TFEU. Its reasoning suggests that there are two main reasons behind the finding. First, exclusive dealing and loyalty rebates were deemed to lack an economic justification other than the exclusion of competition.[147] This is a point that was present in the

[143] Commission Decision 9 June 1976, *Vitamins*, para. 24.

[144] Ibid.: 'The fact of agreeing with purchasers that they will buy all or a very large proportion of their requirements from only one source by its very nature removes all freedom of choice from purchasers in their selection of sources of supply, and ties them to one supplier'.

[145] Ibid.: 'The agreements in question have the further effect of interfering with competition between vitamin manufacturers. The exclusivity established by Roche with its customers denies any access to these customers by other vitamin manufacturers. For quantities of any importance the rate of the rebate given by Roche is such that it is made practically impossible or at the least very onerous for other producers to sell to the customers of Roche'.

[146] Ibid., para. 26.

[147] Case 85/76, *Hoffmann-La Roche*, para. 90: 'Obligations of this kind to obtain supplies exclusively from a particular undertaking, whether or not they are in consideration of rebates or of the granting of fidelity rebates intended to give the purchaser an incentive to obtain his supplies exclusively from the undertaking in a dominant position, are incompatible with the objective of undistorted competition within the [Internal] Market, because – unless there are exceptional circumstances which may make an agreement between undertakings in the context of Article [101] and in particular of paragraph (3) of

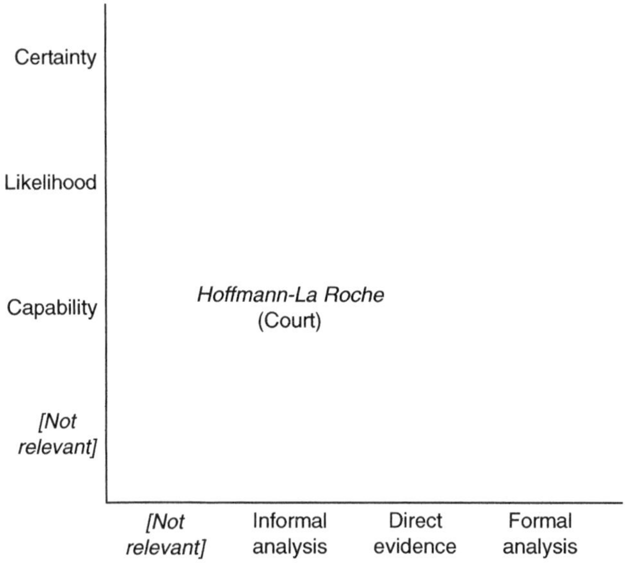

Figure 4.3 *Hoffman La Roche*

Commission decisions, but featured more prominently in the Court judgment. The underlying premise of this claim is that the award of rebates in exchange for exclusivity or quasi-exclusivity would lead to the application of dissimilar prices without reflecting any cost savings. As shown in Figure 4.3, the claim was not substantiated by any formal analysis, nor was it supported by direct evidence of the intent of the firm to exclude competition. Exclusive dealing and loyalty rebates were contrasted with rebates based on volume, in which case price differences can be explained by the economies of scale involved.[148] Second, exclusive dealing and loyalty rebates were understood to be capable of having exclusionary effects. At the very least, they were deemed to contribute to the consolidation of the position of the dominant supplier.[149]

that article, permissible – they are not based on an economic transaction which justifies this burden or benefit but are designed to deprive the purchaser of or restrict his possible choices of sources of supply and to deny other producers access to the market'.

148 Ibid.: 'The fidelity rebate, unlike quantity rebates exclusively linked with the volume of purchases from the producer concerned, is designed through the grant of a financial advantage to prevent customers from obtaining their supplies from competing producers'.

149 Ibid.: 'these practices by an undertaking in a dominant position and especially on an expanding market tend to consolidate this position by means of a form of competition which is not based on the transactions effected and is therefore distorted'.

3.3.2 The Progressive Expansion of the Prohibition Rule

The case law that followed *Hoffmann-La Roche* is marked by two factors. To begin with, it became clear in subsequent cases that the neat divide between loyalty rebates and quantity rebates does not reflect the reality of business transactions. Rebate schemes take a variety of forms in practice, many of which are halfway between the two ideal types on which *Hoffmann-La Roche* was based. As the practice of the Commission would show, some rebates are granted when the customer meets an individualised target. Other schemes are based on the volume supplied, but are not granted in relation to an individual order. Second, the administrative practice of the Commission led to the incremental expansion of the prohibition rule through the progressive softening of the trigger. Rather than lowering the substantive threshold, the scope of the rule was broadened, thereby capturing conduct that could reasonably have been thought to fall outside the prima facie prohibition.

In *Michelin I*, the Commission condemned as abusive a rebate scheme that was not formally conditional upon exclusivity, but upon the customer meeting an individualised sales target. Crucially, the authority rejected claims that the rebates were comparable to the quantity-based schemes deemed prima facie lawful in *Hoffmann-La Roche*. Unlike a system purely conditional on the volume supplied, Michelin's practice was not based on a set of criteria uniformly applicable to all customers, as it varied from one customer to another.[150] In addition, the Commission placed significant emphasis on the fact that the rebate scheme placed 'great pressure' on customers to increase their purchases from the dominant firm. As a result, the practice was deemed to have equivalent effects to a scheme formally conditional upon exclusivity. The pressure on customers came from the uncertainty resulting from the way in which the system was implemented by Michelin. In particular, the Commission attached relevance to the fact that the targets and the bonuses were communicated orally, and not in written form.[151] Finally, the decision argued that the rebate scheme was in any event discriminatory and as such contrary to Article 102(c) TFEU.[152]

The analysis of the Court in *Michelin I* provided the analytical foundations for much of subsequent case law. It is openly acknowledged in the

[150] Commission Decision 81/969/EEC of 7 October 1981 (Case IV.29.491 – *Bandengroothandel Frieschebrug BV/NV Nederlandsche Banden-Industrie Michelin*) OJ (1981) No. L 353/33 ('*Michelin I*'), in particular paras. 42–3.

[151] Ibid., para. 46–47. [152] Ibid., para. 45.

judgment that the rebate scheme at stake was not formally conditional upon exclusivity. As a result, the Court found it necessary to assess 'all the circumstances' surrounding the award of the rebates in order to determine whether, given their nature and operation, they could be likened to a system conditional upon exclusivity. The assessment, in other words, focused on establishing the object of the scheme.[153] The Court identified several factors leading to the conclusion that the practice was in breach of Article 102 TFEU. First, the fact that the amount of the rebates was calculated with respect to the sales made over a period of one year, which was deemed to be 'relatively long'.[154] Second, the relative position of the dominant firm. Finally, the lack of transparency of the scheme was deemed to reduce customers' ability and incentive to deal with Michelin's rivals.[155] This aspect was particularly problematic given the fact that customers risked making losses over the relevant period.[156]

Michelin I suggested that the lawfulness of rebate schemes – and thus the scope of the prohibition rule – would depend on a holistic assessment of a variety of factors. In this sense, the test was not fundamentally different from that suggested by the Commission in *AKZO*. As in *Compagnie Maritime Belge* and *Irish Sugar*, it was not clear from *Michelin I* how the analysis of 'all the circumstances' had to be performed in practice. While the Court held that rebates calculated over a 'relatively long' reference period were likely to be abusive, it did not define any benchmarks in this regard, nor did it explain how to balance the length of the reference period with other factors – such as the transparency of the system – which would suggest that the rebate scheme is unlikely to be problematic. Moreover, *Michelin I* suggested that discrimination claims could always be introduced in the analysis to support a finding of abuse.

The lack of clarity about the scope of the prohibition rule in rebate cases became apparent in *British Airways* and *Michelin II*. The decision in *British Airways*[157] is notable due to the fact that it makes some general

[153] Case 322/81, *Michelin I*, para. 72. In fact, analysis of the Commission decision suggests that the object of the scheme had been the factor driving the analysis in the administrative stage. See in this sense Commission Decision of 7 October 1981, *Michelin I*, paras. 38 ('the discount system is clearly aimed at tying the dealers closely to NBIM and thus making it difficult for other producers to gain a foothold in the market') and 48 ('[t]he aim of NBIM's policy is clearly to bind tyre dealers to NBIM as closely as possible. [. . .] The behaviour at issue distorts competition between tyre producers. Its aim is to restrict the inclination of dealers to obtain their supplies from competing manufacturers').

[154] Ibid., para. 81. [155] Ibid., para. 83. [156] Ibid., para. 84.

[157] Commission Decision 2000/74/EC of 14 July 1999 (Case IV/D-2/34.780 – *Virgin/British Airways*) OJ (2000) No. L 30/1.

statements that go well beyond the position expressed in *Michelin I*. If the legal analysis in *Michelin I* was confined to the facts of the case and sought to establish how the scheme worked in practice, the decision in *British Airways* was based on the premise that any rebate system that seeks to reward loyalty rather than efficiencies is contrary to Article 102 TFEU. In other words, the alleged or presumed purpose of the scheme can be sufficient to establish an abuse. According to the decision, only rebates that are granted in respect of individual orders and that reflect the cost savings made by the dominant supplier would relate to efficiencies and as such be compatible with Article 102 TFEU. Since the rebates granted by British Airways did not depend on the volume of the orders, but on the customer meeting a particular target, they were deemed to be 'clearly related to loyalty rather than efficiencies'.[158] As in *Hoffmann-La Roche*, the decision is not grounded on formal analysis supporting the economic intuition behind this claim. However, the perceived anti-competitive purpose behind the rebate scheme featured prominently not only in the decision,[159] but also in the proceedings before the GC.[160]

The decision in *Michelin II*[161] resulted in the most substantial expansion of *Hoffmann-La Roche*. *Michelin II* involved several practices, including a system of quantity rebates that was found to be in breach of Article 102 TFEU. These rebates differed from the scheme at stake in *Michelin I* in that they did not relate to an individualised target but to a standardised grid that applied uniformly to all customers. Insofar as the award of these rebates was made conditional upon the volume supplied, one could have reasonably argued that they were quantity rebates within the meaning of *Hoffmann-La Roche* and as such prima facie lawful. According to the Commission, however, the logic of *Michelin I* applied equally to individualised and to standardised systems. More importantly, it suggested in the decision – with no support in the case law[162] – that any retroactive scheme granted over a period exceeding three months is in

[158] Ibid., para. 102. [159] See also para. 101.

[160] Case T-219/99, *British Airways plc v Commission*, EU:T:2003:343, para. 288: 'BA can have had no interest in applying its reward schemes other than ousting rival airlines and thereby hindering maintenance of the existing level of competition or the development of that competition on the United Kingdom market for air travel agency services'.

[161] Commission Decision 2002/405/EC of 20 June 2001 (Case COMP/E-2/36.041/PO – *Michelin*) OJ (2002) No. L 143/1 ('*Michelin II*').

[162] For a careful analysis of this point, and, more generally, the case law, see Luc Gyselen, 'Rebates – Competition on the Merits or Exclusionary Practice?' in Claus-Dieter Ehlermann, Isabela Atanasiu (eds), *European Competition Law Annual 2003 - What is an Abuse of a Dominant Position?* (Oxford: Hart Publishing, 2006).

principle contrary to Article 102 TFEU.[163] Beyond exclusionary concerns, the Commission argued that the quantity rebates were unlawful insofar as they were exploitative of customers and led to the partitioning of markets.[164]

From a formal perspective, *British Airways* and *Michelin II* are in line with the principle whereby it is necessary to consider 'all the circumstances' when assessing the lawfulness of rebates that are not conditional on customers obtaining all or most of their needs from the dominant firm. In practice, however, the two decisions strongly suggested that all retroactive rebates granted for purchases exceeding a period of three months are prima facie contrary to Article 102 TFEU. At the very least, it seems very difficult for a dominant firm to claim that the above factors are outweighed by other considerations. Similarly, because only rebates granted in respect of individual orders were deemed prima facie lawful, it is not easy to see how an objective justification for schemes that are granted by reference to a period of time can prove successful in practice under the test.

Controversy followed when the challenges brought against the decisions in *British Airways* and *Michelin II* were dismissed by the GC.[165] The controversy is in part explained by the fact that the practices in the two cases did not appear to have a discernible impact on competition, neither were they likely to have such an impact. While British Airways had a market share that was substantially higher than that of its most immediate rival, this share declined markedly during the relevant period.[166] Direct and indirect available evidence in *Michelin II* suggested that the practices did not have any impact on competition. The dominant firm's market share had declined significantly over a period of 20 years and prices in the relevant market had fallen.[167] Moreover, the informal

[163] Commission Decision of 20 June 2001, *Michelin II*, para. 216.

[164] Ibid., paras. 240–7.

[165] See in particular John Kallaugher and Brian Sher, 'Rebates revisited: anti-competitive effects and exclusionary abuse under Article 82' (2004) 25 *European Competition Law Review* 263; and Denis Waelbroeck, 'Michelin II: A Per Se Rule Against Rebates by Dominant Companies?' (2005) 1 *Journal of Competition Law & Economics* 149.

[166] Commission Decision of 14 July 1999, *British Airways*, para. 107.

[167] Commission Decision of 20 June 2001, *Michelin II*, para. 332, where it is explained that, according to the firm 'in the space of 20 years its shares of the market in new replacement tyres have fallen from [...], and that it has seen a substantial fall on the market in retreaded tyres too; and it states that the prices of truck tyres have fallen by more than [...] in ten years, after allowing for inflation. These falls, Michelin argues, prove that Michelin does not hold a dominant position and has not abused one'.

presumption that rebates aimed at rewarding loyalty have an anti-competitive object, which underpinned both cases, was also criticised for being at odds with mainstream economics. While theoretical and empirical evidence suggests that exclusive dealing and loyalty rebates can have exclusionary effects, there is no support for the assumption that such effects inevitably result from their application.[168] Massimo Motta, who would later become the chief economist at DG Comp, noted in a piece that the dominant firm's behaviour in *Michelin II* was consistent with a pro-competitive strategy.[169]

3.3.3 The Aftermath of *British Airways* and *Michelin II: Post Danmark II* and *Intel*

In the wake of *British Airways* and *Michelin II*, the Commission reconsidered its approach to the enforcement of Article 102 TFEU and resorted to economic expertise.[170] It is in relation to exclusive dealing and rebates that the changes introduced by the Discussion Paper and the Guidance are more profound. As shown in Figure 4.4, the Commission pledged in the Guidance Paper to examine, prior to intervention, the probable impact of practices – including conditional rebate schemes – on equally efficient competitors.[171] In addition, it endorsed a standard of likelihood.[172] In relation to exclusive dealing, the Guidance expressly acknowledges that the practice is capable of having both pro- and anti-competitive effects, and that it is only in certain circumstances that rival foreclosure is likely to be manifested.[173] In relation to rebates, the

[168] Case T-219/99, *British Airways*, para. 183. British Airways argued in its challenge against the Commission decision that '[a] proper analysis of the market share data contradicts rather than supports a finding of dominance. Indeed, BA's market share fell from 47.7% at the beginning of the 1990s to 39.7%. By contrast, the shares of other carriers, notably Virgin and British Midland, have grown rapidly'.

[169] Massimo Motta, 'Michelin II: The Treatment of Rebates' in Bruce Lyons (ed), *Cases in European Competition Policy: The Economic Analysis* (Cambridge: Cambridge University Press, 2009).

[170] See earlier the references to the Discussion and the Guidance Paper.

[171] Guidance Paper, para. 23, where the Commission announced that it would 'normally only intervene where the conduct concerned has already been or is capable of hampering competition from competitors which are considered to be as efficient as the dominant undertaking'.

[172] Ibid., para. 20, where the Commission announced that it would 'normally intervene under Article [102] where, on the basis of cogent and convincing evidence, the allegedly abusive conduct is likely to lead to anti-competitive foreclosure'.

[173] Ibid., paras. 33–6.

no discretion when defining the meaning of the Treaty provisions, including Articles 101 and 102 TFEU. This means, as explained at length in Chapter 2, that the interpretation of these provisions is subject to full review by the EU courts. By holding that the legal test applied by the Commission in *Microsoft I* was not 'manifestly incorrect', the GC applied a lighter standard of judicial scrutiny that appears to be at odds with its duty as a review court. In this sense, it provides an ostensible example of undue deference on an issue of law.

Another key factor that attracted the attention of commentators relates to the interpretation of the notion of indispensability, which is central to the test crafted in *Magill*. As the Court clarified in *IMS Health*, an input is only indispensable where there are 'legal or economic obstacles capable of making it impossible or at least unreasonably difficult' to create alternative solutions.[218] Thus, the mere fact that these alternatives are less advantageous is insufficient to establish an abuse. Insofar as Microsoft's conduct had not led to the elimination of all competition, it is open to question whether access to interoperability information was in fact indispensable for its rivals. In fact, there was evidence suggesting that market entry had actually taken place.[219] The president of the GC at the time of the ruling, Bo Vesterdorf, noted that, by concluding that the Commission's analysis was not (manifestly) incorrect, the *Microsoft I* judgment had redefined the notion of indispensability. Under the approach introduced by the Commission in the case, access to an input may be deemed indispensable if it compromises the 'economic viability' of rivals.[220] Thus, the indispensability condition may be satisfied when less advantageous access might lead to foreclosure.

The Guidance on exclusionary abuses captures how the Commission interpreted the case law following *Microsoft I*. The document does not refer to the 'new product' condition. Instead, it explains that the Commission will intervene when there is evidence that the refusal leads to consumer harm. According to the Guidance, the evaluation of the impact of a practice on consumer harm would involve a balancing exercise aimed at determining whether consumers would be better or worse off following intervention. Under this approach, evidence that the refusal would prevent the emergence of a new product for which there is potential consumer demand is only one of the instances in which action

218 Case C-418/01, *IMS Health*, para. 28.

219 See in this sense Case T-201/04, *Microsoft I*, para. 424.

220 Bo Vesterdorf, 'Article 82 EC: Where Do We Stand after the Microsoft Judgement?' (2008) 1 *Global Antitrust Review* 1.

would be warranted. Article 102 TFEU could also come into play, inter alia, when the practice would be likely to stifle follow-on innovation. As observed by Vesterdorf, this reinterpretation of the 'new product' test leads to a significant expansion of the scope of intervention by competition authorities.[221]

3.4.3 Constructive Refusals to Deal

Discussions around the legal treatment of constructive refusals to deal became important with the liberalisation of network industries during the 1990s. These industries are characterised by the presence of a bottleneck segment that is very costly – and sometimes uneconomical – to duplicate. As a result, network industries are typically subject to a sector-specific regime that requires incumbent operators to provide access to bottleneck facilities – or that mandates the structural or functional separation between the bottleneck and potentially competitive segments. In the presence of such a regime, it is typically not possible – or at least it is significantly more difficult than in other industries – for the operator controlling the bottleneck to engage in an outright refusal to deal. Other mechanisms, more subtle but having the same consequences in practice, may come into play. The most prominent example of a constructive refusal to supply is the so-called 'margin squeeze', whereby leveraging is achieved through the manipulation of the spread between the wholesale price at which access is granted to downstream rivals and the retail price at which the service is offered to end-users.[222] A constructive refusal may take other forms. For instance, the operator controlling the bottleneck may attach unfair terms and conditions to the access obligation, or may withhold or delay the supply of information that is necessary for effective access.

As 'margin squeeze' cases grew in importance in the practice of the Commission, the question arose of whether the legal test that applies to

[221] Ibid., at 8, where he argued that the recrafting of the 'new product condition' would be 'be welcomed by competition authorities' and 9, where he wonders whether a dominant firm 'would be obliged to grant a licence every time another person claims that, if given a licence, its product will be a technical development for which there is potential demand'.

[222] See the definition found in Case C-52/09, *TeliaSonera*, para. 32, where the Court explains that a 'margin squeeze' would exist 'where the spread between the wholesale prices for ADSL input services and the retail prices for broadband connection services to end users were either negative or insufficient to cover the specific costs of the ADSL input services which TeliaSonera has to incur in order to supply its own retail services to end users, so that that spread does not allow a competitor which is as efficient as that undertaking to compete for the supply of those services to end users'.

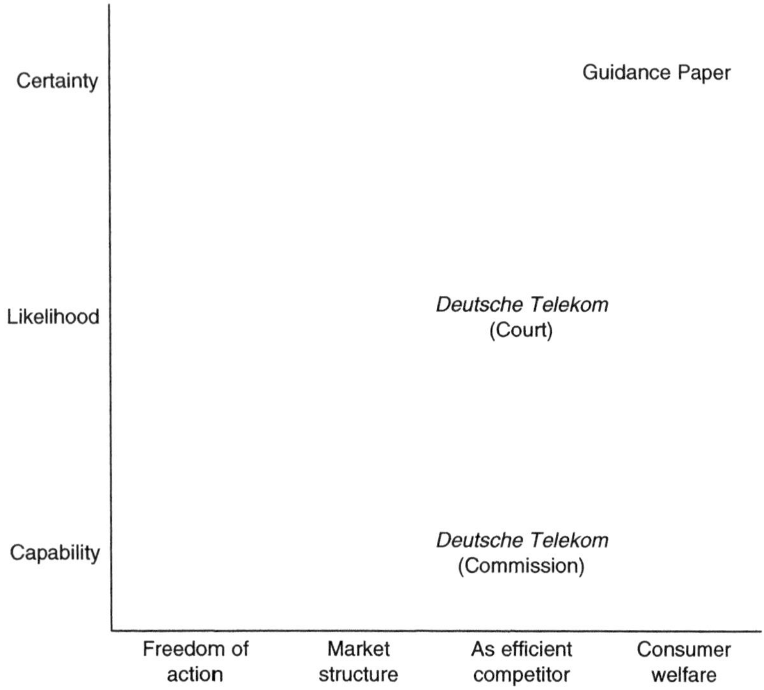

Figure 4.8 'Margin squeeze' abuses in *Deutsche Telekom* and the Guidance Paper

outright and constructive refusals to deal should be the same. The question, in other words, is whether evidence of, at least, the indispensability of the wholesale input is a precondition for intervention in 'margin squeeze' cases. This point of law was not addressed by the Court in the first landmark ruling, *Deutsche Telekom*.[223] This is due to the fact that access to the incumbent's infrastructure was indispensable to provide telecommunications services in the relevant market. As a result, the two conditions discussed in *Bronner* – indispensability and elimination of all competition – were fulfilled in the context of the case. In any event, the Commission did not consider that the said two conditions were prerequisites for intervention in 'margin squeeze' abuses. The decision in *Deutsche Telekom* appeared to endorse a threshold of capability and

[223] Commission Decision 2003/707/EC of 21 May 2003 (Case COMP/C-1/37.451, 37.578, 37.579 – *Deutsche Telekom AG*) OJ (2009) No. L 263/9. Thus, intervention requires evidence that the practice is likely to have an exclusionary effect.

expressed a concern with the exclusion of rivals that were as efficient as the incumbent.[224] As shown in Figure 4.8, the Court departed from the analysis of the Commission in that it clarified that evidence of a 'margin squeeze' (that is, a threshold of capability) is, alone, insufficient to establish an abuse of a dominant position.[225] Accordingly, the likely anti-competitive effects of the practice need to be established on a case-by-case basis.

The question of whether outright and constructive refusals are subject to the same conditions would arise in subsequent cases,[226] and was also addressed in the Guidance Paper. According to the pre-commitment device, outright and constructive refusals to deal should be subject to a common framework. Thus, the Commission would take action in an instance of a 'margin squeeze' in the same circumstances in which an outright refusal to deal would give rise to intervention. More precisely, the authority committed to establishing, in particular, that access is 'objectively necessary' to compete on the relevant downstream market.[227] According to the approach devised in the Guidance, the 'objective necessity' test may be more or less strict depending on whether the refusal concerns an input that has been developed under normal market conditions or, whether, instead, the award of subsidies and/or exclusive rights have been involved. In the latter case, which is typical in the network industries (and thus in 'margin squeeze' cases), the threshold for intervention would be lower.[228]

The question of whether the legal test applying to 'margin squeeze' abuses is the same as that applying to outright refusals to deal was raised

[224] Ibid., para. 180: 'By proving the existence of a margin squeeze, the Commission has therefore done enough to establish the existence of an abuse of a dominant market position'.

[225] See Case C-280/08, *Deutsche Telekom*, para. 250 ('the General Court correctly rejected the Commission's arguments to the effect that the very existence of a pricing practice of a dominant undertaking which leads to the margin squeeze of its equally efficient competitors constitutes an abuse within the meaning of Article [102 TFEU'], and that it is not necessary for an anti-competitive effect to be demonstrated'). Evidence of an exclusionary effect in the case was inferred from the fact that the incumbent's infrastructure was indispensable to provide telecommunications services in the country.

[226] See for instance Commission Decision of 4 July 2007 (Case COMP/38.784 – *Wanadoo España/Telefónica*), para. 299.

[227] Guidance Paper, paras. 80–1.

[228] Guidance Paper, para. 82: 'In certain specific cases, it may be clear that imposing an obligation to supply is manifestly not capable of having negative effects on the input owner's and/or other operators' incentives to invest and innovate upstream, whether ex ante or ex post. The Commission considers that this is particularly likely to be the case where regulation compatible with Community law already imposes an obligation to

explicitly in *TeliaSonera*. In its preliminary ruling, the Court held that, in order to show that a 'margin squeeze' is abusive, it is not necessary to establish that access to the infrastructure is indispensable to compete on the relevant downstream market.[229] Evidence of indispensability, while not a precondition for a finding of abuse, is, according to the judgment, a reliable indicator of the likely exclusionary effects of the practice.[230] At the same time, the Court held that it cannot be ruled out that a 'margin squeeze' has anti-competitive effects even when access to the infrastructure is not indispensable.[231] In the same vein, *TeliaSonera* seemingly endorsed the threshold of likelihood – as opposed to certainty – in relation to the probability of an anti-competitive effect. In this sense, it confirmed the standard set in *Deutsche Telekom*.

In addition, the Court also examined whether it is necessary to show that the conditions for an outright refusal to deal are present before intervening. On this point, the Court followed the submission of the Commission, which argued – in seeming contradiction with the position expressed in its Guidance – that a 'margin squeeze' is an autonomous category of abuse.[232] In the wake of *TeliaSonera*, it is easier to establish that a 'margin squeeze' is abusive than to show that an outright refusal to deal amounts to a violation of Article 102 TFEU.[233] The divergence between the two standards is captured in Figure 4.8. The reasoning of the Court is worth mentioning. It is explained in the ruling that the application of the strict conditions laid down in the case law on refusals to deal would undermine the 'effectiveness' of Article 102 TFEU.[234]

supply on the dominant undertaking and it is clear, from the considerations underlying such regulation, that the necessary balancing of incentives has already been made by the public authority when imposing such an obligation to supply. This could also be the case where the upstream market position of the dominant undertaking has been developed under the protection of special or exclusive rights or has been financed by state resources'.

229 Case C-52/09, *TeliaSonera*, paras. 63–4.

230 Ibid., paras. 69–70.

231 Ibid., para. 72.

232 Ibid., para. 58. See also the Submission of the Commission in Case C-52/09, on file with the author.

233 Cfr. *Pacific Bell Telephone Co v LinkLine Communications, Inc*, 555 U.S. 438 (2009).

234 *TeliaSonera*, para. 58, where the Court argues that requiring evidence of indispensability in 'margin squeeze' cases would 'unduly reduce the effectiveness of Article 102 TFEU'.

3.4.4 Other Forms of Leveraging and the Challenge of Consistency

Leveraging may result from tying and bundling, which are among the most common categories of potentially abusive practices. As generally understood, tying involves conditioning the sale of one product (the so-called 'tying' product) to the acquisition of another one (the 'tied' product). Bundling, in turn, typically defines an instance in which two products are only available as a bundle. Finally, 'mixed bundling' is a term that seeks to capture instances in which customers are given a financial incentive to buy two or more products from the supplier. The legal status of tying has already been discussed above. It is subject to a qualified prohibition rule.[235] As is true of exclusive dealing and pricing below average variable costs, the rule is based on the presumption that tying serves an anti-competitive purpose.[236] Similarly, the threshold of effects is set at the level of capability. As the GC clarified in *Microsoft I*, tying is subject to the prima facie prohibition if it gives an advantage to the dominant firm on the market for the tied product,[237] which is tantamount to saying that it is prima facie prohibited virtually always and everywhere.

As can be seen, the legal test that applies to tying and related conduct is considerably less strict than that applying to refusals to deal. This aspect is important if one considers that the boundaries between the two categories are not clear cut in practice; in other words, whether a given line of conduct amounts to a refusal to deal or to tying is not always a straightforward question. In some cases, the distinction between the two may appear somewhat arbitrary. After all, by refusing to deal with rivals, a firm effectively requires its customers to acquire two or more products from it (which is what tying and bundling seek to achieve). It is particularly difficult to distinguish between the two categories if it is not clear whether the two products are in a vertical relationship (in which case one of the products would be an input) or in a horizontal one (in which case the two products would be at the same level of the value chain). Consider, for instance, a microprocessor and an anti-virus system, which can be said to be both in a vertical (if one considers that the anti-virus is a component running on top of the hardware) and a horizontal (if one considers that the two products are offered as part of a bundle) relationship.[238]

235 See Case T-30/89, *Hilti* and Case T-83/91, *Tetra Pak II*.

236 See in particular Case T-83/91, *Tetra Pak II*, para. 140.

237 Case T-201/04, *Microsoft I*, para. 1054.

238 Commission Decision 26 January 2011 (Case COMP/M.5984 – *Intel/McAfee*).

Against this background, one can expect stakeholders to exploit the blurred boundaries between tying and refusal to deal. The framework crafted in Chapter 2 suggests that a competition authority can be expected to display a preference for construing a borderline case as one of tying, which is a practice subject to a rule. The implications of the unclear divide between tying and refusal to deal became apparent in *Microsoft II*.[239] The case involved the tying of Microsoft's operating system and its web browser. In one sense, the case seemed to involve an obvious tying strategy, as the dominant firm required computer manufacturers to take the operating system together with the web browser. In another sense, the remedies eventually accepted by Microsoft give the impression that the underlying concerns in the case related, above all, to access by the suppliers of an input (a web browser) to an end product (the operating system). This is confirmed by the remedy chosen in the case, which amounted to creating a level playing field in the conditions of access to the operating system by the providers of web browsers.

Similarly, uncertainty around the appropriate legal test in leveraging cases is a prominent aspect of the investigation against Google in relation to its search activities. In its decision, the Commission found that the company had abused its dominant position on the market for online search by favouring its own affiliate on a related market (comparison shopping) and by discriminating against rival services on that same market.[240] Again, this is a leveraging strategy that could well be characterised as a withdrawal of access similar to the one at stake in *Commercial Solvents* but also as a form of tying. It is natural to compare the case with *Commercial Solvents* given that the decision is based on the premise that Google degraded the presentation of rivals' search results once it decided to launch its own comparison shopping service.[241] The case is also comparable to tying in the sense that Google presented its general search results together with its shopping service and gave more prominence to the latter.[242]

239 This point has been explored extensively in Nicolas Petit and Norman Neyrinck, 'Back to Microsoft I and II: Tying and the Art of Secret Magic' (2011) 2 *Journal of European Competition Law & Practice* 117.

240 Commission, 'Commission fines Google €2.42 billion for abusing dominance as search engine by giving illegal advantage to own comparison shopping service' (MEMO/17/1785, 27 June 2017).

241 Ibid.

242 Ibid.: 'Google has systematically given prominent placement to its own comparison shopping service: Google's comparison shopping results are displayed, in a rich format, at the top of the search results, or sometimes in a reserved space on the right-hand side'.

APPENDIX TO CHAPTER 4

Table 4.2 *Challenged prohibition decisions engaging with the notion of abuse*

Decision	First instance	Outcome	Reframes?	Appeal	Outcome	Reframes?
Google Search (Shopping)	T-612/17	Pending	–	–	–	–
Slovak Telekom	T-851/14	Pending	–	–	–	–
Servier	T-691/14 (and others)	Pending	–	–	–	–
Telekomunikacja Polska	T-486/11	Dismiss	No	C-123/16 P	Pending	n/a
Intel	T-286/09	Dismiss	No	C-413/14 P	Set aside	**Yes**
Wanadoo España v Telefónica	T-336/07	Dismiss	No	C-295/12 P	Dismiss	No
Prokent-Tomra	T-155/06	Dismiss	No	C-549/10 P	Dismiss	No
AstraZeneca	T-321/05	**Annul (facts)**	No	C-457/10 P	Dismiss	No
Clearstream	T-301/04	Dismiss	No	–	–	–
Microsoft	T-201/04	**Annul (other)**	No	–	–	–
Wanadoo Interactive	T-340/03	Dismiss	No	C-202/07 P	Dismiss	No
Deutsche Telekom AG	T-271/03	Dismiss	**Yes**	C-280/08 P	Dismiss	**Yes**
DSD	T-289/01	Dismiss	No	C-385/07 P	Dismiss	No
PO-Michelin	T-203/01	Dismiss	No	–	–	–
Soda Ash-ICI	T-66/01	**Annul (facts)**	No	–	–	–
Soda Ash-Solvay	T-57/01	Dismiss (substance)	No	C-109/10 P	**Set aside (other)**	No

Table 4.2 (*cont.*)

Decision	First instance	Outcome	Reframes?	Appeal	Outcome	Reframes?
Virgin/British Airways	T-219/99	Dismiss	No	C-95/04 P	Dismiss	No
TACA	T-191/98	**Annul (law)**	**Yes**	–	–	–
AAMS	T-139/98	Dismiss	No	–	–	–
Alpha Flight Services	T-128/98	Dismiss	No	C-82/01 P	Dismiss	No
Van den Bergh Foods Limited	T-65/98	Dismiss	No	C-552/03 P*	Dismiss	No
Irish Sugar plc	T-228/97	**Annul (facts)**	No	C-447/99 P*	Dismiss	No
HOV-SVZ/MCN	T-229/94	Dismiss	No	C-436/97 P*	Dismiss	No
Cewal, Cowac and Ukwal	T-24/93	Dismiss	No	C-395/96 P and C-396/96 P	Dismiss (substance), Set aside (fine)	No
Tetra Pak II	T-83/91	Dismiss	No	C-333/94 P	Dismiss	No
Magill TV Guide	T-69/89 (and others)	Dismiss	No	C-241/91 P and C-242–91 P	Dismiss	**Yes**
BPB Industries plc	T-65/89	**Annul (facts)**	No	C-310/93 P	Dismiss	No
Tetra Pak I	T-51/89	Dismiss	No	–	–	–
Eurofix-Bauco v Hilti	T-30/89	Dismiss	No	C-53/92 P	Dismiss	No
ECS/AKZO Chemie	C-62/86	**Annul (facts)**	**Yes**	–	–	–
British Leyland	226/84	Dismiss	No	–	–	–
British Telecommunications	41/83	Dismiss	No	–	–	–

GVL	7/82	Dismiss	No	–	–	–
Michelin	322/81	**Annul (facts)**	No	–	–	–
ABG	77/77	**Annul (law)**	**Yes**	–	–	–
Vitamins (Hoffmann-La Roche)	85/76	Dismiss	No	–	–	–
Chiquita (United Brands)	27/76	**Annul (law and facts)**	**Yes**	–	–	–
General Motors Continental	26/75	**Annul (law)**	**Yes**	–	–	–
European sugar industry	40/73 (and others)	**Annul (law and facts)**	**Yes**	–	–	–
Zoja/CSC-ICI	6/73 and 7/73	Dismiss	No	–	–	–
Continental Can Company	6/72	**Annul (facts)**	No	–	–	–

* Order

of the entity. This conclusion is particularly apparent in the instances in which the concerns relate to the creation or the strengthening of a position of single dominance. The case law on Article 102 TFEU and on merger control suggests that the ability of a dominant firm to behave independently of suppliers, customers and competitors – that is, a position which roughly corresponds to the notion of substantial market power[5] – can be established by reference to indirect factors such as market shares and barriers to entry.

These points were discussed explicitly in the challenge brought against the Commission decision in *Ryanair/Aer Lingus*.[6] The acquiring firm argued that the Commission had failed to show that the transaction would harm consumers as a result of an increase in prices and/or a decrease in output. In particular, Ryanair argued that a relationship between prices and the degree of competitive pressure faced by the merging parties had not been established to the requisite legal standard.[7] The GC unambiguously rejected the idea that a declaration of the incompatibility of the transaction with the internal market would have required direct evidence of harm to end-users. The judgment suggests that indirect evidence relating in particular to the elimination of Ryanair's sole source of competitive pressure and to the barriers to entry prevailing on the relevant market were sufficient to conclude that the merger would lead to a significant impediment to effective competition.[8]

The GC came to a similar conclusion in the challenge brought by Deutsche Börse against the Commission decision declaring the incompatibility with the internal market of its planned merger with NYSE Euronext.[9] As in *Ryanair/Aer Lingus*, the firm argued that the Commission had not shown that the transaction would harm a particular parameter of competition. If in the latter it was prices, in *Deutsche Börse/NYSE Euronext* it was innovation. More precisely, the firm claimed that the conclusions drawn by the Commission in this regard were 'manifestly incorrect and unsubstantiated'.[10] The GC dismissed these claims, holding that the analysis of the question in the

[5] See Chapter 4. [6] Case T-342/07 *Ryanair Holdings plc v Commission*, EU:T:2010:280.

[7] Ibid., para. 219, where the GC points out that, according to the applicant, 'the Commission did not demonstrate in the contested decision that the alleged elimination of effective competition between Ryanair and Aer Lingus would harm consumers by leading to increased fares and/or a reduction in the number of flights'.

[8] Ibid., para. 228. [9] Case T-175/12, *Deutsche Börse AG v Commission*, EU:T:2015:148.

[10] Ibid., para. 171.

decision – which focused on the loss of a primary source of 'intensive and unique' competitive pressure between the parties – was sufficient to establish the reduction in innovation entailed by the transaction.[11]

There are no judgments dealing explicitly with instances in which anti-competitive effects were found to exist even though the transaction did not result in the creation or the strengthening of a dominant position.[12] The logic of the case law, however, suggests that anti-competitive effects could also be established by proxy in such a scenario. In the Horizontal Merger Guidelines, the Commission identifies the relevant factors to be considered in this regard.[13] Such factors include, in particular, the closeness of competition, which may result in the elimination of the most important source of competitive pressure between the parties and which already featured in some of the cases discussed above. They also include the possibilities for customers to switch suppliers, the ability of rivals to react to an increase in prices or the ability of the merged entity to hinder the expansion of competitors through its control of essential input.

1.2.2 The Probability of Anti-Competitive Effects

The case law on non-horizontal mergers has clarified that a standard of capability is insufficient to declare the incompatibility of a transaction with the internal market. In other words, the mere plausibility of harm does not give rise to intervention. The Commission and the EU courts have examined several vertical and conglomerate transactions in which one of the parties enjoyed a dominant position on one of the markets. In these cases, the foreclosure of competition on a neighbouring market was a plausible prospect. In *Tetra Laval/Sidel*,[14] for instance, the acquiring firm enjoyed a position of (super)dominance on one of the markets concerned by the transaction; in addition, there were close links between the different markets. When reviewing the Commission decision, the GC concluded that the leveraging and foreclosure were indeed plausible.[15] The Commission considered a comparable scenario in

[11] Ibid., para. 173.

[12] A challenge against a decision of this nature is currently pending. See Case T-399/16, *CK Telecoms UK Investments v Commission*, pending.

[13] Guidelines on the assessment of horizontal mergers under the Council Regulation on the control of concentrations between undertakings OJ (2004) No. OJ C 31/5 ('Horizontal Merger Guidelines').

[14] Case T-5/02, *Tetra Laval BV v Commission*, EU:T:2002:264.

[15] Ibid., paras. 192–9 (in para. 199, the GC concluded that the Commission 'did not commit a manifest error of assessment in finding that it would be possible for the merged entity to engage in leveraging practices').

Microsoft/Skype.[16] It noted in its decision that, following the acquisition, Microsoft, which most probably enjoyed a dominant position on the market for operating systems for PCs,[17] had the ability to eliminate competition.[18]

Had the standard of capability been deemed sufficient, the factors discussed above (dominance on one market, close links between the relevant markets) would have, alone, justified intervention. This approach would be in line with that followed in relation to certain practices in the context of Article 102 TFEU, in particular tying and exclusive dealing.[19] It is clear from the applicable case law, however, that it is not sufficient to show that anti-competitive effects are a plausible consequence of the merger. It is necessary to identify, in addition, the mechanism(s) through which anti-competitive effects would be manifested, that the new entity would have an incentive to adopt this behaviour and that, in addition, the implementation of the said mechanism(s) would have anti-competitive effects. This is an analytical framework that stems clearly from the GC ruling in *Tetra Laval.*[20]

In its appeal judgment in *Tetra Laval*, the Court noted that the analysis of the anti-competitive effects of non-horizontal mergers makes it necessary to consider various – plausible – scenarios that may unfold in the wake of the transaction and to identify which of these is the 'most likely'.[21] Put differently, the Court held that, for intervention to be justified, a scenario of foreclosure must be not only plausible, but more probable than other plausible scenarios. In this sense, the Court hinted at the endorsement of what has sometimes been called the 'relative plausibility' theory.[22] Subsequent case law appears to confirm this conclusion. The GC indeed took a similar position in a series of judgments, which

[16] Commission Decision of 7 October 2011 (Case COMP/M.6281 – *Microsoft/Skype*).

[17] Ibid., para. 133. [18] Ibid., para. 143.

[19] See in this sense Chapter 4 and in particular Case 85/76, *Hoffmann-La Roche & Co. AG v Commission*, EU:C:1979:36; Case T-30/89 *Hilti AG v Commission*, EU:T:1991:70; and Case T-201/04, *Microsoft Corporation v Commission* EU:T:2007:289.

[20] Case T-5/02, *Tetra Laval BV*, paras. 154–62.

[21] Case C-12/03 P, *Commission v Tetra Laval BV*, EU:C:2005:87, para. 43 ('the prospective analysis consists of an examination of how a concentration might alter the factors determining the state of competition on a given market in order to establish whether it would give rise to a serious impediment to effective competition. Such an analysis makes it necessary to envisage various chains of cause and effect with a view to ascertaining which of them are the most likely').

[22] For an application of this approach to EU competition law, see Ioannis Lianos and Christos Genakos, 'Econometric Evidence in EU Competition Law: An Empirical and Theoretical Analysis' in Ioannis Lianos and Damien Geradin (eds.), *Handbook of*

include the challenges brought against the Commission decisions in *Ryanair/Aer Lingus* and *Deutsche Börse/NYSE Euronext*, mentioned above.

A separate but related issue concerns whether it is sufficient to show that a particular scenario is indeed the most plausible one or whether, in addition, it is necessary to establish that it meets a requisite level of probability, measured in absolute terms. In other words, the question that remains is that of whether intervention is warranted simply because the scenario of harm is the most likely, even if the absolute probability of it occurring is relatively low, or whether, instead, a minimum threshold of probability is required. In this regard, some of the judgments appear to endorse an absolute threshold of likelihood – which, according to the definition given in Chapter 2, would correspond to a probability of >50 per cent. This appears to be the position at which the Court hinted in *Kali & Salz*. The case concerned, inter alia, the question of whether Regulation 4064/89 encompassed the notion of collective dominance, which raises similar issues to those encountered in the context of non-horizontal mergers.[23] In that case, the Court held that the inquiry must establish whether the transaction is likely to have anti-competitive effects.[24] The threshold of likelihood is also endorsed by the Commission in its Guidelines.[25] The vocabulary of the GC in *Tetra Laval*, on the other hand, could well be interpreted as suggesting a higher threshold. According to that judgment, intervention would require evidence that the transaction would, 'in all likelihood' have anti-competitive effects. This threshold comes closer to one of certainty. Alternatively, this vocabulary may simply reflect that, given the nature of non-horizontal mergers, establishing the probable impact of a merger on competition requires particular care.

European Competition Law – Enforcement and Procedure (Cheltenham: Edward Elgar, 2013).

[23] This point would be reiterated in subsequent judgments on non-horizontal mergers. See in particular, Case T-5/02, *Tetra Laval*, para. 155.

[24] Joined Cases C-68/94 and C-30/95, *France and Société commerciale des potasses et de l'azote and Entreprise minière et chimique v Commission*, EU:C:1998:148 ('*Kali & Salz*'), para. 170: 'It follows from the sixth, seventh, tenth and eleventh recitals in the preamble that the Regulation, unlike Articles [101 and 102] of the Treaty, is intended to apply to all concentrations with a Community dimension in so far as they are likely, because of their effect on the structure of competition within the Community, to prove incompatible with the system of undistorted competition envisaged by the Treaty'.

[25] Horizontal Merger Guidelines, paras. 3–4.

Figure 5.2 Analysis of effects in EU merger control

1.2.3 The Time Horizon

As already pointed out, the analysis of mergers is by definition prospective. This inevitably raises the question of the time horizon that needs to be considered when the anti-competitive effects of a transaction are evaluated. The question, in other words, is how far into the future the analysis can or must venture. The temporal dimension of the analysis is discussed in the case law, in particular in relation to non-horizontal mergers. The GC suggested in *Tetra Laval* that intervention in such cases would only be justified where it can be shown that, 'in the relatively near future', they can give rise to the leveraging of a dominant position to a neighbouring market.[26] On the other hand, there is nothing in the case law that suggests that a precise time frame (for instance, a period of two or three years) has been defined in this regard. In *Tetra Laval*, decided in 2001, developments

[26] Case T-5/02, *Tetra Laval*, paras. 148 and 151.

until 2005 were considered, but there is nothing in the GC and Court judgments that suggests that this is a general rule. It would seem that the temporal aspects are inevitably – if implicitly – considered in the assessment of the likely anti-competitive effects of a transaction. Indeed, the ECJ suggested in *Tetra Laval* that the more the analysis ventures into the future, the more challenging it is for a competition authority to show that anti-competitive effects are likely.[27]

2 Institutional Context

2.1 Overview

EU merger control differs from the enforcement of Articles 101 and 102 TFEU in that preliminary references play only a very marginal role in the shaping of the scope of the Regulation.[28] Virtually all cases have reached the Court through direct actions against Commission decisions. In the current enforcement landscape, a second aspect that makes EU merger control stand out from behavioural provisions relates to the institutional setup. Under Regulation 139/2004, all concentrations having a 'Union dimension' are to be notified to the Commission. Inevitably, only a very small fraction of such cases have reached the EU courts. At the time of writing, the Commission had decided on the compatibility with the internal market of 6,457 transactions.[29] Of these, it has been possible to trace 78 actions brought since the entry into force of Regulation 4064/89.

These figures, however, do not provide a faithful picture of the relationship between the Commission and the EU courts in the field of

[27] See Case C-12/03 P, *Tetra Laval*, para. 44, where the Court indicates that '[t]he analysis of a "conglomerate-type" concentration is a prospective analysis in which, first, the consideration of a lengthy period of time in the future and, secondly, the leveraging necessary to give rise to a significant impediment to effective competition mean that the chains of cause and effect are dimly discernible, uncertain and difficult to establish'.

[28] It has been possible to trace only two preliminary references concerning the interpretation of Regulation 139/2004. These are Case C-248/16 *Austria Asphalt GmbH & Co OG v Bundeskartellamt*, EU:C:2017:643; and Case C-633/16 *Ernst & Young P/S v Konkurrencerådet*, pending.

[29] These figures have been obtained from the website of the European Commission, which includes a set of statistics and a search form. The data, last updated on 15 September 2017, includes compatibility decisions adopted in accordance with Article 6 of the two versions of the Merger Regulation (merger falling outside the scope of the Regulation, merger deemed compatible with the internal market and merger deemed compatible with conditions) and Article 8 (prohibition, unconditional approval and approval with conditions).

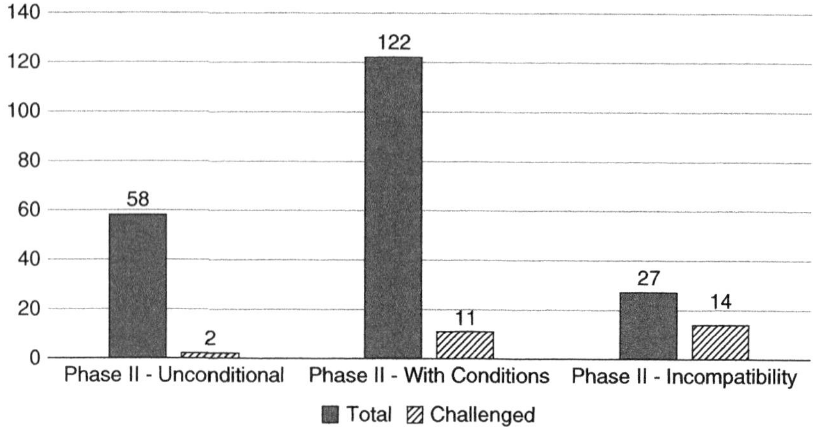

Chart 5.1 Challenges against Phase II decisions (including pending cases)

merger control. The vast majority of transactions are not a plausible source of competition concerns, but are examined by the Commission due to the mandatory notification system put in place by Regulation 139/2004. These transactions are unconditionally cleared in Phase I by the Commission. A more meaningful approach to determine how contentious merger cases are is to focus on decisions adopted in Phase II – that is, in relation to concentrations that were deemed to 'raise serious doubts' as to their compatibility with the internal market.[30] This subset of cases – which does not include all challenged Commission decisions, as some Phase I decisions have been brought before the GC[31] – can be found in Chart 5.1.

[30] In accordance with Article 6(1)(c) of Regulation 139/2004, 'where the Commission finds that the concentration notified falls within the scope of this Regulation and raises serious doubts as to its compatibility with the common market, it shall decide to initiate proceedings'.

[31] It has been possible to trace a total of 12 Phase I Decisions that have been challenged before the GC. These are Commission Decision of 3 August 2016 (Case COMP/M.7978 – *Vodafone/Liberty Global/Dutch JV*); Commission Decision of 7 October 2011 (Case COMP/M.6281 – *Microsoft/Skype*); Commission Decision of 21 May 2010 (Case COMP/M.5786 – *Française des Jeux/Groupe Lucien Barrière/JV*); Commission Decision of 12 November 2009 (Case COMP/M.5549 – *EDF/Segebel*); Commission Decision of 29 April 2011 (Case COMP/M.5047 – *REWE/ADEG*); Commission Decision of 29 May 2006 (Case COMP/M.4071 – *Apollo/AKZO Nobel IAR*); Commission Decision of 21 December 2004 (Case COMP/M.3605 – *Sovion/HMG*); Commission Decision of 11 February 2004 (Case No COMP/M.3280 – *Air France/KLM*); Commission Decision of 11 November 2003 (Case COMP/M.2621 – *SEB/Moulinex*); Commission Decision of 5 September 2000 (Case COMP/M.2045 – *Salzgitter/Mannesmann-Röhrenwerke*);

When analysing Chart 5.1 (and Table 5.1 in the Appendix), it makes sense to pay attention, first, to decisions declaring the incompatibility of a concentration with the internal market. While the analogy is imperfect, these decisions are the closest in nature and purpose to prohibition decisions adopted in accordance with Articles 101 and 102 TFEU. As in the case of the latter, the consequence for the merging parties is that they are precluded from carrying out the transaction. Chart 5.1 shows that around half of incompatibility decisions have been challenged before the EU courts. This figure does not strike one as being fundamentally at odds with the proportion of challenges against prohibition decisions in the context of Articles 101 and 102 TFEU. Unsurprisingly, the number of direct actions against decisions declaring the compatibility, with conditions, of a transaction is lower. Again, however, the figure does not appear to be manifestly out of line with decisions fulfilling a comparable role in other areas of EU competition law. Suffice it to think, in this sense, of the proportion of challenges against decisions granting an exemption within the meaning of Regulation 17,[32] and of commitment decisions adopted under Regulation 1/2003.[33]

2.2 Assessment

According to a popular narrative, administrative action in the field of EU merger control has traditionally been subject to effective judicial review.[34] This would be so in spite of the fact that the review of concentrations typically involves complex economic assessments. It has been argued that the formal application of the marginal standard of review, even when invoked, has not prevented the EU courts from carefully scrutinising the legal and factual aspects of Commission decisions,

Commission Decision of 21 March 2000 (Case COMP/JV.37 – *BSkyB/Kirch Pay TV*); and Commission Decision of 27 November 1992 (Case IV/M.259 – *British Airways/TAT*).

[32] See Chapter 3. [33] See Chapter 6.

[34] See for instance Matteo F. Bay and Javier Ruiz Calzado, 'Tetra Laval II: the Coming of Age of the Judicial Review of Merger Decisions' (2005) 28 *World Competition* 433; Kyriakos Fountoukakos, 'Judicial Review and EC Merger Control: Reflections on the Effectiveness of the System with Regard to the Standard of Review and Speed' (2007–08) 10 *Cambridge Yearbook of European Legal Studies* 133, at 142 ('the Community Courts, and in particular the CFJ as the court hearing actions at first instance, have provided effective judicial review in the mergers field'); Marc Jaeger, 'The Standard of Review in Competition Cases Involving Complex Economic Assessments: Towards the Marginalisation of the Marginal Review? (2011) 2 *Journal of European Competition Law & Practice* 295, at 301 ('the General Court exercised a thorough, meticulous and precise review').

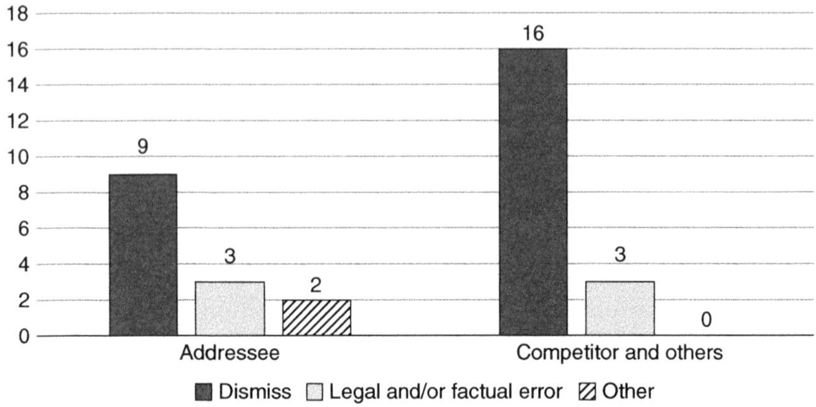

Chart 5.2 Actions against final compatibility decisions, by applicant and outcome in first instance

sometimes leading to their annulment.[35] A systematic overview of the relevant case law helps understand this widespread perception. It also confirms that the annulment of a Commission decision in first instance is not an exceptional outcome. A look at Chart 5.2 shows that over a third (40 per cent) of challenges brought by the addressees of a final decision on the compatibility of a merger with the internal market has proved successful. This figure is in line with the percentage observed across all EU law in a comprehensive study conducted by Tridimas and Gari.[36]

The rate of annulment is significantly lower where the applicant is a competitor or another third party – as seen in Chart 5.2, it sits at around 18 per cent. This outcome is unsurprising if one takes a look at the outcome of comparable challenges in other areas of EU competition law. Complainants challenging rejection decisions in the context of Article 102 TFEU are also less successful than the addressees of prohibition decisions. As pointed out above, several challenges have been brought against Phase I decisions concluding that there were no serious doubts about the compatibility of the transaction with the internal market. The low rate of annulment by third parties tends to be

[35] See in this sense Fernando Castillo de la Torre and Eric Gippini Fournier, *Evidence, Proof and Judicial Review in EU Competition Law* (Cheltenham: Edward Elgar, 2017), 6.046–6.048.

[36] See Takis Tridimas and Gabriel Gari, 'Winners and Losers in Luxembourg: A Statistical Analysis of Judicial Review Before the ECJ and the CFI (2001–2005)' (2010) 35 *European Law Review* 131.

exacerbated by challenges brought by other applicants, such as consumer associations, workers' representatives or local authorities.[37] In the same vein, admissibility issues feature more prominently in these cases.[38]

Chart 5.3 provides a different perspective on this same question. Unsurprisingly, it shows that the vast majority of decisions ruling on the compatibility of mergers with the internal market have been annulled for reasons relating to the application of the substantive criterion.[39] In particular, it appears that the EU courts have not hesitated to refine or alter the legal framework devised by the Commission. As will be examined in greater detail below, the EU courts reframed the approach to the assessment of the lawfulness of vertical and conglomerate mergers, and defined the instances in which horizontal transactions are likely to lead to the emergence of a collective dominant position. It is also possible to identify a series of judgments questioning the legal characterisation of facts in the decision, even though this is the privileged realm of the 'complex economic assessments' for which the Commission enjoys a margin of discretion. This is the case, inter alia, of rulings like *Impala*[40] and *Schneider Electric*.[41]

It has been possible to trace 14 appeals in cases relating to the application of Regulations 4064/89 and 139/2004. However, only a small fraction of these appeals relates to decisions on the compatibility of a merger with the internal market. As a result, it is difficult to draw any meaningful conclusions from such a small sample. If one considers the nature of mergers and the incentives of firms involved in them, it is not surprising that the figure is lower than in the context of Articles 101 and 102 TFEU. This said, it is worth noting that the appeal

[37] See for instance Case T-224/10, *Association belge des consommateurs test-achats ASBL v Commission*, EU:T:2011:588; Case T-132/10, *Communauté de communes de Lacq v Commission*, EU:T:2011:413; and Case T-12/93, *Comité Central d'Entreprise de la Société Anonyme Vittel and Comité d'Etablissement de Pierval and Fédération Générale Agroalimentaire v Commission*, EU:T:1995:78.

[38] Applications against decisions ruling on the compatibility with the internal market of a concentration that were declared inadmissible are the following: Case T-315/10, *Groupe Partouche v Commission*, EU:T:2012:21; Case T-224/10, *Association belge des consommateurs test-achats ASBL v Commission*; and Case T-350/03, *Wirtschaftskammer Kärnten and best connect Ampere Strompool GmbH v Commission*, EU:T:2006:257.

[39] The picture is a different one when one considers all the challenges brought against EU merger control. Still, it appears that around half of the challenges relate to the application of the substantive criterion by the Commission.

[40] Case T-464/04, *Independent Music Publishers and Labels Association v Commission*, EU:T:2006:216 ('*Impala*').

[41] Case T-310/01, *Schneider Electric SA v Commission*, EU:T:2002:254.

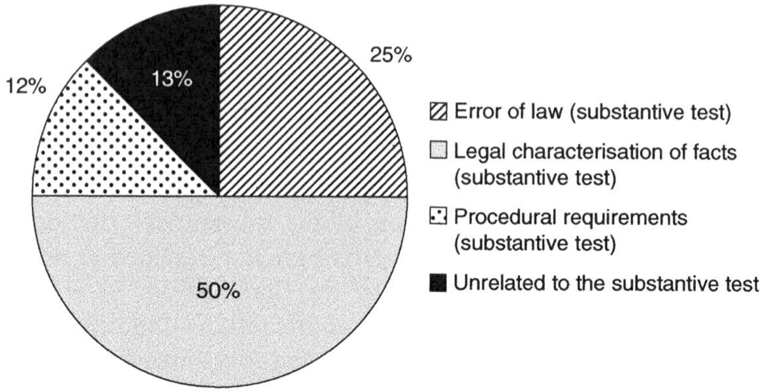

Chart 5.3 Annulment of final compatibility decisions in first instance, by type

brought by the Commission against the GC ruling in *Tetra Laval/Sidel*, which raised issues relating to the standard of proof and to the legal framework for the assessment of non-horizontal mergers, was dismissed by the Court.[42] Of the two appeals brought by the original addressees of the decision, one of them – brought against the GC ruling in *Impala*[43] – was successful.

3 Dynamic Analysis

3.1 Overview

3.1.1 Patterns in the Case Law and Administrative Practice

One key aspect in which EU merger control differs from Articles 101 and 102 TFEU is that it is based on secondary legislation. This difference makes it possible to examine the behaviour of the Commission at two different levels: the stage at which the substantive criterion is defined in the Regulation and the stage at which its scope is interpreted. These two separate levels also capture the dual role of the Commission in the EU system as the institution in charge of proposing legislation[44] and the authority in charge of enforcing competition law. In its first role, the Commission is expected to advance legislation that

[42] Case C-12/03 P, *Tetra Laval*. The substantive questions are examined at length below.

[43] Case C-413/06 P, *Bertelsmann AG and Sony Corporation of America v Independent Music Publishers and Labels Association*, EU:C:2008:392.

[44] See in this sense Articles 103 and 352 TFEU.

the Council[45] will find persuasive and palatable. In its second role, which is the one that this volume has examined so far, its interpretations of competition law provisions are subject to scrutiny by the EU courts.

A dynamic analysis reveals a similar pattern of behaviour at the two levels. The proposals for a Regulation to the Council sought to define the scope of the Commission powers in a relatively broad way. The proposals that preceded the adoption of Regulation 4064/89 did not revolve around dominance. The relevant question under the test originally proposed by the Commission was whether the merger hindered or prevented 'effective competition'.[46] As already pointed out, the compromise that was eventually reached with the Council set the threshold of appreciability at a higher level, thereby substantially reducing the scope of the powers of the Commission. However, the latter was subsequently able to persuade the legislator to adopt a test – 'significant impediment to effective competition' – that is closer to the one envisaged in its initial proposals.[47] Accordingly, the authority is now in a position to control the creation or strengthening of market power in the context of both collusive and non-collusive oligopolies.[48] The dynamic analysis below shows that, prior to the introduction of the new test in 2004, the Commission had explored the outer boundaries of

45 In accordance with Article 103 TFEU, the 'appropriate regulations or directives to give effect to the principles set out in Articles 101 and 102 shall be laid down by the Council'. In accordance with Article 352 TFEU, 'the Council, acting unanimously on a proposal from the Commission and after obtaining the consent of the European Parliament, shall adopt the appropriate measures'.

46 See in this sense Proposal for a Regulation (EEC) of the Council on the control of concentrations between undertakings COM(73) 1210 final; Amended proposal for a Council regulation on the control of concentrations between undertakings (merger control regulation) COM(81)773 final; Amended proposal for a Council Regulation on the control of concentration between undertakings COM(84) 59 final; Amended proposal for a Council Regulation (EEC) on the control of concentrations between undertakings COM(88) 97 final; Amended proposal for a Council Regulation (EEC) on the control of concentrations between undertakings COM(88) 734 final.

47 In its 1973 proposal, for instance, the question would be whether the merger gives the new entity 'the power to hinder effective competition in the common market or in a substantial part thereof'. In the December 1989 proposal, in turn, intervention would depend on whether the merger creates or strengthens 'a position as a result of which the maintenance or development of effective competition would be impeded in the common market or in a substantial part thereof'.

48 For an overview of the question, see Giorgio Monti, 'The New Substantive Test in the EC Merger Regulation – Bridging the Gap Between Economics and Law?' (2008) 10 *Cambridge Yearbook of European Legal Studies* 263.

the notion of dominance. In this sense, the two levels (legislative proposal and enforcement) are, at least to some extent, interchangeable.

The endorsement of a broader substantive criterion in Regulation 139/2004 is not the final step in the review of the scope and reach of EU merger control. Following the legislative change, the Commission has advanced proposals to expand the scope of the Regulation in different directions. First, it floated the idea of taking action not only in relation to transactions leading to a change in control, but also in relation to minority shareholdings.[49] Secondly, it has launched a consultation in which it discusses the possibility of defining alternative notification thresholds so that certain transactions that currently fall outside the scope of the merger control regime would be subject to review at the EU level.[50] The latter is a response to the concern that firms' turnover is not necessarily a reliable indicator of the cross-border significance of mergers in some industries.[51]

At the second level, that is, the interpretation of the scope of the substantive criterion as defined in the Regulation, a dynamic analysis suggests that the Commission has displayed a tendency to advance an expansive interpretation of the scope of its powers. This is most obviously apparent in relation to the notion of dominance as laid down in Regulation 4064/89. It was not obvious from the letter and the legislative history of the relevant provision that Article 2 of the Regulation gave the Commission powers to control the creation or strengthening of collusive oligopolies (that is, of a position of collective dominance). However, the authority advanced this interpretation – which was not expressly rejected in the Regulation – in its administrative practice, and would ultimately be validated by the Court in *Kali & Salz*.[52] The boundaries of the notion of collective dominance remained unclear until the GC defined a set of operational criteria in *Airtours*.[53]

Similarly, it was not immediately obvious that a substantive criterion based on the notion of dominance would be broad enough to capture

[49] Commission, 'Towards more effective EU merger control' COM (2014) 449 final.
[50] Commission, 'Mergers: Commission seeks feedback on certain aspects of EU merger control' (IP/16/3337, 7 October 2016).
[51] Ibid.: 'acquisitions of target companies that do not yet generate significant turnover but that have a high market potential, which may be reflected in a high purchase price, do not have to be notified to the Commission'.
[52] Joined Cases C-68/94 and C-30/95, *Kali & Salz*.
[53] Case T-342/99, *Airtours plc v Commission*, EU:T:2002:146.

vertical and conglomerate mergers. As already pointed out, these transactions do not in themselves result in the creation or strengthening of a position of dominance. However, the Commission adopted, from the outset, a steady stream of decisions that were based on the assumption that non-horizontal mergers were subject to Regulation 4064/89. Eventually, the EU courts would accept the principle that vertical and conglomerate transactions could be controlled by the Commission. At the same time, it laid down a series of principles constraining administrative action and going, in this sense, beyond what the authority had defined in its decisions.

A comprehensive analysis of cases relating to the substantive criterion in merger control reveals a difference of views between the Commission and the EU courts concerning the appropriate divide that exists between the aspects that pertain to the legal test as such and about those that pertain to the legal qualification of facts. This difference may be important in practice. As already pointed out, the legal qualification of facts sometimes involves complex economic assessments over which the Commission enjoys a margin of appreciation and which are thus subject to marginal review. On the other hand, the authority does not enjoy any discretion in relation to the definition of the legal test, that is, of the conditions that must be met to establish the incompatibility of a merger with the internal market.

In this regard, the early decision-making practice of the Commission suggests that the authority advanced a relatively broad understanding of the issues that pertain to the legal qualification of facts – and thus over which it may enjoy some discretion. In some key decisions, the arguments were framed in a way that suggested that the conditions to establish a significant impediment to effective competition are not part of the legal test as such. From this perspective, the conditions under which, for instance, a non-horizontal merger would result in the creation of a dominant position would not be, strictly speaking, an issue of law. Accordingly, the Commission could invoke a margin of appreciation not only in relation to the application of the conditions but also to the definition of the legal test as such. Second, the administrative practice under Regulation 4064/89 suggests that the Commission had a preference for unstructured standards (that is, a 'checklist' approach)[54] requiring

[54] Daniel Gore, Stephen Lewis, Andrea Lofaro and Frances Dethmers, *The Economic Assessment of Mergers under European Competition Law* (Cambridge: Cambridge University Press, 2013), pp. 335–7. See also Nicolas Petit, 'The "Oligopoly Problem" in

a case-by-case assessment of how the various conditions are to be applied and weighed against one another. In this sense, its behaviour is not fundamentally different from that described in Chapter 4.

Another notable aspect of EU merger control is the role of exogenous constraints on administrative action in the definition of substantive principles. This becomes apparent, first, in the behaviour of the EU courts. When defining some fundamental substantive aspects of EU merger control, the EU courts relied upon mainstream economic theory. In *Airtours*, the GC unambiguously ruled that the notion of collective dominance had to be interpreted in line with the economic idea of tacit collusion. In *Tetra Laval* and subsequent rulings, the Court endorsed mainstream principles by starting from the assumption that non-horizontal mergers are generally innocuous, if not beneficial, for competition, and that the set of conditions under which they harm the competitive process is relatively narrow.

The impact of mainstream economics can also be noted in the behaviour of the Commission. In this sense, the evolution of the administrative practice is not fundamentally different from the shift observed in the context of Articles 101 and 102 TFEU. It is possible to discern an incremental trend towards the incorporation of insights from economic theory and practice. In relation to horizontal mergers, this trend is reflected, in particular, in the acknowledgement of the limits of structural factors (such as market shares) as a proxy for the impact of transactions on effective competition. In relation to non-horizontal mergers, the evolution of the administrative practice reflects increased awareness of the fact that these transactions can lead to efficiency gains and that these could be negated if firms were penalised for becoming more efficient than their rivals. As shown in Figure 5.3, this trend has resulted in a shift in the understanding of the notion of effects. As the administrative practice evolved, effects became equated less with the market structure and more with the impact on equally efficient competitors.

3.1.2 Case Selection

The dynamic analysis below focuses on the three categories of concentrations: those giving rise to the creation and strengthening of a collective dominant position, non-horizontal mergers and those leading to a significant impediment to effective competition without them resulting

EU Competition Law' in Ioannis Lianos and Damien Geradin (eds.), *Handbook of European Competition Law – Substantive Aspects* (Cheltenham: Edward Elgar, 2013).

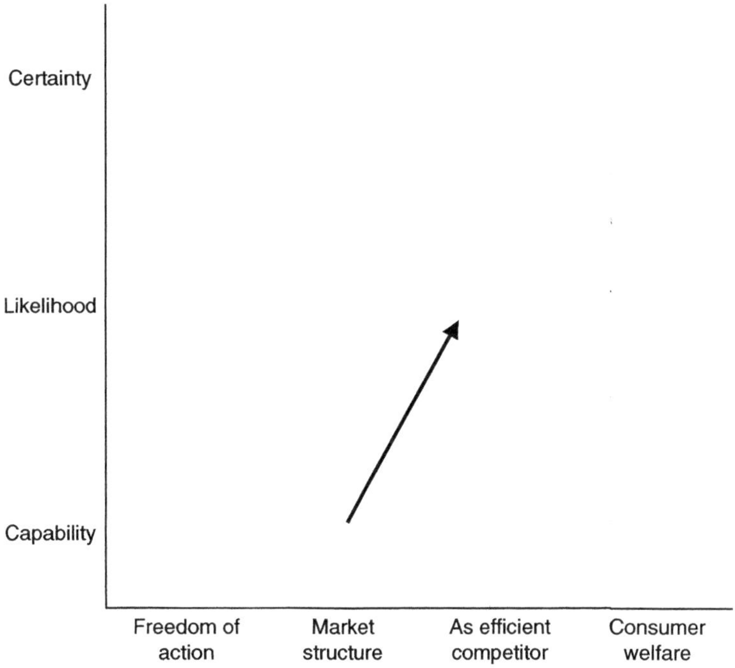

Figure 5.3 Evolution in the assessment of merger effects by the Commission

in the creation or the strengthening of a position of dominance. The choices seem obvious for several reasons. The issues raised by these transactions have been the most relevant for the definition of the substantive criterion applying in EU merger control. Moreover – and this is something that becomes already apparent from the discussion above – the three questions make it possible to examine, from a dynamic perspective, the behaviour of the Commission at the level of the drafting of legislation and the level of the interpretation of the provision.

3.2 *Collective Dominance and Tacit Collusion*

3.2.1 The Commission Approach to Collective Dominance under Regulation 4064/89

In the case law of the EU courts, the notion of collective dominance refers to an instance in which the members of a tight oligopoly have the ability and incentive to coordinate their behaviour, and thus to adopt a common course of conduct on the relevant market, without necessarily resorting to an agreement or a concerted practice.[55] This notion, typically – at the very least in the field of merger control – has come to be associated with the economic concept of tacit collusion.[56] The enforcement of the successive Regulations to instances of oligopolistic interdependence, and the definition of the notion of collective dominance around a distinct concept that captures a consensus position, is the outcome of a process in which the Commission tested the boundaries of Regulation 4064/89, both from a legal and an economic perspective.

The question of whether the said Regulation could be enforced to prevent the creation or the strengthening of a collective dominant position was in fact not a straightforward one. The letter of Article 2, which encapsulated the substantive criterion for the assessment of concentrations, did not expressly rule out that Regulation 4064/89 was applicable to the anti-competitive effects resulting from the interaction between the members of an oligopoly. It left the issue open to interpretation by the EU courts. On the other hand, the Regulation and its Preamble could be interpreted as suggesting that the substantive scope of Article 2 was confined to the creation and strengthening of positions of single dominance. In particular, Article 2(1) gave the impression that the compatibility of transactions was to be assessed by reference to the market position of the merging parties.[57] Similarly, the Preamble laid down a presumption of compatibility for concentrations where the market share falls below 25 per cent.[58] Arguably, the fact that the substantive

[55] See in this sense the Horizontal Merger Guidelines, para. 39: 'In some markets the structure may be such that firms would consider it possible, economically rational, and hence preferable, to adopt on a sustainable basis a course of action on the market aimed at selling at increased prices. A merger in a concentrated market may significantly impede effective competition, through the creation or the strengthening of a collective dominant position, because it increases the likelihood that firms are able to coordinate their behaviour in this way and raise prices, even without entering into an agreement or resorting to a concerted practice within the meaning of Article [101] of the Treaty'.

[56] See in this sense Luis Ortiz Blanco, *Market Power in EU Antitrust Law* (Oxford: Hart Publishing, 2011); and, in particular, Nicolas Petit, *Oligopoles, collusion tacite et droit communautaire de la concurrence* (Bruxelles: Bruylant, 2007).

[57] Article 2(1)(b) indeed referred to the 'the market position of the undertakings concerned and their economic and financial power'.

[58] It was indicated in the preamble that 'concentrations which, by reason of the limited market share of the undertakings concerned, are not liable to impede effective competition may be presumed to be compatible with the common market; whereas, without prejudice to Articles 85 and 86 of the Treaty, an indication to this effect exists, in particular, where the market share of the undertakings concerned does not exceed 25% either in the common market or in a substantial part of it'.

criterion was narrowed down from the early legislative proposals submitted by the Commission also supports this conclusion.

The application of Regulation 4064/89 to tight oligopolies was a complex issue for two additional reasons. One complication related to the scope of the powers enjoyed by the Commission. From an economic perspective, there is a consensus about the instances in which tacit collusion is likely to arise and be sustained.[59] Against this background, the immediate question was whether administrative action should be constrained by the limits that would logically derive from economic theory. The question, in other words, was whether a competition authority could raise concerns about coordination in a tight oligopoly even when mainstream positions would suggest that tacit collusion is unlikely to be sustained. In the same vein, it was open to question – at least in theory – whether the competition authority enjoys (some) discretion over the conditions under which a collective dominant position arises or whether the issue is subject to the full review of courts. It may be argued that, insofar as it involves complex economic assessments, the task lies primarily with the authority, which would benefit from a margin of appreciation.

A third challenge related to the actual assessment of collective dominant positions in concrete scenarios. The analysis of the impact of these practices on competition is necessarily more complex than the assessment of non-coordinated effects (and in particular the creation or strengthening of a position of single dominance). This is so because the anti-competitive impact of the transaction does not depend, alone, on the behaviour of the merged entity. It would in addition be necessary to show not only that all players on the market would have an incentive to coordinate their conduct, but that they would have the ability to do so on a sustainable basis. As a result, a competition authority faces issues of proof that may not be present (or may be far less prominent) in other contexts.

After some cases in which the question was raised but the issue left open,[60] the Commission, in line with the behaviour observed in other areas, advanced an expansive interpretation of the scope of Regulation

[59] Marc Ivaldi, Bruno Jullien, Patrick Rey, Paul Seabright and Jean Tirole, *The Economics of Tacit Collusion*, Final Report for DG Competition (March 2003).

[60] See in this sense Commission Decision 91/595/EEC of 31 July 1991 (Case No IV/M.12 – *Varta/Bosch*) OJ (1991) No. L 320/26; Commission Decision of 18 December 1991 (Case No IV/M.165 – *Alcatel/AEG Kabel*); Commission Decision of 27 April 1992 (Case IV/M.202 – *Thorn EMI/Virgin*). These cases are discussed in Antoine Winckler and

4064/89. In *Nestlé/Perrier*[61] it argued that, absent remedial action, the concentration would have given rise to the emergence of a position of 'duopolistic dominance' on the French market for bottled sourced water. In its analysis, the Commission rejected the arguments of Nestlé to the effect that Regulation 4064/89 did not cover collective dominant positions. As it did in the context of Article 102 TFEU (suffice it to think of a case like *Continental Can*), it referred to the system of undistorted competition created by virtue of the Treaty to justify the application of the Regulation beyond instances of single dominance.[62] Similarly, the Commission argued that collective dominance can impede effective competition.[63] The transaction, which was cleared with remedies, was challenged by the employees of the firm. However, the GC did not go beyond procedural matters in its analysis.[64]

Some of the challenges mentioned above were already apparent in *Nestlé/Perrier*. On the one hand, it was unclear from the decision how the Commission intended to apply Article 2 of the Regulation to instances of collective dominance. In particular, it was not clear whether it intended to examine the question on a case-by-case basis (that is, following a 'checklist' approach)[65] or whether, instead, it intended to apply a fixed set of operational conditions across the board. Under a 'checklist' approach, the conditions to establish a position of collective dominance would pertain to the legal characterisation of facts, and thus would give the Commission a margin of appreciation. In other words, it would be an approach under which the authority would enjoy some leeway to decide, on a case-by-case basis, the exact boundaries of the notion of collective dominance. Under the second approach, the conditions would be part of the legal test, that is, an issue of law in the strict sense of the word. A second challenge came from the fact that *Nestlé/Perrier* did not clarify the requisite threshold of effects. In particular, the decision left open the

Marc Hansen, 'Collective Dominance under the EC Merger Control Regulation' (1993) 30 *Common Market Law Review* 787.

61 Commission Decision 92/553/EEC of 22 July 1992 (Case No IV/M.190 – *Nestlé/Perrier*) OJ (1992) No. L 356/1.

62 Ibid., para. 113. 63 Ibid., para. 114.

64 Case T-12/93, *Comité Central d'Entreprise de la Société Anonyme Vittel and Comité d'Etablissement de Pierval and Fédération Générale Agroalimentaire v Commission.*

65 For an analysis of the question, see Europe Economics, 'Study on Assessment Criteria for Distinguishing between Competitive and Dominant Oligopolies in Merger Control', Report for the Directorate General for Enterprise (May 2001).

question of whether a threshold of plausibility would be sufficient to take action.[66]

In *Kali & Salz*, the Court declared unambiguously – and in line with the position of the Commission – that Regulation 4064/89 applied to concentrations leading to the creation or the strengthening of a collective dominant position. In this regard, the Court departed from the position of the Advocate General, for whom the letter of the Regulation and its legislative history suggested that it was only intended to apply to positions of single dominance.[67] In relation to the other two issues, however, the ruling in *Kali & Salz* did not address all questions with equal clarity. The Court recognised that the Commission enjoys 'certain discretion' in relation to 'assessments of an economic nature'.[68] It was not clear from the ruling whether this discretion extended to the definition of the conditions under which the creation or the strengthening of a position of collective dominance – as defined by the Court[69] – is to be expected, or whether discretion was confined to the legal characterisation of facts in the context of the particular case.

The uncertainty around these questions was not dissipated when the Commission decision in *Gencor* was challenged before the GC.[70] This judgment clarified that the notion of collective dominance within the meaning of Regulation 4064/89 covered – as the Commission argued in the case – instances of tacit collusion. In this sense, the requisite economic links for a collective dominant position to exist need not be of a structural nature, contrary to what some Article 102 TFEU rulings suggested at the time.[71] Thus, such a position can be established if it is shown that the relevant market is conducive to sustained coordination among the members of the oligopoly. On the other hand, the GC did not clarify whether the Commission enjoys some discretion over the

66 See Winckler and Hansen, 'Collective Dominance under the EC Merger Control Regulation', 828.

67 Opinion of AG Tesauro in Joined Cases C-68/94 and C-30/95, *France and Société commerciale des potasses et de l'azote and Entreprise minière et chimique v Commission*, EU:C:1997:54 ('*Kali & Salz*'), paras. 78–98.

68 Joined Cases C-68/94 and C-30/95, *Kali & Salz*, para. 223.

69 It would seem that the Court assessed the creation or strengthening of a collective dominant position by reference to the framework crafted by the Commission. See in this sense ibid., para. 180.

70 Case T-102/96, *Gencor Ltd v Commission*, EU:T:1999:65.

71 Ibid., paras. 273–83. The applicant referred to Joined Cases T-68/89, T-77/89 and T-78/89, *Società Italiana Vetro SpA, Fabbrica Pisana SpA and PPG Vernante Pennitalia SpA v Commission*, EU:T:1992:38.

definition of the conditions under which collective dominance is likely to emerge and/or over the application of these conditions.

The lack of clarity on this point was readily identified at the time by González Díaz, then a civil servant in charge of the assessment of mergers. He noted that the GC, in *Gencor*, did not question either the 'theoretical framework' or the 'basic criteria' identified by the Commission to establish collective dominance.[72] Indeed, both the GC and the applicants in the case accepted the principles laid down in the contested decision without challenging them. The applicants did not argue that the conditions identified by the Commission were not in line with the case law and/or economic theory; they argued instead that they were not in line with past administrative practice. The GC, in turn, did not define the benchmark against which the lawfulness of the decision would be assessed. The judgment provides a high-level definition of the concept, and then goes on to review the application of the conditions that the Commission itself deemed relevant. Thus, the GC failed to examine whether these conditions, or the underlying approach to the assessment of collective dominance in the decision, were the correct framework to establish a position of collective dominance.

3.2.2 *Airtours* and Mainstream Economics

The uncertainties around the scope of the notion of collective dominance and about its assessment in concrete scenarios would be dissipated in *Airtours*. In that case, the Commission blocked a transaction in an industry in which, mainstream economic theory suggested, tacit collusion was unlikely to arise and/or be sustained. The case concerned a merger between two tour operators based in the UK.[73] As noted by several commentators at the time, this is a sector that presents certain characteristics that limit the ability of the members of the oligopoly to coordinate their conduct on a lasting basis.[74] Suffice it to mention that the product affected by the transaction is not a homogenous one; that

[72] F. Enrique González Díaz, 'Recent Developments in EC Merger Control Law – The Gencor Judgment' (1999) 22 *World Competition* 3.

[73] Commission Decision 2000/276/EC of 22 September 1999 (Case IV/M.1524 – *Airtours/ First Choice*) OJ (2000) No. L 93/1.

[74] See in particular Juan Briones and Jorge Padilla, 'The Complex Landscape of Oligopolies under EU Competition Policy – Is Collective Dominance Ripe for Guidelines?' (2001) 24 *World Competition* 307, at 309–310 ('Leisure travel services and holiday packages generally do not seem to present the characteristics of mature, stable markets where the leading players face similar cost and demand conditions, and the products present little

demand for it is volatile; and, more importantly, that oligopolists lacked the mechanisms to retaliate against firms deviating from a common course of conduct.

According to the Commission, these factors did not necessarily exclude the finding that the transaction created or strengthened a position of collective dominance. The *Airtours* decision appeared to suggest that a finding of collective dominance may still be possible if it can be shown that the operation increases the incentives of the oligopolists to coordinate their conduct. As observed by commentators at the time, this position entails a deviation from mainstream positions in two main ways. On the one hand, the analysis of the Commission appeared to lower the requisite threshold of probability of an anti-competitive effect. The decision implied that intervention could be justified if coordination is a plausible (as opposed to likely) outcome. On the other hand (and perhaps more importantly), the Commission appeared to downplay the relevance of the factors relating to the ability (as opposed to the incentive) of firms to coordinate their conduct.

From an economic perspective, one key consequence of the position expressed by the Commission in *Airtours* is that a finding of collective dominance would be possible in virtually every oligopolistic market insofar as firms generally have an incentive to coordinate their conduct (in the same way that they typically have an incentive to deviate from it).[75] In this sense, the decision seemingly failed to acknowledge that the ability to coordinate is what gives the concept of tacit collusion a distinct and operational meaning. From a legal perspective, the interpretation of the concept of collective dominance sketched by the Commission in *Airtours* became a source of uncertainty. Once the legal concept departed from the boundaries defined by the economic notion of tacit collusion, it became difficult to anticipate the instances in which a concentration in a tight oligopoly would raise concerns. If the factors identified by the Commission in its 'checklist' were to be applied on a case-by-case basis in an unstructured way, any merger could be blocked, at least in theory.

scope for differentiation'); and 'The Airtours case', Lexecon Competition Memo (November 1999).

75 Briones and Jorge Padilla, 'The Complex Landscape of Oligopolies under EU Competition Policy', at 311 ('It is indeed difficult to conceive a situation where the members of an oligopoly would not have an objective incentive to constrain capacity down to the level of optimal production by a monopolist').

This is the background against which the GC examined the legality of the Commission decision in *Airtours*. The judgment is notable in that the GC made it explicit, from the outset, that the legal concept of collective dominance was to be interpreted in line with the economic notion of tacit collusion. In this same vein, it laid down the framework for the assessment of the phenomenon in concrete cases. The GC's approach in the case represented a departure from the behaviour observed in *Gencor* or *Kali & Salz*, where the EU courts accepted as given the conditions and analysis set out in the decision. The approach in *Airtours* suggests that review courts may be more willing to depart from the applicable legal framework defended by the competition authority where economic theory provides a sound operational benchmark (in particular when the administrative authority ostensibly departs from it). In this sense, the behaviour of the GC in *Airtours* is comparable to that observed in *AKZO*, where the Court resorted to an economically informed test that had become a golden standard.

The three conditions laid down by the GC in *Airtours*[76] place an emphasis on the ability of the members of the oligopoly to coordinate their conduct on a sustainable basis. In this sense, the GC pointed out that it would not be sufficient to show that coordination is a profitable course of conduct for the remaining firms. It would be necessary to establish, in addition, that each of the firms has the 'means of knowing whether the other operators are adopting the same strategy and whether they are maintaining it' and that there are 'adequate deterrents to ensure that there is a long-term incentive in not departing from the common policy'.[77] The annulment of the decision seemed inevitable considering that the Commission decision was grounded, in several key respects, on conflicting premises about the meaning and scope of the notion of collective dominance. The judgment emphasised that the industry presented a degree of volatility that was incompatible with sustained collusion.[78] It also acknowledged, in the same vein, that the industry was subject to exogenous shocks,[79] and that some of the practices made it difficult to monitor the behaviour of rivals.[80] The evolution of market shares in the preceding years, in turn, suggested that the industry was competitive and thus sat at odds

[76] Case T-341/99, *Airtours*, para. 62. [77] Ibid. [78] Ibid., in particular paras. 134–47.
[79] Ibid., paras. 137–45. [80] Ibids., paras. 157–80.

with the assumption that firms lacked the ability and incentive to compete with each other.[81]

Following the annulment of the *Airtours* decision, the Commission took measures on the substantive and the institutional side. From a substantive perspective, it issued, immediately following the adoption of Regulation 139/2004, a set of Guidelines dealing with the assessment of coordinated effects in the context of horizontal mergers.[82] Demand for a soft law instrument had been recurrent following the uncertainties created by *Airtours* and similar decisions.[83] The Horizontal Merger Guidelines are in line with the position taken by the GC and represent an unambiguous commitment to the interpretation of the notion of collective dominance in line with mainstream economic principles. The same approach to collective dominance was endorsed in another soft law instrument, applicable to non-horizontal mergers and published in 2008.[84]

The administrative practice that followed the *Airtours* decision has not been questioned on fundamental grounds. The challenge brought by Impala against the Commission Decision in *Sony/BMG*[85] did not change the basic principles that apply to these transactions. The dispute – and the disagreement between the GC[86] and the Court[87] – concerned the legal characterisation of facts, not the definition of the analytical framework as such. In fact, the appeal judgment appeared to confirm some of the key aspects that led to the annulment of the *Airtours* decision. In particular, the Court endorsed the conditions set out by the GC and emphasised that the various factors that are conducive to tacit collusion must not be examined in isolation – or following a 'checklist' or 'mechanical' approach – but as part of a coherent conceptual framework.[88]

The institutional developments that followed the *Airtours* judgment are, if anything, more relevant. They revealed a willingness to endorse

[81] Ibid., paras. 109–19. [82] Horizontal Merger Guidelines OJ (2004) No. C 31/5.

[83] See in this sense Briones and Jorge Padilla, 'The Complex Landscape of Oligopolies under EU Competition Policy'.

[84] Guidelines on the assessment of non-horizontal mergers under the Council Regulation on the control of concentrations between undertakings OJ (2008) No. C 265/6 ('Non-Horizontal Merger Guidelines'), para. 19.

[85] Commission Decision 2005/188/EC of 19 July 2004 (Case No COMP/M.3333 – *Sony/BMG*) OJ (2005) No. L 62/30.

[86] Case T-464/04, *Impala*. [87] Case C-413/06 P, *Impala*.

[88] Ibid., para. 125: 'it is necessary to avoid a mechanical approach involving the separate verification of each of those criteria taken in isolation, while taking no account of the overall economic mechanism of a hypothetical tacit coordination'.

mainstream economic principles in a way that is more profound than the adoption of pre-commitment devices. In a speech delivered a few months after the *Airtours* ruling, Commissioner Mario Monti announced that DG Comp was considering the creation of an office of a chief competition economist that would head a team of experts and would provide support and independent advice to the various case teams.[89] In his speech, the Commissioner made an explicit reference to the 2002 judgments annulling the three GC decisions, including *Airtours*.[90] The position would be created a year later, in 2003.[91] As part of the activities of the office, the Economic Advisory Group on Competition Policy intended to provide advice on some policy issues (including the review of the policy of the Commission towards unilateral practices and non-horizontal mergers).

3.3 *Non-Horizontal Mergers*

3.3.1 Non-Horizontal Mergers and the Scope of EU Merger Control

The analytical framework described in Section 1 of this chapter can be applied more readily to horizontal than to non-horizontal mergers. In the context of a horizontal merger, the various meanings that can be attached to the notion of anti-competitive effects (market structure, impact on equally efficient competitors, consumer welfare) are discrete points in a continuum. In this sense, they are not fundamentally at odds with one another. Thus, a change in the market structure resulting from the elimination of a competitor can be taken as a – more or less accurate – proxy for its impact on the various parameters of competition and on consumer welfare. Once the competitive constraint coming from a direct rival is eliminated, it is not unreasonable to presume that the new entity will have the ability and the incentive to raise prices. The use of these

[89] Mario Monti, 'EU Competition Policy' (Fordham Annual Conference on International Antitrust Law and Policy, New York, 31 October 2002).

[90] In fact, the creation of the office of the Chief Competition Economist is widely considered to be the consequence of the annulment of the Commission decisions in *Airtours* and *Tetra Laval*. In his abovementioned speech, the Commissioner noted that '[w]e are increasingly confronted with the need to investigate complex cases, which require in-depth fact-finding and rigorous economic and/or econometric analysis. The CFI Judgements confirm this need. We are therefore discussing measures aimed at further strengthening the economic expertise capabilities of the Competition DG'.

[91] See Lars-Hendrik Röller and Pierre A. Buigues, 'The Office of the Chief Competition Economist at the European Commission' (May 2005).

proxies is misleading and thus problematic in the context of a non-horizontal merger. This is so for two main reasons.

To begin with, the change in the market structure entailed by a non-horizontal transaction is not a powerful indicator of the elimination of a competitive constraint and thus of an increase in the market power of the merged entity. Because the merging parties are not in a direct competitive relationship, the ability and incentive of the remaining firms to compete may remain wholly unaffected by the concentration. If anything, a change in the market structure in the context of a non-horizontal merger may well lead to a decrease in prices. This is so not only because such mergers do not, in and of themselves, reduce the competitive constraints faced by firms, but because they are also known to be a source of efficiency gains. For instance, it is known that a vertical merger can bring prices down by effectively addressing what is known as the double marginalisation problem.[92] A conglomerate merger involving complementary products, in turn, can allow the merged entity to exploit the economies of scope generated by the transaction.

The practical consequence of the above is that neither harm to consumers nor the elimination of a competitive constraint in the markets affected by the transaction can be presumed from the change in the market structure entailed by a merger. By the same token, it is not obvious to assume that non-horizontal concentrations fall within the scope of EU merger control. After all, they do not in themselves – or at least not directly – have anti-competitive effects. Such effects can only be expected where the merged entity has the ability and incentive to engage in a foreclosure strategy. If there is evidence that market foreclosure is a likely outcome, the competitive constraints coming from rivals could be eliminated or disappear. Put differently, the effects of the non-horizontal merger could, in these circumstances, be the same as those observed in the context of a horizontal concentration.

There is an additional factor that further complicates the assessment of non-horizontal mergers. The very foreclosure concerns that may justify intervention may also give rise to pro-competitive effects. Pro- and anti-

[92] See in this sense the Non-Horizontal Merger Guidelines, para. 13: 'In vertical relationships for instance, as a result of the complementarity, a decrease in mark-ups downstream will lead to higher demand also upstream. A part of the benefit of this increase in demand will accrue to the upstream suppliers. An integrated firm will take this benefit into account. Vertical integration may thus provide an increased incentive to seek to decrease prices and increase output because the integrated firm can capture a larger fraction of the benefits'.

competitive effects, in other words, cannot be dissociated from one another in this context; they are two sides of the same coin.[93] Rivals may be foreclosed from the relevant market due to the very efficiency gains resulting from the transaction. For instance, the new entity may be in a position to offer a better, integrated product, which substantially improves existing goods offered by rivals. In *Intel/McAfee*, for instance, the Commission pointed out that the transaction could allow the merged entity to embed security solutions directly in the microprocessors.[94] As a result of this very improvement, rivals, following the merger, may lack the ability and incentive to compete effectively on the market. If the elimination of competition is the consequence of the superior efficiency of the merged entity, examining the impact of the transaction on the market structure does not provide a reliable idea about its impact on consumer welfare. In fact, if intervention seeking to protect the market structure penalises efficiency, it may well make consumers worse off.

Against this background, it seems clear that the meaning that is given to the notion of effects can have a very significant impact on the shaping of EU merger control law. It is also clear that it is a challenge to define the notion in a way that captures adequately the ambivalent (pro- and anti-competitive) nature of non-horizontal mergers. For instance, an approach to anti-competitive effects that equates the notion with rival foreclosure and ignores the efficiency potential of vertical and conglomerate transactions lends itself easily to criticism. This approach would amount to an endorsement of the 'efficiency offence' insofar as the pro-competitive aspects of the transaction would be relied upon to justify a negative outcome.[95] It would also be criticised for being at odds with mainstream economics. In any event, alternative approaches are not

[93] This is a point elaborated in Simon Bishop, Andrea Lofaro and Francesco Rosati, 'Turning the tables: why vertical and conglomerate mergers are different' (2006) 27 *European Competition Law Review* 403.

[94] Commission Decision of 26 January 2011 (Case COMP/M.5984 – *Intel/McAfee*).

[95] On the concept of 'efficiency offence', see Philippa Watson, 'Portfolio Effects in EC Merger Law' (2003) 48 *Antitrust Bulletin* 781; and Massimo Motta and Helder Vasconcelos, 'Efficiency gains and myopic antitrust authority in a dynamic merger game' (2005) 23 *International Journal of Industrial Organization* 777. See also Mario Monti, 'Review of the EC Merger Regulation – Roadmap for the reform project' (Conference on Reform of European Merger Control, Brussels, June 4, 2002), where the commissioner stated that 'there is no such thing as a so-called "efficiency offence" in EU merger control law and practice. In other words, the Commission does not rely on the fact that efficiencies resulting from a merger are likely to have the effect of reducing or eliminating competition in the relevant market (for example, by enabling lower prices to be charged to customers), as a ground for opposing a proposed transaction'.

without difficulties. If effects are equated with consumer welfare, for instance, the evaluation of transactions in concrete scenarios would involve a case-by-case balancing of its pro- and anti-competitive effects.[96] Such an approach may not be easily administrable.

3.3.2 Commission Practice under Regulation 4064/89

A look at the practice of the Commission reveals that, from the outset, the authority considered that Regulation 4064/89 was applicable to non-horizontal transactions. Some examples can be traced back to the very early days of the system[97]. In *ICI/Tioxide*, the Commission examined for the first time the compatibility with Regulation 4064/89 of a vertical merger.[98] The transaction involved the acquisition of control of a producer of titanium dioxide by its largest customer. After considering the horizontal aspects, the Commission examined the likelihood of foreclosure. In this regard, it noted that the position of the downstream company would not be strengthened as a result of the transaction, as paint producers would have alternative sources of supply and titanium dioxide is not an important input in terms of costs.[99] In *Matsushita/MCA*, the Commission considered for the first time the compatibility of a conglomerate transaction with the internal market. The concentration involved a producer of videocassette tape recorders and a media company.[100] The Commission argued that the conglomerate effects of mergers fell within the scope of Article 2 of the Regulation.[101] In the specific circumstances of the case, however, it concluded that leveraging was an unlikely prospect.[102]

One of the themes that emerges from this early practice relates to the assessment of efficiencies. The vocabulary used by the Commission in *Matsushita/MCA* suggests that the competitive advantages gained by the parties (that is, their superior efficiency) may be a concern and could justify intervention. According to the decision, the relevant question when examining the effects of a conglomerate transaction is whether the merged entity would be in such an 'advantageous position' that

[96] See in this sense Simon Bishop, Andrea Lofaro, Francesco Rosati and Juliet Young, *The Efficiency-Enhancing Effects of Non-Horizontal Mergers* (Report prepared by RBB Economics for the Directorate General for Enterprise and Industry, 2005).

[97] For an overview, see Frank L. Fine, 'The Appraisal Criteria of the EC Merger Control Regulation' (1991) 12 *European Competition Law Review* 148.

[98] Commission Decision of 28 November 1990 (Case IV/M.23 – *ICI/Tioxide*).

[99] Ibid., paras. 18–20.

[100] Commission Decision of 10 January 1991 (Case IV/M.37 – *Matsushita/MCA*).

[101] Ibid., para. 6. [102] Ibid., paras. 11–2.

a dominant position would be created in one of the horizontally related markets.[103] Hints at the endorsement of an 'efficiency offence' would become recurrent in subsequent years. Commentators[104] tend to illustrate this idea by reference to a series of mergers in the drinks and spirit industry, including *Coca-Cola/Amalgamated Beverages*[105] and *Guinness/Grand Metropolitan.*[106] In the latter, the concerns expressed by the Commission related not only to the horizontal overlaps it identified, but to the fact that the transaction would give rise to 'portfolio effects', that is, that it would harm competition due to the merged entity's unparalleled presence across all major categories of spirits. According to the decision, this competitive advantage, which rivals would have been unable to match, would have led, absent remedial action, to the creation of a dominant position on one of the product markets.[107]

The analytical approach towards non-horizontal mergers during this early period is summarised in Figure 5.4. One notable aspect is that there is no systematic analysis of the ability and incentive of the merged entity to engage in a foreclosure strategy. Accordingly, concerns could be raised without considering whether rivals would be marginalised as a result of the transaction. The mere fact that the merged entity would enjoy a competitive advantage – or the mere prospect of a foreclosure strategy – was deemed sufficient to conclude to the creation or strengthening of a dominant position on one or more of the relevant markets. Under this approach, the fact that the merged entity would be in a position to lower its prices, for instance, would justify intervention, and this irrespective of whether lower prices would in fact intensify (and not harm) rivalry among the remaining firms. On the other hand, the Regulation did not leave any room – at least not formally – for the assessment of the efficiency gains generated by a transaction.[108] As shown in the figure, the focus of the

[103] Ibid., para. 14: 'It is therefore necessary to consider whether MEI will, after the takeover of MCA, be in such an advantageous position that the creation of a dominant position on future video equipment markets (as increasingly affected by HDTV technology) is likely'.

[104] See in particular Barry Nalebuff and David Majerus, 'Bundling, Tying, and Portfolio Effects: Part 2 – Case Studies' (2003) DTI Economics Paper No. 1.

[105] Commission Decision 97/540/EC of 22 January 1997 (Case IV/M.794 – *Coca-Cola/Amalgamated Beverages GB*) OJ (1997) No. L 218/15.

[106] Commission Decision 98/602/EC of 15 October 1997 (Case IV/M.938 – *Guinness/Grand Metropolitan*) OJ (1998) No. L 288/24.

[107] Ibid., paras. 91–103.

[108] Green Paper on the Review of Council Regulation (EEC) No. 4064/89 COM(2001) 745, para. 170.

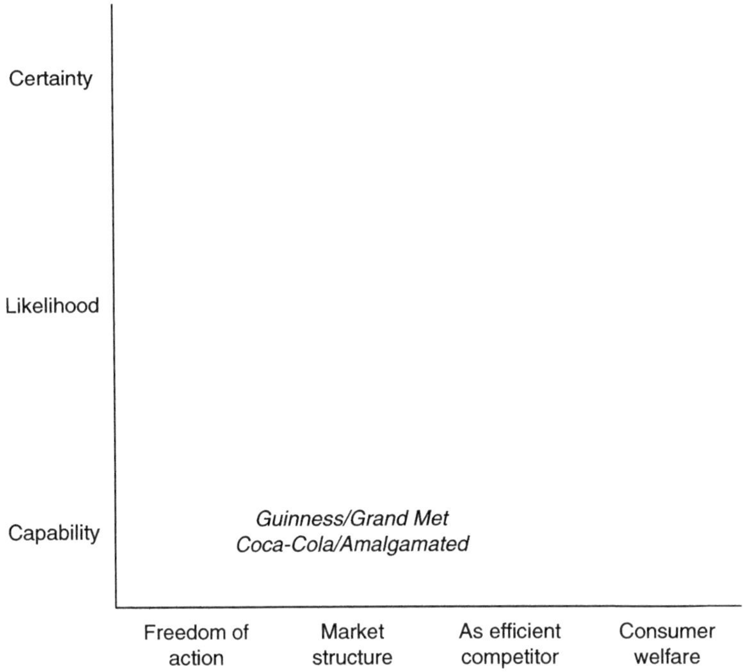

Figure 5.4 The assessment of conglomerate mergers before *Tetra Laval*

analysis is on the market structure. Because the creation and/or strengthening of a dominant position was inferred from the mere existence of a competitive advantage or from the mere prospect of a foreclosure strategy, the analysis of the anti-competitive effects of the merger did not go beyond a threshold of plausibility.

3.3.3 *Tetra Laval, GE/Honeywell* and Mainstream Economics

In the challenges brought against the Commission decisions in *Tetra Laval/Sidel*[109] and *General Electric/Honeywell*,[110] the EU courts confirmed the applicability of Regulation 4064/89 to non-horizontal mergers insofar as these transactions could create or strengthen a dominant position.[111] However, the analytical framework crafted by the GC – validated, by and large, on appeal by the ECJ – differed in fundamental

[109] Commission Decision 2004/124/EC of 30 October 2001 (Case No COMP/M. 2416 – *Tetra Laval/Sidel*) OJ (2009) No. L 43/13.

[110] Commission Decision 2004/134/EC of 3 July 2001 (Case COMP/M.2220 – *General Electric/Honeywell*) OJ (2004) No. L 48/1.

[111] Case T-5/02, *Tetra Laval*, paras. 146–7; and Case C-12/03, *Tetra Laval*, paras. 37–51.

ways from the approach favoured by the Commission. It is therefore not surprising that the GC found that the analysis in the two abovementioned decisions was vitiated by manifest errors of assessment, which in the case of *Tetra Laval/Sidel* led to the annulment of the decision. Judicial review was directly inspired from mainstream economic principles. In particular, the GC noted that the change in the market structure entailed by a non-horizontal merger does not necessarily have anti-competitive effects[112] and that such transactions may turn out to be pro-competitive.[113]

As a preliminary point, the GC emphasised the need to establish that the merger would lead to the creation or the strengthening of a dominant position in the foreseeable future. This analysis presupposes the identification of a mechanism through which foreclosure would occur and of the incentive of the merged entity to engage in an anti-competitive strategy. Only following these steps could the analysis proceed to the anti-competitive effects of the transaction. In this regard, the EU courts conceded that, even when plausible, foreclosure may not occur, and that a scenario in which competition is foreclosed is not necessarily the only plausible one. In other words, the review courts made it clear that the mere plausibility of a foreclosure strategy is insufficient to take action. It is in this context that the issues of proof and probability described above become of particular importance.

The divergence between the approach favoured by the Commission and that endorsed by the EU courts is best illustrated by reference to *GE/Honeywell*. Even though the decision was not annulled, the GC found that the analysis of the non-horizontal aspects of the transaction did not stand up to scrutiny. According to the Commission, the concentration was a source of competition concerns, inter alia, because the merged entity would have the ability and incentive to engage in a variety of bundling strategies.[114] The thrust of the case was based on the idea,

[112] Ibid., para. 150: 'The Court observes that, in principle, a merger between undertakings which are active on distinct markets is not usually of such a nature as immediately to create or strengthen a dominant position due to the combination of the market shares held by the parties to the merger. The factors which are of significance for the relative positions of competitors within a given market are generally to be found within the market itself, namely in particular the market shares held by the competitors and the conditions of competition on the market. It does not follow, however, that the conditions of competition on a market can never be affected by factors external to that market'.

[113] Ibid., para. 155 ('the effects of a conglomerate-type merger are generally considered to be neutral, or even beneficial, for competition on the markets concerned').

[114] Ibid., paras. 350–404.

already present in decisions like *Guinness/Grand Metropolitan*, that the said entity would enjoy a unique position vis-à-vis its customers due to the complementary nature of the products covered by the merger and its leading position on several of the relevant markets.[115]

In spite of these advantages, the GC noted, from the outset, that bundling strategies, while not wholly implausible, did not appear to be prima facie likely on the relevant markets insofar as they went against the '*modus operandi*' of the sector.[116] One necessary consequence is that an 'additional commercial effort' would be required from the merged entity to ensure the success of these strategies. In relation, for instance, to pure bundling, the GC stressed that compelling customers to acquire a set of complementary products need not be viable or profitable, as the latter may develop counterstrategies, or be more inclined to acquire a rival product as a result.[117] Another consequence is that any claims about the likelihood of changes to the '*modus operandi*' in the industry following the merger would need to be established convincingly by the Commission. In relation to technical bundling, for instance, the GC noted that such a strategy had not yet been implemented in the relevant market. As a result, remedial action cannot be justified simply because the prospect of the merged entity engaging in it is deemed plausible. The Commission would need to carry out an analysis based on the features of the relevant market and to show not only why such a development would be likely, but also why it would result in the creation or the strengthening of a dominant position.[118]

Equally interesting is to consider the way in which the Commission framed the discussion about the substantive criterion in its appeal against the GC judgment in *Tetra Laval* before the ECJ. As in *GE/Honeywell*, there were major differences between the approach of the Commission and that set out in the first instance judgment. According to the decision in *Tetra Laval*, the change in the market structure immediately brought

[115] Ibid., para. 349: 'The complementary nature of the GE and Honeywell product offerings coupled with their respective existing market positions will give the merged entity the ability and the economically rational incentive to engage in bundled offers or cross-subsidisation across product sales to both categories of customers'.

[116] Case T-210/01, *General Electric Company v Commission*, EU:T:2005:456, para. 415.

[117] Ibid., para. 423 ('if the merged entity were to adopt the extreme commercial stance represented by pure bundling, which is tantamount to a threat to refuse to supply, customers might prefer to use another product, even an inferior one, instead of the former Honeywell's EGPWS, rather than accept an engine which is not their engine of choice').

[118] Ibid., paras. 427–30.

about by the transaction, and the fact that the entity would have the ability and the incentive to foreclose competition, justified a finding of incompatibility with the internal market.[119] Inevitably, the GC, which endorsed a different analytical framework, found that the factors identified by the Commission were insufficient to substantiate a prohibition decision. In its analysis, the review court repeatedly pointed out that the Commission had not established that the merger would have led, in the foreseeable future, to the creation of a dominant position on the relevant neighbouring markets.[120]

Interestingly, the primary argument raised by the Commission in its appeal did not relate to the interpretation of Regulation 4064/89 but to the requisite standard of proof for the review of administrative action. The Commission suggested that the annulment of the decision was due to the endorsement by the GC of a standard of proof departing from the one introduced by the Court in *Kali & Salz*. According to the Commission, the 'convincing evidence' standard allegedly introduced in the first instance judgment ignored the margin of appreciation of the authority when it engages in complex economic assessments. In addition, the introduction of a more stringent standard would result in the review court substituting its own views for those of the Commission, which would go beyond the control of the legality of administrative action.[121] In doing so, the administrative authority framed the issue as one pertaining to the legal characterisation of facts – as opposed to being an issue of law.

[119] Commission Decision 2004/124/EC of 30 October 2001, *Tetra Laval/Sidel*, para. 330: 'In the light of the above factors, the proposed transaction would create a market structure providing considerable scope for anti-competitive effects arising from the merged entity's simultaneous dominant and leading position in carton and PET equipment respectively'. The Commission would reiterate this argument in its appeal before the Court. See also Frances Dethmers, Ninette Dodoo and Anna Morfey, 'Conglomerate Mergers Under EC Merger Control: An Overview' (2005) 1 *European Competition Journal* 265, at 283: 'Prior to the Court's ruling in Tetra Laval, the Commission concluded that a finding of pre-merger dominance and the existence of some conglomerate links (giving the merged entity the ability to pursue strategic behaviour) would by themselves be sufficient for a finding of anti-competitive effects'.

[120] Case T-5/02, *Tetra Laval*, for instance paras. 235 ('[i]t follows that, as regards the barrier technology market, the evidence in the contested decision is not sufficient as a matter of law to show that, if the anticipated leveraging were to take place, the foreseeable consequences would be sufficiently far-reaching to enable the merged entity to achieve a dominant position on that market by 2005'); 251; and 283.

[121] Case C-12/03, *Tetra Laval*, para. 27.

Implicit in this ground of annulment – and, indeed, in the whole of the appeal – was, however, the idea that the legal framework devised by the GC in its judgment was based on an erroneous interpretation of Article 2 of Regulation 4064/89. Formally, the Commission chose to challenge a minor aspect of the said framework,[122] as well as some issues pertaining to the legal characterisation of facts.[123] At the same time, the authority appeared to argue that the GC had departed from prior case law by suggesting that the change in the market structure entailed by a concentration cannot, in and of itself, justify intervention.[124] According to the Commission, there would be no reason to distinguish between horizontal and non-horizontal mergers in this regard. This argument echoes the premises on which the annulled decision was based. Because the Court endorsed the essence of the GC's approach, it put an end to the debate around this question.

The Commission embraced mainstream economic principles in the Guidelines on non-horizontal mergers that followed the adoption of Regulation 139/2004.[125] This instrument, issued in 2008, makes it clear that the competitive advantages resulting from a non-horizontal merger do not justify intervention in and of themselves. In fact, the Commission acknowledges that a competitive advantage acquired by the new entity may spur competition on the relevant market by forcing rivals to develop counterstrategies.[126] In this sense, the document distinguishes between 'foreclosure' and 'anticompetitive foreclosure'. The difference between the two concepts seeks to emphasise that intervention is only justified where a foreclosure strategy can be expected to marginalise rivals to such an extent that the new entity would not be subject to effective competitive constraints in the post-merger scenario.[127] Moreover, there seems to be no trace of the idea of an

[122] Ibid., paras. 58–63. The Commission challenged the idea that it is necessary to take into account the deterrent effect of Article 102 TFEU when evaluating the likely impact of a transaction on competition.

[123] Ibid., paras. 90–106.

[124] See in this sense Case C-12/05 P, *Tetra Laval*, para. 60: 'The Commission submits, moreover, that the Court of First Instance's approach is mistaken in that it is based on unwarranted distinctions between different types of mergers, which are contrary to Article 2 of the Regulation. It criticises paragraph 154 of the judgment under appeal, in which the Court of First Instance took the view that it is not the structure resulting from the merger transaction itself which creates or strengthens a dominant position within the meaning of Article 2(3) but rather the future conduct of the merged entity'.

[125] Non-Horizontal Merger Guidelines. [126] Ibid., paras. 39–67.

[127] Ibid., para. 18. The Commission distinguishes between 'foreclosure', whereby 'actual or potential rivals' access to supplies or markets is hampered or eliminated as a result of the

'efficiency offence'. If anything, the possibility of claiming that the efficiencies resulting from the transaction outweigh any anti-competitive effects is now made explicit.[128]

3.4 *Non-Collusive Oligopolies*

3.4.1 The 'Oligopoly Gap' in Regulation 4064/89

The so-called 'oligopoly gap' in EU merger control was readily identified as soon as Regulation 4064/89 was adopted. Writing at a time when it was not clear whether the Regulation encompassed the notion of collective dominance, Ridyard noted that there was no compelling reason, from an economic perspective, to leave transactions outside of the scope of EU merger control simply because they would not lead to the creation or the strengthening of a dominant position.[129] Under a single dominance test, however, a merger between the second and third largest firms on the market would not be caught by the relevant legislation even when the joint share of the two firms amounts to 49 per cent.[130] The extension of the scope of the dominance test to capture instances of tacit collusion is only a partial remedy for the 'oligopoly gap'. It has long been understood that a merger may have anti-competitive effects even when the relevant market is not conducive to coordinated conduct.[131] In non-collusive oligopolies, a merger may give the new entity (and possibly its rivals) the ability and the incentive to increase prices unilaterally, even when the transaction does not result in the creation or strengthening of a dominant position.

If it was clear since *Kali & Salz* that instances of tacit collusion were caught by Regulation 4064/89, the question of whether the scope of this legislation was broad enough to cover unilateral effects in the absence of

merger, thereby reducing these companies' ability and/or incentive to compete', and which does not give rise to intervention as such, and 'anticompetitive foreclosure', as a result of which the merging parties are 'able to profitably increase the price charged to consumers'.

[128] Ibid., para. 21.

[129] Derek Ridyard, 'Joint Dominance and the Oligopoly Blind Spot Under the EC Merger Regulation' (1992) 13 *European Competition Law Review* 161.

[130] Ibid., at 161, where he notes that the 'oligopoly blind spot' could 'in principle leave the Commission powerless to prevent a merger which brought together two firms with respectively 25 and 24 per cent of a market, if their main competitor accounted for the remaining 51 per cent'.

[131] Europe Economics, 'Study on Assessment Criteria for Distinguishing between Competitive and Dominant Oligopolies in Merger Control'.

dominance had to wait until *Airtours*. The expansive interpretation of the notion of collective dominance advanced by the Commission in that decision could be interpreted – and was interpreted at the time – as an attempt to expand its scope beyond tacit collusion, so as to encompass any anti-competitive effect arising in oligopolistic markets.[132] The rejection of the Commission's approach in this sense suggested that there was indeed an 'oligopoly gap' in Regulation 4064/89. Following the ruling in *Airtours*, there were reasons to believe that the only way in which the said gap could be addressed was through the review of the substantive criterion for the assessment of concentrations.[133]

3.4.2 The Closing of the 'Oligopoly Gap' in Regulation 139/2004

The Commission had initiated the process for the review of Regulation 4064/89 before *Airtours* was rendered. A few months prior to the judgment, in December 2001, it issued a Green Paper discussing, inter alia, the substantive issues involved in the review. The Commission evaluated the advantages and disadvantages of moving away from a test based on dominance to one based on a substantial lessening of competition (or SLC), which is the applicable framework under the US Clayton Act.[134] The Green Paper did not display a clear willingness to move away from a dominance-based framework. According to the Commission, the fundamental advantage of the SLC test is that it would bring in line the substantive assessment of mergers across jurisdictions.[135] While it also acknowledged that the new test would be less rigid than one based on dominance and as such more economics oriented,[136] the Commission noted that it could be a source of legal uncertainty due to its open-ended nature.[137] From the perspective of enforcement, on the other hand, the

[132] See for instance Ioannis Kokkoris, *Merger Control in Europe: The Gap in the ECMR and National Merger Legislations* (Oxford: Routledge, 2011), p. 2 ('The Commission's argumentation was not clear on whether it was attempting to capture non-collusive oligopolies by expanding the notion of collective dominance or whether it misunderstood concerns related to non-collusive oligopolies with collective dominance').

[133] See in this sense Ortiz Blanco, *Market Power in EU Antitrust Law*, p. 200.

[134] Green Paper on the Review of Regulation 4064/89, paras. 159–72.

[135] See in particular para. 160: 'From a procedural viewpoint, the main reason proposed in favour of such a re-evaluation is that it could allow an alignment of the Merger Regulation's appraisal criteria with those applied in other major jurisdictions, such as the US, Canada and Australia, which rely on a concept of substantial lessening of competition ("the SLC-test"). Such an alignment towards a global standard for merger assessment holds certain attractions'.

[136] Ibid., para.165. [137] Ibid.

authority expressed the view that the dominance test had not given rise to any major loopholes in practice. According to the Green Paper, the authority had not encountered a single instance of a 'gap case' such as the one mentioned above – that is, of a merger falling short of the dominance threshold in a non-collusive oligopoly.[138]

The Proposal for a Regulation issued in January 2003[139] confirmed the impression that the Commission was not keen on moving away from the dominance test. At the same time, it showed that the authority was willing to make clear that 'gap cases' in non-collusive oligopolies would be subject to the new legislation. According to the proposal, the notion of dominance is flexible enough to encompass such cases. In this sense, the Commission advocated the approach it had consistently followed in this and other areas of EU competition law. It was possible, according to the Commission, to further expand the scope of the notion of dominance. After all, it noted in the proposal, the Court had not expressly ruled on – and thus not excluded – whether the notion of dominance encompassed 'gap cases'.[140] The authority found support for this idea in the fact that the Court had traditionally favoured a teleological interpretation of EU law, and arguably placed greater emphasis on preventing distortions of competition than on a literal reading of a particular provision.[141] Against this background, the Commission proposed to amend Article 2 of the Regulation so as to clarify that the notion of dominance in the context of merger control would cover 'gap cases'.[142]

Instead of seeking to stretch the boundaries of an existing concept beyond recognition, the legislature eventually opted, as explained

[138] Ibid., para. 166.

[139] Proposal for a Council Regulation on the control of concentrations between undertakings ('The EC Merger Regulation') COM(2002) 711 final OJ (2003) No. C 20/4.

[140] Ibid., para. 54: 'the Court of Justice has not explicitly ruled on, and therefore not explicitly excluded, the possibility of addressing the effect of mergers in (non-collusive) oligopolies with no single firm being significantly larger than the others under the current dominance test'.

[141] See in this sense the footnote to para. 54, where the Commission argues that 'the Court has shown a willingness to adopt a teleological interpretation of the notion of dominance in order not to deprive it of its *effet utile*. Such a teleological interpretation has been particularly applied in the context of the ECMR'. In this regard, it referred to the approach followed by the Court in *Kali & Salz*.

[142] The Commission proposed to introduce a new Article 2(2) to the Regulation, pursuant to which '[f]or the purpose of this Regulation, one or more undertakings shall be deemed to be in a dominant position if, with or without coordinating, they hold the economic power to influence appreciably and sustainably the parameters of competition, in particular, prices, production, quality of output, distribution or innovation, or appreciably to foreclose competition'.

above, for the adoption of a new substantive criterion. The relevant question under Regulation 139/2004 is whether a merger is likely to lead to a significant impediment to effective competition (hereinafter, the 'SIEC test'). The creation and the strengthening of a dominant position is no longer the only instance that justifies action; it is simply the typical scenario giving rise to intervention.[143] As noted by the Commission in its Green Paper, the introduction of a new test had a potentially ambivalent impact on legal certainty. In a sense, it is positive, as it would avoid attaching different meanings to the notion of dominance under Article 102 TFEU and merger control.[144] In another sense, its impact could be negative, insofar as the new concept had not been fleshed out by the courts and the administrative authority. In addition, an open-ended notion such as SIEC could allow the Commission to take action against virtually any merger in an oligopolistic market.

In order to address concerns with legal certainty, the Commission issued a set of Guidelines on horizontal mergers in 2004. These Guidelines provide the factual scenarios that may lead to anti-competitive effects in the absence of dominance, which formally justified the move away from the test set out in Regulation 4064/89.[145] The document identifies the instances in which concentrations between competitors give rise to 'non-coordinated effects' and which are not necessarily related to the creation or the strengthening of a dominant position. Accordingly, the joint market share of the merging parties is just one of the factors to consider in the analysis. Other factors that may lead to a SIEC include, inter alia, the closeness of competition between the parties, the limited possibilities for customers to switch suppliers and the inability of rivals to increase supply in the event of a price rise.[146]

[143] Articles 2(2) and 2(3) of Regulation 139/2004 point out that a significant impediment to effective competition might arise 'in particular as a result of the creation or strengthening of a dominant position'.

[144] In its proposal, the Commission conceded that the expansion of the dominance test under the Merger Regulation would have the effect of introducing divergent definitions of the notion.

[145] See in this sense Recital 25 of the Preamble to Regulation 139/2004, which appears to reflect a concern with concentrations in oligopolistic markets 'involving the elimination of important competitive constraints that the merging parties had exerted upon each other, as well as a reduction of competitive pressure on the remaining competitors, may, even in the absence of a likelihood of coordination between the members of the oligopoly, result in a significant impediment to effective competition'.

[146] Horizontal Merger Guidelines.

3.4.3 The Practice of the Commission under Regulation 139/2004

According to the Commission, the first true 'gap case' in which the principles of the Guidelines were implemented is *T-Mobile Austria/tele.ring.*[147] The transaction did not result in the creation of a market leader, let alone a dominant one. However, the Commission concluded that tele.ring was T-Mobile Austria's closest competitor. More precisely, it argued that tele.ring was the 'maverick firm' and as such the most important competitive constraint on the two largest providers of mobile phone services in Austria.[148] The transaction was only cleared following remedies suggested by the parties. *T-Mobile Austria/tele.ring* was followed by a steady stream of 'gap cases'.[149] The first 'gap case' leading to a prohibition decision related to the merger between UPS and TNT.[150]

The administrative practice of the Commission since 2004 does not seem to have tempered the concerns voiced when the SIEC test was introduced. Some commentators have been vocal about the lack of legal certainty to which, in their view, it has given rise.[151] According to this perception, the Commission would be in a position to block virtually any merger – in particular any horizontal merger – in an oligopolistic market. After all, every merger between rivals entails the loss of a source of competitive pressure, and can thus plausibly affect one or several

147 Commission Decision of 26 April 2006 (Case No COMP/M.3916 – *T-Mobile Austria/ Tele.ring*). The Commission claims this is its first case in the Staff Working Document accompanying the White Paper 'Towards more effective EU merger control' SWD(2014) 221 final.

148 Ibid., paras. 72–3.

149 The Commission refers to the following cases in the Staff Working Document: For instance Commission Decision of 6 June 2006 (Case COMP/M.4141 – *Linde/BOC*); Commission Decision of 12 December 2006 (Case COMP/M.4187 – *Metso/Aker Kvaerner*); Commission Decision of 3 October 2007 (Case COMP/M.4844 – *Fortis/ ABN Amro*), Commission Decision of 22 December 2008 (Case COMP/M.5224 – *EDF/British Energy*); Commission Decision of 23 November 2011 (Case COMP/ M.6203 – *Western Digital/ Hitachi*); Commission Decision 12 December 2012 (Case COMP/M.6497 – *Hutchison/ Orange*).

150 Commission Decision of 30 January 2013 (Case No COMP/M.6570 – *UPS/ TNT Express*). See, for an analysis, Giorgio Castaldo and Aurélie Belzunces, 'UPS/TNT Express: First "Gap Case" Prohibition' (2015) 6 *Journal of European Competition Law & Practice* 709.

151 James S. Venit, 'Widening the "Gap" – The Substantial Lessening of the Commission's Evidentiary Burden and the Demise of Coordinated Effects under the SIEC Test and §§24/25 of the Horizontal Merger Guidelines' (2015) 11 *European Competition Journal* 291.

parameters of competition. As explained above, these views are not fundamentally different from the criticism of the 'checklist' approach that the Commission followed in cases like *Airtours*. In the two cases, the concerns relate to the absence of a structured standard with clear boundaries that can be anticipated by stakeholders. It is possible to identify four primary factors underlying this perception, which are examined hereinafter in turn.

The first of these factors is the absence of any meaningful safe harbours in EU merger control. In theory, one could think of two potential safe harbours in the system, one found in the Green Paper and another one in the letter of Regulation 139/2004. In its legislative proposals, crystallised in the Green Paper, the Commission suggested that the canonical example of a 'gap case' is one involving the second and third largest firms on the market. Accordingly, one could argue that mergers between smaller players (say, the third and fourth largest players in an industry) are presumptively compatible with the internal market – or presumed not to have appreciable effects on competition. It is not possible to infer the existence of such a presumption from the practice of the Commission. Some examples show that transactions are scrutinised irrespective of the relative position of the parties on the relevant market. *Orange/Jazztel*, in the telecommunications sector, is a case in point.[152] A second potential safe harbour is to be found in the Preamble to Regulation 139/2004, which points out that mergers are presumed compatible with the internal market where the joint market share of the parties falls below 25 per cent.[153] However, this presumption has not precluded the Commission from requiring remedies in transactions falling below that threshold,[154] which does not seem to play a meaningful role in practice.

In one sense, it is unsurprising, and arguably desirable, that intervention in merger cases takes place even when the market share falls below 25 per cent and/or where the transaction concerns relatively small players. If a transaction is likely to lead to an increase in market power, there is no reason why the relative position of the parties on the relevant market, or their joint market share, should preclude intervention. Consistency across provisions is another reason that pleads against considering these factors. In the context of Article 101(1) TFEU, an agreement may very well be found to restrict competition

[152] Commission Decision of 19 May 2015 (Case M.7421 – *Orange/Jazztel*).
[153] Recital 25 of the Preamble to Regulation 139/2004.
[154] Commission of 12 December 2012 (Case COMP/M.6497 – *Hutchison 3G Austria/ Orange Austria*).

in circumstances similar to the cases discussed above. The Guidelines on horizontal co-operation agreements provide several examples in this regard.[155] There appears to be no reason why functionally equivalent transactions should be treated differently under Article 101(1) TFEU and Regulation 139/2004.

In another sense, there are reasons to believe that, absent some guarantees, the potentially broad reach of EU merger control could be problematic. The single most important difference between EU merger control and Article 101(1) TFEU (and which explains the ongoing controversy around the former) has to do with the way in which the balancing of pro- and anti-competitive effects is addressed in the context of each regime. As far as agreements are concerned, Article 101(3) TFEU plays – and has always played – a central role in the structure and enforcement of the provision. Thus, it has long been understood that an agreement may be deemed compatible with Article 101 TFEU not only when it falls outside the scope of the first paragraph but when it fulfils the conditions set out in the third. In this sense, a finding that an agreement is restrictive of competition within the meaning of Article 101(1) TFEU has never been understood to lead, almost inevitably, to its prohibition. In fact, the tendency on the part of the Commission to attach a broad meaning to the notion of restriction of competition meant in practice that, for a long time, the thrust of the analysis was performed under Article 101(3) TFEU.

The system introduced by virtue of Regulation 1/2003, in turn, is based on the idea that a substantial number of agreements having appreciable restrictive effects on competition – in particular a large number of borderline cases – are compatible with Article 101 TFEU because they satisfy the conditions set out in Article 101(3) TFEU even though they are caught by the first paragraph.[156] Firms, under the current regime, are expected to self-assess the compatibility of their practices with Article 101 TFEU. This self-assessment exercise

[155] Guidelines on the applicability of Article 101 of the Treaty on the Functioning of the European Union to horizontal co-operation agreements OJ (2011) No. C 11/1, for instance, paras. 162–82, where the Commission considers the restrictive effects of joint production agreements. The safe harbour for these agreements is set at 20 per cent.

[156] Suffice it to mention that, in accordance with Article 1(2) of Council Regulation (EC) No. 1/2003 of 16 December 2002 on the implementation of the rules on competition laid down in Articles 81 and 82 of the Treaty OJ (2003) No. L 1/1 '[a]greements, decisions and concerted practices caught by Article 81(1) of the Treaty which satisfy the conditions of Article [101(3)] of the Treaty shall not be prohibited, no prior decision to that effect being required'.

necessarily comprises the evaluation of the pro-competitive aspects of their agreement. The Commission, in turn, devotes its enforcement efforts to what it perceives to be the most harmful infringements. In this institutional context, the risk that Article 101(1) TFEU may be given an overly broad meaning in borderline cases is not particularly important. In fact, borderline cases are unlikely to face direct case-by-case scrutiny by the Commission. Through the adoption of Guidelines and Block Exemption Regulations, the authority has identified the instances in which some of these agreements are likely to fulfil the conditions of Article 101(3) TFEU.

In theory, the so-called 'efficiency defence' could fulfil, in the context of merger control, the same role that Article 101(3) TFEU fulfils in relation to agreements. Thus, a merger could be cleared if the likely anti-competitive effects are deemed outweighed by the efficiency gains it generates. This would mean that some transactions leading prima facie to a significant impediment to effective competition could be unconditionally approved because they are on the whole pro-competitive. The balancing of pro- and anti-competitive effects of mergers would be particularly important in borderline cases such as *Orange/Jazztel*. The administrative practice of the Commission is at odds with this theory. The 'efficiency defence' has played a marginal role, if at all, since 2004.[157] In practice, a prima facie finding of a SIEC is understood to lead, almost inevitably, to a finding of incompatibility (absent remedies proposed by the parties). A systematic analysis of all concentrations cleared without conditions in Phase II shows that there is not a single case in which the Commission was ready to claim that the efficiencies generated by the transaction outweighed the anti-competitive effects resulting from it. Efficiency gains have been considered in the analysis of transactions with relative frequency, in particular in Phase II cases.[158] However, such

[157] For an analysis of this question, see Petri Kuoppamäki and Sami Torstila, 'Is there a future for an efficiency defence in EU merger control?' (2015) 41 *European Law Review* 687. The authors find that, overall, efficiency defence counts for 3 per cent of all cases, and for 31 per cent of Phase II cases).

[158] Efficiency claims were considered, at least to some extent, in Commission Decision of 8 January 2016 (Case COMP/M.7630 – *Fedex/TNT*); Commission Decision of 2 September 2013 (Case COMP/M.6360 – *Nynas/Shell/Harburg Refinery*); Commission of 4 September 2012 (Case COMP/M.6314 – *Telefónica UK/Vodafone UK/Everything Everywhere/JV*); Commission Decision of 13 July 2011 (Case COMP/M.6101 – *UPM/Myllykoski and Rhein Papier*); Commission Decision of 21 January 2010 (Case COMP/M.5529 – *Oracle/Sun Microsystems*); Commission Decision of 17 December 2008 (Case COMP/M.5141 – *KLM/Martinair*); Commission Decision

gains have always been acknowledged in cases in which the Commission concluded that the transaction was unlikely to have anti-competitive effects in the first place.[159]

A second factor behind the marginal role of the 'efficiency defence' in EU merger control (and, more generally, behind the perception of legal uncertainty) relates to the institutional framework, which is not particularly conducive to the balancing of the pro- and anti-competitive effects of transactions. The existence of a system of compulsory notification means that the Commission will systematically scrutinise borderline cases having a Union dimension. Given the time constraints that are inherent in the system, the merging parties in such borderline cases face, for all practical purposes, a choice between a declaration of incompatibility and a conditional approval following the submission of remedies addressing the competition concerns identified by the Commission. Thus, any merger in which the efficiency gains could outweigh any anti-competitive effects is likely to be cleared with conditions offered by the parties.

The third factor explaining ongoing criticism relates to the inherent fallibility and complexity of the instruments applied to establish the likely effects of transactions, in particular in 'gap cases'. A prospective analysis of the impact of a merger on prices requires the use of econometric tools that are by definition sensitive to the assumptions upon which they are based. For this reason, it is not easy for the merging parties to challenge the findings of the Commission. The choice of the econometric tool and the findings deriving from their use are the privileged realm of the complex economic assessments, for which the Commission enjoys a margin of appreciation. As a result, the judicial review of the assessment of non-coordinated effects – at least in 'gap cases' – can be expected to be marginal. This fact, in turn, can be expected to reduce the likelihood of a challenge.

of 2 July 2008 (Case COMP/M.4942 - *Nokia/Navteq*); Commission Decision of 14 May 2008 (Case COMP/M.4854 – *TomTom/Tele Atlas*).

[159] In *Fedex/TNT*, the Commission considered at length (paras. 498–588) the efficiency claims made by the parties and argued that they would have been sufficient to outweigh any anti-competitive effects. In any event, the Commission argued that no such effects were likely in the first place. In *Nynas/Shell/Harburg Refinery* the Commission concluded that the transaction would most probably lead to an increase in supply capacity. In any event, the Commission had found that the failing division defence applied in the context of the case. In *Oracle/Sun Microsystems*, the Commission briefly (paras. 755 and 957) identified several potential efficiencies, which were not analysed in detail due to the fact that no anti-competitive effects were found. A similar attitude was displayed in *TomTom/Tele Atlas* and *Nokia/Navteq*.

The fourth factor is a corollary of the third. The leeway enjoyed by the Commission means that it can structure its enforcement activity around a set of proxies for the incompatibility of mergers with the internal market. These proxies would not dispense it from the need to establish negative effects on a case-by-case basis, but can be relied upon as the basis for a presumption of harm. In this sense, some authors have voiced concerns about the fact that a presumption of incompatibility of '4 to 3' mergers in tight oligopolies may be on the verge of emerging in the practice of the Commission.[160] Accordingly, the starting point of the analysis would be that an oligopoly of three players or fewer would not be effectively competitive, and that the approval of the merger in that context is conditional upon the parties preserving, via remedies, the conditions of competition existing prior to the transaction.

[160] Joan de Sola-Morales, 'Counting Sheep: Is The "4-to-3 or Fewer" Distinction Becoming a Corridor-Talk Presumption?' (Kluwer Competition Law Blog, December 6, 2016).

APPENDIX TO CHAPTER 5

Table 5.1 *Challenged decisions on the compatibility of concentrations with the internal market (Regulations 4064/89 and 139/2004)*

Decision	Type	First instance	Applicant	Outcome	Appeal	Outcome
Vodafone/Liberty Global/ Dutch JV	Phase I Conditions	T-370/17	Competitor	Pending	–	–
HeidelbergCement/ Schwenk/Cemex Hungary/Cemex Croatia	Phase II Incompatible	T-380/17	Merging party	Pending	–	–
Hutchison 3 Italy/ Wind/JV	Phase II Conditions	T-19/17	Competitor	Pending	–	–
Hutchison 3 G UK Investments Limited/ Telefónica	Phase II Incompatible	T-399/16	Merging party	Pending	–	–
Telefonica Deutschland/ E-Plus	Phase II Conditions	T-305/15 and T-307/15	Competitor	Pending	–	–
Liberty Global/Ziggo	Phase II Conditions	T-394/15	Competitor	Pending*	–	–
UPS/TNT Express	Phase II Incompatible	T-194/13	Merging party	**Annul (other)**	C-265/17	Pending

Deutsche Börse AG/NYSE Euronext	Phase II Incompatible	T-175/12	Merging party	Dismiss	–	–
Microsoft/Skype	Phase I Unconditional	T-175/12	Competitor	Dismiss	–	–
Française des jeux/Groupe Lucien Barrière/JV	Phase I Unconditional	T-315/10	Competitor	Dismiss (inadmissible)	–	–
EDF/Segebel	Phase I Conditions	T-224/10	Other third party	Dismiss (inadmissible)	–	–
Lufthansa/Austrian Airlines	Phase II Conditions	T-162/10	Competitor	Dismiss	–	–
REWE/ADEG	Phase I Conditions	T-405/08	Competitor	Dismiss	–	–
Ryanair/Aer Lingus	Phase II Incompatible	T-342/07	Merging party	Dismiss	–	–
Apollo/Akzo Nobel, IAR	Phase I Unconditional	T-282/06	Competitor	Dismiss	–	–
Sovion/HMG	Phase I Unconditional	T-151/05	Other third party	Dismiss	–	–
EDP/ENI/GDP	Phase II Incompatible	T-87/05	Merging party	Dismiss	–	–
Sony/BMG	Phase II Unconditional	T-464/04	Competitor	Annul (legal characterisation)	C-413/06 P	**Set aside**
Air France/KLM	Phase I Conditions	T-177/04	Competitor	Dismiss	–	–

Table 5.1 *(cont.)*

Decision	Type	First instance	Applicant	Outcome	Appeal	Outcome
Lagardère/Natexis/VUP	Phase II Conditions	T-279/04	Competitor	Dismiss	C-551/10 P	Dismiss
Verbund/EnergieAllianz	Phase II Conditions	T-350/03	Other third party	Dismiss (inadmissible)	–	–
DaimlerChrysler/Deutsche Telekom/JV)	Phase II Conditions	T-48/04	Competitor	Dismiss	–	–
SEB/Moulinex	Phase I Conditions	T-114/02 and T-119/02	Competitor	**Annul (legal characterisation)**	–	–
Haniel/Cementbouw/JV	Phase II Conditions	T-282/02	Competitor	Dismiss	C-202/06 P	Dismiss
Schneider/Legrand	Phase II Incompatible	T-310/01	Merging party	**Annul (legal characterisation)**	–	–
Tetra Laval/Sidel	Phase II Incompatible	T-5/02	Merging party	**Annul (law)**	C-12/03 P	Dismiss
General Electric/ Honeywell	Phase II Incompatible	T-209/01 and T-210/01	Merging party	Dismiss	–	–
Salzgitter/Mannesmann-Röhrenwerke	Phase I Unconditional	T-374/00	Competitor, Other third party	Dismiss	–	–
MCI WorldCom/Sprint	Phase II Incompatible	T-310/00	Merging party	**Annul (other)**	–	–

BskyB/Kirch Pay TV	Phase I Conditions	T-158/00	Competitor	Dismiss	–	–
Airtours/First Choice	Phase II Incompatible	T-342/99	Merging party	**Annul (law)**	–	–
Coca-Cola/Amalgamated Beverages GB	Phase II Unconditional	T-125/97	Merging party	Dismiss (inadmissible)	–	–
Kesko/Tuko	Phase II Incompatible	T-22/97	Merging party	Dismiss	–	–
Gencor/Lonrho	Phase II Incompatible	T-102/96	Merging party	Dismiss	–	–
RTL/Veronica/Endemol	Phase II Incompatible	T-221/95	Merging party	Dismiss	–	–
Procter & Gamble/ VPSchickedanz (II)	Phase II Conditions	T-290/94	Competitor	Dismiss		
Kali + Salz/MdK/ Treuhand	Phase II Conditions	C-68/94 and C-30/95	Competitor, Other third party	**Annul (legal characterisation)**	–	–
British Airways/TAT	Phase I Conditions	T-2/93	Competitor	Dismiss	–	–
Nestlé/Perrier	Phase II Conditions	T-96/92 and T-12/93	Other third party	Dismiss	–	–

* The ruling in this case was adopted as this book was going to press. Not included for the sake of consistency.

PART III

Implications

6

The Shaping of EU Competition Law: Past and Prospects

1 The Behaviour of the Commission

The preceding three chapters reveal a pattern in the decision-making practice of the Commission. This pattern has unfolded both in the crafting of legal tests – that is, in one-shot interactions – and in the way in which the authority has engaged with the relevant case law – that is, in repeated interactions. The identification of the phenomenon is valuable for two main reasons, which are examined hereinafter. First, it contributes to the understanding of the factors underpinning the substantive peculiarities of EU competition law. It would seem that the behaviour of the Commission plays a more important role than generally conceded in this regard. Several key features of the system can indeed be directly traced to the choices made by the authority. Second, the analysis of the phenomenon is valuable insofar as it exposes the vulnerabilities of the system, which may not be adequately equipped to deal with some sources of inconsistent enforcement and legal uncertainty.

1.1 Summary of the Main Findings

1.1.1 One-Shot Interactions

The analysis of one-shot interactions reveals a tendency by the Commission to shape the scope of prima facie prohibitions in a relatively expansive manner. Arguably, this behaviour is common to any administrative agency, in any field, that acts both as an investigator and decision-maker. When shaping the scope of the provisions dealing with the free movement of goods and services, for instance, it is well documented that the Commission sought to define them, from the outset, relatively broadly.[1] In EU competition law, the observed tendency has

[1] Joseph Weiler, 'The Constitution of the Common Market Place: Text and Context in the Evolution of the Free Movement of Goods' in Paul Craig and Gráinne de Búrca (eds.), *The Evolution of EU Law* (Oxford: Oxford University Press, 1999).

been manifested in a variety of ways over the years and across provisions. In general, the administrative practice reflects a preference for rules over standards, as well as a tendency to blur the line between the two. In the context of Article 102 TFEU, the Commission expressed a preference for the former over the latter. A dominant theme in its pre-Guidance decisions is in fact the idea that the – presumed or established – purpose behind a given line of conduct can be sufficient, in and of itself, to take action under Article 102 TFEU. The positions it took in *Michelin II*, where it dismissed as irrelevant evidence showing that the contentious practices had failed to have a perceptible impact on the market, and in *Deutsche Telekom*, where it held that evidence of an anti-competitive effect is not necessary to establish the abusive nature of a 'margin squeeze', are clear examples in this regard.

The technique developed in the context of Article 101 TFEU is different, but had identical consequences in practice. Because the Commission traditionally equated a restriction in the freedom of action of the parties with a restriction of competition, a very large number of agreements was in principle caught by Article 101(1) TFEU, whether by object or effect. It is in fact not easy to trace in the traditional practice a coherent or systematic approach to distinguish between these two categories. In practice, the analysis of effects operated as a qualified rule, in the sense that only agreements with an insignificant impact on competition were likely to be deemed to fall outside the scope of Article 101(1) TFEU. Under this interpretation of the provision, it is for the authority itself to decide which agreements are de minimis and thus fail to have appreciable restrictive effects.

If a qualified rule applied in practice across the board, this is in part because the Commission did not systematically evaluate the conditions of competition that would have prevailed in the absence of the agreement. The virtual irrelevance of the counterfactual is a consistent feature in Article 101 TFEU enforcement. In the context of Article 102 TFEU, claims relating to the counterfactual have been tersely dismissed by arguing that the conditions of competition could have improved in the absence of the practice, and that this possibility was sufficient to exclude the claims from the analysis.[2] Another factor that has led to the blurring of the line between rules and standards is the inclination to set the

[2] Commission Decision 2002/405/EC of 20 June 2001 (Case COMP/E-2/36.041/PO – *Michelin*) OJ (2002) No. L 143/1 ('*Michelin II*'), para. 333; and Commission Decision 2000/74/EC of 14 July 1999 (Case IV/D-2/34.780 – *Virgin/British Airways*) OJ (2000) No. L 30/1, para. 107.

threshold of effects at the level of capability. Thus, the mere tendency of a practice to restrict competition was deemed sufficient to intervene. This is the basis of pre-Guidance Article 102 TFEU case law. A similar approach was observed in the context of EU merger control. The fundamental idea underlying *Tetra Laval/Sidel* and *General Electric/Honeywell* is that action in the context of a non-horizontal merger requires evidence that the change in the market structure makes the leveraging of a dominant position plausible, as opposed to likely.

A second pattern in one-shot interactions is the tendency of the Commission to craft unstructured legal tests that give the authority or claimant greater leeway in the context of a particular case. Pursuant to this approach, a prohibition is established in light of a 'checklist' of several indicators, which may or may not be relevant in a given instance. This tendency is manifested, first, in the preference for rules with a 'soft' trigger. The analysis of predatory pricing in the original *AKZO* decision is an example in this sense. The Commission proposed to establish the abusive nature of aggressive pricing policies in light of a set of indicators, not all of which would be relevant in the context of a particular case. For instance, the Commission argued that evidence of pricing below a given cost benchmark is not necessary. The relevance of the various factors was not to be defined in advance, but ex post, on a case-by-case basis. A similar approach can be found in the definition of standards in EU merger control. The 'checklist' approach to the assessment of collective dominance in *Airtours* comes to mind immediately.

A third pattern relates to the way in which the Commission has established the purpose behind a practice and, by the same token, has engaged with formal analysis. Traditionally, the presumed or established rationale behind the practice played a significant role when drawing the line between pro- and anti-competitive conduct. The Commission did not necessarily resort to formal analysis in individual cases. For instance, the administrative practice on 'loyalty-inducing' rebates was grounded on the idea that target-based and retroactive rebate schemes presumptively lack an economic justification and are thus implemented to prevent customers from obtaining supplies from other producers. However, this presumption was not informed by formal analysis – which leads to the opposite conclusion.[3] This inclination has only been tempered with the

[3] A discussion of mainstream positions can be found, for instance, in Massimo Motta, 'Michelin II: The Treatment of Rebates' in Bruce Lyons (ed.), *Cases in European Competition Policy: The Economic Analysis* (Cambridge: Cambridge University Press, 2009).

progressive introduction of mainstream economic principles in the analysis of practices. However, the shift towards formal analysis appears, to this day, far from complete. In *Cartes Bancaires*, the Commission came to conclusions about the object behind the practice without taking into account the dynamics of the relevant market, which suggested the contentious restraints might serve a pro-competitive purpose – as the ECJ would point out in its appeal against the decision.[4]

1.1.2 Repeated Interactions

An across-the-board analysis suggests that the Commission has given a relatively expansive or narrow interpretation to EU courts' rulings depending on their impact on the scope of its powers. Again, this is arguably a pattern observed in all administrative authorities with similar characteristics. Where a ruling places significant constraints on subsequent intervention, the authority may be inclined to circumvent it or depart from it. Think, for instance, of predatory pricing. The administrative action that followed *AKZO* was based on the idea that an aggressive pricing campaign can amount to an abuse even when there is no evidence of sales below cost, which directly contradicts the Court's ruling in that case. The reaction that followed the *Delimitis* case exemplifies this same reaction in the realm of Article 101 TFEU. Instead of examining the compatibility of exclusive dealing obligations in accordance with the conditions set out by the Court in that ruling, the Commission relied upon its traditional approach, whereby any such agreement that is not de minimis is restrictive of competition, whether by object or effect.

Another technique to reduce the impact of the case law in the administrative practice consists of acknowledging the EU courts' judgments but interpreting them narrowly in its practice. The aftermath of *Nungesser* illustrates this approach well. As explained in Chapter 3, that ruling confirmed an issue of principle relating to the evaluation of the counterfactual. In addition, it suggested that agreements providing for the licensing of intellectual property fall, in certain circumstances, outside the scope of Article 101(1) TFEU. In its subsequent practice, the Commission would deny the relevance of *Nungesser* in the individual cases it examined. A Block Exemption Regulation, on the other hand, allowed it to define the instances in which licensing agreements are

[4] Case C-67/13 P, *Groupement des cartes bancaires v Commission*, EU:C:2014:2204, paras. 73–4.

compatible with Article 101(3) TFEU. In *Hoffmann-La Roche*, to mention an Article 102 TFEU case, the Court ruled that volume-based rebates do not amount to an abuse of a dominant position. The administrative practice that would follow was premised on the principle that this rule applied only to the rebates tied to a particular transaction and justified by economies of scale.[5]

Conversely, the Commission has interpreted favourable precedents in a relatively expansive manner. This behaviour has been observed, first, in instances in which the Court laid down a prohibition rule. Typically, the Commission has expanded the scope of the rule by 'softening' the trigger. The prima facie prohibition of exclusive dealing and of rebates conditional upon exclusivity, for instance, was progressively expanded to other schemes having the same effect in practice (in *Michelin I*) and then to any 'loyalty-inducing' scheme (in *British Airways* and in *Michelin II*). This behaviour has also been displayed in the definition of standards, as several examples from EU merger control show. If in *Kali & Salz* the Court accepted the principle that positions of collective dominance fell under the scope of Regulation 4064/89, the Commission would explore the outer boundaries of the notion in *Airtours*. Before the adoption of Regulation 139/2004, moreover, the authority considered the possibility – later abandoned – of expanding the scope of the notion of single dominance to encompass instances in which non-coordinated effects result from a merger that does not lead to the emergence of a market leader.[6]

1.1.3 Horizontal Issues

There are three main horizontal conclusions that can be drawn from the analysis of one-shot and repeated interactions. First, the analysis suggests that the patterns in the behaviour of the Commission have been consistently displayed over time. In this sense, it does not seem obvious to argue that the observed conduct is transitory, or the inevitable manifestation of the understanding of the discipline prevailing at the time of the decision. Some patterns persisted even when consensus positions had moved in a different direction, or when they supported a different view. The decision in *Airtours*, for instance, was adopted when the phenomenon of tacit collusion in oligopolies was well understood by mainstream economists, as the reaction that followed the prohibition of the merger

[5] See in this sense Case C-163/99, *Portugal v Commission*, EU:C:2001:189.

[6] Proposal for a Council Regulation on the control of concentrations between undertakings ('The EC Merger Regulation') COM(2002) 711 final OJ (2003) No. C 20/4.

showed. When the Commission adopted the controversial decisions in *British Airways* and *Michelin II*, it had long been known that rebate schemes – even loyalty rebate schemes – are plausibly pro-competitive and can only have anti-competitive effects in certain circumstances.

Over time, the administrative practice that followed the annulment of the decisions in *Airtours* and *Tetra Laval*, on the one hand, and the adoption of Regulation 1/2003, on the other, would distinguish more clearly between rules and standards. In the context of Article 101 TFEU, the Commission committed to equating restrictive effects with the creation or strengthening of market power. In the context of Article 102 TFEU, it committed to evaluating the anti-competitive impact of most exclusionary practices, even in relation to conduct that would not require such an assessment under the case law. In spite of this shift in policy, the behaviour of the Commission did not change fundamentally. In the context of Article 101 TFEU, the administrative practice in the past decade has focused markedly on agreements that it deems restrictive by object. As suggested in Chapter 3, the preference for rules over standards does not seem to be only the result of a focus on 'fact-intensive' cases. The Commission has chosen the 'by object' label in relation to practices that it examined for the first time. More importantly, the controversies raised by some of these cases are similar to those observed in the past case law. The issue of the counterfactual features prominently in them.

It is possible to discern a similar pattern in the context of Article 102 TFEU. Since the mid-2000s, the Commission has examined practices that did not fall neatly into pre-defined categories. However, the preference for rules over standards, and for a threshold of capability in the assessment of effects, can also be observed in relation to them. *Motorola*, for instance, is based on the idea that it is prima facie abusive for a holder of a standard-essential patent to bring an injunction against a firm implementing the technology.[7] In *Servier*, it concluded that a pharmaceutical company had developed a strategy aimed at delaying the entry of generic producers.[8] An important issue in the case relates to the ability of generic producers to enter the market. It was not clear, in particular, that in the absence of the practices, generic producers would likely have constrained the behaviour of the pharmaceutical company. This fact did not prevent

[7] Commission Decision of 29 April 2014 (Case AT.39985 – *Motorola – Enforcement of GPRS Standard Essential Patents*).

[8] Commission Decision of 9 July 2014 (Case AT.39612 – *Perindopril (Servier)*).

the Commission from taking action, which was based on a standard of capability.

A second transversal conclusion is that exogenous constraints on administrative action have proved to be more effective than endogenous ones. The traditional approach to the enforcement of Article 101(1) TFEU, for instance, was overhauled not because it appeared to be at odds, in several fundamental respects, with the case law, but because the Commission deemed it appropriate to define its policy around mainstream economic principles. Similarly, the adoption of a relatively risk-averse approach to the enforcement of Article 102 TFEU since the mid-2000s was not so much the consequence of the constraints deriving from the case law – the boundaries of which had progressively expanded – but because it sought to set its enforcement priorities in a way that captured consensus positions. Finally, the annulment of three decisions in the early 2000s in the field of merger control was interpreted by the Commission as a mandate to embrace formal economic analysis and to ensure that administrative action was compatible with it.[9]

Finally, it appears that many of the features that have generally been associated with the EU competition law system can be rationalised as a predictable consequence of the behaviour of an authority with the characteristics of the Commission. EU competition law has, over the years, been criticised by some commentators for being overly formalistic and for ignoring the lessons of economic analysis. For many years, it became commonplace to read that EU competition law aimed at protecting competitors, not competition. There has been a series of attempts to explain these alleged features by reference to the ideological environment prevailing in Europe, and in particular to ordoliberalism.[10] This study shows that formalism, and the reluctance to embrace economic analysis, allow a competition authority to define

[9] Lars-Hendrik Röller and Pierre A. Buigues, 'The Office of the Chief Competition Economist at the European Commission' (May 2005).

[10] For an example of representative work discussing the role of ordoliberalism in EU competition law, see David Gerber, *Law and Competition in Twentieth Century Europe: Protecting Prometheus* (Oxford: Oxford University Press, 1998); Liza Gormsen, *A Principled Approach to Abuse of Dominance in European Competition Law* (Cambridge: Cambridge University Press, 2010); and Philip Marsden, 'Some Outstanding Issues from the European Commission's Guidance on Article 102 TFEU: Not-so-faint echos of Ordoliberalism' in Federico Etro and Ioannis Kokkoris (eds.), *Competition Law and the Enforcement of Article 102* (Oxford: Oxford University Press, 2010).

the scope of its powers in a relatively expansive manner. In this sense, it provides an alternative explanation for the abovementioned features. This explanation, moreover, avoids the methodological difficulties of the ordoliberal account[11] and helps explain other observed patterns (such as the EU courts' willingness, from the outset, to embrace economic insights).

1.2 The Commission in a Changing Institutional and Substantive Landscape

The decentralisation of EU competition law enforcement, facilitated and encouraged by Regulation 1/2003, is a source of new challenges that are still only imperfectly studied and understood. One aspect that has become apparent in the past decade is that the behaviour of the Commission, as described in Part II, is now manifested in institutional settings that were less prominent during the formative years of the discipline. In particular, the past decade has seen a steady stream of preliminary references coming from disputes that had originated in investigations conducted by an NCA. As a result, the interaction between the Commission and the Court can be expected to revolve more often around such proceedings. Similarly, Regulation 1/2003 has introduced new enforcement instruments through which the authority can advance its policy – and against which, as a result, its behaviour can be examined. A second aspect that has become apparent relates to the substantive aspects of the discipline. Due to the evolution of EU competition law, there are some questions that are of fundamental relevance in the new institutional landscape, but on which the case law sheds little or no light. These two aspects are examined in turn.

[11] The attempts to explain the features of EU competition law by reference to ordoliberalism have often been criticised for their lack of rigour in the explanation of the fundamental tenets of this school of thought. In addition, accounts of the relationship between ordoliberalism and EU competition law often fail to acknowledge that ordoliberal scholars do not adhere to a monolithic set of policy prescriptions. For an overview of the evolution of ordoliberal thinking and of disagreements among ordoliberals at discrete points in time, see Peter Behrens, 'The Ordoliberal Concept of "Abuse" of a Dominant Position and its Impact on Article 102 TFEU', available at http://ssrn.com/ and Heike Schweitzer, 'The History, Interpretation and Underlying Principles of Section 2 Sherman Act and Article 82 EC' in Claus-Dieter Ehlermann and Mel Marquis (eds.), *European Competition Law Annual 2007: A Reformed Approach to Article 82 EC* (Oxford: Hart Publishing, 2008).

1.2.1 Substantive Gaps and the Changing Institutional Landscape

There is a mismatch between the substantive and enforcement choices made by the Commission during the formative years of the discipline and the demands of the EU competition law system following the adoption of Regulation 1/2003. Some substantive gaps relating to the interpretation of Articles 101 and 102 TFEU have emerged as a result. These are questions that are relevant in the new institutional landscape but for which the existing case law and administrative practice fail to provide clear guidance. One of the substantive gaps concerns the divide between restrictions by object and by effect in the context of Article 101(1) TFEU. Even though there is case law in which the Court explicitly concluded that some agreements were not restrictive of competition by their very nature – suffice it to think in this sense of *Delimitis*,[12] *Asnef-Equifax*[13] or *Pronuptia*[14] – as well as case law where the opposite conclusion was reached,[15] there is still considerable uncertainty about the appropriate way to draw the line between rules and standards in this area.

This question has acquired particular relevance once the Commission committed, in line with the case law (and at odds with its traditional approach), to assessing the restrictive effects of practices by reference to the market power enjoyed by the parties and their impact on the market structure. The divide between rules and standards has widened as a result of this choice. In the new enforcement landscape, the qualification of an agreement as restrictive by object – that is, the choice of rules over standards – has a major impact on the ease with which a prima facie infringement can be established. As already mentioned, any authority, in such circumstances, is likely to express a preference to follow the 'by object' route. This pattern of behaviour, in turn, can be expected to further contribute to the existing uncertainty about the instances in which a practice is restrictive of competition by its very nature.

The uncertainty about the divide between rules and standards in the aftermath of the adoption of Regulation 1/2003 is in part explained by the traditional approach of the Commission, whereby all agreements were

[12] Case C-234/89, *Stergios Delimitis v Henninger Bräu AG*, EU:C:1991:91.

[13] Case C-238/05 *Asnef-Equifax, Servicios de Información sobre Solvencia y Crédito, SL v Asociación de Usuarios de Servicios Bancarios*, EU:C:2006:734.

[14] Case 161/84, *Pronuptia de Paris GmbH v Pronuptia de Paris Irmgard Schillgallis*, EU:C:1986:41.

[15] See for instance Case C-286/13 P, *Dole Food Company, Inc. and Dole Fresh Fruit Europe v Commission*, EU:C:2015:184; and Case C-8/08, *T-Mobile*.

subject, in practice, to a qualified rule that dispensed it from the need to clarify the difference between 'by object' and 'by effect' infringements. It is possible to think of two additional factors at play, one of which is the consistent tendency of the authority to downplay some aspects of the case law – such as the need to engage in an analysis of the counterfactual. The other factor relates to the enforcement priorities of the Commission in the past decade. As already noted, the overwhelming majority of prohibition decisions adopted by the authority after Regulation 1/2003 concluded that the agreement under consideration was restrictive by object.

The example of *Cartes Bancaires*, discussed in Chapter 3, suggests that the dominance of 'by object' infringements in the administrative practice of the past decade is not necessarily the consequence of the choice of the most serious or clear-cut infringements. Indeed, the agreement examined in *Cartes Bancaires* did not fall into any categories of agreements deemed restrictive by their very nature. This is not an isolated instance. Among the decisions adopted by the Commission in the past decade, those dealing with the so-called pay-for-delay agreements,[16] whereby a pharmaceutical company pays a generic producer to delay the market entry of the latter, provide an additional illustration. These cases are different from plain vanilla market-sharing cartels in that they involve the exploitation of intellectual property rights. If one assumes that the patents are valid and in force, a pharmaceutical company does not necessarily achieve, by means of an agreement, anything that it would not have been able to achieve by means of an injunction.[17] In this sense, it is not certain that the practice is capable of restricting competition that would have existed in its absence.

In addition, it is widely understood – as the Commission itself has held in its Guidelines on technology licensing – that the settlement of

[16] See in this sense Commission Decision of 9 July 2014, *Servier*; Commission Decision of 10 December 2013 (Case AT.39685 – *Fentanyl*); Commission Decision of 19 June 2013 (Case AT.39226 – *Lundbeck*). On pay-for-delay agreements, see Scott Hemphill, 'Paying for Delay: Pharmaceutical Patent Settlement as a Regulatory Design Problem' (2006) 81 *New York University Law Review* 1553.

[17] For an analysis of this question, see Romano Subiotto and Jacopo Figus Diaz, 'Reverse Payment Patent Settlements as Restrictions of Competition by Object' (2017) 8 *Journal of European Competition Law & Practice* 27. See, by analogy, the logic of rulings like Case 193/83, *Windsurfing International Inc. v Commission*, EU:C:1986:75; Case 35/83, *BAT Cigaretten-Fabriken GmbH v Commission*, EU:C:1985:32, which, as explained in Chapter 3, appear to be based on the logic whereby agreements that remain within the scope of intellectual property right are not as such contrary to Article 101(1) TFEU.

intellectual property disputes can be pro-competitive and efficiency-enhancing.[18] These were the reasons that led the US Supreme Court to conclude, in *Actavis*, that pay-for-delay agreements do not amount to a per se restraint of trade.[19] According to the available evidence, moreover, the Commission, when it first looked into them, did not consider these agreements to be caught by Article 101(1) TFEU, or at least not to be restrictive of competition by their very nature.[20] Eventually, however, the authority would present them as blatant infringements of the provision. Accordingly, it found them to fall within the scope of the prohibition and imposed a fine on the firms.

The preliminary references submitted by national courts also support the conclusion that the criteria to identify agreements that restrict competition by object have never been fleshed out with sufficient clarity. The question of whether an agreement is caught, by its very nature, by Article 101(1) TFEU has indeed been raised frequently since the mid-2000s. The practices around which the question revolved varied widely, ranging from crisis cartels[21] and exchanges of information[22] to non-compete obligations[23] and selective distribution agreements.[24] The references submitted to the Court give an idea of the factors around which there is uncertainty. It appears, first, that there is not a clear sense

[18] Guidelines on the application of Article 101 of the Treaty on the Functioning of the European Union to technology transfer agreements OJ (2014) No. C 89/3, para. 235: 'Settlement agreements in the context of technology disputes are, as in many other areas of commercial disputes, in principle a legitimate way to find a mutually acceptable compromise to a bona fide legal disagreement. The parties may prefer to discontinue the dispute or litigation because it proves to be too costly, time-consuming and/or uncertain as regards its outcome. Settlements can also save courts and/or competent administrative bodies effort in deciding on the matter and can therefore give rise to welfare enhancing benefits'.

[19] *FTC v Actavis, Inc.*, 570 U.S. ___, 133 S. Ct. 2223.

[20] This issue is documented in Michael Clancy, Damien Geradin and Andrew Lazerow, 'Reverse-Payment Patent Settlements in the Pharmaceutical Industry: An Analysis of US Antitrust Law and EU Competition Law' (2014) 59 *Antitrust Bulletin* 153; and Romano Subiotto, 'Legal Assessment of Patent Settlement Agreements Containing "Reverse" Payments' (Fordham IP Conference, New York, 5 April 2013).

[21] Case C-209/07, *Competition Authority v Beef Industry Development Society Ltd and Barry Brothers (Carrigmore) Meats Ltd*, EU:C:2008:643 ('*BIDS*').

[22] Case C-8/08, *T-Mobile Netherlands BV, KPN Mobile NV, Orange Nederland NV and Vodafone Libertel NV v Raad van bestuur van de Nederlandse Mededingingsautoriteit*, EU:C:2009:343.

[23] Case C-345/14, *SIA 'Maxima Latvija' v Konkurences padome*, EU:C:2015:784.

[24] Case C-439/09, *Pierre Fabre Dermo-Cosmétique SAS v Président de l'Autorité de la concurrence and Ministre de l'Économie, de l'Industrie et de l'Emploi*, EU:C:2011:649; Case C-230/16, *Coty Germany GmbH v Parfümerie Akzente GmbH*, pending.

of the requisite threshold of effects to establish a 'by object' infringement. This is a question raised, for instance, in *T-Mobile*.[25] In the same vein, another issue that features prominently relates to whether the concept of restriction by object encapsulates a presumption of anti-competitive effects.[26]

Preliminary references are also valuable in that they suggest that the behaviour of the Commission is likely to be observed at the national level. The majority of references addressing the divide between 'by object' and 'by effect' infringements originated in proceedings before an NCA. In all disputes, the NCAs had defended that the agreement was restrictive by its very nature – that is, they favoured rules over standards. In some cases, the finding that the agreement amounted to a 'by object' breach was difficult to dispute. This is true, for instance, of *BIDS*, which concerned the legal status of what was, in essence, a crisis cartel.[27] Other cases were more controversial. In *Maxima Latvija*, for instance, the NCA had come to the conclusion that an agreement that amounted to an exclusivity obligation within the meaning of *Delimitis* was restrictive by object.[28] *Coty*, in turn, concerned a set of obligations imposed in the context of a selective distribution agreement and aimed at preserving the brand image of the contractual product.[29] Crucially, the Commission had taken the view in its Guidelines on vertical restraints that the obligations at stake in the latter case fall outside the scope of Article 101(1) TFEU.[30]

A second substantive gap concerns the analysis of effects, in the context of both Articles 101 and 102 TFEU. On the one hand (and contrary to what is true in the field of merger control), the administrative practice

[25] Case C-8/08, *T-Mobile*, para. 31 ('the concerted practice must simply be capable in an individual case, having regard to the specific legal and economic context, of resulting in the prevention, restriction or distortion of competition within the common market. Whether and to what extent, in fact, such anti-competitive effects result can only be of relevance for determining the amount of any fine and assessing any claim for damages').

[26] Case C-345/14, *Maxima Latvija*, para. 19, where the Court noted that 'certain collusive behaviour, such as that leading to horizontal price-fixing by cartels, may be considered by their nature as likely to have negative effects, in particular on the price, quantity or quality of the goods and services, so that it may be considered redundant, for the purposes of applying Article 101(1) TFEU, to prove that they have actual effects on the market'.

[27] Case C-209/07, *BIDS*, para. 11. [28] Case C-345/14, *Maxima Latvija*, paras. 5–6.

[29] Request for a preliminary ruling from the Oberlandesgericht Frankfurt am Main (Germany) lodged on 25 April 2016 – Coty Germany GmbH v Parfümerie Akzente GmbH (Case C-230/16) OJ (2016) No. C 260/21. See also Opinion of AG Wahl in Case C-230/16, *Coty Germany GmbH v Parfümerie Akzente GmbH*, EU:C:2017:603.

[30] Guidelines on vertical restraints OJ (2010) No. C 130/1, para. 54. Final report on the E-commerce Sector Inquiry SWD(2017) 154 final.

provides relatively limited examples in which the impact of a practice against firms' ability and/or incentive to compete has been assessed. The examples in which effects have been evaluated, moreover, are not particularly useful to shed light on some of the most relevant aspects of the analysis. Often, the relevant Article 101(1) TFEU decisions were annulled because the Commission had not duly considered the counterfactual.[31] In this sense, the decisions failed at a relatively early stage and could not provide guidance on subsequent steps in the assessment. Article 102 TFEU cases, in turn, failed to provide meaningful insights beyond the specifics of the case. In 'margin squeeze' cases like *Deutsche Telekom*, for instance, the anti-competitive effects could be safely inferred from the fact that the infrastructure that was the instrument of the abuse was indispensable for downstream rivals.[32] The same can be said of outright refusal to deal cases like *Magill, Microsoft I* or *Clearstream*.

Preliminary references in which the legality assessment requires an evaluation of the effects of the practice, in turn, are either relatively abstract or not capable of shedding much light on the question. References are not always rich in details. As a result, principles can only be enunciated in relatively general terms. This is typically the case where the national court fails to provide sufficient factual information. In *Maxima Latvija*, for instance, the Court did not (and could not, given the information given by the referring court) go beyond replicating the principles set out in *Delimitis*.[33] Even where the ECJ has come to conclusions about the outcome of a case, the analysis has remained relatively succinct. In *Post Danmark I*, for instance, it did not rule out that the practice could have exclusionary effects, but noted, in a single paragraph, that the facts available to it suggested that rivals' ability and incentive to compete had been unaffected by the practice.[34] Other cases are not

[31] See for instance Case T-328/03, *O2 (Germany) GmbH & Co. OHG v Commission*, EU:T:2006:116. The case law in which the analysis of effects is somewhat relevant is relatively scarce and does not shed much light. The single most important case in this sense in recent years is Case C-382/12 P, *MasterCard Inc. and Others v Commission*, EU:C:2014:2201, where the issue raised on appeal was relatively narrow (it concerned the notion of objective necessity). In Case T-65/98, *Van den Bergh Foods Ltd v Commission*, EU:T:2003:281, the interest of the issue of effects was limited due to the high market share enjoyed by the firm.

[32] Case C-280/08 P, *Deutsche Telekom AG v Commission*, EU:C:2010:603, para. 255.

[33] Case C-345/14, *Maxima Latvija*, paras. 25–31.

[34] Case C-209/10, *Post Danmark A/S v Konkurrencerådet*, EU:C:2012:172 ('*Post Danmark I*'), para. 39.

representative, either because effects were particularly likely or, conversely, particularly unlikely. Some references concerned recently liberalised network industries and thus related to segments with natural monopoly features, around which foreclosure tends to be particularly likely. This was the factual scenario at stake in, for instance, *TeliaSonera* and *Post Danmark II*.[35] Arguably, the references in which the most interesting issues were raised involved agreements with limited coverage that were unlikely to have anti-competitive effects. A steady stream of references concerning the compatibility with Article 101(1) TFEU of agreements between petrol suppliers and individual stations has reached the Court in the past two decades.[36]

There are three aspects relating to the analysis of effects that have not been fully clarified in the abovementioned cases. The first aspect relates to the requisite threshold of effects. It is clear that, as far as practices subject to a rule are concerned, it is sufficient to show that anti-competitive effects are plausible. The vocabulary is sometimes more ambiguous in the context of 'by effect' cases, which require evidence of a negative impact on competition as a precondition to establish a prima facie infringement. As noted by several commentators, the expressions 'capable' and 'likely' have occasionally been used interchangeably in 'by effect' cases, which casts doubts as to whether evidence of plausibility is enough across the board.[37] If that is true, there would be no meaningful difference between practices subject to a rule and those subject to a standard.

A second, related, aspect concerns the time horizon that should be considered in the analysis. As explained in Chapter 5, this is an issue that has been addressed in EU merger control, but not in the context of Articles 101 and 102 TFEU. While the Court has repeatedly held that it is not necessary to wait for the anti-competitive effects of a practice to materialise,[38] and that EU competition law provisions cover both actual and potential effects, it is not clear how far the forecast can venture into

[35] In Case C-23/14, *Post Danmark A/S v Konkurrencerådet*, EU:C:2015:651 ('*Post Danmark II*'), the industry had only been partially liberalised (some of the incumbent's activities were protected by exclusive rights), which made anti-competitive effects even more likely.

[36] See in particular Case C-384/13, *Estación de Servicio Pozuelo 4, S.L., v Galp Energía España, S.A.U.*, EU:C:2014:2425; Case C-506/07, *Lubricantes y Carburantes Galaicos SL v GALP Energía España SAU*, EU:C:2009:504; and Case C-214/99, *Neste Markkinointi Oy v Yötuuli Ky and Others*, EU:C:2000:679.

[37] For a detailed analysis of this question, see Renato Nazzini, *The Foundations of European Union Competition Law: The Objective and Principles of Article 102* (Oxford: Oxford University Press, 2011), pp. 294–301.

[38] Case C-23/14, *Post Danmark II*, para. 66; Case C-52/09, *TeliaSonera*, para. 64.

the future. The issue can be of practical importance, in particular from the perspective of the rights of defence. If action can be grounded on a speculative theory of harm that might or might not unfold in the distant future, it is difficult to see how it could be disproved by firms. The key question, against this background, is whether the principles set out by the Court in *Tetra Laval*, which would effectively address these concerns, apply across competition law provisions.

A final issue relates to the causal link between the practice and the impact it has allegedly had (or is likely to have). *Post Danmark II* provided an important clarification in that it held that Article 102 TFEU is only triggered when the anti-competitive effects are 'attributable' to the behaviour of the dominant firm.[39] This requirement is consistent with the relevant Article 101(1) TFEU case law, which has consistently required authorities and claimants to establish anti-competitive effects against the relevant counterfactual. This question has also been emphasised in the field of merger control, where the failing firm defence has long provided an example of an instance in which there is no causal link between the elimination of a source of competitive pressure and the transaction.[40] In the context of Articles 101 and 102 TFEU, however, there are no cases in which the principle enunciated in *Post Danmark II* is fleshed out.

1.2.2 The Rise of Commitment Decisions

Of all institutional innovations introduced by virtue of Regulation 1/2003, the so-called commitment decisions are those that have attracted the greatest amount of commentary and controversy.[41] As explained in

[39] Case C-23/14, *Post Danmark II*, para. 47.

[40] On the failing firm defence in merger control, see Joined Cases C-68/94 and C-30/95 *France v Commission*, EU:C:1998:148 ('*Kali & Salz*') and Guidelines on the assessment of horizontal mergers under the Council Regulation on the control of concentrations between undertakings OJ (2004) No. OJ C 31/5, paras. 89–91.

[41] For a representative sample of the literature, see Melchior Wathelet, 'Commitment Decisions and the Paucity of Precedent' (2015) 6 *Journal of European Competition Law & Practice* 553; Niamh Dunne, 'Commitment Decisions in EU Competition Law' (2014) 10 *Journal of Competition Law & Economics* 399; Philip Marsden, 'The Emperor's Clothes Laid Bare: Commitments Creating the Appearance of Law, While Denying Access to Law', *CPI Antitrust Chronicle*, October 2013(1); Heike Schweitzer, 'Commitment Decisions under Art. 9 of Regulation 1/2003: The Developing EC Practice and Case Law' in Claus-Dieter Ehlermann, Mel Marquis (eds.), *European Competition Law Annual 2008 – Antitrust Settlements under EC Competition Law* (Oxford: Hart Publishing, 2010); and John Temple Lang, 'Commitment Decisions and Settlements with Antitrust Authorities and Private Parties under European Antitrust Law' (2006) 32 *Annual Proceedings of the Fordham Corporate Law Institute* 265.

the preceding chapters, this instrument allows the Commission to put an end to proceedings by means of a formal decision making the commitments offered by the parties binding upon them. This possibility did not formally exist under Regulation 17.[42] In spite of this fact, it would be inaccurate to assume that commitment decisions have greatly altered the enforcement landscape. This is a point emphasised, among others, by Wils.[43] While the Commission was not empowered to adopt formal decisions accepting commitments, the – formal or informal – closure of proceedings following the remedies offered by the parties was a frequent and important aspect of the practice of the authority. In addition, commitment decisions have emerged as the instrument that has filled the gap left by the demise of exemptions. In fact, they work in many ways like the latter. This is not surprising. The practices with which the Commission deals by means of a commitment decision are similar in their nature, purpose and impact to those that would have qualified for an exemption under Regulation 17. As explained in Chapter 3, both instruments are suitable for conduct that has ambivalent effects on competition – as opposed to, for instance (and in particular), cartels.

Commitment decisions have become controversial for several reasons. The first and most obvious of these reasons is that they have become a central instrument in the decision-making practice of the Commission. As shown in Chart 6.1, a significant amount of decisions adopted in any given year are commitment decisions. According to some commentators, this is an outcome that the Commission itself did not anticipate when it adopted Regulation 1/2003.[44] These commentators have explained that this instrument was expected to be used only sparingly by the authority. The popularity of commitment decisions to address concerns in 'law-intensive' cases should not come as a surprise, however, if one considers the framework laid down in Chapter 2. It is indeed reasonable for an authority like the Commission to prefer negotiated outcomes over decisions formally establishing an infringement.

A second reason behind the controversy around commitment decisions relates to the way in which the instrument engages with the

42 Regulation No. 17: First Regulation implementing Articles 85 and 86 of the Treaty OJ (1962) No. 13/204.

43 Wouter Wils, 'Ten Years of Commitment Decisions Under Article 9 of Regulation 1/2003: Too Much of a Good Thing?', available at http://ssrn.com/.

44 See in this sense John Temple Lang, 'Commitment Decisions and Settlements with Antitrust Authorities and Private Parties under European Antitrust Law'.

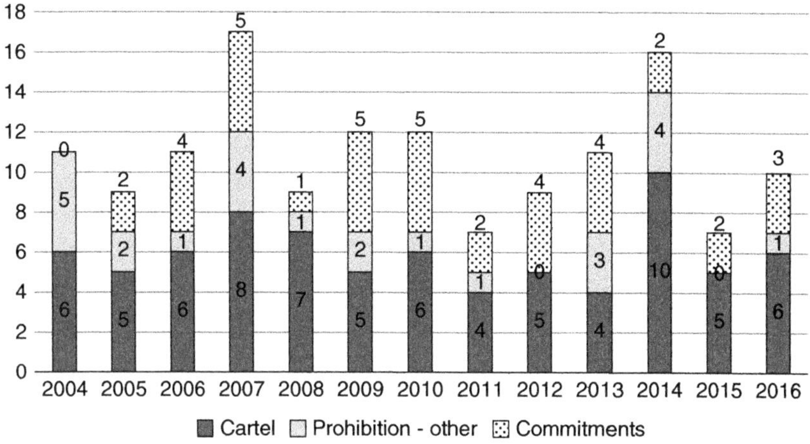

Chart 6.1 Decisions adopted since 2004, three main types

substance of the provisions. As already explained in Chapter 2, commitment decisions do not express a view on whether the practices under consideration are in breach of Articles 101 and 102 TFEU – at least not so formally. These decisions make the remedies binding upon firms and state that, as a result, there are no longer grounds for the Commission to continue with the investigation. In this sense, they are, first and foremost, a tool that aims to provide transparency to stakeholders while allowing the authority to make effective use of its resources. The substantive analysis is inevitably succinct as a result. It is confined to a 'preliminary assessment' in which the Commission outlines the concerns that justified the opening of an investigation.[45] Some commentators regret the absence of a fully fledged legal analysis. From this perspective, the flexibility allowed by commitment decisions would come at the expense of legal certainty.[46] According to this view, the availability of a formal instrument would not represent a substantial improvement relative to the regime implemented by virtue of Regulation 17.

A third aspect of the controversy relates to the institutional consequences of the rise of commitment decisions. Due to their nature, it is

[45] The need to conduct a preliminary assessment is enshrined in Article 9 of Council Regulation (EC) No. 1/2003 of 16 December 2002 on the implementation of the rules on competition laid down in Articles 81 and 82 of the Treaty OJ (2003) No. L 1/1.

[46] See for instance Wathelet, 'Commitment Decisions and the Paucity of Precedent' and Marsden, 'The Emperor's Clothes Laid Bare: Commitments Creating the Appearance of Law, While Denying Access to Law'.

relatively unlikely that these decisions will be challenged before the EU courts. This is a conclusion that is supported by the findings in Part II, and which explains the preferences of the authority. The experience since the adoption of Regulation 1/2003 confirms this intuition. Out of a total of 40 decisions adopted at the time of writing, only four of them have been challenged before the GC. What is more, challenges have become less likely following the Court ruling in *Alrosa*, mentioned in Chapter 2.[47] The Court concluded in that judgment that the intensity of the review needs to adapt to the nature of the instrument. Insofar as the Commission enjoys discretion to define its enforcement priorities, a decision stating that there are no longer grounds for it to continue with the investigation can only be subject to marginal review.[48]

Even though the outcome in *Alrosa* appears to be consistent with prior case law dealing with the areas in which the Commission enjoys discretion, some authors have deplored the negative implications it is claimed to have. Because they are only subject to marginal review, the substantive approach underpinning commitment decisions would not be subject to effective judicial scrutiny. As a result, the system would not be adequately equipped to address attempts by the Commission to stretch the boundaries of Articles 101 and 102 TFEU. Eventually, the absence of full judicial review would lead to the outcomes identified in Chapter 2 – namely, inconsistent and unpredictable enforcement. These effects would be exacerbated by the fact that commitment decisions do not provide a clear statement of the law and of the legal characterisation of facts.

There is already anecdotal evidence that has been advanced in support of these claims. Several commentators have sought to show that commitment decisions allow the Commission to depart from the applicable precedents.[49] Similarly, it has been argued that the remedies that the commitments agreed upon by firms go beyond what would have been necessary to address the concerns raised by the Commission.[50] The latter question is in fact at the origin of Court ruling in *Alrosa*.[51] This line of research is valuable in that its underlying intuitions raise the same issues that this volume seeks to verify, that is, whether the Commission displays

47 Case C-441/07 P, *Commission v Alrosa Company Ltd*, EU:C:2010:377.

48 Ibid., para. 42.

49 For a discussion, see Dunne, 'Commitment Decisions in EU Competition Law', at 421–4.

50 Pablo Ibáñez Colomo, 'On the Application of Competition Law as Regulation: Elements for a Theory' (2010) 29 *Yearbook of European Law* 261.

51 See in this sense Case C-170/06, *Alrosa Company Ltd v Commission*, EU:T:2007:220, paras. 62–4.

a consistent tendency to interpret the scope of its powers relatively broadly. As a result of this pattern of behaviour, commitment decisions can make the system more vulnerable. The vulnerability of the system would be exacerbated by the prospect of fines. In the current institutional landscape, commitments may be perceived as a more acceptable outcome, for several reasons, than a prohibition decision providing for a fine. As a result, firms may be inclined to propose commitments even when it is unclear that the practice raising concerns constitutes an infringement of Articles 101 and/or 102 TFEU.

The approach that was followed in Part II can also be applied to examine systematically these concerns. As already pointed out, a total of 40 decisions have been adopted by the authority at the time of writing. As shown in Chart 6.2, decisions are evenly shared. Eighteen of them concern the application of Article 101 TFEU; 20 concern the application of Article 102 TFEU; and two concern the application of the two provisions. Charts 6.3 and 6.4, as well as Table 6.1 in the Appendix, provide a more detailed overview of the sort of cases that have been dealt with via commitments. Among Article 101 TFEU decisions, it appears that the landscape is dominated by cases that can be labelled as horizontal co-operation agreements. The industries and the objectives of co-operation are very diverse, ranging from copyright-collecting societies[52] to airline alliances.[53] Another sizeable range of cases concerns vertical agreements. In particular, the Commission has adopted a series of decisions relating to the practices implemented by car manufacturers in the aftermarkets for their products.[54] Other cases defy an easy categorisation.[55]

When looking at Article 102 TFEU cases in Chart 6.4, the most noticeable pattern is the pre-eminence of cases relating to (outright and constructive) refusals to deal, which represent nine of the 20 decisions

[52] Commission Decision of 4 October 2006 (Case COMP/C2/38.681 – *The Cannes Extension Agreement*).

[53] Commission Decision of 12 May 2015 (Case AT.39964 – *Air France/KLM/Alitalia/Delta*); Commission Decision of 23 May 2013 (Case COMP/AT.39595 – *Continental/United/Lufthansa/Air Canada*); and Commission Decision of 14 July 2010 (Case COMP/39.596 – BA/AA/IB).

[54] Commission Decision of 13 September 2007 (Case COMP/E-2/39.143 – *Opel*); Commission Decision of 13 September 2007 (Case COMP/E-2/39.142 – *Toyota*); Commission Decision of 13 September 2007 (Case COMP/E-2/39.141 – *Fiat*); and Commission Decision of 13 September 2007 (Case COMP/E-2/39.140 – *DaimlerChrysler*).

[55] See for instance Commission Decision of 25 July 2013 (Case AT.39847 – *E-Books*), which looks more like a collective boycott than an efficiency-enhancing arrangement.

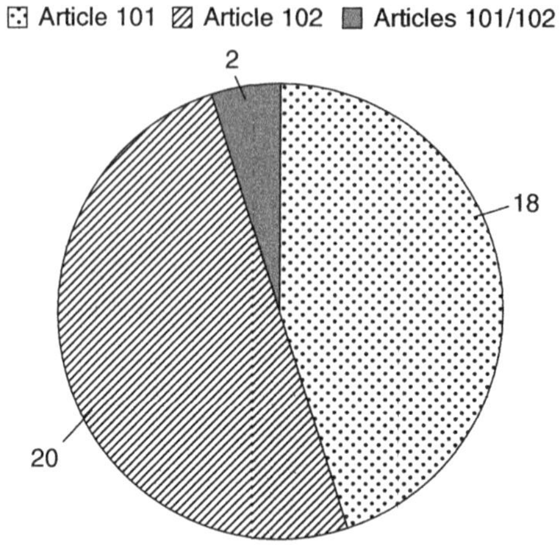

Chart 6.2 Commitment decisions, by provision

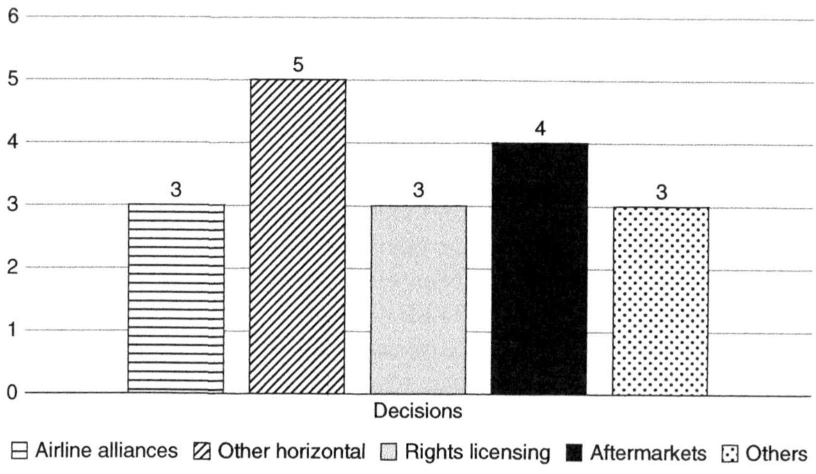

Chart 6.3 Article 101 TFEU commitment decisions, by issue

considered (or around 45 per cent).[56] The majority of these cases concern practices in the energy sector[57] – gas and electricity – but also in other

[56] This chart includes proceedings dealing with both Articles 101 and 102 TFEU.

[57] Commission Decision of 29 September 2010 (Case COMP/39.315 – *ENI*); Commission Decision of 4 May 2010 (Case COMP/39.317 – *E.ON Gas*); Commission Decision of 3 December 2009 (Case COMP/39.316 – *Gaz de France*); Commission Decision of 18 March 2009 (Case COMP/39.402 – *RWE Gas Foreclosure*).

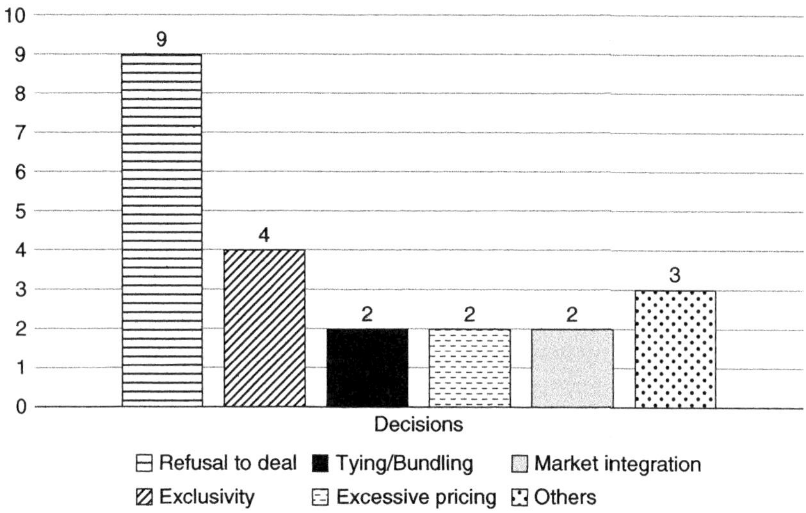

Chart 6.4 Article 102 (and 101/102) TFEU commitment decisions, by issue

network industries[58] and in technology markets.[59] This pattern is remarkable if one considers that only in exceptional circumstances does a refusal to deal amount to an abuse of a dominant position. Six of the decisions concern more traditional abusive categories – tying and exclusive dealing.[60] Finally, there are two decisions dealing with excessive prices.[61] Behaviour that does not clearly fall within the usual categories includes practices aimed at limiting parallel trade[62] or the ability of customers to resell a good.[63]

The substantive analysis conducted by the Commission in individual cases shows that commitment decisions are not always used in relation to practices that would amount to a clear-cut infringement, or that fall

[58] Commission Decision of 18 December 2013 (Case COMP/AT.39678 – *Deutsche Bahn I* and Case COMP/AT.39731 – *Deutsche Bahn II*).

[59] See for instance Commission Decision of 20 December 2012 Case AT.39654 – *Reuters Instrument Codes*); and Commission Decision of 13 December 2011 (Case COMP/C-3/39.692 – *IBM Maintenance Services*).

[60] See for instance Commission Decision of 16 December 2009 (Case COMP/C-3/39.530 – *Microsoft (tying)*) ('*Microsoft II*'); and Commission Decision of 22 February 2006 (Case COMP/B-2/38.381– *De Beers*).

[61] Commission Decision of 15 November 2011 (Case COMP/39.592 – *Standard & Poor's*); and Commission Decision of 9 December 2009 (Case COMP/38.636 – *Rambus*).

[62] Commission Decision of 14 April 2010 (Case COMP/39.351 – *Swedish Interconnectors*).

[63] Commission Decision of 10 December 2015 (Case AT.39767 – *BEH Electricity*).

squarely within the scope of existing categories. There are some cases in which, indeed, there were no obvious precedents indicating that the practice was a prima facie violation of Articles 101 and/or 102 TFEU. What is more, commitment decisions have sometimes been relied upon even though administrative action seemed unwarranted. In some instances, the theory of harm advanced by the Commission appeared to move beyond the boundaries defined in the case law. In other instances, the concerns raised appeared to contradict the position expressed by the Commission in a pre-commitment device.

The *Paramount* decision is an example of administrative action seemingly contradicting the boundaries defined in the case law.[64] In essence, the case raises the same issues that the Court already addressed in *Coditel II.* As explained in Chapter 3, the Court held in that judgment that an agreement that provides for absolute territorial protection is not as such caught by Article 101(1) TFEU where the protection it affords does not go beyond the protection that intellectual property rights alone would afford. In *Paramount*, the Commission raised concerns, inter alia, about the clauses in a licensing agreement prohibiting a broadcaster the unauthorised Internet transmission of copyright-protected works outside the area covered by the licence and about the clauses requiring the licensor to introduce similar clauses in other licensing agreements.[65] The authority took this position even though the protection afforded by virtue of the agreement did not go beyond the protection afforded by virtue of the copyright system.

One would have expected the outcome of *Paramount* and *Coditel II* to have been the same. In fact, the investigation into licensing agreements between film studios and broadcasters, which is at the origin of the *Paramount* decision, initially left clauses relating to Internet transmission outside of its scope. This fact can be interpreted as suggesting that they were deemed unproblematic in light of the relevant case law.[66] Against this background, it would have been reasonable for the Commission to explain why it had come to the preliminary view that the contentious clauses amounted to a 'by object' infringement in spite of the principles set out in *Coditel II.* However, the *Paramount* decision is silent on the question, and simply restates the principle whereby agreements aimed at restricting

[64] Commission Decision of 26 July 2016 (Case AT.40023 – *Cross-Border Access to pay-TV*).
[65] Ibid., paras. 46–9.
[66] Joaquín Almunia, 'Statement on Opening of Investigation into Pay TV Services' (Brussels, 13 January 2014).

trade between Member States are contrary to Article 101(1) TFEU by their very nature.

ENI[67] is an example of a case that does not contradict the boundaries defined in the case law, but expands them. The decision is based on the preliminary conclusion that the behaviour by an incumbent in the energy sector amounted to a refusal to supply that breached Article 102 TFEU. The single most notable aspect of the case relates to a practice that has been labelled 'strategic underinvestment'.[68] According to the Commission, a decision by a vertically integrated operator not to invest in infrastructure could constitute an abuse of a dominant position. The authority noted in *ENI* that there was 'long-term capacity demand' from third parties to gain access to the dominant firm's infrastructure.[69] In spite of this fact, the company took its investment decisions based on its own needs alone, according to the decision. Thus, the purpose of this business strategy was not driven by the profitability of its transport capacity activities, but by the aim of protecting itself from competition on the downstream market.[70]

The reasoning of the Commission in *ENI* is notable in several respects. Contrary to the case law dealing with the potentially abusive nature of a refusal to deal, the authority did not challenge a refusal *stricto sensu*, but the firm's decision not to build the infrastructure in the first place. It is in this sense that *ENI* can be said to stretch the boundaries of the relevant precedents. While the applicable case law supports the proposition that a refusal to give access to existing capacity may, in exceptional circumstances, be in breach of Article 102 TFEU, it does not obviously support the view that a refusal to invest in new capacity may amount to an abuse. Second, the existing case law could be interpreted as suggesting that the absence of capacity could arguably justify a refusal, and thus rule out the application of Article 102 TFEU.[71] In this sense, the very

[67] Commission Decision of 29 September 2010, *ENI*.

[68] On the notion of strategic underinvestment, see Pietro Merlino and Gianluca Faella, 'Strategic Underinvestment as an Abuse of Dominance under EU Competition Rules' (2013) 36 *World Competition* 513; and Frank Maier-Rigaud, Federica Manca and Ulrich von Koppenfels, 'Strategic underinvestment and gas network foreclosure – the ENI case' (2011) 1 *Competition Policy Newsletter* 18.

[69] Commission Decision of 29 September 2010, *ENI*, para. 56. [70] Ibid., para. 58.

[71] For an opinion supporting this conclusion, see Robert O'Donoghue and Jorge Padilla, *The Law and Economics of Article 102 TFEU*, 2nd edn. (Oxford: Hart Publishing, 2013), p. 564. The authors refer in this sense to Commission Decision 94/119/EC of 21 December 1993 concerning a refusal to grant access to the facilities of the port of Rødby (Denmark) OJ (1994) No. L 55/52.

behaviour that the Commission considered to be problematic in *ENI* could be said to fall outside the scope of the prohibition, as being objectively justified in light of precedents like *Magill* or *IMS Health*.

The *E.On* saga shows that, as suggested above, commitment decisions can be adopted in cases where there are no clear precedents supporting a finding of infringement.[72] The Commission challenged in this decision, inter alia, the policy of the dominant firm – which controlled an electricity transmission network in Germany – when acquiring balancing energy. According to the authority, the practice sought to favour its own production affiliate and discriminated against third parties, which were offering their energy in a 'more competitive environment'.[73] The decision speculates that E.On might have been interested in inflating the costs of its own transmission division to achieve this objective. This aspect of the decision is notable in several respects. First, there is nothing in the decision that suggests that the Commission had come to the preliminary conclusion that the practice was abusive in light of the conditions set out in *Magill* or *Bronner*. In fact, there is no reference to the actual or likely impact of the behaviour on competition.

Insofar as it does not mention the anti-competitive effects of the discriminatory conduct, the decision could be interpreted as suggesting that vertically integrated firms are under a general duty not to favour their own affiliate against rivals, or that discrimination is prima facie abusive by its very nature. However, it seems difficult to argue, in light of the relevant precedents, that there is something inherently abusive in the fact that a dominant firm seeks to favour its own interests at the expense of rivals. These are positions for which there is no obvious support in the case law. In fact, if one considers that some practices, like a refusal to deal, can also be seen as a form of discrimination, it is not clear whether such a principle can be inferred from Article 102 TFEU.[74] More generally, nothing in the case law suggests that dominant firms are under a general duty to subsidise rivals, or to ensure that they are able to remain on the market.

Finally, the *Microsoft II* (tying) decision is an example of a commitment decision seemingly going against the position expressed by the Commission in a pre-commitment device. In its Guidance Paper, the authority

[72] Commission Decision of 26 November 2008 (Case COMP/39.388 – *German electricity wholesale market* and COMP/39.389 – *German Electricity Balancing Market*).

[73] Ibid., para. 51.

[74] Pablo Ibáñez Colomo, 'Exclusionary Discrimination under Article 102 TFEU' (2014) 51 *Common Market Law Review* 141.

committed to examining tying and bundling practices in a manner consistent with consensus views. This commitment involved, first, revisiting one of the most contentious aspects of the case law on tying. This practice is only abusive where it involves two separate products.[75] In this regard, there is a divergence between the consensus and the case law. According to the GC in *Microsoft I*, evidence that some manufacturers are specialised in offering the tied product is evidence that the two are separate for the purposes of the application of Article 102 TFEU.[76] According to the mainstream (as reflected in the Guidance), two products are only deemed separate where the tying product is commonly sold without the tied product.[77] Second, the pre-commitment made in the Guidance Paper departs from the case law in relation to the assessment of anti-competitive effects. If in *Microsoft I* the GC ruled that a 'distribution advantage' on the market for the tied product is sufficient to conclude that the practice is capable of having such effects,[78] the Guidance Paper advocates a careful assessment of whether foreclosure is a likely outcome in the relevant economic and legal context.[79]

Microsoft II provided an opportunity to test the principles set out in the Guidance Paper. The decision in the case was adopted about a year after the pre-commitment device was issued. However, there are fundamental contradictions between the two. Rather than endorsing the consensus positions embraced in the Guidance, the Commission followed the case law, in particular the GC ruling in *Microsoft I*. It is not immediately obvious to argue – were one to follow the consensus approach – that operating systems (the tying product in the case) and web browsers (the

[75] Guidance on the Commission's enforcement priorities in applying Article 82 of the EC Treaty to abusive exclusionary conduct by dominant undertakings OJ (2009) No. C 45/7.

[76] Case T-201/04, *Microsoft Corporation v Commission*, EU:T:2007:289 ('*Microsoft I*'), para. 927 ('according to the case-law the fact that there are on the market independent companies specialising in the manufacture and sale of the tied product constitutes serious evidence of the existence of a separate market for that product').

[77] See in this sense the principle set out in Herbert Hovenkamp, *Federal Antitrust Policy – The Law of Competition and its Practice*, 4th edition (Saint Paul: West Publishing, 2011): 'Thus the basic test for tying: the alleged tying and tied items are separate products if the tying item is commonly sold separately from the tied item in a well functioning market. [U]nder the basic test someone claiming that an automobile manufacturer [. . .] unlawfully tied tires to cars would have to show that under ordinary competitive conditions cars are commonly sold without their tires'. See also Guidance Paper, para 51: 'Two products are distinct if, in the absence of tying or bundling, a substantial number of customers would purchase or would have purchased the tying product without also buying the tied product from the same supplier'.

[78] Case T-201/04, *Microsoft I*, para. 1054.

[79] Guidance Paper, para. 20.

tied product) are separate products.[80] Due to the pervasiveness of the Internet, consumers expect operating systems to be equipped with web browsers. In spite of this fact, the Commission claimed that the web browser and the operating system were separate products.[81] Nowhere is the rationale for this conclusion explained in this decision and nowhere does the Commission examine whether there is separate demand for the operating system without the web browser. Regarding the assessment of the anti-competitive effects, the decision merely notes, in an approach that mirrors that of the GC in *Microsoft I*, that the integration of the two products gave an 'artificial distribution advantage' to the web browser of the dominant operator[82] and that this advantage could not be offset by rivals.[83]

As can be seen, these examples suggest that there may be merit in claims that commitment decisions make it possible for the Commission to deviate from the logic of existing precedents or to address unexplored issues without being required to provide a fully-fledged legal analysis and without being exposed to judicial review. Three of the above examples have an aspect in common that is valuable to fully explain the behaviour of the Commission – and to understand in part the controversies around the use of the instrument by the authority. These three cases cannot be entirely understood without considering that they were initiated at the same time that two Commission-wide initiatives were under way. The *Paramount* decision, for instance, was adopted in the context of the Digital Single Market Strategy, which is aimed at bringing down barriers to online cross-border economic activity in the EU. A priority in this sense has been to ensure that consumers are in a position to access the content of their choice irrespective of their location within the EU. In this sense, *Paramount* – and the broader *Cross-Border Pay-TV* investigation[84] – deals with the heart of the Commission-wide initiative.

[80] It is indeed difficult to think that, in an era of ubiquitous access, operating systems would be sold without a web browser. In fact, the very remedy accepted in *Microsoft II* suggests that the sale of an operating system without a web browser was not considered an adequate one by the Commission.

[81] Commission Decision of 16 December 2009, *Microsoft II*, paras. 32 and 36.

[82] Ibid., para. 39: 'the Commission preliminarily considered that the tying of Internet Explorer to Windows was liable to foreclose the market for web browsers and that the tying gave Internet Explorer an artificial distribution advantage that other web browsers were unable to match'.

[83] Ibid., para. 45.

[84] See in this sense Case AT.40023 – *Cross-border access to pay-TV, pending*. At the time of writing, the proceedings against five film studios and Sky UK are still open. Commission,

ENI and *E.On*, on the other hand, must also be understood in the context of the liberalisation of energy markets. The two are part of a series of decisions adopted by the Commission following the launch of a sector inquiry into electricity and gas markets. This sector inquiry, in turn, took place at the same time that the adoption of EU-wide legislation in the field was being considered. The parallels and substantive overlaps between the sector inquiry and the individual cases, on the one hand, and legislation, on the other, are significant. The concern with vertical integration and its impact on competition and the emergence of an internal market for gas and electricity, which is central to *ENI* and *E.On*, is also a key aspect of the regulatory framework. In this sense, the competition cases reflect the preferred approach of the Commission, which would not be fully enshrined in the liberalisation package.[85]

Commitment decisions have proved to be a valuable and flexible instrument in EU competition law. In the current institutional landscape, they are arguably indispensable, in the same way that decisions with commitments in Phase I are necessary in the field of merger control. At the same time, they are part of a peculiar setting which may exacerbate some features of the Commission behaviour as discussed in Part II. The tendency to construe the scope of prima facie prohibitions in a relatively broad manner, and to shift the burden of proof, can be expected to be more frequently displayed where the authority is not required to provide a fully-fledged legal analysis of the provision and where judicial review is unlikely (and in any event confined to manifest errors of assessment). These questions, which can have tangible consequences for the evolution and consistency of the EU competition law system, must be taken into consideration.

'Antitrust: Commission sends Statement of Objections on cross-border provision of pay-TV services available in UK and Ireland' (IP/15/5432, 23 July 2015).

85 Concerning the so-called 'third energy package' see, in particular Directive 2009/73/EC of the European Parliament and of the Council of 13 July 2009 concerning common rules for the internal market in natural gas and repealing Directive 2003/55/EC OJ (2009) No. L 211/94; Directive 2009/72/EC of the European Parliament and of the Council of 13 July 2009 concerning common rules for the internal market in electricity and repealing Directive 2003/54/EC OJ (2009) No. L 211/55. Unlike the Commission Decision in *E.On*, the third energy package did not require the ownership unbundling of some segments of the value chain. For an analysis of the legislation, see Angus Johnston and Guy Block, *EU Energy Law* (Oxford: Oxford University Press, 2012).

1.2.3 The Changing Interactions with the EU Courts

One of the consequences of the decentralised application of Articles 101 and 102 TFEU is that the majority of this enforcement now takes place at the national level, through the activity of NCAs and national courts.[86] As a result, annulment proceedings have become a relatively less prominent setting in which to examine the behaviour of the Commission and the Court. This reality is not only due to the increased activity at the national level, but to the practical importance of commitment decisions, which make challenges against administrative action less likely. Other institutional settings are on the rise. To begin with, one can expect preliminary references to increase in importance, if not necessarily in quantitative terms, at least in qualitative ones. It was noted in Chapter 4 that the majority of references in Article 102 TFEU cases traditionally concerned questions of peripheral relevance for the understanding of the notion of abuse – or for the provision at large. In recent years, however, national courts have submitted some questions of principle addressing fundamental issues around the notion of abuse. These include, as already explained, the legal status of 'margin squeeze' practices,[87] of selective price cuts[88] and of standardised rebate schemes.[89] Similarly, it has been noted in this chapter that questions and contributions relating to the boundaries between restrictions by object and by effect are coming as much from preliminary references, if not more, as from annulment proceedings.

If preliminary references become more important in relative terms, one can expect the behaviour of the Commission to be manifested in new ways. For instance, the authority may carefully choose the timing of its decisions in anticipation of preliminary rulings. If its decisions are published ahead of a preliminary ruling, it may be able to avoid any potential endogenous constraints. It is possible to think of two examples showing how the timing can impact these constraints. In both, the Commission issued a prohibition decision shortly before a Court judgment addressing the same point of law. Moreover, the two decisions set

[86] See Commission, 'Ten Years of Antitrust Enforcement under Regulation 1/2003: Achievements and Future Perspectives' COM(2014) 453. According to the figures provided, the Commission adopted, between May 2004 and September 2013, 122 decisions. During the same period, national authorities adopted 665 decisions. See also the figures and analysis found in Wouter Wils, 'Ten Years of Regulation 1/2003 – A Retrospective' (2013) 4 *Journal of European Competition Law & Practice* 293.

[87] Case C-52/09, *TeliaSonera*.

[88] Case C-209/10, *Post Danmark I*.

[89] Case C-23/14, *Post Danmark II*.

the threshold for intervention at a significantly lower level than the preliminary ruling. *Microsoft I*, for instance, was issued a month before *IMS Health*, in which the Court reiterated that the conditions set out in *Magill* are cumulative and which defined the benchmark against which the lawfulness of the decision was to be assessed. It was explained at length earlier how the *Microsoft I* decision departed from this understanding of Article 102 TFEU. Similarly, the Commission adopted a decision in 2014[90] on a new point of law – concerning namely the instances in which an injunction brought by the holder of a patent essential to a standard amounts to an abuse – that would be addressed by the Court the following year in a preliminary ruling.[91] Again, the interpretation of the notion advanced by the authority appeared to be broader.

The Commission has the power to make submissions to the Court in the context of preliminary reference proceedings. This is another tool through which it can advance its interpretation of EU competition law provisions. For the purposes of this study, the tool is particularly valuable insofar as it makes it possible to examine whether the Commission displays, in preliminary reference proceedings, a behaviour that is consistent with that displayed in the context of annulment actions. Submissions, moreover, can be compared against the case law and also against the pre-commitment devices, such as Guidelines, issued by the authority. In this sense, they make it possible to evaluate whether the interpretations of EU competition law provisions advanced in the context of a preliminary reference are consistent with the constraints that it has committed to impose upon itself. As shown in Part II, the possibility to make submissions has always existed. However, it may become significantly more important in the new enforcement landscape.

Some of the submissions made by the Commission in Article 102 TFEU references suggest that the authority may depart, in a preliminary reference procedure, from the approach endorsed in a pre-commitment device. As already explained, the reference in *TeliaSonera* concerned, inter alia, whether evidence of indispensability is a necessary condition to establish the abusive nature of a 'margin squeeze'. In the Guidance Paper, the Commission committed to examining this practice as a constructive refusal to supply, which would make indispensability

[90] Commission Decision of 29 April 2014, *Motorola*.

[91] Case C-170/13, *Huawei Technologies Co. Ltd v ZTE Corp. and ZTE Deutschland GmbH*, EU:C:2015:477.

(or 'objective necessity', which is the term used in the document) a precondition for intervention.[92] In *TeliaSonera*, however, the Commission expressed a different view.[93] According to its submission, it would be inappropriate to view a 'margin squeeze' as a constructive refusal to deal. Such an interpretation of Article 102 TFEU, the authority argued, would amount to requiring evidence of indispensability in any abuse case. This is the argument that would be followed by the Court.[94]

Post Danmark I is another example in which the Commission appeared to depart from the logic of the Guidance Paper. As explained in detail in Chapter 4, the fundamental question raised in that case was whether a policy of selective price cuts can be deemed abusive in and of itself or only where the prices applied are predatory within the meaning of *AKZO*. The position expressed in the Guidance Paper suggested that action in a selective pricing case would be warranted if (and only if) prices fall below a relevant cost benchmark. The authority's submission in *Post Danmark I*, however, endorsed a different understanding of Article 102 TFEU. The Commission suggested that a policy of selective price cuts implemented by a super-dominant firm – such as Post Danmark in that case – is prima facie abusive if the difference in price lacks an objective justification.[95] The rationale for intervention under this approach is the presumed anti-competitive intent of the dominant firm.

In the new institutional context, the Commission may also influence the evolution of Articles 101 and 102 TFEU through its exchanges with national courts. In accordance with Article 15(3) of Regulation 1/2003, it can become involved in competition law

[92] Guidance Paper, paras. 80 and 81. In para. 81, the Commission explained that it would 'consider these practices [including 'margin squeeze' practices] as an enforcement priority if all the following circumstances are present:

the refusal relates to a product or service that is objectively necessary to be able to compete effectively on a downstream market,
the refusal is likely to lead to the elimination of effective competition on the downstream market, and
the refusal is likely to lead to consumer harm'.

[93] See also the Submission of the Commission in Case C-52/09, on file with the author.

[94] Case C-52/09, *TeliaSonera*, para. 58: 'if *Bronner* were to be interpreted otherwise, in the way advocated by TeliaSonera, that would, as submitted by the European Commission, amount to a requirement that before any conduct of a dominant undertaking in relation to its terms of trade could be regarded as abusive the conditions to be met to establish that there was a refusal to supply would in every case have to be satisfied, and that would unduly reduce the effectiveness of Article 102 TFEU'.

[95] Submission of the Commission in Case C-209/10, on file with the author.

proceedings at the national level where it considers that the coherent application of Articles 101 and 102 TFEU so requires.[96] A submission to the French Supreme Court in the aftermath of *Cartes Bancaires* provides a valuable example of how the Commission's role as amicus curiae may operate in practice. The case in question originated in a decision of the French NCA finding that the inter-entity fees set by a group of banks were not justified. This decision was subsequently quashed by the Cour d'appel de Paris.[97] In its submission, the Commission argued, inter alia, that the pro-competitive justifications for an agreement are of no relevance for the qualification of an agreement as restrictive by object, as they can only be taken into consideration under Article 101(3) TFEU.[98] This position is compatible with a relatively expansive understanding of the discipline. At the same time, it is not immediately obvious how to reconcile it with the case law discussed in Chapter 3, including *Cartes Bancaires* itself, which suggests that a clause that is a plausible means to achieve a pro-competitive objective is not restrictive of competition by object.

2 The Behaviour of the EU Courts

2.1 *Summary of the Main Findings*

The findings of Part II are not obviously compatible with the view that the EU courts are systematically deferential to the Commission. This is true irrespective of the way in which the question is examined. It is possible to find examples of instances in which the GC and the ECJ articulated with clarity the legal test against which the

[96] Article 15(3) of Regulation 1/2003 reads as follows: 'Competition authorities of the Member States, acting on their own initiative, may submit written observations to the national courts of their Member State on issues relating to the application of Article 81 or Article 82 of the Treaty. With the permission of the court in question, they may also submit oral observations to the national courts of their Member State. Where the coherent application of Article 81 or Article 82 of the Treaty so requires, the Commission, acting on its own initiative, may submit written observations to courts of the Member States. With the permission of the court in question, it may also make oral observations'.

[97] Decision of the Autorité de la concurrence of 20 September 2010 (Case 10-D-28). See also Judgment of the Paris Court of Appeal of 23 February 2012 and of the *Cour de Cassation* of 14 April 2015, available at www.autoritedelaconcurrence.fr/user/avisdec.php?numero=10D28.

[98] Submission of the Commission to the Cour de Cassation of 17 February 2015, available at http://ec.europa.eu/competition/court/mif_17022015_fr.pdf.

lawfulness of administrative action was to be assessed. Some judgments are even explicit about the rationale underlying the test. The conclusion would not be different if one were to take the annulment of Commission decisions as a proxy for the alleged deferential attitude of the EU courts. Decisions have indeed been quashed with relative regularity. In the context of Article 101 TFEU, the EU courts have often challenged the analytical framework of the Commission. In merger control, they questioned some fundamental choices made by the authority. This impression is confirmed when the figures are examined closely and are disaggregated, as has been done in Part II.

2.1.1 Variation in the Behaviour of the EU Courts

The analysis of one-shot interactions reveals that the EU courts have regularly engaged with the substantive analysis conducted by the Commission. In this sense, their behaviour does not appear to be compatible with claims of systematic or undue deference. Examples of rulings in which the EU courts are explicit about the rationale behind intervention, the applicable legal test and the legal characterisation of facts can be found across the board. The approach to the assessment of mergers in EU competition law, for instance, has been defined in a series of rulings handed down by the GC, in particular *Airtours* and *Tetra Laval*. In the context of Article 102 TFEU, the Court enunciated a clear rule, as well as the underlying logic, in cases like *Hoffmann-La Roche* and *AKZO*. In the context of Article 101 TFEU, the case law did not always coincide with the premises on which the analysis of the Commission rested, and this fact has occasionally led to the annulment of the administrative decision.

If one can identify a difference in the behaviour of the EU courts from one case or one area to another, this difference relates more to the resilience of the case law than to an allegedly deferential attitude. There is significant variation in this regard across provisions. As far as the interpretation of the notion of restriction of competition is concerned, the principles laid down in the early cases have proved resilient, and guided the evolution of subsequent case law to this day. The failure on the part of the Commission to consider the counterfactual, for instance, has regularly led to the annulment of decisions. *Nungesser* and *European Night Services* are obvious examples in this regard. Similarly, the tendency on the part of the Commission to equate a restriction of a firm's freedom of action with a restriction of competition has not been validated by the Court, even in cases where the substantive findings were not questioned.

The case law dealing with the notion of abuse has proved to be less resilient. The observed lack of resilience has been manifested in three ways. When looked upon from a dynamic perspective, it appears, first, that the rationale and tests laid down in the context of a particular case have not been followed in subsequent rulings raising similar or identical issues. As a result, precedents are not reliable indicators of the outcome of a ruling. In several instances, the EU courts did not appear to question the deviation from the applicable case law. Suffice it to mention the rule in *AKZO*, the logic of which is grounded on formal analysis and was spelled out by the Court. This rule was not followed in subsequent cases like *Irish Sugar* and *Compagnie Maritime Belge*. In the latter, the EU courts appeared to be satisfied with the idea that the specific factual circumstances of the case justified the application of an alternative analytical framework. Similarly, the standard applying to outright refusals to deal, introduced in *Magill* and confirmed in *IMS Health*, was not expanded to constructive refusals – in particular where they take the form of a 'margin squeeze'. This is so in spite of the fact that the Commission took the view in the Guidance that constructive and outright refusals should be subject to the same legal framework.

The absence of resilience has been manifested in the context of Article 102 TFEU in another way. In some instances, a rule has been expanded beyond its original scope, without the EU courts articulating the rationale for the expansion and its limits. *Michelin II* illustrates this phenomenon particularly well. As explained in Chapter 4, the case is notable in that the Commission expanded to standardised rebate schemes a rule originally confined to rebates conditional upon exclusivity. The scheme in *Michelin II* was based on volume, which is a factor that could have been reasonably interpreted as suggesting that it was prima facie lawful.[99] While there was no reason to rule out from the outset a finding of abuse, the case seemingly exceeded the boundaries defined in previous cases. In spite of this fact, the GC did not deem it necessary to explain or clarify in any detail why the rule could be expanded, without more, to rebates that apply equally to all customers and thus depend on the quantity supplied.[100]

[99] At least, the Court held in *Hoffmann-La Roche* – without elaborating on the point – that rebates conditional upon volume are compatible with Article 102 TFEU.

[100] This issue was raised by a leading Commission official, who suggested the need to be explicit about this point. See Luc Gyselen, 'Rebates – Competition on the Merits or

Finally, there are instances in which the EU courts have come close to recognising deference to the Commission over the definition and application of the legal test. This attitude is remarkable insofar as the system established by virtue of the Treaty does not recognise any discretion to the administrative authority on issues of law. The *Microsoft I* case provides a concrete example of such an instance, which has been discussed in detail in the preceding chapters. The analysis of the GC and that of the Commission in that case differed. The former examined the lawfulness of the practice in light of the principles set out in *Magill* and *IMS Health*. At the same time, it recognised some leeway to the Commission when defining the scope of the test in question. Remarkably, the GC concluded that the reinterpretation of the test – whereby the 'new product' condition became an assessment of whether the refusal limited technical development – was not 'manifestly incorrect'. In this sense, the GC appeared to hold the legal analysis of the Commission to a 'reasonableness' test, as opposed to a 'correctness' one.

2.1.2 Explaining Variation in One-Shot Interactions: The Impact of Formal Analysis

When the case law is examined from a static perspective, the most obvious tentative explanation for variation in the behaviour of the EU courts appears to be the influence of formal analysis, and in particular by the principles deriving from mainstream economics. More precisely, it would seem that the EU courts are more willing to articulate the rationale behind intervention and to lay down an explicit legal test where the underlying issue has already been the subject of formal analysis. This appears to be the case, in particular, where formal analysis has been or can be readily converted into an operational rule or standard. For the same reasons, the likelihood that the EU courts will depart from the framework endorsed by the Commission, and will challenge some aspects of the decision, is also higher if the EU courts perceive administrative action to be at odds with consensus positions.

This factor is a constant across provisions. It has been explained how, in the context of Article 102 TFEU, the Court departed from the test laid down by the Commission in *AKZO*. If the authority endorsed a 'checklist approach' that required a case-by-case assessment, the Court adopted

Exclusionary Practice?' in Claus-Dieter Ehlermann, Isabela Atanasiu (eds.), *European Competition Law Annual 2003: What Is an Abuse of a Dominant Position?* (Oxford: Hart Publishing, 2006).

a test that was grounded on economic analysis and that made it possible to identify instances in which the behaviour could be safely presumed to be a strategy to eliminate competition. The substantial differences between the analysis of the Commission and the Court in *Magill* have also been emphasised. If administrative action failed to engage with the fundamental issue raised by the case – whether, and in what circumstances, a refusal to license an intellectual property right amounts to an abuse of a dominant position – the judgment acknowledged the potentially unintended consequences of intervention and crafted a legal test inspired from literature that had taken such factors into consideration.

Similarly, the evolution of EU merger control cannot be understood without the impact of formal economic analysis on the behaviour of the GC and thus on its inclination to review administrative action. While the ECJ accepted the principle that Regulation 4064/89 was applicable to concentrations creating or strengthening a collective dominant position, the GC reacted where the Commission attempted to construe the notion in a way that ignored the operational boundaries logically deriving from mainstream economics. Similarly, the redefinition of the principles applying to the assessment of non-horizontal mergers was crafted around the consensus position, according to which such transactions typically have neutral or positive effects of competition and intervention requires the articulation of a theory of harm.

2.1.3 Explaining Variation in Repeated Interactions: Path Dependence

A systematic review, from a dynamic standpoint, of the administrative practice and the resulting case law suggests that the behaviour of the EU courts is remarkably path-dependent. The evolution of the law suggests that the choices made at a relatively early stage have a significant impact on the evolution of the law. Thus, the marginal tendency to defer to the substantive analysis of the Commission in period 1 appears to increase the likelihood of deference in period 2. This marginal tendency seems to be amplified in subsequent periods. As a result of this phenomenon, one can identify two main ways in which the EU courts appeared to have responded to the tendency of the Commission to define the scope of prohibitions in a relatively expansive manner. In some areas, the resilience of the case law has been the norm and the tendency has been to preserve the principles on which this case law is based. In other areas, resilience is the exception, and the route followed is one of deference to the authority. Inevitably, deference leads to fluctuations in the case law.

Evidence of resilience can be found in Article 101 TFEU case law. Some of the principles introduced by the Court have guided the shaping of the notion of restriction of competition over the decades. This case law is peppered with annulments of Commission decisions deviating from these principles. The path followed in the context of Article 102 TFEU is, conversely, one of deference in dynamic interactions. Accordingly, the evolution of the law is driven by the fluctuations that necessarily followed the attempts by the Commission to deviate from – or expand the scope of – prior rulings. During the past four decades, the notion of abuse has meandered in line with the practice of the authority. When deference is the norm, the dismissal of actions challenging administrative action is routine.

Several factors may explain the relative resilience of the case law. One factor that stands out in this regard is the ratio of annulment actions to preliminary references. An analysis of Article 101 and 102 TFEU rulings suggests that the principles of the case law may be more resilient where they are introduced and/or reiterated in a series of preliminary rulings, and thus where the ratio of preliminary rulings to annulment actions is higher. Conversely, a low ratio seems to have had the effect of weakening such principles and/or making them subject to more fluctuations over time. Preliminary references, in other words, appear to 'pull' towards resilience, whereas annulment actions 'pull' towards fluctuations in the case law. This intuition is sketched in Chapter 2. A second related factor is the timing of the decisions. The path followed by the case law may vary depending on whether the principles are first enunciated (and subsequently followed) in a preliminary reference – where they are often spelled out explicitly – or an annulment action instead.

In the context of Article 101 TFEU, the idea that a restriction of competition cannot be equated with a restriction in the freedom of action was introduced in a series of early preliminary rulings and was progressively strengthened over time. To take a concrete example, the framework for the analysis of exclusive dealing agreements, which was sketched in two references (*Brasserie de Haecht* and *Delimitis*), proved resilient when a series of Commission decisions departed from it in the 1990s. In spite of the observed resilience, the analysis of Article 101(1) TFEU case law also reveals that administrative action can lead to fluctuations in the EU courts' approach and interpretation of competition law provisions. It is possible to identify, in the context of Article 101(1) TFEU case law, a 'gravity effect', whereby administrative action 'pulls' towards the interpretations favoured by the authority. In other words, an overview of the case law suggests that the substantive analysis found in Commission decisions influences the EU courts, thereby leading to occasional – and temporary – variations.

The 'gravity effect' observed in the context of Article 101(1) TFEU can be illustrated by reference to two examples. It makes sense to mention, first, the contrast between *Windsurfing*, in which the Court reviewed a Commission decision, and *Bayer v Süllhöfer*, adopted in the context of a preliminary reference. The two cases examined the same issue – the status of no-challenge clauses under Article 101(1) TFEU. The analytical framework, however, is different in each case. In *Windsurfing*, the Court appeared to suggest that no-challenge clauses are prima facie prohibited insofar as they restrict the freedom of action of the licensee. As explained in Chapter 3, this position would be rectified in *Bayer v Süllhöfer*, in which the ECJ insisted, in line with the case law, on the need to consider the economic and legal context of the agreement to establish whether it is caught by Article 101(1) TFEU. A similar fluctuation can be observed in the analysis of selective distribution agreements. While some passages in *Metro I* gave the impression that the Court was equating a restriction of competition and a restriction in the distributors' freedom of action, a series of preliminary references on the same point of law during the early 1980s suggested a return to the analytical framework consistently applied over the years.

The degree of resilience is not the same in the context of Article 102 TFEU. For the same reason, the 'gravity effect' of administrative action is considerably stronger. This divergence may well be explained by the two factors mentioned above. As explained in Chapter 4, preliminary rulings engaging with the notion of abuse were delivered once a body of case law had already developed. The first reference dealing with the legal status of rebates (*Post Danmark II*), for instance, was submitted to the Court decades after the first decisions on the matter had been adopted by the Commission. Second, cases reaching the EU courts through direct actions are more important in qualitative and quantitative terms. For every preliminary reference on a given point of law, there were several annulment actions. The rule laid down in *AKZO*, for instance, was not followed by a series of preliminary rulings strengthening its underlying logic and approach. Instead, it was followed by annulment proceedings in which the Commission departed from it. These cases 'pulled' the analysis away from the logic of *AKZO* and closer to the 'checklist approach' that the authority had originally defended. The inconsistency that emerged in the case law would only be adequately addressed by the Court more than a decade later in *Post Danmark I* – a preliminary ruling.

2.1.4 Explaining Variation: Other Factors

It is possible to think of alternative explanations for the observed variation in the behaviour of the EU courts and thus the relative resilience of the case law. If there are different perceptions about the nature and scope of the different provisions, it seems natural that they are interpreted in divergent ways, and that, by the same token, the EU courts display more tolerance for fluctuations in the evolution of the provisions. In this sense, one cannot exclude that the peculiar evolution of Article 102 TFEU, and the deference shown towards attempts by the Commission to recraft, or depart from, the applicable legal test, may be a consequence of the way in which the provision in question is understood by the EU courts. As explained in Chapter 4, the Court held, in an oft-repeated statement (sometimes misunderstood),[101] that dominant firms have a 'special responsibility' not to impair 'genuine undistorted competition'.

Against this background, the possibility exists that the observed deference displayed in Article 102 TFEU cases simply reflects the fact that the EU courts consider that a certain leeway to the authority – that is, a degree of substantive fluctuation – is justified given its substantive scope of application. Considering that Article 102 TFEU is relevant only where the conditions of competition are already weakened, the articulation of clear rules and standards may limit the ability of an authority to take action where the competitive process may otherwise suffer. From this perspective, construing cases narrowly, and confining the analysis to the specific circumstances of the case, may make it possible to ensure that Article 102 TFEU remains effective. The fact that the emergence of dominant positions can be expected to be relatively rare in open-market economies may also justify some tolerance vis-à-vis the fluctuation of substantive principles. Since no two dominant positions are likely to be the same, and since the characteristics of the relevant market can vary significantly from one case to another, allowing the Commission to craft ad hoc legal tests adapting to the circumstances of each case may be deemed justified.

The observed resilience of Article 101(1) TFEU case law may also be, at least in part, the consequence of a particular perception of the scope and role of the provision. Since agreements between independent firms are

[101] This is a point raised by Schweitzer, 'The History, Interpretation and Underlying Principles of Section 2 Sherman Act and Article 82 EC'.

ubiquitous, and the majority of them concern operators with no significant market power, it is natural to place an emphasis on the definition of clear principles that make it possible to anticipate the rationale and direction of administrative action. In fact, the flexible and pragmatic interpretation of Article 101(1) TFEU displayed by the Court in its preliminary rulings could very well be explained as an attempt to ensure that EU competition law is not overly cumbersome on ordinary, pro-competitive transactions involving non-dominant firms. The same can be said in relation to mergers, which are rarely ever a source of competition concerns and are known to be a plausible source of efficiency gains.

A second factor that might have played a role in the evolution of the law is the frequency with which the scope of a given notion is litigated before the EU courts. In this sense, it appears from Part II that the notion of abuse under Article 102 TFEU has been relatively more contentious than the notion of restriction of competition within the meaning of Article 101(1) TFEU. As already explained, there is a substantial number of decisions challenged before the EU courts in which the restrictive nature of the agreement is not seriously disputed. The opposite is true in the context of Article 102 TFEU. Against this background, the centrality of the notion of abuse in annulment proceedings may make the EU courts more careful to question a decision, as doing so is more likely to interfere with the central policy choices of the authority. The fact that there are fewer Article 102 TFEU cases in absolute terms may reinforce this perception.

2.2 The EU Courts and the Challenge of Consistency

2.2.1 Mapping the Frictions in the Case Law

It has been explained above why there seems to be no support for the idea that the EU courts have been consistently deferential to the Commission. At the same time, it seems difficult to dispute that there are variations in the attitude towards judicial review, which has not been uniform. Inevitably, these variations have resulted in the emergence of inconsistencies. The dynamic inconsistencies in the assessment of potentially anti-competitive conduct have led to a situation in which the interpretation and enforcement of EU competition law is not always coherent. The EU courts do not always assess the lawfulness of practices in accordance with the same principles. In addition, there are static inconsistencies in the approach to a given line of conduct. The same – or a functionally equivalent – practice may be treated differently depending on the provision that applies to it. It is submitted that these inconsistencies are among the most important reasons why some aspects of EU competition law enforcement continue to be controversial.

One area that has become a persistent source of incoherence relates to the way in which the EU courts address the divide between rules and standards. In the context of Article 101(1) TFEU, the EU courts typically rely on formal analysis to consider whether the agreement has as its object the restriction of competition. This approach is encapsulated in the idea whereby it is necessary to consider the 'economic and legal context' of which the agreement is part before coming to conclusions in this sense. The analysis of the economic and legal context might suggest, as in *Nungesser*, that the agreement may be necessary to preserve the licensor's incentives to invest and innovate; or it might suggest, as in *Pronuptia*, that it can be an effective device to expand a successful business model without capital investment on the part of the franchisor. This case law is also clear in stating that an agreement must at least be capable of restricting competition for it to be caught by Article 101(1) TFEU.

There is case law in the context of Article 102 TFEU that is consistent with this approach to the divide between rules and standards. *AKZO* and *Post Danmark I* provide valuable examples in this sense. As already explained, the Court resorted in *AKZO* to formal analysis as a means to identify – directly or by proxy – the instances in which it would be appropriate to presume that the practice served no purpose other than the exclusion of competition. By clarifying in both cases that Article 102 TFEU is concerned with the exclusion of equally efficient competitors, moreover, the Court endorsed a standard of capability. This approach, however, is not a universal one under the provision. There are some cases in which the Court concluded that the purpose of the practice was anti-competitive, but did not seek to ground its position on formal analysis. The case law on exclusive dealing and on tying springs to mind in this regard. Similarly, there is case law – including *Irish Sugar* and *Compagnie Maritime Belge* – that suggests that a practice may be subject to a rule even when it is not capable of driving rivals out of the market.

An inevitable consequence of the lack of coherence is the rise of static inconsistency within Article 102 TFEU. Practices that are equivalent in their nature, objective purpose and potential anti-competitive effects are not always treated alike. Suffice it to compare in this regard the way in which standardised rebates, on the one hand, and target rebates, on the other, are treated by the Court. It is well understood that the difference between these schemes is not one of principle, but of degree.[102] As a result, they are likely to be used in the same circumstances. In fact, the very factual background of *British Airways* and *Michelin II* illustrates this idea well. However, standardised and target rebates are not subject to a single analytical framework. While the latter appear to be subject to a rule, volume-based schemes are examined in accordance with a standard, which takes account of their likely impact on competition, since *Post Danmark II*.[103]

The lack of coherence in Article 102 TFEU case law has resulted in inconsistencies across EU competition law provisions. Perhaps the most obvious example relates to the treatment of tying under, respectively, Article 102 TFEU and EU merger control. Under the former, tying is subject to a rule. Accordingly, the mere fact that anti-competitive foreclosure is a plausible outcome of the practice (or, as the GC held in *Microsoft I*, the fact that tying gives a 'distribution advantage' to the dominant firm on the market for the tied product) is sufficient to take action. Plausibility, however, would not suffice to intervene in a merger case. As explained in Chapter 4 (in light of *Tetra Laval*), action under Regulation 139/2004 requires the identification of the mechanism through which foreclosure would occur, as well as evidence that such an outcome is likely. The fact that the merged entity enjoys a dominant position on the market for the tying product is insufficient in this regard.

Evidence of the inconsistent approach to tying under the two provisions was provided by the merger in *Microsoft/Skype*, discussed in Chapter 5.[104] The compatibility of this transaction with the internal market was considered by the Commission shortly after *Microsoft II*. The setting in the two cases was very similar, as was the underlying issue and the competition concerns. Indeed, *Microsoft/Skype* was potentially problematic insofar as it could strengthen Skype's 'artificial distribution advantage' on desktop PCs. If this transaction had been examined under the principles set out in Article 102 TFEU, it would have been declared to be incompatible with the internal market. However, the Commission noted that, in spite of the dominance enjoyed by Microsoft on the market for the tying product, the foreclosure of competition was an unlikely outcome. In particular, it

[102] For an analysis of this question, see Opinion of AG Wahl in Case C-413/14 P, *Intel Corp. v Commission*, EU:C:2016:788, para. 100.
[103] Case C-23/14, *Post Danmark II*, paras. 30–46.
[104] Commission Decision of 7 October 2011 (Case COMP/M.6281 – *Microsoft/Skype*).

suggested that the transaction would have imperceptible effects on competition.[105] This is an argument that, in light of the GC ruling in *Microsoft I*, would not have been relevant in the context of Article 102 TFEU.[106]

A similar tension can be identified in relation to the treatment of exclusive dealing under Articles 101 and 102 TFEU. As explained in Chapter 3, the Court resorted to formal analysis to conclude that the practice was not restrictive of competition by object under the first of the provisions. The plausible pro-competitive justifications played a crucial role in this regard. Under Article 102 TFEU, on the other hand, the Court held in *Hoffmann-La Roche* that the practice is prima facie prohibited irrespective of its effects. As pointed out above, the presumption that the practice serves an anti-competitive purpose is at the origin of this rule, which applies to this day.[107] The tension between these two provisions was manifested in *Van den Bergh Foods*,[108] which considered the status of a set of de facto exclusivity obligations under both. The analysis conducted by the GC under Article 101 TFEU, which carefully sought to establish the foreclosure effects of the practice, would not have been necessary under Article 102 TFEU.[109]

2.2.2 EU Courts' Reaction to Frictions in the Case Law

When addressing inconsistencies, the EU courts respond prudently and incrementally. Instead of proclaiming a major departure from the relevant precedents, they clarify the scope of provisions on a case-by-case

[105] Ibid., paras. 159–69. The Commission pointed out, in particular, that Skype was, at the time of the decision, already pre-installed in a substantial number of PCs (para. 161). In addition, it noted that there is a tendency on the part of consumers to use operating systems from devices other than PCs, which would have reduced the negative impact of any foreclosure strategy implemented by Microsoft.

[106] See in this sense Case T-201/04, *Microsoft I*, para. 1054. If anything, the fact that Skype was already pre-installed in a significant number of computers could have strengthened the case for intervention under the approach taken by the GC in *Microsoft I*, insofar as it would have consolidated the distribution advantage enjoyed by the application. In any event, arguments relating to the appreciability of anti-competitive effects are not relevant in the context of Article 102 TFEU, as the Court would confirm in Case C-23/14, *Post Danmark II*, para. 73 ('fixing an appreciability (de minimis) threshold for the purposes of determining whether there is an abuse of a dominant position is not justified').

[107] Case C-413/14 P, *Intel Corp. v Commission*, EU:C:2017:632, para. 137.

[108] Case T-65/98, *Van den Bergh Foods*. For an analysis of this tension, see O'Donoghue and Jorge Padilla, *The Law and Economics of Article 102 TFEU*, pp. 431–2.

[109] This point is to some extent acknowledged in para. 159 of the judgment, where the GC notes that the factors that lead to the analysis of effects in the context of Article 101 TFEU are not relevant under Article 102 TFEU.

basis. The EU courts' reaction, if it takes place, is not immediate. It may take decades. Consider the example of exclusive dealing under Article 102 TFEU. Following *Delimitis*, dominant firms challenging administrative action have consistently pointed out that the rule in *Hoffmann-La Roche* is grounded on a premise that does not withstand formal analysis. In particular, applicants in abuse cases have noted for decades that exclusive dealing obligations can be observed in competitive markets and that firms can resort to it for reasons that are unrelated to the elimination of competition. In fact, *Delimitis* provides a valuable example in this sense. The exclusive dealing obligations at stake in that dispute had been imposed by a firm which, with a 6 per cent market share, could not hope to foreclose competition. Claims identifying the tension between *Delimitis* and *Hoffmann-La Roche* were brought forward in cases like *British Plasterboard*[110] and *Intel*.[111]

For many years, arguments pointing to this friction were summarily dismissed without addressing the fundamental underlying issue. In its judgments in *British Plasterboard* and *Intel*, the GC merely took the view that the conclusions drawn by the Court in the context of Article 101 TFEU could not be expanded, without more, to Article 102 TFEU, and this due to the 'special responsibility' that the said provision imposes upon dominant firms.[112] It was necessary to wait until 2017 (almost 40 years since *Hoffmann-La Roche*) to see the Court openly acknowledge some of the implications of *Delimitis*. The appeal judgment in *Intel* clarified that dominant firms are entitled to provide evidence showing that exclusion is implausible in the economic and legal context of which the practice is part.[113] This clarification appears to take into consideration that exclusive dealing and related conduct do not invariably result in exclusion, even when implemented by dominant firms.

An equally prudent and incremental approach can be noted where the Court has been called upon to react to the inconsistencies in the case law addressing predatory pricing concerns. It has already been explained that the authority did not apply the principles set out in *AKZO* in *Irish Sugar*

[110] See Case T-65/89, *BPB Industries Plc and British Gypsum Ltd v Commission*, EU:T:1993:31 ('*British Plasterboard*'), paras. 66–7.

[111] Case T-286/09, *Intel Corp. v Commission*, EU:T:2014:547, paras. 89–90.

[112] In *British Plasterboard*, the Court noted, in para. 67, that the factors considered by the Court in *Delimitis*, 'which apply in a normal competitive market situation, cannot be unreservedly accepted in the case of a market where, precisely because of the dominant position of one of the economic operators, competition is already restricted'.

[113] Case C-413/14 P, *Intel*, para. 138.

and *Compagnie Maritime Belge*. When confronted with the friction between *AKZO* and subsequent administrative practice, the EU courts justified the inconsistency by pointing to the specific factual circumstances of the case at hand. In *Irish Sugar*, the GC appeared to argue that, where market integration is at stake, a policy of selective price cuts can be abusive even if it does not involve below-cost pricing.[114] In addition, it pointed to the very high market shares enjoyed by the dominant firm in its domestic market. In *Compagnie Maritime Belge*, it referred to the characteristics that it considered to be unique to the industry in question (maritime transport) and the superdominant position of the collectively dominant firms to justify the outcome. The inconsistency that emerged as a result of the latter two rulings would only be addressed a decade later, in *Post Danmark I*.

2.2.3 Explaining the EU Courts' Attitude

The prudent and incremental attitude on the part of the EU courts should not come as a surprise. One can reasonably expect courts – any court – to have a preference for a legal test that has been consistently applied for several decades. As noted in Chapter 2, judges may value stability as much as consistency, if not more. Accordingly, they may only be prepared to depart from a line of case law in the name of consistency where they are persuaded that it is obviously wrong, or that the benefits of overruling clearly outweigh the benefits of preserving the status quo.[115] One should note, in addition, that a lag between the development of a consensus among stakeholders and a reaction of the EU courts is arguably inevitable. A court may only be willing to refine its case law – or to introduce clarifications – where some positions have become part of the mainstream. The inconsistency between *Delimitis* and *Hoffman-La Roche* was only partially acknowledged following a lively debate in the literature that suggested the convenience of clarifying some aspects of the operation of the legal test.[116]

[114] Case T-228/97, *Irish Sugar plc v Commission*, EU:T:1999:246, para. 185.

[115] For two examples in which the Court may have reached the conclusion that, indeed, the benefits of departing from the relevant precedents may outweigh the advantages of stability, see Joined Cases C-267/91 and C-268/91, *Criminal proceedings against Bernard Keck and Daniel Mithouard*, EU:C:1993:905; and Case C-10/89, *SA CNL-SUCAL NV v HAG GF AG*, EU:C:1990:359.

[116] The debate became particularly lively following the GC judgment in *Intel*. See in this sense Wouter Wils, 'The Judgment of the EU General Court in Intel and the So-Called "More Economic Approach" to Abuse of Dominance' (2014) 37 *World Competition* 405; Richard Whish, '*Intel v Commission*: Keep Calm and Carry on!' (2015) 6 *Journal of*

It is equally unsurprising that, when the EU courts consider that there is merit in addressing the observed inconsistencies, they often choose to do so in an indirect or implicit manner. The example of the preliminary reference in *Post Danmark I*, in which the Court addressed the inconsistency brought about by *Irish Sugar* and *Compagnie Maritime Belge*, is a valuable one in this sense. While it does not address the issue directly, the ruling unambiguously endorses the test laid down in *AKZO*. The same approach has been followed in the treatment of rebate schemes. There is a difference between the analysis performed by the Court in *Post Danmark II* and that found in previous cases like *British Airways*. In the latter, the analysis of effects is confined to the impact of the scheme on customers' freedom of action. In *Post Danmark II*, the analysis extended to other considerations, including the coverage of the practice or the extent of the dominant position enjoyed by the firm. In addition, the Court endorsed a standard of likelihood in the case. However, the divergence was not explicitly acknowledged.

A second reason behind the attitude of the EU courts may have to do with the fact that the outcome of individual systems may sometimes matter more than consistency. Administrative action sometimes seeks to provide a response to an exceptional or unusual practice. Such cases rarely provide the ideal circumstances in which to refine or clarify the scope of the law and thus may lead to inconsistencies. For instance, it is not difficult to think of the reasons why a finding of abuse in cases like *Irish Sugar* and *Compagnie Maritime Belge* may come across as intuitively correct, or why a review court may hesitate to challenge the findings of the authority. In the two cases, there was evidence which either suggested that the practice was part of an overall strategy to exclude a rival (as is true of the latter),[117] that the firms suspected that it was prohibited (as in the case of the former)[118] or that the circumstances of the case justified a departure from the standard legal test.

European Competition Law & Practice 1; Patrick Rey and James Venit, 'An Effects-Based Approach to Article 102: A Response to Wouter Wils' (2015) 38 *World Competition* 3; Nicolas Petit, 'Intel, Leveraging Rebates and the Goals of Article 102 TFEU' (2015) 11 *European Competition Journal* 25; and Damien Geradin, 'Loyalty Rebates after Intel: Time for the European Court of Justice to Overrule Hoffman-La Roche' (2015) 11 *Journal of Competition Law & Economics* 579.

[117] Joined Cases C-395/96 P and C-396/96 P, *Compagnie Maritime Belge Transports SA, Compagnie Maritime Belge SA and Dafra-Lines A/S v Commission*, EU:C:2000:132, para. 119.

[118] Case T-228/97, *Irish Sugar*, para. 183.

The reluctance to engage with the substantive aspects of a decision may be more likely to be observed in an institutional setting in which the thrust of enforcement lies with a specialist authority acting in the public interest. In such a setting, review courts may perform their function on the assumption that, by carefully choosing which cases to pursue, the authority will be in a position to minimise and manage the consequences of any substantive inconsistencies. Review courts may, in other words, trust that exceptional cases remain exceptional and thus do not affect the coherence and predictability of the system. From this perspective, the observed inconsistency between the *Microsoft* saga – decided under Article 102 TFEU – and *Microsoft/Skype* would seem less problematic than one would have assume. The *Microsoft* saga would simply be a response to an extreme situation – a firm holding a quasi-monopoly position – and understood by review courts as such.

2.3 The Future of Judicial Review between Law and Economics

2.3.1 Judicial Review on Issues of Law

There are two questions that any debate about the future of judicial review in EU competition law cannot avoid. An ever-present one relates to whether the judicial oversight of issues of law (and fact) is effective – or, if one prefers, whether the EU courts consistently exercise 'full review' within the meaning of *Menarini*. The conclusions of this study confirm the importance of the question. A systematic overview of the Commission practice suggests that administrative authorities may display a tendency to circumvent or minimise endogenous constraints on administrative action. The observed tendency can become – and has become – a source of substantive inconsistencies and legal uncertainty. In addition, the behaviour of the EU courts when reviewing administrative action has not been uniform. Even if the issue is not obvious to establish directly, some concrete examples – including *Microsoft I*, where the GC appeared to give deference to the Commission on a point of law – suggest that the intensity of judicial review may fluctuate from one case to the other.

A second question relates to the ongoing changes in the institutional structure through which the law is enforced. The choices made, and/or the attitudes displayed by the EU courts during the formative years of the discipline may not lead to the same outcomes in a decentralised setting. Deference on points of law and the perpetuation of inconsistencies within and across EU competition law provisions may seem relatively unproblematic where an expert authority can be trusted to carefully prioritise cases and intervene only where the public interest is likely to be advanced. Where, on the other hand, the thrust of enforcement lies with national courts and authorities – not all of which have the resources or the expertise of the Commission – some of the unintended effects of deference and inconsistency (namely legal uncertainty and opportunistic behaviour) become more frequent and more pressing concerns.

These two questions can be condensed into a single central claim: effective judicial review has become, if anything, even more important following the adoption of Regulation 1/2003. Evaluating whether judicial review is effective in general and in individual cases is, by the same token, equally crucial. Against this background, it is worth identifying a set of hallmarks of the intensity with which administrative action is scrutinised. To begin with, one would expect review courts to verify whether the authority has spelled out with clarity the overarching rationale(s) behind intervention in a given case, and whether administrative action is consistent with the declared rationale. As already explained, the Commission has occasionally been ambiguous on these two points. This attitude has allowed it to justify intervention simultaneously on two separate grounds – for instance, exclusion and exploitation; inter-brand competition and market integration. Due to this ambiguity, the legal status of certain practices has never been fully clarified. For instance, it is not entirely clear, to this day, whether loyalty rebates are deemed abusive, always and everywhere, insofar as they are assumed to lead to *exploitative* discrimination within the meaning of Article 102(c) TFEU. It is equally unclear how legal analysis is to be adjusted when market integration is at stake.

Second, one would expect a review court to articulate some fundamental principles that apply transversally across practices and provisions. This exercise could assist the task of judicial review by making it possible to identify decisions that are erroneous and a source of incoherence. Suffice it to mention some examples of the sort of principles that may assist courts in this sense and enhance legal certainty. In the context of Article 101 TFEU, for instance, it is well established that a restriction in the freedom of action is neither a sufficient nor a reliable indicator of a restriction of competition. Similarly, the Court has consistently held that 'competition' within the meaning of Article 101(1) TFEU must be understood as the competition that would have existed in the absence of the practice. Finally, the departure of firms that are less attractive for end-users from the point of view of, inter alia, prices, quality and innovation is prima facie unproblematic under Article 102 TFEU. It would be for the Commission to explain convincingly, in the context of a particular case, why it seeks to depart from these principles, or why they are not applicable.

Third, one would expect the EU courts to spell out clearly and explicitly the legal test against which administrative action is to be assessed. If the Commission has identified more than one dimension of competition, one would expect the EU courts to spell out the legal test that applies to each of these dimensions – inter-brand rivalry, intra-brand rivalry, or market integration. If there was a disagreement in the course of the administrative phase about the applicable legal test, this disagreement should ideally be acknowledged and resolved by the review court. Disagreements may concern, for instance, whether a given precedent is applicable in the circumstances of the case. If the EU courts endorse the approach taken by the Commission and the applicable legal test is contentious, it would be appropriate to clarify why one approach is favoured over the other.

The articulation of a legal test by a review court has two main dimensions. It involves, first, laying down the conditions under which the practice under consideration would give rise to intervention and, second, explaining the logic behind the choice. If, for instance, the legality of a practice is subject to a rule, one would expect the EU courts to explain why a rule is applicable in the context of the case as well as the choices made when crafting it. This is one of the areas where there is greater scope for progress in the case law. The criteria relied upon to distinguish between restrictions by object and by effect have not always been spelled out with clarity and have to be inferred from an analysis of individual cases. Similarly, where the practice is subject to a standard, one would expect the EU courts to clarify the requisite threshold of effects and the meaning attached to the notion of competition. Again, this is an area in which there is some uncertainty, in particular in relation to the assessment of effects under Articles 101 and 102 TFEU.

Finally, it would be desirable to bring more clarity to the aspects of administrative action that are subject to limited review. While it is clear that the Commission enjoys discretion in the definition of its policy, which comprises the decision to reject a complaint or to make commitments binding upon the firms proposing them, the scope of the notion of 'complex economic assessments' over which the authority enjoys a margin of appreciation remains relatively obscure. The logic of the case law suggests that the scope of this notion should be confined to two aspects of administrative action: the methodology followed to identify facts – for instance, the use of a particular technique to define the market, or to forecast the impact of a horizontal merger on prices – as well as the facts established in accordance with the said methodology.

2.3.2 Economic Consensus and Judicial Review

The conclusions that follow from Part II dispel some commonly held views about how the EU courts engage with economic analysis. It has already been explained why it does not seem accurate to claim that the case law is, as a rule, at odds with mainstream positions. Formal analysis has informed the shaping of rules and standards. The case law cannot be fully understood without its contribution. There are in fact several examples that show that often – arguably, more often than not – the impetus towards the introduction of economic analysis has come from the EU courts. Part II hints at another, more fundamental, conclusion. If one examines carefully the behaviour of the EU courts, it appears not only that they are less likely to be deferential to the Commission where the analysis of the authority contradicts mainstream economic principles, but that consensus positions have been relied upon to define the substantive boundaries of administrative action.

Some cases indeed suggest that, whenever it ignores mainstream views, the Commission commits an error of assessment in the definition of the substantive scope of a provision. In this sense, formal economic analysis is not only an exogenous factor, but also a tool that informs the definition of endogenous constraints on administrative action. Put differently, consensus positions appear to have a substantive dimension. This idea can be inferred from the way in which the EU courts have engaged with them. In cases like *Airtours* or *Tetra Laval*, the GC did not argue that it was preferable to make a choice in favour of mainstream positions. Instead, it presented consensus positions – relating, respectively, to the instances in which tacit collusion might arise and in which non-horizontal mergers can be expected to harm rivals' ability and incentive to compete – as the appropriate benchmark against which administrative action had to be scrutinised. A similar attitude can be observed in the ECJ ruling in *Cartes Bancaires*. As explained in Chapter 3, the Court acknowledged that the activity concerned by the practice had the characteristics of a two-sided platform and that these characteristics had consequences for the qualification of the agreement as restrictive by object or effect.

In doing so, it endorsed the economic theory of two-sided markets[119] without questioning or disputing its validity and relevance for the case.

One can think of several reasons why it would be reasonable to ensure that the (endogenous) substantive boundaries of the system are informed by consensus positions. Arguably, it is an indispensable ingredient of effective judicial review. If an authority were given the leeway to ignore the consensus, it would enjoy, in practice, the discretion to define the legal framework to which administrative action would be subject. Suppose that administrative action were based on the idea – at odds with mainstream views – that conglomerate mergers typically lead to restrictive effects and that, accordingly, a qualified prohibition rule is appropriate for such transactions. A legal challenge against this assumption would necessarily rely on the flawed economic premises underlying the legal framework. Thus, if the courts were to give discretion to the authority in this regard, they would be shielding administrative action from effective judicial review.

The debate that followed the Commission decision in *Airtours* is a good illustration of these ideas. As explained in Chapter 5, economists noted at the time that the attempt by the authority to stretch the boundaries of the notion of collective dominance allowed it to challenge virtually any concentration taking place in an oligopolistic market. The case rested on the premise that the crucial issue when establishing a position of collective dominance is whether the members of the oligopoly would have an incentive to raise prices, and not so much of whether they would have the means to coordinate and sustain a price increase. Because the incentives to collude can be safely presumed to exist in an oligopolistic market, it was indeed difficult to imagine instances in which the test crafted by the Commission would fail. By the same token, the approach defended by the authority amounted to turning an issue of law into one of policy that would give discretion to the authority.

Two corollaries appear to follow naturally from the above. One of them is that, as a matter of law, the Commission cannot deviate from consensus positions when laying down a legal test. This is a point that has not been addressed explicitly by the EU courts. This said, there are some questions over which, the case law suggests, the Commission does not appear to enjoy a margin of appreciation. These include the following:

[119] See also the Opinion of AG Wahl in Case C-67/13 P, *Groupement des cartes bancaires v Commission*, EU:C:2014:1958, para. 3, which refers expressly to the economic literature on two-sided markets.

the assessment of the business rationale behind the implementation of the practice under consideration (that is, whether the practice has a plausible pro-competitive rationale) and the definition of the circumstances in which anti-competitive effects (such as, for instance, tacit collusion or rival foreclosure) can be expected to arise. Think, for instance, of exclusive dealing. It would seem that the Commission enjoys no discretion when deciding whether or not this practice (or any other practice) is implemented for reasons other than the exclusion of competition and when identifying the circumstances in which it can have anti-competitive effects. These questions are not part of the 'complex economic assessments' that have been discussed above.[120] They are not matters of policy either. The behaviour displayed by the EU courts, which do not hesitate to depart from the analysis displayed by the Commission when these questions arise, supports these conclusions. For instance, the Court concluded in *Cartes Bancaires* that the GC had failed to 'observe the standard of review required under the case-law' when evaluating the business rationale behind the practice.[121]

Arguably, administrative action that fails to incorporate consensus positions is arbitrary and unreasonable, and as such manifestly erroneous. Consensus in any academic discipline, including economics, is incrementally developed over the years. Accordingly, an administrative authority could only ignore the lessons learned in the context of this incremental process if it were in a position to rebut the fundamental tenets of the mainstream and show why it is incorrect. If an administrative authority does not have the means to do so – and it is reasonable to presume that it does not – one can claim that it is bound by such positions in its practice. For the same reasons, it would be arbitrary and unreasonable for the Commission to make administrative action revolve around an analytical framework that has been dismissed or is known to be incorrect and/or insufficiently nuanced. For instance, it would be arbitrary and unreasonable for the Commission to rely on the premise that non-horizontal mergers are generally anti-competitive, or that tacit collusion typically arises in tight oligopolies with just three competitors.

One can take the argument even further and think of a second corollary. One could indeed argue not only that administrative action cannot disregard formal analysis, but also that the EU courts should, as a rule,

[120] For an attempt to make sense of the concept, see Andriani Kalintiri, 'What's in a Name? The Marginal Standard of Review of "Complex Economic Evaluations" in EU Competition Enforcement' (2016) 53 *Common Market Law Review* 1283.

[121] Case C-67/13 P, *Cartes Bancaires*, para. 91.

define the scope of EU competition law provisions in a way that endorses consensus positions. This is so not only for the reasons already exposed, but because it would be an effective mechanism to identify and remedy effectively any inconsistencies in the case law. As the analysis above shows, the main areas of friction are the result of the uneven endorsement of mainstream economic principles across practices and provisions. For instance, this factor alone can explain the observed tension between the *Microsoft* Article 102 TFEU saga and *Microsoft/Skype*, or between *Hoffmann-La Roche* and *Delimitis*. The practical implication of this principle would be that Courts need to actively address, in an incremental manner, the observed frictions in the case law.

APPENDIX TO CHAPTER 6

Table 6.1 *Commitment decisions adopted by the European Commission*

Decision	Provision	Area	First instance	Applicant	Outcome
E-book MFNs and related matters	Article 102 TFEU	Others	–	–	–
Cross-border access to pay-TV (Paramount)	Article 101 TFEU	Rights licensing	T-873/16	Third party	Pending
CDS Information Market	Articles 101 and 102 TFEU	Refusal to deal	–	–	–
Container Shipping	Article 101 TFEU	Other horizontal	–	–	–
BEH Electricity	Article 102 TFEU	Market integration	–	–	–
Air France/KLM/Alitalia/Delta	Article 101 TFEU	Airline alliances	–	–	–
Samsung – Enforcement of UMTS standard essential patents	Article 102 TFEU	Others	–	–	–
Visa MIF	Article 101 TFEU	Other horizontal	–	–	–
Deutsche Bahn I and II	Article 102 TFEU	Refusal to deal	–*	–	–
Ebooks (Penguin)	Article 101 TFEU	Others	–	–	–
Continental/United/Lufthansa/Air Canada	Article 101 TFEU	Airline alliances	–	–	–
CEZ	Article 102 TFEU	Refusal to deal	–	–	–
Rio Tinto Alcan	Articles 101 and 102 TFEU	Tying/Bundling		–	–
Reuters Instrument Codes	Article 102 TFEU	Refusal to deal	T-76/14	Third party	Dismiss

Table 6.1 *(cont.)*

Decision	Provision	Area	First instance	Applicant	Outcome
Ebooks	Article 101 TFEU	Others	–	–	–
Siemens/Areva	Article 101 TFEU	Other horizontal	–	–	–
IBM Maintenance Services	Article 102 TFEU	Refusal to deal	–	–	–
Standard and Poor's	Article 102 TFEU	Excessive pricing	–	–	–
ENI	Article 102 TFE	Refusal to deal	–	–	–
BA/AA/IB	Article 101 TFEU	Airline alliances	–	–	–
E.ON Gas	Article 102 TFEU	Refusal to deal	–	–	–
Swedish Interconnectors	Article 102 TFEU	Market integration	–	–	–
Long-term contracts France	Article 102 TFEU	Exclusivity	–	–	–
Microsoft (tying)	Article 102 TFEU	Tying/bundling	–	–	–
Rambus	Article 102 TFEU	Excessive pricing	–	–	–
Gaz de France	Article 102 TFEU	Refusal to deal	–	-	-
Ship Classification	Article 101 TFEU	Other horizontal	–	–	–
RWE gas foreclosure	Article 102 TFEU	Refusal to deal	–	–	–
German electricity wholesale market and balancing market	Article 102 TFEU	Others	–	–	–
Distrigaz	Article 102 TFEU	Exclusivity	–		–
Opel	Article 101 TFEU	Aftermarkets	–	–	–
Toyota Motor Europe	Article 101 TFEU	Aftermarkets	–	–	–
Fiat	Article 101 TFEU	Aftermarkets	–	–	–
DaimlerChrysler	Article 101 TFEU	Aftermarkets	–	–	–

The Cannes Extension Agreement	Article 101 TFEU	Other horizontal	–	–	–
REPSOL C.P.P.	Article 101 TFEU	Others	T-274/06	Third party	Dismiss
Joint selling of the media rights to the FA Premier League	Article 101 TFEU	Rights licensing	–	–	–
De Beers	Article 102 TFEU	Exclusivity	T-170/06	Third party	**Annul (law)****
Coca-Cola	Article 102 TFEU	Exclusivity	–	–	–
Joint selling of the media rights to the German Bundesliga	Article 101 TFEU	Rights licensing	–	–	–

* An action was brought during the administrative procedure; see Case T-289/11 and Case C-583/13

** First instance ruling set aside on appeal; see Case C-441/07 P

7

Conclusions

1 The Evolution of EU Competition Law

The question of whether the institutional features of EU competition law have an impact on its substantive evolution inspired this monograph. The findings suggest that the former is indeed a factor driving and shaping the latter. An administrative authority that is both investigator and decision-maker can exercise significant influence on a legal discipline. This conclusion should not come as a surprise. It is natural – and arguably desirable – that a decision-making body seeks to define its powers in a relatively expansive manner. If EU competition law provisions are given a broad scope of application, the ability of the authority to tackle harmful practices is maximised. It is also unsurprising that review courts show an occasional inclination to give deference on issues of law. Where there are two or more reasonable answers to a legal issue, they may be inclined to side with the interpretation advanced by the administrative authority. This behaviour may be displayed even when – as in the EU law system – the authority in question enjoys no discretion on issues of law. The level of expertise of the administrative body, or the fact that it acts in the public interest, may also favour this inclination.

A systematic review of the case law and the administrative practice is valuable in that it suggests that an analysis of the behaviour of the Commission over the years can contribute significantly to the understanding of some of the distinct features of the EU competition law system. The EU regime has been criticised in the past for being, allegedly, overly formalistic, and for not paying sufficient attention to the impact of practices on competition. It has also been claimed that EU competition law (or some aspects thereof) is at odds with economic analysis. More often than not, the tendency among commentators has been to explain these features by reference to the ideological climate prevailing in Europe. A popular approach has been to attribute these alleged features to some academic schools of thought.

These explanations are generally incomplete in that they tend to ignore the institutional context in which substantive choices are made and the structure of EU competition law enforcement. It is submitted that the distinct features of the EU regime could be rationalised as a logical side effect of the behaviour of an authority with the characteristics of the Commission. What is more, this interpretation of the evolution of the EU competition law system may have more explanatory power than alternative accounts, which are typically fraught with methodological difficulties. In this sense, one cannot ignore that, from the perspective of an administrative authority, formalism is convenient. It is an effective means to ease the burden required to establish a prima facie prohibition. The traditional approach of the Commission to the enforcement of Article 101 TFEU, which equated a restriction of competition with a restriction in the firms' freedom of action, shows how formalism can allow an authority to shift the burden of proof to firms. This example is all the more valuable if one considers that there was nothing inevitable – ideologically or otherwise – about the substantive choices made by the Commission. In fact, these choices were contested as inadequate from the outset, and the Court departed in several fundamental respects from them in its earliest rulings.

Similarly, it would not be surprising to see an administrative authority develop a sceptical attitude vis-à-vis economic analysis if consensus views have the effect of constraining its discretion, or of limiting the scope of its powers. Accordingly, this reluctance may well explain the traditional paucity of economic analysis in the practice of the Commission and, by extension, in the EU competition law system. In this regard, this monograph contradicts some views that feature the authority as the main driver towards the endorsement of mainstream ideas in EU competition law. The EU courts have frequently been behind the introduction of legal tests informed by economic analysis. The example of the annulment of the *Airtours* decision is one that comes to mind immediately. The test crafted in *AKZO*, which departed from the 'checklist' approach advocated by the Commission in the case, is another one. More generally, the insistence of the EU courts on the counterfactual – in particular in the context of Article 101 TFEU – reflects a concern with the understanding of the economic realities in which practices are implemented. This concern predated the so-called 'more economics-based approach', but captures its essence.

The monograph sheds light on two other factors that tend to attract less attention from commentators. It shows, first, that substantive inconsistencies have emerged in the EU competition law system over the years. Like practices are not always treated alike, whether within or across provisions. Suffice it to think, in this sense, of the way in which tying concerns are addressed, respectively, in the context of Article 102 TFEU and of EU merger control, or the divergent approaches to the analysis of exclusive dealing under, respectively, Articles 101 and 102 TFEU. It is submitted that inconsistencies – inevitable in any legal system – have been fuelled, first, by some of the choices made by the Commission in one-shot and repeated interactions and, second, by fluctuations in the degree of oversight of administrative action by the EU courts. This phenomenon impacts negatively on the coherence and predictability of the system, and is one that deserves the attention of commentators and stakeholders.

Secondly, the systematic review of the case law and the decision-making practice of the Commission suggests that exogenous factors – in particular economic analysis – constrain administrative action more effectively than endogenous factors. On the one hand, where there is a consensus among economists, deference by the EU courts is significantly less likely. The case law suggests that an interpretation of the scope of a provision that ignores mainstream views is deemed unreasonable by the GC and the ECJ and as such very unlikely to survive judicial scrutiny. On the other hand, economic analysis has been a major driver of changes in the behaviour of the Commission, more than endogenous constraints. The authority reconsidered its approach to the enforcement of Articles 101 and 102 TFEU not because its practice was at odds with the case law, but because it intended to bring it in line with mainstream economics. It would seem, from this perspective, that formal analysis is, for the Commission, an effective factor in preserving the legitimacy of administrative action – even if the practical implications are not significant.

The structure of EU competition law enforcement does not seem to be optimally equipped to address some of the expected consequences of the behaviour of its actors. This reality should be acknowledged in legal and policy discussions. First, it appears that not all decisions adopted by the Commission can credibly be expected to be subject to effective review. In particular, commitment decisions provide a framework in which the interpretation of Articles 101 and 102 TFEU is unlikely to be subject to meaningful judicial oversight. Thus, commitment decisions can exacerbate some of the implications of inconsistent enforcement, namely legal uncertainty. The frequent recourse to this instrument makes this concern a particularly pressing one. Second, the substance of competition law provisions was shaped in an era in which the Commission was responsible for the thrust of enforcement. In a decentralised institutional framework in which enforcement lies primarily with national courts and authorities, the potential for substantive divergence is much greater. In addition, some of the factors that limited the practical consequences of static and dynamic inconsistency in the past – such as the ability of the Commission to prioritise cases – are not present.

2 An Agenda for Future Research

The preceding chapters were comprehensive in the sense that they sought to consider all the relevant case law and administrative practice. At the same time, they were limited in scope, and this at least for two reasons. First, they only examined the behaviour of the Commission and the EU courts in relation to three substantive concepts. Some conditions for the application of EU competition law provisions – such as the existence of an agreement within the meaning of Article 101 TFEU or of a dominant position under Article 102 TFEU – and, more generally, other substantive matters, were not part of the analysis. Second, the interpretation and enforcement of EU competition law at the national level has not been scrutinised. An analysis of other substantive conditions – the first issue – would make it possible to test whether the Commission has displayed a similar tendency across the board. An analysis of the second issue (the application of EU competition law at the national level) would make it possible to consider whether the behaviour of NCAs differs from that of the Commission – and whether there are variations in their behaviour depending on the institutional setting in which national authorities exercise their powers. Finally, this monograph provides a template for comparative work. Institutional differences in competition law regimes across the world may lead to substantive divergences, which can in turn be mapped.

2.1 Substantive Aspects

The principles laid down in this monograph could be extended to the assessment of other substantive conditions of EU competition law. Some of these are obvious candidates for the expansion of the analysis. The notions of agreement and concerted practice within the meaning of Article 101 TFEU spring to mind immediately. Depending on how these notions are fleshed out, the scope of the powers of an authority – or the ease with which it can establish an infringement – will vary. The notion of agreement, to begin with, can be defined in a way that encompasses conduct that seems unilateral in nature – such as a decision by a manufacturer to stop supplying a product to its distributors. The scope of the notion of concerted practice, in turn, could be broader or narrower depending on whether it is understood to encompass parallel behaviour as such, or whether additional factors are deemed necessary.

If one considers the notion of agreement, a preliminary analysis suggests that, indeed, the Commission may have progressively tested the outer boundaries of the notion by attempting to capture conduct that is arguably unilateral in nature. *Sandoz*[1] and *AEG-Telefunken*[2] are notable milestones in the decision-making practice of the authority. In any event, the case that best captures this tendency is *Bayer-Adalat*,[3] where the Commission sought to argue – in a way that did not seem to be manifestly at odds with the case law – that a decision by a manufacturer to limit the amounts supplied to its distributors amounted to an agreement within the meaning of Article 101(1) TFEU. The EU courts reacted by annulling the decision,[4] thereby clarifying that some firms' strategies aimed at restricting trade between Member States are not caught by that provision.

A superficial look at the approach to the notion of concerted practice is suggestive of a similar inclination. The analysis of these notion raises two separate issues, one substantive and the second one evidentiary. The substantive issue relates to whether tacit collusion amounts, in and of itself, to a concerted practice within the meaning of Article 101(1) TFEU. If this first question is answered in the negative, the second one relates to whether evidence of a concerted practice can be established indirectly, by relying, inter alia, on the parallel behaviour among the members of the oligopoly. In *Woodpulp II*,[5] the Court held, first, that tacit collusion is not sufficient, in and of itself, to establish a concerted practice; and second, that only where a concerted practice is the only plausible explanation for parallel conduct is it possible for an authority to dispense

[1] Case 277/87, *Sandoz prodotti farmaceutici SpA v Commission*, EU:C:1989:363.

[2] Case 107/82, *Allgemeine Elektrizitäts-Gesellschaft AEG-Telefunken AG v Commission*, EU:C:1983:293.

[3] Joined Cases C-2/01 P and C-3/01 P, *Bundesverband der Arzneimittel-Importeure eV and Commission*, EU:C:2004:2; and Case T-41/96, *Bayer AG v Commission*, EU:T:2000:242.

[4] Commission Decision 96/478/EC of 10 January 1996 (Case IV/34.279/F3 – *Adalat*) OJ (1996) L 201/1.

[5] Joined Cases C-89/85, C-104/85, C-114/85, C-116/85, C-117/85 and C-125/85 to C-129/85, *A. Ahlström Osakeyhtiö and others v Commission*, EU:C:1993:120.

itself from the need to show that there is contact between the parties. The practical consequence of the judgment is that it makes it considerably more difficult for an authority to prove the existence of a concerted practice. Attempts by the Commission to show that coordination is the only plausible explanation for parallel behaviour have failed.[6] As with the notions of abuse and restrictions of competition, however, such difficulties can be at least partially circumvented through commitment decisions. The *Container Shipping* case[7] is a good example in this regard. Even though it was not clear whether the unilateral price announcements deemed problematic by the Commission amounted to a concerted practice within the meaning of *Woodpulp II*, the authority was able to obtain commitments from the firms subject to the investigation.[8]

The concepts and approaches developed by the Commission in its fight against cartels – a *sui generis* area of competition law enforcement – provide another setting in which to examine the behaviour of the authority. Cartel-busting raises unique challenges for any competition agency. One of them relates to the difficulty of establishing, to the requisite legal standard, that cartel conduct has indeed taken place. Ensuring adequate deterrence is another challenge. It would be natural for an authority to react to this dual challenge by crafting legal notions so as to maximise deterrence and be able to establish cartel conduct by proxy – or in light of indirect indicators. Several examples reveal some of the techniques crafted by the Commission in this regard, which give an idea, in turn, of how this behaviour may be displayed in practice. The doctrine of the 'single continuous infringement',[9] pursuant to which the authority can conclude that a series of distinct anti-competitive agreements and/or concerted practices are manifestations of one and the same cartel, is one of them. Another technique has been developed by the Commission in the context of the calculation of the fines. A controversial doctrine in this sense concerns the liability of parent

[6] See for instance Case AT.39520 – *Cement and related products*, closed.

[7] Commission Decision of 31 August 2016 (Case AT.39850 – *Container Shipping*).

[8] For an analysis of the question, see Luis Ortiz Blanco, 'A Reasonable Solution, for No Problem? Advance Rate Increase Announcements under EU Competition Law' (Chillin' Competition, 28 July 2016).

[9] See, on this question, David Bailey, 'Single, Overall Agreement in EU Competition Law' (2010) 47 *Common Market Law Review* 473; and Julian Joshua, 'Single Continuous Infringement of Article 81 EC: Has the Commission Stretched the Concept Beyond the Limit of its Logic?' (2009) 5 *European Competition Journal* 451.

companies for cartel conduct undertaken by a subsidiary,[10] which, in practice, can prove to be a valuable policy instrument to increase the amount of the sanctions in individual cases and thus to maximise their deterrent effect.

2.2 *Institutional Aspects*

The decentralisation of the enforcement of EU competition law opens several research avenues. It is possible to adopt the approach of this monograph to examine the behaviour of national courts and authorities in charge of the application of Articles 101 and 102 TFEU – and possibly national merger control regimes. An expansion of the analysis in this direction is valuable for several reasons. As already pointed out, it would make it possible to verify whether national authorities consistently display behaviour that is comparable to that of the Commission. The key questions that would be answered in this regard include whether NCAs show a preference for rules over standards, and whether they adopt a risk-prone attitude when engaging with the EU courts' case law and that developed at the national level.

One of the fundamental contributions of this exercise would come from the fact that there are appreciable differences between the Commission and other national authorities in several major respects. The model of an authority that is in charge of both the investigation and the adoption of decisions is widespread in Europe and beyond. At the same time, the design and internal check and balances may vary from one authority to the other. There are, in particular, important differences regarding the composition of the decision-making body and its involvement in the proceedings. These differences provide a valuable starting point for comparative work. It would make sense to explore whether these institutional differences have an impact on an authority's inclination to adopt a risk-prone attitude when shaping the scope of EU competition law provisions, or when choosing between rules and standards. Intuition suggests that the greater the internal checks and balances

[10] See for instance Sebastian Felix Janka, 'Parent Company Liability in German and EU Competition Law: Two Worlds Apart?' (2016) 7 *Journal of European Competition Law & Practice* 614; Lukas Solek and Stefan Wartinger, 'Parental Liability: Rebutting the Presumption of Decisive Influence' (2015) 6 *Journal of European Competition Law & Practice* 73; and Aitor Montesa and Angel Givaja, 'When Parents Pay for their Children's Wrongs: Attribution of Liability for EC Antitrust Infringements in Parent-Subsidiary Scenarios' (2006) 29 *World Competition* 555.

and the more marked the division between investigators and decision-makers within an organisation, the more risk-averse an authority can be expected to become.

When trying to make sense of the behaviour of national authorities, the attitude displayed by the review courts is, to be sure, another factor that should be considered. In this regard, there are significant institutional variations from one national system to another. The courts (or tribunals) in charge of the review of administrative action can be generalist or specialised courts. For instance, Article 101 and 102 TFEU decisions adopted by the French *Autorité de la Concurrence* are reviewed by a generalist court, the *Cour d'appel de Paris.*[11] By contrast, decisions adopted by the UK Competition and Markets Authority are reviewed by the specialist Competition Appeal Tribunal.[12] These institutional differences provide a valuable starting point for comparative research work. The question of whether generalist courts are more or less inclined to defer to the authority than specialist ones is a particularly interesting one.

It is intuitively appealing to claim that a generalist court is, as a rule, more inclined to defer to the administrative authority on issues of law. As argued by Ginsburg and Wright,[13] however, the issue is probably less straightforward than it appears. It is undeniable that the gap in terms of expertise between a generalist court and an administrative authority is greater. Similarly, a generalist court may be less interested than a specialist tribunal in a matter that is highly technical, and less legal (or formalistic) than others. At the same time, generalist courts – or at least some of them – may be eager to assert their hierarchy vis-à-vis administrative authorities. In addition, such courts may not share – or may even be hostile to – the policy objectives and views of the agency. Conversely, specialist tribunals may be more inclined to give deference (or to avoid questioning the substantive choices made by the authority) because they share values and expertise with it. Finally, it is equally possible that both generalist and specialist bodies are equally proactive, but that their proactivity is manifested in different ways – one set of courts may focus on formal issues and the other on substantive matters. Ultimately, these are all empirical questions.

[11] Article L464-7 of the French Commercial Code.

[12] See Section 12 and Schedule 2 of the Enterprise Act 2002.

[13] Douglas H. Ginsburg and Joshua D. Wright, 'Antitrust Courts: Specialists Versus Generalists' (2013) 36 *Fordham International Law Journal* 788.

2.3 *Beyond EU Competition Law*

2.3.1 The Evolution of US Antitrust and EU Competition Law

An obvious extension of the analysis found in this monograph is the comparison that inspired it in the first place. It was suggested in Chapter 1 that the substantive differences between the US and EU regimes could be explained by reference to the framework in which each of the systems operates. In this regard, the tentative conclusions of this study suggest that, indeed, institutional factors play a role in the divergent evolution of the law on both sides of the Atlantic. Differences in this sense can be attributed not only to the peculiarities of the US system but also – and this is the intended contribution of the monograph – to some factors that are specific to the EU framework. It is possible to identify a series of questions around which a comparative research agenda between the two most important jurisdictions in the field could revolve.

The dominance of private over public enforcement is one of the most salient features of US antitrust. As a result, it seems unsurprising that the administrability of rules and standards is one of the aspects that dominates discussions in that country,[14] and one that is explicitly discussed even in rulings.[15] This issue has been far less prominent in Europe, and when it has been invoked, it has been used selectively. For instance, administrability concerns have occasionally been raised to justify the use of rules over standards, such as the prima facie prohibition of exclusive dealing under Article 102 TFEU,[16] but ignored in other respects. To mention an obvious example, concerns with administrability were not raised to challenge the unstructured standards applied by the Commission in cases like *Microsoft I* (and in particular the analysis of the impact of the refusal to deal on 'follow-on innovation') or *British Airways*

[14] See, among the vast literature on the question, Herbert Hovenkamp, *The Antitrust Enterprise: Principle and Execution* (Cambridge: Harvard University Press, 2005), at 43–56; and Frank Easterbrook, 'The Limits of Antitrust' (1984) 63 *Texas Law Review* 1. See also Judd Stone and Joshua Wright, 'Antitrust Formalism is Dead! Long Live Antitrust Formalism!: Some Implications of *American Needle v. NFL*' (2009–2010) *Cato Supreme Court Review* 369, where the authors point out that the concern with administrability was common to both Harvard and Chicago scholars.

[15] See for instance *Town of Concord, Mass. v Boston Edison Co.*, 913 F.2d 17 (1st Cir. 1990); and *Leegin Creative Leather Products, Inc. v. PSKS, Inc.*, 551 U.S. 877 (2007), Breyer, J., dissenting.

[16] Wouter Wils, 'The Judgment of the EU General Court in Intel and the So-Called "More Economic Approach" to Abuse of Dominance' (2014) 37 *World Competition* 405.

(where the authority concluded that the rebate scheme in question had a 'loyalty-inducing' effect).[17]

In a different vein, it seems intuitively correct to argue that, where private disputes dominate the enforcement landscape, consistency is much more valued than in a system that revolves around a public authority. In the latter, the consequences of substantive inconsistency can be tempered by a public authority that carefully chooses which cases to pursue. This institutional difference may explain why the debate around the objectives of competition law acquired a scale and a prominence in the US that is unlikely to be seen in Europe. The monograph hints at another conclusion in this regard. In a system that revolves around private enforcement, courts may value consistency more than effective enforcement. In other words, they may value law over optimal policy choices. Accordingly, they may be ready to concede that preserving legal certainty inevitably means leaving some harmful practices out of the reach of the system.

A final line of research could focus on the choices made by authorities. Irrespective of the overarching institutional framework, it may well be the case that US authorities display instincts that are not fundamentally different from those of the Commission. Assuming that this is the case, any substantive divergences between the two systems would be the consequence, at least in part, of the different attitude displayed by the review courts on each side of the Atlantic or, more generally, to the institutional setting. The intuition behind this line of research is inspired by some anecdotal evidence from recent developments in the field. Suffice it to mention two examples. At the time of writing, the legal status of pay-for-delay agreements in the pharmaceutical sector is different in the US and the EU. This fact is not due, however, to the divergent substantive approaches taken by authorities. In *Actavis*, the FTC took the view that pay-for-delay agreements are presumptively anti-competitive.[18] Its position was similar to that defended by the Commission in *Lundbeck*. If the GC upheld the approach of the authority in the latter case, the US Supreme Court concluded that a situation such as the one considered by the FTC in *Actavis* should be subject to a standard (rule of reason).[19] *Rambus* is

[17] For a discussion of this last question, see Pablo Ibáñez Colomo, '*Post Danmark II*, or the Quest for Administrability and Coherence in Article 102 TFEU', available at http://ssrn.com.

[18] *In re Androgel Antitrust Litigation* (No. II), 687 F. Supp. 2d 1371, 1379 (ND Ga. 2010).

[19] *FTC v Actavis*, Inc., 570 U.S. ___, 133 S. Ct. 2223 (2013).

another example in which both US and EU authorities attempted to take action in a novel and relatively controversial case. While the efforts made by the FTC were quashed on appeal,[20] the Commission managed to obtain commitments from the firm.[21]

2.3.2 Transnational Competition Law

The proliferation of competition law regimes across the world multiplies the possibilities of research revolving around the behaviour of administrative authorities and review courts. Beyond expanding the scope of the comparative analysis, the framework crafted in the monograph can make a contribution to knowledge by providing a template for the evaluation of the performance of competition authorities. This is an area of research that has grown in popularity in recent years. Some of the recent efforts in this sense include the framework developed by Delgado, Otero and Pérez-Asenjo,[22] on the one hand, and Iacobucci and Trebilcock, on the other.[23] This line of research acknowledges, as a starting point, that the most obvious measures of performance – the number of decisions adopted, amount of the fines imposed or success before review courts – are not necessarily reliable indicators. Similarly, they acknowledge the difficulty – and the limits – of a pure ex post analysis based on economic factors, such as the contribution to economic welfare.

The analytical framework developed in this monograph has the potential to contribute to this literature in two main ways. First of all, it may make it possible to incorporate some considerations that would otherwise prove elusive, including concepts such as legal certainty and the question of whether authorities incorporate consensus positions. By examining how authorities shape the scope of substantive provisions, and how they behave over time, one can determine whether their behaviour is – statically and dynamically – consistent, and thus whether administrative action can be anticipated with ease. Similarly, it is possible to examine whether they incorporate economic analysis when ruling on the lawfulness of practices. Finally, the analytical framework devised in

[20] *Rambus, Inc. v FTC*, 522 F.3d 456, 469 (D.C. Cir. 2008).

[21] Commission Decision of 9 December 2009 (Case COMP/38.636 – *Rambus*).

[22] Juan Delgado, Héctor Otero and Eduardo Pérez-Asenjo, 'Assessment of antitrust agencies' impact and performance: an analytical framework' (2016) 4 *Journal of Antitrust Enforcement* 323.

[23] Edward Iacobucci and Michael Trebilcock, 'Evaluating the Performance of Competition Agencies: The Limits of Assessment Methodologies and Their Implications', available at http://gclc.coleurope.eu.

the monograph makes it possible to assess not only the behaviour of administrative authorities, but also the responses of review courts to that behaviour.

3 The Court-Agency Relationship in Administrative Law

Even though it is not likely to be seen in this light by all readers, this monograph is, in a sense, also a study in administrative law. It may contribute to the understanding of issues relating, in general, to the relationship between courts and agencies. Major theoretical and empirical advances have been made in the past 20 years in this area, which can shed much light on the dynamics in EU competition law. In particular, formal tools have been developed to model the behaviour of administrative authorities and review courts.[24] In addition, considerable efforts have been made to develop measures to assess the intensity of the judicial review of administrative action.[25] This monograph confirms some of the lessons that can be drawn from these lines of research. They can be summarised as follows.

One lesson to be drawn from this study is that any debate about whether administrative agencies should be given deference by review courts seems incomplete if dynamic considerations, on the one hand, and the incentives of authorities, on the other, are ignored. Put differently, arguments in favour of deference cannot disregard the fact that administrative authorities act strategically and adapt to the behaviour of review courts. Thus, the question of whether it is appropriate to defer to the reasonable interpretation of an authority cannot be examined as a one-shot game, thereby ignoring the interaction with the review courts and the legal uncertainty that may result from the introduction of inconsistencies in the system. This monograph suggests that approaches to the question that one may label as primarily doctrinal or principled can be

[24] See for instance Yehonatan Givati and Matthew Stephenson, 'Judicial Deference to Inconsistent Agency Statutory Interpretations' (2011) 40 *Journal of Legal Studies* 85; Yehonatan Givati, 'Strategic Statutory Interpretation by Administrative Agencies' (2010) 12 *American Law and Economics Review* 95; and Matthew Stephenson, 'The Strategic Substitution Effect: Textual Plausibility, Procedural Formality, and Judicial Review of Agency Statutory Interpretations' (2006) 120 *Harvard Law Review* 528.

[25] See for instance Joshua Fischman, 'Measuring Inconsistency, Indeterminacy, and Error in Adjudication' (2014) 16 *American Law and Economics Review* 40.

expected to lose their influence over time insofar as they lack explanatory power.[26]

A second lesson is that the quantitative analysis of judicial review cannot rely exclusively – in fact, not even primarily – on the rate of annulment of decisions by review courts. The use of annulments as a proxy for the intensity of the review of administrative action is popular in quantitative studies.[27] This monograph has exposed its many limits. Arguably, one of the key methodological suggestions is that the analysis of court-agency relationships may not be properly undertaken without engaging, at least to some extent, with substantive matters. If there is an idea that transpires clearly from this work it is that inconsistencies in the interpretation and enforcement of a body of law appear to be more reliable indicators of the behaviour of courts and authorities than the rate of annulment of a particular decision. In this sense, it joins a strand of the literature – cited above – that has formally modelled agencies' reactions to deference.

[26] For two examples of these approaches, see Paul Daly, 'Deference on Questions of Law' (2011) 74 *Modern Law Review* 694; and Jaime Arancibia, *Judicial Review of Commercial Regulation* (Oxford: Oxford University Press, 2011).

[27] See for instance the abundant literature that emerged following the introduction of the *Chevron* doctrine – laid down in *Chevron U.S.A., Inc. v Natural Resources Defense Council, Inc.*, 467 U.S. 837 (1984), including Thomas Miles and Cass Sunstein, 'Do Judges Make Regulatory Policy? An Empirical Investigation of *Chevron*' (2006) 73 *University of Chicago Law Review* 823. See also, by the same authors, Thomas Miles and Cass Sunstein, 'The Real World of Arbitrariness Review' (2008) 75 *University of Chicago Law Review* 761.

INDEX